PROGRAMMING IN C

PROGRAMMING IN C

Lawrence H. Miller

University of Southern California
Information Sciences Institute

Alexander E. Quilici

University of California, Los Angeles

John Wiley & Sons

New York • Chichester • Brisbane • Toronto • Singapore

To my mother, Erin and RGM

To my parents, Robert and Alice Quilici

Cover: Computer art created and photographed by Helen Iranyi.

Library of Congress Cataloging in Publication Data:

Miller, Lawrence H.
    Programming in C.

    1. C (Computer program language)   I. Quilici,
Alexander E.   II. Title.
QA76.73.C15M553   1986   005.13'3   85-26602
ISBN 0-471-81875-5

Printed in the United States of America

10 9 8 7 6 5 4 3 2 1

PREFACE

C is like a Porsche: powerful, efficient, and compact. Programming in C, like driving a Porsche, can be interesting, exciting, and fun—once you have mastered it and can use its capabilities to the fullest. In this book, we try to provide enough information to make programming in C as enjoyable for you as it is for us. We introduce each of C's features, show the common ways to put them together, and teach how to *use* the language, showing how to write readable, modifiable, efficient, and portable programs. Our treatment of the language is thorough and includes complete coverage of the standard libraries and the preprocessor. While discussing the various language features, we present the shortcuts, idioms, and stylistic problems the reader is likely to encounter in existing code.

We do not assume any prior experience with C. However, we do assume some practice with a high-level programming language, or at least some knowledge of how variables, statements and procedures work. As we go along, we note the similarities with and differences from other languages such as Pascal, FORTRAN, and BASIC. When our programs are drawn from topics that the reader may not be familiar with, we take care to explain not only the programs but the ideas behind them and the algorithms as well.

EXAMPLES AND CASE STUDIES

Since the only way to learn how to write good C programs is to study well-written ones, we have included many examples and case studies. Our examples not only illustrate language features but also reinforce general principles of good programming style. For instance, many of the functions written in our early examples are used to build more interesting programs later, illustrating modularity and the resusability of code—concepts central to C's philosophy. Our case studies consolidate and reinforce earlier material and illustrate real-world applications. Within all our programs, we avoid sacrificing clarity for conciseness.

v

The programs and functions used as examples and case studies are diverse and include:

- Interactive and display-oriented programs: the Game of Life, an indexed data base, and a histogram producer.
- Implementations of sorting and searching algorithms: insertion sort, quicksort, tree sort, radix sort, sequential search, and binary search.
- Our versions of useful tools for copying files, stripping duplicate lines, counting words, and line numbering.
- Implementations of standard libraries: the string library and the character-testing functions.
- Additional functions that we have found to be useful: an alternative to the standard library's input handling and a package for sets.

FEATURES OF OUR PRESENTATION

In addition to the numerous examples and case studies the text contains several pedagogical aids. Exercises after each section test comprehension of the material covered in that section and encourage further exploration. There are many illustrations to provide needed pictorial descriptions of pointers, data structures, and the behavior of algorithms. Finally, each chapter ends with a summary box that provides design insights, stylistic guidelines, and programming hints that aid the reader in building useful C programs.

ORGANIZATION

Chapter 1 is a tutorial introduction to the language. Through a series of example programs, each adding several new language constructs, we present many of C's basic data types and control structures and introduce functions and parameter passing.

With this tutorial out of the way, we start to delve into the details of C's data types and control structures. Chapter 2 describes C's basic data types and operators, concentrating on differences between C and other high-level languages. We give special attention to assignment, prefix, postfix, and bitwise operators and to automatic type conversions and casting. Chapter 3 discusses arrays, strings, and pointers, emphasizing the relationships between them. The standard string library functions are introduced and used in writing a useful tool that detects duplicate input lines. Chapter 4 examines C's statements, illustrating each with an example showing its most appropriate uses and concluding with a histogram program that ties together the concepts covered thus far.

We then examine features of C that support the writing of larger programs. Chapter 5 discusses functions, examining the way they can communicate with each other through parameter passing and return values. In addition, the closely related topics of recursion and pointers to functions are described and illustrated with binary search and the nucleus of a function plotter. Chapter 6 discusses program structure, introducing storage classes, header files, separate compilation, and methods of implementing abstract data types. These concepts are illustrated with several useful modules including an alternative to the standard I/O library's input handling, and an implementation of sets. Chapter 7 describes the preprocessor, showing its use in making programs easier to read and debug, as well as more efficient.

Next, we examine more complex user-defined data structures. Chapter 8 returns to arrays, concentrating on multidimensional and ragged arrays and the efficient use of pointers to access them. We also introduce dynamic storage allocation and use it in a program to sort strings. The chapter ends with a closer examination of C's declarations, explaining their often confusing syntax. Chapters 9 and 10 introduce structures and unions, illustrating their use in defining static data structures like tables, and in constructing dynamic data structures such as linked lists and trees. Chapter 10 ends with a program requiring dynamic data structures: a C program cross-referencer.

We conclude by discussing the writing of real-world programs. Chapter 11 focuses on the relationship between C programs and the outside world, describing command line arguments and files, providing complete coverage of the standard I/O library. The ideas of the chapter are brought together in the implementation of an indexed data base for names, addresses, and phone numbers. Chapter 12 provides techniques for writing more portable and efficient programs, illustrating them through two significant case studies: radix sort and the Game of Life. The appendixes summarize library functions and describe the binary, octal, and hexadecimal base systems.

Lawrence H. Miller
Marina del Ray, CA

Alexander E. Quilici
Santa Monica, CA

ACKNOWLEDGMENTS

We are grateful to several insightful individuals who have had a significant influence on our views about programming and teaching. Dennis Ritchie's clear thinking has given us C and, as a result, has made program development a pleasant experience. Niklaus Wirth and Brian Kernighan, through their classic books, have shown us the power of structured programming and the intelligent development and use of tools. Lastly, Ken Thompson and Dennis Ritchie created UNIX[1], providing us with a comfortable environment for programming and for writing.

Special thanks go to our friends and colleagues for improving this book. In particular, David Smallberg provided many perceptive comments and criticisms and in countless late night discussions directed us to elegant solutions to our problems. Jeff Rothenberg at the Rand Corporation, Eric Anderson at the USC Information Sciences Institute, and Arthur Goldberg and Karen Dorato at UCLA have been using drafts of the manuscript and have contributed valuable suggestions. David G. Kay's enthusiasm for teaching and writing is contagious, and his inspiration is noticeable throughout this book. Marcy Swenson and Richard Wolpert aided us in putting together the appendixes. We also thank our students at UCLA, especially Tai Lue and Bruce McCorkendale, for their patience with our earlier drafts and for pointing out mistakes and painfully unclear explanations.

Finally, we cannot imagine how we could have completed this book without the encouragement and support we received from Rita Grant-Miller and Collette Zee. And, as always, we are in debt to Colonel Vigorish for providing us with financial aid, and to Dr. Ruth Westheimer for making our evenings more exciting.

L.H.M.
A.E.Q.

C O N T E N T S

CHAPTER 8   ARRAYS AND POINTERS REVISITED   227

CHAPTER 9   CONSTRUCTED DATA TYPES   259

CHAPTER 10   LINKED DATA STRUCTURES   281

CHAPTER 11   C AND THE OUTSIDE WORLD   319

CHAPTER 12   PORTABILITY AND EFFICIENCY   351

C H A P T E R 1

INTRODUCING C PROGRAMMING

We begin with a tutorial introduction to C. Through a series of example programs, each using several new language constructs, we introduce many of C's fundamental data types, operators, and control structures. While doing so, we examine the use of predefined library functions to perform both formatted and character-at-a-time input and output, and discuss the process of actually compiling, loading, and executing C programs. The chapter concludes by introducing user-defined functions and showing how they can communicate through parameter passing and return values.

1.1

A FIRST C PROGRAM

Believing in the idea that we learn by seeing and doing, we will start right out by examining a C program. The program in Figure 1.1 prints the interest accumulated in a bank account over a period of 10 years, with an initial deposit of $1000 and assuming an interest rate of 10 percent.

When we compile and run this program, we produce the output shown in Figure 1.2. The program first writes a header giving the current year

```
/*
 * Generate a table showing interest accumulation.
 */

#define PRINCIPAL       1000.00         /* start with $1000 */
#define IRATE           0.10            /* interest rate of 10% */
#define PERIOD          10              /* over 10-year period */
main()
{
  int    year;                         /* year of period */
  float  sum;                          /* total amount */

  sum = PRINCIPAL;
  year = 0;
  printf ("Year\tTotal at %.2f%%\n\n", IRATE * 100.0);
  while (year <= PERIOD)
  {
    printf ("%d\t\t    $ %.2f\n", year, sum);
    sum = sum * IRATE + sum;
    year = year + 1;
  }
}
```

FIGURE 1.1 A program that calculates interest.

and the interest rate, and then prints the total amount of money in the account at the end of each year in the period. To do our calculations, we used a simple interest rate compounding formula:

Amount at end of year = amount at start of year × interest rate + amount at start of year

Year	Total at 10.00%
0	$ 1000.00
1	$ 1100.00
2	$ 1210.00
3	$ 1331.00
4	$ 1464.10
5	$ 1610.51
6	$ 1771.56
7	$ 1948.72
8	$ 2143.59
9	$ 2357.95
10	$ 2593.74

FIGURE 1.2 Output generated when running the interest rate accumulator.

1.1.1 ANALYSIS OF INTEREST PROGRAM

The first lines of the program begin with /*, the C start-of-comment marker. Anything between the opening /*, and a closing */ is taken as a comment. The first piece of the program is a brief comment block describing the program. In general, comments can appear anywhere blank spaces can occur – at the end of a line, at the beginning, or even in the middle – as long as they do not appear in the middle of a keyword or identifier.

The next three lines begin with the symbol # followed by the word define; #define is a mechanism for defining constants. The way C handles #defines is interesting and important; they are interpreted by a *preprocessor*. Each time a #define is seen by the preprocessor, the value associated with the name is remembered. Then whenever the name occurs in the program, it is replaced with its corresponding value. After the preprocessor has finished its replacements, the program is passed to the compiler. The compiler never sees the names in the #define statements. That is why we use #define for constants.

The syntax (that is, the way the statement is constructed) of #define is so simple that we will use it in virtually every program we write. In fact, #define is more powerful than we have indicated here; it is a general mechanism that allows the preprocessor to replace the given string of characters with another string. For now, we will use it to define constant values. In this simple form, its use requires the keyword #define to begin in column one, followed by the name we are defining, followed by its value:

```
#define        NAME        value
```

We use italics (*NAME, value*) to indicate symbols that are generic; the programmer provides the name and its value.

In Figure 1.1 we have used #define for the values that are constants for the program: the initial principal amount PRINCIPAL, the interest rate IRATE, and the number of years over which we wish to calculate the accumulating value, PERIOD. The preprocessor replaces each use of PRINCIPAL in the program with its defined value (1000.00) and performs a similar action for the other two defined constants. We have used all uppercase names for constants because this system makes it easier to spot them. The #defines can occur anywhere in a program but are usually placed at the beginning. Chapter 7 describes the complete preprocessor in detail.

The Main Program

The lines after the #defines define a function with the name main. Program execution begins with a call to main, so every program must have a function with this name. The parentheses after the word main indicate that it is a function that takes no parameters. Chapter 11 shows that `main` can indeed take arguments, and we will see how they are defined and used.

Other functions can appear before or after `main`, but there must be exactly one `main` function per program. In contrast to some programming languages, however, it does not matter where the main function is defined. Our program consists of just the one function, `main`, which, in turn, consists of data declarations and statements. We group all statements that belong together under `main` using the statement grouping symbols { and }.

Data Definitions

In C, the types of all variables must be declared before they are used. Variable declarations appear at the beginning of a function. In Figure 1.1 the declarations

```
int        year;
float      sum;
```

tell the compiler that `year` is an `int` (an abbreviation for the word *integer*) and `sum` is a `float` (a *floating point* or *real* number). These declarations are required because, among other reasons, the amount of storage actually used by a variable depends on its type. Further, accuracy and the range of values differs between types.

The range of values for the various types depends on the machine on which the program runs. Table 1.1 lists the standard numerical predefined types and their range of representations on a typical computer's word size. The table divides the world into 16-bit and 32-bit machines. The 16-bit machines include the IBM-PC, the PDP-11, the Macintosh, and most micros. The 32-bit machines include the VAX, the IBM mainframes, and most full-size computers.

In addition to the basic numerical types of Table 1.1, C provides character and pointer (address) data types, allows arrays and structures of any data type, and allows us to devise new data types from the standard types.

There are two basic numerical representation forms: integer and real

TABLE 1.1 Predefined C data types and typical machine representations

Data Type	16-bit machines	32-bit machines
char	8	8
short	16	16
int	16	32
long	32	32
float	32	32
double	64	64

(or floating point). Among these, there are also multiple forms. For integers, they are `short`, `int`, and `long`; for reals, they are `float` and `double`. Integer forms are used when exact 'whole' numbers are needed, since their representation is exact within the range of integers that a given word size can represent. They are also used when speed of arithmetic operations is important, since most operations are faster with integers. Different sizes are provided for storage efficiency and for program portability, a topic we discuss in considerable depth in Chapter 12.

Reals are numbers with a decimal point. Their accuracy depends on the machine's representation. Typically, a `float` represents about 7 significant digits, with exponents generally ranging from about −38 to +38. The `doubles` allocate more storage for the real, and this storage is usually given to the fractional part of the number. Thus, `doubles` usually represent about 14 significant digits. There are both automatic and explicit ways to convert from one form to another.

In Chapter 2 we will consider built-in data types in more detail, pointing out that the range of values of a particular type can vary from machine to machine. Notice in Table 1.1 that the basic integer representation varies from 16 to 32 bits. With one bit required for the sign, the range of an `int` using a 16-bit representation is from −32,768 to +32,767 (that is, -2^{15} to $+2^{15} - 1$). On a 32-bit machine, however, `ints` range from −2,148,483,648 to +2,148,483,647 (that is, from -2^{31} to $+2^{31} - 1$). Care must be taken to select an appropriate data type if a program written on one computer is to run on another.

Executable Statements

The statements that are executed when a function is called follow any variable declarations. The first statements in `main` in Figure 1.1 are

```
sum = PRINCIPAL;
year = 0;
```

These are assignment statements and work in the conventional way. The first assigns the value defined for the constant `PRINCIPAL` (1000.00) to the variable `sum`; the second sets the variable `year` to 0.

The next statement is an output statement that writes the header line

```
printf ("Year\t   Total at %.2f%%\n", IRATE * 100.0);
```

`printf` is a predefined function for performing formatted output. Predefined means that it is a function that has already been written and compiled for you, and is linked together with your program after it compiles. In C, all input and output is performed by library functions. Together, these functions comprise the standard I/O library.

Formatted output means that the function takes two classes of arguments. The first, between the double quotation marks, is the formatting control string. The second is a list of values to be printed according to the formatting control. In general, anything in the format specification (between the quotation marks) is printed as is. However, instructions for formatting numerical and string output are indicated using the % formatting codes: %d is used to print a decimal integer and %f a floating point value. If no size is given, enough space is used to print the entire value. In the interest program we have specified a format of %.2f, which tells the compiler that we want floating point output, with two places to the right of the decimal point and enough space for all places to the left. The value of the expression IRATE * 100.0 is calculated and is printed with two digits to the right of the decimal point. Since we also want to print a percent sign in the heading, we use two percent signs (%%) to indicate that a single percent is to be printed.

printf is a fairly conventional output formatting function and quite simple to use. The various output formats are described in detail in Appendix 6. Perhaps you have noticed the obscure \n at the end of the formatting string. Characters with backslashes are special nonprinting characters. \n is used to indicate that a newline is wanted. Without this, output continues on the same line as the previous output. There are many nonprinting characters in any machine's character set, and the backslash quoting method is used to indicate a desired function. For example, the tab character is indicated by \t. Other output formats will be seen in Chapter 2.

For each value to be printed, there must be a formatting instruction, and these instructions must appear in the correct order. We see this in the second printf statement:

```
printf ("%d\t\t    $ %.2f\n", year, sum);
```

where we print the values of year and sum. The first variable in the output list is year, and its value is printed using the %d specification. Then two tab characters are printed, followed by a dollar sign and a space. The next variable is sum, and its value is printed using the %.2f format. Finally, a newline is written.

Before we leave printf, we should point out that in certain cases there are more efficient ways to produce output. These methods are presented in Chapter 11, along with other functions in the standard I/O library.

Most of the work of the program is accomplished in a while loop:

```
while (year <= PERIOD)
{
        printf ("%d      $ %.2f\n", year, sum);
        sum = sum * IRATE + sum;
        year = year + 1;
}
```

`while` is a mechanism for repeating a statement or a group of statements. The syntax of a `while` loop is

```
while (expression)
    statement;
following-statement;
```

The expression in parentheses is evaluated and if the condition is true, *statement* is executed. This process repeats until the condition is false, when we skip to *following-statement*.

In this case whenever `year` is less than or equal to `PERIOD`, we want to execute the three statements

```
printf ("%d\t\t    $ %.2f\n", year, sum);
sum = sum * IRATE + sum;
year = year + 1;
```

We do this by grouping the statements together using the statement grouping indicator `{` to start the group and `}` to end it. The first statement in the group does the printing; the second updates `sum`, and the last updates `year`. We exit the loop when `year` is greater than `PERIOD`.

C has the usual arithmetic operators (+, −, *, /), along with several others, examined later in this chapter and in Chapter 2. The operators * and / have higher precedence than + and −, but as with most other programming languages, the order of evaluation can be changed by using parentheses.

Two additional points should be made about this first C program. First, each statement terminates with a semicolon. However, statement groups and `#defines` do not. Secondly, C has a rather free format. We have used one particular indentation style, but you are free to use others. Many C environments include program formatters, so that whatever accidents occur in creating the program can be corrected by using one of these tools.[1]

1.2
COMPILING AND RUNNING A PROGRAM

Creating a program typically requires the use of several facilities, such as text editors, compilers, file system utilities, and others. Figure 1.3 diagrams the typical program-building, compiling, and running cycle, showing the use of some of these tools.

---

[1] In UNIX a program called *cb* (standing for "C Beautifier!") and a program called *indent* are available.

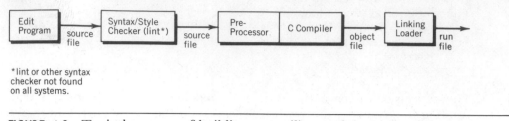

*lint or other syntax
checker not found
on all systems.

FIGURE 1.3 Typical process of building, compiling and running a C program.

The program is first created with an interactive text editor. Then the source file is compiled using the C compiler.

Figure 1.3 shows a preliminary step before compiling, preprocessing. This is an automatic step in compiling programs, that expands the `#defines` and replaces their names with their values throughout the program. The preprocessor also does preliminary syntax checking.

At this point, the expanded version of the program is passed to the compiler proper. If there are no errors in the compilation of the program, an intermediate form of the program, known as an *object module*, is produced. An object module or file contains the compiled code, but this code may contain references to functions that the code did not define, called *externals* (such as to `printf` in Figure 1.1).

Now the linking loader must reconcile any externals. It does this by looking in a standard location that contains a library of precompiled standard functions. The compiled definition of the `printf` function is found in this library and is linked together by the linking loader (usually invoked automatically by the C compiler) with the object module to produce a runnable program. The runnable program is the sole output of this pipeline.

Many of these steps can be modified by the use of flags to the compiler. You should read the compiler documentation to discover the details of your own system.

EXERCISES

1-1 Compile and run the interest rate program (Figure 1.1) on your own computer. □

1-2 In order to introduce you to the error messages your compiler provides, remove a terminating semicolon from one of the statements in the interest rate program (Figure 1.1). How helpful are the error messages? □

1-3 Remove a needed parenthesis from the interest rate program and then compile the program. You will probably discover that the error messages from your C compiler are not very helpful. You should begin building a list of messages and their true meaning. □

1-4 Experiment with different values for the constants `PRINCIPAL`, `IRATE`, and `PERIOD`. □

1-5 What happens if `sum` is declared as an `int` rather than a `float`? Test your conjecture by changing the declaration of `sum` and rerunning the program. □

1-6 Does your C compiler distinguish between uppercase and lowercase letters? Answer this question by adding the following declaration to the interest rate program after the declaration of `year`:

```
int  YEAR;
```

Does the compiler accept this new declaration, or does it complain about multiply defined names? □

1.3

EXTENDING THE SAMPLE PROGRAM — INPUT AND ADDITIONAL CONTROL STRUCTURES

We would like to make the interest accumulation program a bit more flexible. Rather than hard-wiring the initial amount of money (`PRINCIPAL`), the interest rate (`IRATE`), and the number of years (`PERIOD`), we request these values from an interactive user and read them as input. To do this, we use another function from the standard I/O library, `scanf`, the input analog of `printf`. As with `printf`, there are two sets of arguments to `scanf`. The first, in quotation marks, is the formatting control string and uses conventions similar to those of `printf`: `%d` indicates a decimal integer, `%f` a floating point, and so on. The rest of the arguments list the variables to which input is assigned. Unlike `printf`, however, `scanf` does not recognize the special formatting descriptions that start with `\` such as `\n`. In fact, when searching for a value, `scanf` ignores line boundaries and simply looks for the next appropriate character.

Importantly, `scanf` indicates whether the input was completed successfully and when the end of the input file has been reached. `scanf` does this because it is a function that returns a value — the number of values correctly read from the input or the special value EOF (a predefined constant), meaning that the end of the input file has been reached. Since scanf returns the number of values correctly read, we can compare this value with the expected number, to determine if an error has occurred. An error may occur, for example, when we are reading an integer value and an alphabetic character is entered.

When we read a value into a variable, scanf does not use the *name* of the variable, but rather its *address*. Fortunately, there is a simple operator for indicating the address of a variable. If we have declared year to be an int and we wish to read a value for year, we use scanf as follows:

```
scanf("%d", &year);
```

The symbol & before the variable name year is an operator that returns the address of the variable. If you forget the address operator &, unexpected results occur. We will see why when we consider how parameters work in functions in Chapter 5.

With this preliminary review out of the way, we can extend the interest accumulator to allow input from the user. This time, we ask the user to enter the interest rate, principal, and period, and then read these values using scanf. Since we are reading three values, we expect scanf to return a value of three. If scanf returns something other than three, either there has been an error in the input or we have reached the end of the input file. In either case, we print a simple message and terminate the program. This version is shown in Figure 1.4.

When we run the new version of the program, we produce similar output as before, shown in Figure 1.5. What the user types is shown in italics.

1.3.1 ANALYSIS OF THE INTERACTIVE INTEREST PROGRAM

Since the values used in the program are now variables, we no longer use the #defines for IRATE, PRINCIPAL, and PERIOD. Instead, we make them variables by declaring their types along with the program's other variables:

```
int    period,                 /* length of period */
       year;                   /* year of period */
float  irate,                  /* interest rate */
       sum;                    /* total amount */
```

We have declared period and year to be ints and irate and sum to be floats.

The first executable statement in the program is a printf, asking the user to enter values of the interest rate, the principal, and the period.

```
/*
 * Generates a table showing interest accumulation.  Allows the
 * user to input the interest rate, principal, and period.
 */
main()
{
    int    period,              /* length of period */
           year;                /* year of period */
    float irate,                /* interest rate */
          sum;                  /* total amount */

    printf ("Enter interest rate, principal, and period: ");

    if (scanf ("%f %f %d", &irate, &sum, &period) == 3)
    {
        printf ("Year\t    Total at %.2f%%\n\n", irate * 100.0);

        for (year = 0; year <= period; year++)
        {
            printf ("%5d\t      $ %10.2f\n", year, sum);
            sum += sum * irate;
        }
    }
    else
        printf ("Error in input.  No table printed.\n");
}
```

FIGURE 1.4 Second implementation of the interest rate accumulator. Here the information is input from the user.

Since we want to write the prompt and leave the cursor on the same line, the format string of the `printf` does not contain the newline character `\n`.

```
Enter interest rate, principal and period:  .10      10000      10
Year    Total at 10.00%

    0  $    10000.00
    1  $    11000.00
    2  $    12100.00
    3  $    13310.00
    4  $    14641.00
    5  $    16105.10
    6  $    17715.61
    7  $    19487.17
    8  $    21435.89
    9  $    23579.47
   10  $    25937.42
```

FIGURE 1.5 Output from the second implementation of the interest rate accumulator.

```
printf ("Enter interest rate, principal, and period:    ");
```

Input into the variables `irate`, `sum`, and `period` is accomplished using `scanf`. To see if the input was read correctly, we test `scanf`'s return value with an `if` statement:

```
if (scanf ("%f %f %d", &irate, &sum, &period) == 3)
{
    printf ("Year\t    Total at %.2f%%\n\n", irate * 100.0);

    for (year = 0; year <= period; year++)
    {
        printf ("%5d\t    $ %10.2f\n", year, sum);
        sum += sum * irate;
    }
}
else
    printf ("Error in input.  No table printed.\n");
```

The `if` statement has a simple form:

```
if (expression)
    statement1
else
    statement2
```

First, the expression in parentheses is evaluated (the parentheses are required). If the condition is true, *statement1* is executed; if it is false, *statement2* is executed. Notice that there is no keyword `then` before *statement1*. The `else` *statement2* is optional. As with the `while` statement, braces can be used around a group of statements whenever we show a single statement.

In Figure 1.4 we want to read values for the three variables `irate`, `sum`, and `period`, and so we expect `scanf` to return three. We test the value of `scanf` using the test-for-equality operator, the double equal sign (`==`). In addition to testing for equality, we can test for inequality (`!=`), less than (`<`), greater than (`>`), less than or equal (`<=`), and greater than or equal (`>=`).

Putting this all together, if `scanf` in Figure 1.4 returns three, we execute the group of statements that follows it, writing the heading and computing the balances for the various years. If `scanf` does not return three, we have an error on input, and we execute the `else` part of the `if` statement, printing an appropriate error message.

The relational operators (tests for equality, inequality, and the others) are conventional in their use, except that they return an integer value: *true* is represented by one, *false* by zero. Consequently, C is more general than other programming languages in its use of tests within a `while` or `if` statement. Any arithmetic expression may be used, not just one of the relational tests. If the expression is zero, it is interpreted as false; if it is nonzero (positive or negative) it is interpreted as true.

The `for` Loop

Once the values for interest rate, principal amount, and number of years have been entered, we want to print the current year and total amount of money and then update the total, once for each year, from the first to the entered number of years. We capture this notion of a repetition of a statement in the `for` loop. Most other programming languages have a similar construct, which contains the idea of a loop index that is initialized to some starting value and is incremented or decremented each time through the loop. The loop terminates when a stopping condition is met. The C `for` contains these ideas but is really much more general. Its basic form is:

```
for (Start1 ; Test2 ; Action3)
    Loop body
```

Start1, *Test2*, and *Action3* are any C expressions.

When a `for` is executed, *Start1* is evaluated first (this is usually a loop initialization, such as `year = 0`). *Test2* is evaluated next (this is usually the loop index bounds test, such as `year <= period`). If *Test2* evaluates to true (or any nonzero value) the statements in the loop body are executed; if it evaluates to false (or zero), the `for` loop exits. As with the `while` and `if` statements, braces are used if there are multiple statements within the loop body.

If the loop does not exit (that is, if *Test2* is nonzero), after the loop body is executed, *Action3* is evaluated and the cycle is repeated. Usually *Action3* increments the loop counter.

In Figure 1.4, we initialize `year` to zero, and then compare to see whether it is less than or equal to `period`. If it is, we enter the body of the loop, and if not, we exit the loop. Upon completing the loop, we add one to `year`, evaluate *Test2* again, and repeat the process.

```
for (year = 0; year <= period; year++)
{
    printf ("%5d\t   $ %10.2f\n", year, sum);
    sum += sum * irate;
}
```

The astute reader will have noticed a most bizarre form for *Action3* in the `for` loop of Figure 1.4: `year++`, along with a similarly strange construct at the end of the `for` loop

```
sum += sum * irate;
```

The `++` and `+=` are shorthand operators for adding values to a variable.

year++ is a short way of writing `year = year + 1` and `sum += sum * irate` is short for `sum = sum + (sum * irate)`.

These shorthand operations are provided because incrementing by one is a common operation. Similarly, adding a value other than one is also quite common. C also supports a double minus operator, `--`, which subtracts one from a variable, and other assignment operators such as `-=`, which performs analogously to `+=`. These shorthand operators are provided because they save some typing, because they more clearly show the operation, and because some compilers can produce more efficient code. They are examined in detail in Chapter 2.

EXERCISES

1-7 The input-directed interest accumulator (Figure 1.4) did not do any range or error checking on the values entered by the user. Add a constant `MAXPERIOD` and check (with an appropriate `if` statement) that the number of years entered is less than or equal to `MAXPERIOD`. Similarly, add a check to see that the principal amount entered is greater than zero. If either of these bounds is violated, print an appropriate error message and terminate the program. □

1-8 What happens if the braces around the `for` loop's body in Figure 1.4 are left off? Try compiling and running to find the answer. □

1.4

ARRAYS

C supports arrays of the predefined data types and constructed types (we will consider constructed types in later chapters). An array is a collection of values, all of which are of the same underlying type, such as `int` or `float`.

An array is declared by giving the type of its elements, the array name, and the number of elements. The number of elements in the array is enclosed in brackets following its name and must be an integer. For example,

```
int    a[100];
```

defines an array called `a`, consisting of 100 ints. In C all arrays are indexed from zero, and in this example we access `a` from `a[0]` to `a[99]`.

Any expression that evaluates to an integer can be used as an array subscript. Here are some examples (where i and j are ints):

```
a[0]
a[10]
a[27 * 3]
a[i]
a[i * j]
```

We will illustrate the use of arrays by writing a program that reads integers and keeps them sorted in an array. The sorting technique is known as *insertion sort*[2]; it is easy to understand and to program, usually works with little debugging effort, and is suitable when the number of values to sort is fewer than about 50 to 100.

Insertion sort works by assuming that the array is already sorted and trying to find the appropriate place to insert a new value. We compare the new value with the last element in the array, the largest. If the value is less than this largest one, we shift it over one place and compare it with the next value. Eventually, the new number will be larger than some value in the array and thus will indicate the appropriate place to insert this new value. Alternatively, the new value will be smaller than every value in the array and thus will go into the first position. Therefore, the entire operation can be characterized as "compare, shift; compare, shift . . ." until we find the appropriate place. The technique is diagrammed in Figure 1.6.

Figure 1.7 is the program used to accomplish insertion sort. In Figure 1.8 we show a sample collection of input values and the output generated by the program. As long as we have more numbers to read, we will continue reading them and inserting into the array. Of course, we may eventually run out of room, since we only preallocate MAXVALS array elements, so we include an additional check during input to be certain that we read only MAXVALS numbers (MAXVALS is a program constant and is set to 100 via a #define statement). When we exceed MAXVALS numbers or reach the end of the input file, we print out the array in order.

1.4.1 ANALYSIS OF INSERTION SORT

The insertion sort program, Figure 1.7, starts with a new statement:

```
#include <stdio.h>
```

[2] Though this is not the fastest sorting routine (it has the property that the computing time increases as the *square* of the number of values to be sorted − double the number of values and the computing time goes up by a factor of four, triple the number and the computing time goes up by a factor of nine), it is reasonable for small number of values to be sorted.

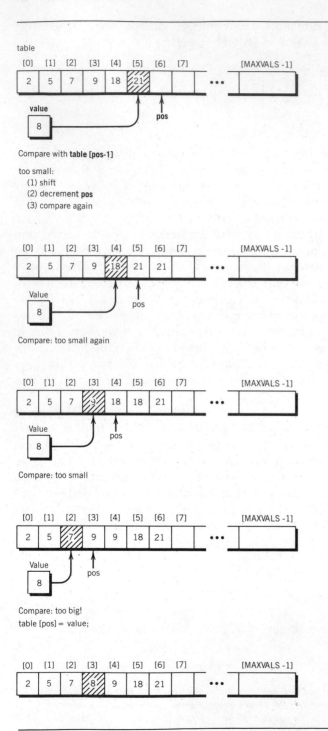

FIGURE 1.6 Stages in insertion sort. The new value is eventually put between the seven and the nine.

```
/*
 * Read a table of values and sort them using "insertion sort."
 */
#include <stdio.h>
#define  MAXVALS          100          /* maximum number of values to sort */

main()
{
  int numvals = 0,                  /* number of values currently in table */
      pos,                          /* index into table */
      table[MAXVALS],               /* table of values */
      value;                        /* current value */

  while (numvals < MAXVALS && scanf ("%d", &value) != EOF)
  {
    /* Find place for new element, shifting other elements over. */

      for (pos = numvals; pos > 0 && value < table[pos - 1]; pos--)
        table[pos] = table[pos - 1];

    /* Insert element, updating element counter */

      table[pos] = value;
      numvals++;
  }

    /* Reached end of input file - print in order */

    for (pos = 0; pos < numvals; pos++)
      printf ("%d\n", table[pos]);
}
```

FIGURE 1.7 Insertion sort program – builds an array of integers in sorted order.

which is another preprocessor directive. In this case, the file named *stdio.h* is included in the program. This is a system-supplied *header* file (thus the suffix name .h) that contains many of the definitions used by the library

15	−45
97	9
−45	15
123	18
18	21
9	97
21	123

(a) Sample input data　　　　*(b) Output from the insertion sort program*

FIGURE 1.8 Sample input and output produced by the insertion sort program, Figure 1.7.

functions for low-level input and output processing (thus the prefix *stdio*, which stands for standard input/output). The exact location of this file is system dependent. The angle brackets surrounding its name instruct the preprocessor to look in various standard locations where header files are likely to be found.

Why do we need to include *stdio.h* in this program, since the program in Figure 1.7 is so similar in its declarations and control structures to the previous programs in this chapter? The answer is that we use the predefined constant `EOF`, a value returned by `scanf` when the end of the input file is detected. In most C compilers, `EOF` is defined to be minus one, but since this is system dependent, it is included in *stdio.h* and we test for it directly. We will discuss the use of `scanf` in this program in more detail later.

Data Declarations

We have used a new form in our data declarations:

```
int numvals = 0,        /* number of values in table */
    pos,                /* index into table */
    table[MAXVALS],     /* table of values */
    value;              /* current value */
```

We declare `numvals` to be an `int` and initialize it to zero. We do this by assigning a value to a variable at the point where it is declared. There are restrictions on the types of variables that can be initialized in this way, but this is an efficient means of giving values to variables that have to be initialized during run time; if a variable is not initialized, you should assume that it contains garbage.

We have also declared `table` to be an array. We do this by including square brackets after its name, and including the size of the array within the brackets. Thus, the type of `table` is "array of `int`," and a declaration such as

```
int     table[MAXVALS];
```

allocates storage for `MAXVALS` integers, indexed from 0 to $MAXVALS - 1$ (0 to 99 here).

We access an array element by specifying its index. The index within the square brackets can be any expression that can be interpreted as an integer. Normally, reals and strings are not allowed as array indexes, although we will consider the construction of array indexes more fully in Chapter 3. It should be noted that there is no run-time array bounds checking. If you attempted to access a location such as `table[-10]`, neither the compiler nor the run-time environment would note this error.

You are responsible for doing your own bounds checks during the running of your program.[3]

The while Loop

We control reading of insertion sort's input values with a while loop. There are two conditions that must be true for the loop body to be executed: numvals must be less than MAXVALS (so that we do not insert past the upper array bounds) and scanf must not return EOF (so that we stop when we have read all the input):

```
while (numvals < MAXVALS && scanf ("%d", &value) != EOF)
```

The double ampersands (&&) represent the logical AND operator. Logical OR is also available and is indicated by double vertical bars (||). When we are testing more than one conditional combined with logical AND, the leftmost one is tested first. Only if this one is true (nonzero) is the next conditional tested. A similar situation holds for logical OR: only if the first conditional is false (zero) is the second tested. As a result, in the while loop we first test numvals < MAXVALS. If this is false, we do not perform the second test. Specifically, scanf is not called. Only when the first test is true is scanf called and compared with EOF. The result is that we read a value only if there is room to store it in the array.

Notice again that scanf takes two sets of arguments. The first indicates the format of the input data (in this case a single decimal integer, indicated by "%d") and the second the list of addresses of the variables to be read. We use the address of value, indicated by &value, in the parameter list of scanf. Here, however, we are assuming that the input contains no errors, and we compare the value of scanf not with one (the number of values we expect to read), but with the predefined constant EOF, the value scanf will return if the end of the input file is reached. The symbol != is the inequality operator, read as "not equal." Therefore, only when both conditions, numvals < MAXVALS and scanf not equal to EOF, are true do we enter the while loop body.

The for Loop

We want to compare value with each entry in the array, starting with the largest, or last, entry and shift values one place whenever value is smaller than the entry we are comparing. Eventually, value will be greater than

---

[3] The action of C in this situation is interesting. In Pascal, for example, illegal array accesses can also occur; they cause the program to terminate. In C you are forced to do what you should do anyway to protect your programs – guard against illegal array access.

or equal to an entry in the array, or we will have reached the beginning of
`table`. In that case, we insert `value` into the newly created hole. We do
this with a `for` loop, whose entire body consists of a single statement, and
whose terminating expression is a logical AND of two conditions; if either
one is false, the loop terminates. Notice also that we use the shorthand
decrement operation `pos--`:

```
for (pos = numvals; pos > 0 && value < table[pos - 1]; pos--)
    table[pos] = table[pos - 1];
```

A great deal is taking place within this `for` loop; we suggest that you try
working through it by hand to see its effect.[4]

An Aside on `scanf`

`scanf` is a useful function, but there are several limitations that may pre-
clude its use in production programs. Unfortunately, because of the way
`scanf` is written, there is no easy way to scan over illegal input; it remains
on the illegal character, returning the same error indication over and over.
In Chapters 6, 11, and 12, we will consider low-level input in detail and
develop solutions to this problem.

Because `scanf` can read an arbitrary number of values with differing
types, the underlying implementation is extremely large and cumbersome.
We can often produce code that is more condensed and works more
quickly by writing special-purpose versions of `scanf`, and we will do this in
Chapters 6 and 9. The methods needed are brief and surprisingly simple,
and they can reduce the size of the compiled code by one third or more,
and the running times of programs by equally large amounts.

EXERCISES

1-9 Add additional code to the insertion sort program, Figure 1.7, in order to
count the number of elements moved. After printing the entire sorted
array, print out this count of the number of element movements. For a
random set of n input values, this number should be approximately
$n(n + 1)/2$. Compare your result with this expected result.   □

1-10 Rewrite the insertion sort program so that it sorts the values from high to
low. There are two ways to do this, so try to implement both methods.   □

---

[4] Insertion sort is an enjoyable algorithm to implement because it is so natural. If you give
someone one suit of a deck of cards and ask that the cards be sorted, the person will usually
do something resembling insertion sort – compare the next card with each in turn, until the
right place is found and then move everything over to make room for the new card.

1-11 C's `for` loop is significantly more general than that of most other languages. Write an insertion sort program in another language with which you are familiar and compare the programs. Which is easier? Which is more compact? □

1-12 In Figure 1.7 we tested `scanf` for EOF, but we did not test to see that the value returned from `scanf` is one, which it should be because we are reading one number each time. Add input error-checking code to Figure 1.7 so that your program treats any non-one return from `scanf` as if it were the end of the file. □

1-13 Write an insertion sort program that first finds the appropriate place to insert the new value, and then shifts everything after it one place before inserting the value. □

1.5

CHARACTER INPUT AND OUTPUT

C allows us to manipulate characters, as well as numbers. A character is indicated by enclosing it in single quotation marks, such as

```
'a', 'A', 'l', '9'
```

Different computers provide different characters. However, almost all computers' character sets allow both upper- and lowercase letters, digits, some punctuation, and control, or non-printing, characters.

Just as there are prewritten routines for formatted input and output of numerical and string data, so there are predefined functions for character I/O. The two character-equivalent functions of `scanf` and `printf` are `getchar` and `putchar`, respectively.

`getchar` takes no arguments and returns as its value a single character — the next character in the input stream. Like `scanf`, `getchar` will return the special value EOF if the end-of-file character is entered. `getchar` is guaranteed to return a value that is the integer representation of the character in the local character set, or the special value EOF. As we saw earlier, EOF is usually minus one, a value that does not represent a character.

Similarly, `putchar` takes an integer that represents a legal character, and writes it as a character to the standard output. If the number does not represent a legal character, anomalous results will occur. Usually the least significant bits (equivalent to the local character representation) are examined, but the results vary from machine to machine. It is the programmer's responsibility to provide a value that represents a legitimate character. `putchar` does not return a value and should never fail.[5]

As a result of the need for an "extended" character set (that is, one that includes `EOF`), we usually deal with variables declared as `int`s when reading character data. We can see this in Figure 1.9, a program that echoes its input to its output, one character at a time. Such a program is useful if we have the ability to direct the standard input or standard output to different files, since it can then be used to copy one file to another. The program reads characters using `getchar` and writes them with `putchar` until `getchar` returns `EOF`. This program is interesting because it shows how transformations of input are built using more basic pieces.[6]

Try compiling and running the program in Figure 1.9 to see how it works on your system. Some operating systems buffer the characters from the terminal until carriage return is typed. In that case, after typing a complete line plus carriage return, the entire line will be echoed (Figure 1.10a). If your operating system does not buffer lines, then each character will be repeated as it is typed (Figure 1.10b).

1.5.1 ANALYSIS OF CHARACTER COPYING

By now you should be familiar with many of the usual C constructs. Reading Figure 1.9, you should be starting to think in terms of programming paradigms – those structures and declarations that are used over and over

```
/*
 * Copy the input to the output.
 */
#include <stdio.h>

main()
{
  int c;                  /* next character */

  while ((c = getchar()) != EOF)
    putchar(c);
}
```

FIGURE 1.9 A program that copies its input to its output.

[5] In fact it can fail if the character is being written to a file. The details are presented in Chapter 11.

[6] In UNIX the file-copying program *cp* functions almost in this way, except that it includes additional code to handle named files or directories on the command line.

```
Now is the time                          NNooww  iiss  tthhee  ttiimmee
Now is the time
for all good men                         ffoorr  aallll  ggoooodd  mmeenn
for all good men
to come to the aid                       ttoo  ccoommee  ttoo  tthhee  aaiidd
to come to the aid
of their party.                          ooff  tthheeiirr  ppaarrttyy..
of their party.

            (a)                                      (b)
```

FIGURE 1.10 (*a*) Output from Figure 1.9 when input is being line buffered. (*b*) Output when lines are not buffered.

again. And in Figure 1.9 we see that the file *stdio.h* is included at the very beginning:

```
#include <stdio.h>
```

We include this file because `getchar` and `putchar`, as well as `EOF`, are defined there. As previously noted, the declaration for the character to be read via `getchar` must include `EOF`, which is outside any character set; we declare `c` as an `int`.

The program itself is a single `while` loop that reads a single character and tests for `EOF`. Note that reading the character and assigning to `c` occur within the loop's test:

```
(c = getchar()) != EOF
```

This works because assignment (=) is an operator; it performs an assignment and returns the value assigned. In this case, a character is read and its integer representation is assigned to `c`. After the assignment, the value of `c` is compared with `EOF` to determine if the loop should exit. If `c` is not `EOF`, the loop body is entered; we simply write the character.

The parentheses around `c = getchar()` are necessary because the precedence of assignment is very low and would otherwise cause the statement to be interpreted as

```
c = (getchar() != EOF)
```

which is not the result we intended at all.

To further illustrate character handling, as well as the now familiar `printf`, we will write a small program (Figure 1.11) that writes each line in the input with a line number. Like Figure 1.9, this program will read a character at a time (until the end of the file) and write the character to the standard output. We will also remember the previous character typed, so that when a character is ready to be printed, if its previous character was a

```
/*
 * Copy the input to the output, giving each line a number.
 */

#include <stdio.h>

main()
{
  int c,                                    /* next character */
      lastch = '\n',                        /* pretend starting new line */
      lineno = 0;                           /* lines printed so far */

  while ((c = getchar()) != EOF)
  {
    if (lastch == '\n')
    {                                       /* hit end of line */
      lineno++;
      printf("%6d ", lineno);
    }
    putchar(c);
    lastch = c;
  }
}
```

FIGURE 1.11 Program that copies its input to its output, placing a line number at the start of each line.

carriage return (\n), we will know that we are at the start of a new line and will print the line number. Notice that this is just an extension of the function provided in Figure 1.9, the program that copied its input to its output.

Line numbering is a useful capability and is surprisingly simple to accomplish. However, it makes sense only if the operating system buffers its input lines and if we have the ability to redirect the standard input and output.[7]

Figure 1.12 shows the result of running the line-numbering program on itself.

EXERCISES

1-14 In Figure 1.9, we used parentheses to get the precedence right on

```
(c = getchar()) != EOF
```

[7] In UNIX, if we have compiled the program into a file named *number*, we can create a line-numbered version of *infile*, called *outfile*, by entering *number < infile > outfile*

Describe the effect of

```
c = getchar() != EOF
```

(*Hint*: Remember, a conditional test returns zero for false, one for true.) □

1-15 Notice that blank lines are numbered in Figure 1.12. Rewrite the line-numbering program (Figure 1.11) so that blank lines are counted but not numbered. □

1-16 Add page numbering to the line-numbering program, Figure 1.11. That is, place a line with "PAGE N" at the beginning of each page, with a blank line between the page numbering line and the next line from the input. Assume that a page has a maximum of 66 lines (use a constant PGLINE). □

1.6

FUNCTIONS

In our programs so far, we have used only the single function main. However, when we write larger programs, it is necessary to break them up into

```
 1 /*
 2  * Copy the input to the output, giving each line a number.
 3  */
 4
 5 #include <stdio.h>
 6
 7 main()
 8 {
 9   int c,                                  /* next character */
10       lastch = '\n',                      /* pretend starting new line */
11       lineno = 0;                         /* lines printed so far */
12
13   while ((c = getchar()) != EOF)
14   {
15     if (lastch == '\n')
16     {                                     /* hit end of line */
17       lineno++;
18       printf("%6d ", lineno);
19     }
20     putchar(c);
21     lastch = c;
22   }
23 }
```

FIGURE 1.12 Output with line numbers added by the program.

smaller, more efficient, more manageable pieces. Functions provide a way of packaging code and giving the package a name that can be referred to by other functions and the main program. In fact, a program in C is a collection of one or more functions, including `main` (which must be present in each program). Functions are used because they allow common, single-purpose routines to be neatly packaged and their capabilities made available to the main program, without the main program having to know how their task is accomplished internally. In fact, we have already used functions that were prewritten and compiled for us, `printf` and `scanf`, without knowing how they perform their job.

Functions in C are assumed to return a value (type `int` unless we declare them to be otherwise). We can ignore the returned value, in which case a function behaves like a procedure in other languages (such as Pascal). The syntax of a function definition is quite similar to the syntax of the `main` function that occurs in every program.

```
type-identifier   function-name   (parameters)
    type declarations for parameters
    {
        local declarations

        function body
    }
```

Here *type-identifier* is the type of the value that the function returns. If no type is specified, `int` is assumed. If the function has parameters, they are indicated in the parameter list; if there are no parameters, the parentheses are still needed to indicate to the compiler that this is a function definition. The parameter list names the parameters but gives no type information; this is indicated in the next part of the function, where the type of each parameter is declared.

Any variables that are local to the function (such as loop counters and array indexes) are declared in the *local declarations*. A local variable's value can be accessed only within the function where it is declared. Finally, the body of the function is written. Notice the use of statement grouping brackets ({ and }), which are required even if the function has no body. If the function is to return a value, a `return` statement is used.

In order to illustrate the use of functions and parameter-passing mechanisms, we will write a small program (Figure 1.13) with two functions – one that reads data into an array and another that prints the array in reverse order. Although simple, the functions in Figure 1.13 demonstrate different aspects of function use and will prove instructive as a guide for writing your own functions. Further, we will use the input-reading function `get_data` again later in the book. The program reads integers into an array `a`, and then prints them out in reverse order. We use two functions called from `main` to do this. The first, `get_data`, reads numbers into an array. The second, `reverse_print`, prints the values

```
/*
 * Read values and print out in reverse order.
 */
#define MAXARRAY        1000             /* max values in array "a" */

main ()
{
    int a[MAXARRAY],                     /* input array */
        nvals;                           /* number of values in "a" */

    nvals = get_data (a, MAXARRAY);      /* read values */
    printf ("Values in reverse order:\n\n");
    reverse_print (a, nvals);            /* print them in reverse order */
}

/*
 * Read integers from the std. input.  Terminate on end of file, illegal input,
 * or if the number of values exceeds "max".  Returns the number of values read.
 */
int get_data (vals, max)
int vals[], max;
{
    int n = 0;                           /* values read */

    while (n < max && scanf ("%d", &vals[n]) == 1)
        n++;
    return n;
}

/*
 * Print the values in "vals[n-1]" through "vals[0]"        */
 */
reverse_print (vals, n)
int vals[], n;
{
    int i;                               /* index into array */

    for (i = n - 1; i >= 0; i--)
        printf ("%d\n", vals[i]);
}
```

FIGURE 1.13 Program that reads values and prints them out in reverse order.

from the last to the first element. The entire program, showing where the functions are defined and how they are called, is shown in Figure 1.13.

1.6.1 ANALYSIS OF REVERSE

The main program has a simple structure: get the data for the array and print them. It does this by calling two functions, get_data and reverse_print. The underscore (_) is part of the function name; it is a legal character and can occur anywhere in a name. We use the underscore to make the function name more readable. An alternative is to use uppercase and lowercase, such as GetData.

The Function get_data

get_data has two arguments: the array where the input values are to go and the number of values to read, in this case the size of the array. In addition, the function returns n, the number of values in the array (that is, the array vals contains values at vals[0] through vals[n−1]). Notice that in Figure 1.13 the parameters to the functions are named in the function header and that the header *does not* end in a semicolon.

```
int get_data (vals, max)
```

The header is followed with the declarations of the function's parameters. vals is an array of integers and max is an integer, and both are declared in the next line:

```
int vals[], max;
```

It is not necessary to declare the size of one-dimensional arrays passed to functions, since it is the address of the first element that is copied to the function. The compiler can address the array with this information.[8]

When we call a function, a copy of each argument is made and any changes to the argument value apply only to the copy within the function. This parameter-passing mechanism is known as *call by value* because the *value* is copied to the function. Thus, max can be changed within get_data without affecting the parameter passed to the function. Because the address of an array is passed instead of the entire array, arrays are not copied and changes to an array parameter affect the array in the calling function.

return statement. The expression is the value returned.

```
   return n;
```

We call a function by specifying its name, and providing a list of values

---

[8] Since it is the address of the first element of the array that is passed, the compiler knows how much storage to allocate – the amount necessary to hold a single address. In the main program, the compiler actually allocated sufficient storage to hold the entire array.

for its parameters. We call `get_data` and assign its value to a variable `nvals` in `main` with

```
nvals = get_data (a, MAXARRAY);
```

When `get_data` exits, `nvals` is the number of values read into `a`; that is, the elements `a[0]` through `a[nvals−1]` contain valid data. If no values have been entered, `nvals` will be zero.

The Function `reverse_print`

`reverse_print` takes two arguments, the array to be printed and the number of values in the array. The array is printed in reverse order using `i` as an index. Since `i` is declared within `reverse_print`'s body, it is local to `reverse_print`.

```
reverse_print (vals, n)
int vals[], n;
{
    int i;                          /* index into array */

    for (i = n − 1; i >= 0; i−−)
    printf ("%d\n", vals[i]);
}
```

Since the size of an array parameter is not specified in the declaration, any size array (of the specified type) can be passed. This makes `reverse_print` fairly general; it can be used to print any sized array of integers in reverse order.

EXERCISES

1-17 Write a function, `search`, that finds the location of a value in an array. The function should take three parameters: the value to be found, the array to be searched, and the size of the array. The function should return an `int`, the index where the value is found. If the value is not in the array, the function should return minus one.   □

1-18 Rewrite the sorting program (Figure 1.7) so that it calls upon three functions:

a. `get_data` from this section.

b. `print_data`, similar to `reverse_print`, except that it prints the array from first to last, that is, from `a[0]` to `a[n−1]`.

c. A new function, `sort`, that takes two parameters, an array of ints and the number of values in the array, and returns the array sorted from high to low.

The program will read values using get_data and then call sort to sort the array. After returning from sort, the array is printed via a call to print_data. □

1-19 Write a function, sum, that computes and returns the sum of the first n elements in an array of ints. □

1-20 A function named dummy with no body is defined by

```
dummy ()
{
}
```

When might such a function be useful? □

STYLE IN C

At the end of each chapter we will include a "Style Summary" similar to this one, summarizing the main points of the chapter and their relationship to writing understandable programs. Oriented most often to the more experienced C programmer, these hints and insights should grow in importance as your experience with C grows. For this chapter, we provide some suggestions that will make it easier to start writing readable and understandable C programs.

- Use #define for symbolic constants. If their values need to be changed, only one line of the program (the #define) must be altered.
- Use all uppercase names for constants and mixed-case names or the underline character (_) for variables and function names. Names such as GetData or get_data are easier to read than singlecase names without underlining (as in getdata). This also makes it easy to spot names known only to the preprocessor.
- C can be a concise, compact language. Unfortunately, the meaning of a piece of code can easily become obscured with the overuse of the shorthand operators such as ++, --, +=, and -=. Never hesitate to use more traditional constructions in order to keep the operation and purpose of the code clear.

- Watch out for the double equal sign (==) used for the test of equality. If we want to test whether two values, A and B, are equal in an if statement, we do it as shown on the left below. On the right we show a very common mistake, using a single equal sign, which has a very different meaning.

```
if (A == B)                          if (A = B)
    statement1                           statement1
else                                 else
    statement2                           statement2
```

What is the difference? The first compares A and B, evaluating to true or false depending on whether or not they are equal. The second is an *assignment* that also returns a value as a side effect. The value of B is assigned to A, and A's new value is the value of the assignment. This will always be evaluated as true (nonzero), unless B is zero.

- Use functions to keep your programs concise and modular. Functions shorten the main program and thus clarify its overall functioning. As with all identifiers, a function's name should indicate its purpose. Functions should be relatively short (50 to 100 lines), and should be liberally commented.

- To allow the programmer full access to the underlying machine, C provides minimal error checking. Programmers are assumed to know what they are doing. It is the programmer's responsibility to check array bounds and parameter types, and a few careful checks can save large amounts of debugging time.

CHAPTER 2

BASIC DATA TYPES AND OPERATORS

In Chapter 1 we introduced the basic data types **int** and **float**, as well as several different operators. In this chapter we discuss these data types and operators in more detail, and provide descriptions and examples of other data types and operators we had previously ignored. We pay special attention to C's shorthand and bit-manipulation operators, which are not found in most other programming languages. The chapter concludes with a look at the rules for C's automatic type conversions and the rules for constructing variable names. This chapter is a reference manual on the built-in data types and on the operations that can be performed on them.

2.1

BUILT-IN TYPES AND VALUES

There are three built-in data types in C, with several variations: integers, reals and characters. The differences in the numerical types (integers versus reals) results from different storage representations and different machine instructions for handling them. Each numerical type comes in different sizes, allowing you to select the number of bits (or range of values) that is appropriate for your needs.

2.1.1 INTEGERS

Integers, as we saw in Chapter 1, are whole numbers with a range of values supported by a particular machine. Generally, integers occupy one word of storage, but since the word size of machines varies over a wide range (typically 16, 32, or 36 bits), we are not certain how big an integer can be. To provide some control and to save storage space when values are in a more restricted range, C has three classes of integer storage: short, int, and long, in both signed and unsigned forms. Usually a short is 16 bits, an int is 32 bits, and a long is also 32 bits, but this depends on the machine your program runs on. Thus, a short can be used to save space when you can guarantee that a value will always be in a small range, and a long can be used to store larger values. Table 2.1 lists the sizes of shorts, ints, and longs on typical machines.

Integers can be either signed or unsigned. Signed integers use one bit for the sign of the number. A signed int (or just int, the default) uses 1 bit for the sign and 15 bits for the magnitude of the number on 16-bit machines or 31 bits for the magnitude on 32-bit machines. On a 16-bit machine, an int can store a value in the range from −32,768 to +32,767 (that is, -2^{15} to $+2^{15} - 1$).

Unsigned integers (declared unsigned int, unsigned short, or unsigned long) use all the bits for the magnitude and are always nonnegative.[1] On a 16-bit machine all 16 bits are used, so any value in the range from 0 to 65,535 (0 to $2^{16} - 1$) can be represented. Unsigned types are used to increase the range of representable values when it is known that a variable will always be nonnegative, as, for example, a loop counter. Unsigned integer arithmetic is straightforward when two unsigned values are combined; however, when an unsigned integer is combined with a signed integer, automatic conversions take place, as discussed in Section 2.3.

Integer constants are expressed as a string of digits, with a minus sign for negative numbers. If the number is too large for an int, it is automat-

TABLE 2.1 Integer representation on typical computers.

Data Type	Number of Bits			
	DEC PDP-11	DEC VAX	IBM-PC	Apple Macintosh
short	16	16	16	16
int	16	32	16	16
long	32	32	32	32

[1]Most compilers allow the type of integer to be omitted from the declaration. A variable declared as unsigned is assumed to be an unsigned int.

ically stored as a `long`. You can force a number to be a `long` by placing the letter 'l' or 'L' after it. For example, `32767L` is a `long` constant. There is no such thing as a `short` or `unsigned` constant; C will automatically make it an `int`.

In addition to decimal (base 10) numbers, integers can be specified in either octal (base 8) or hexadecimal (base 16). A leading zero indicates an octal number; a number prefixed by '0x' or '0X' indicates a hexadecimal (hex for short). Regardless of how a value is indicated, however, it is stored in its binary equivalent. For example, the decimal value 63, the octal 077, or the hex 0x3f are all stored as 0 . . . 0111111. The octal and hexadecimal number systems are described in Appendix 1.

The data types `short`, `int`, and `long` are called *integral* types. They can be read or printed using `scanf` and `printf` using the `%d` formatting string. Normally, integers are printed in decimal (base 10) format, even if they have been defined as octal or hex values. To read or print an integral value in octal using `scanf` or `printf` use `%o`; to read or print in hex, use `%x`. Unsigned integers are printed using the `%u` format specifier. Reading or printing a `long` requires the modifier l (`%ld` for a long decimal, `%lo` for a long octal, `%lx` for a long hex value, and `%lu` for a long unsigned value). Similarly, reading or printing a `short` requires the modifier h.

Figure 2.1*a* shows typical declarations and assignments of these data types, along with `printf` statements for printing some of the values. Figure 2.1*b* shows the output of the program in Figure 2.1*a*.

EXERCISES

2-1 Write a program to determine the largest and smallest values for an `int`, `short`, and `long` on your computer. □

2-2 Repeat the previous exercise for `unsigned` values. □

2-3 Carelessness in the use of constants can lead to unexpected program results. What are the base 10 values of the following constants: 0377, 0x377, 377? □

2-4 Write a program that reads a value (using `scanf`) and prints it in base 10, hex, and octal. □

2.1.2 REALS

Reals, or floating point numbers, are stored in 32 bits (on all 16-bit and 32-bit machines), with a machine dependent number of bits for the frac-

```
main ()
{
    int     a = 17,
            b = -197,
            c = 0xa7c;              /* a hex value, 2684 decimal */
            d = 01777;              /* an octal value, 1023 decimal */

    short   s = 32,
            t = -32767,
            u = -1;

    long    l = 15L,                /* the 'L' is redundant - stored as type of "l" */
            m = -455,
            n = 156765341;          /* too big for an int on 16 bit machines */

    unsigned int    ui = 157,
                    uj = 0xff,
                    uk = -15;       /* careful - machine dependent */

    printf("a: %d b: %d c: %d\n", a, b, c);
    printf("s: %d t: %d u: %d\n", s, t, u);
    printf("l: %ld m: %ld n: %ld\n", l, m, n);
    printf("ui: %u uj: %u uk: %u\n", ui, uj, uk);

    /* Print 'c' in both decimal and hex format */

    printf("c (base 10): %d  c (base 16): %x\n", c, c);
}
```

(a) *Sample declarations and* printf *formats*

```
a: 17 b: -197 c: 2684
s: 32 t: -32767 u: -1
l: 15 m: -455 n: 156765341
ui: 157 uj: 255 uk: 4294967281
c (base 10): 2684  c (base 16): a7c
```

(b) *Output when run on a 32-bit machine*

FIGURE 2.1 Sample declarations and assignments using shorts, ints, and longs

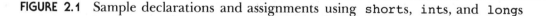

tion and the number of bits for the exponent. A typical representation uses 23 bits for the fraction and 9 bits, including the sign, for the exponent, as in Figure 2.2.

Real numbers are normally written with a decimal point, such as 13.45 or −211.0, but they may also be written in "e" notation, giving both a fraction and an exponent to base 10, as shown in Figure 2.3. "e" notation is similar to scientific notation, replacing the times sign and the base with the letter "e," as we see in Figure 2.3.

```
0  1  •••  8 9     •••    31
┌─┬──────────┬──────────────────┐
│S│ exponent │     fraction     │
└─┴──────────┴──────────────────┘
```

FIGURE 2.2 A typical floating point representation. Bit 0 is the sign of the fraction; bits 1-8 are the exponent (excess 128); bits 9-31 are the fraction.

Reals are defined using the `float` declaration and have about 7 significant digits. When greater significance is needed, a `double` can be used. `doubles` use 64 bits per value, with additional bits going to the fraction. Typical representations for `doubles` give 14 significant digits.

`floats` and `doubles` are specified in floating point notation, and are read with `scanf` using the `%f` formatting string for `floats` and `%lf` for `doubles`. With `printf`, `%f` is used to print both `floats` and `doubles`. If the "e" notation is desired (1.3e5 instead of 130000), use `%e`. The default number of digits printed using these formats is compiler dependent. The examples in Figure 2.4*a* and *b* were run on a DEC VAX, a 32-bit machine. Try them on your own machine to see what the defaults are.

2.1.3 CHARACTERS

We usually think of characters as letters of the alphabet, but they encompass even more than that. In fact, a character value can be any member of a machine's character set. The available characters and their internal representation depend on the machine on which the program runs. The most common character sets are ASCII (American Standard Code for Information Interchange) and EBCDIC (Extended Binary Coded Decimal Interchange Code). ASCII is the character set used on most personal, micro, and minicomputers, as well as several large mainframes, while EBCDIC is used on large IBM mainframes. ASCII characters are seven bits but are usually put into an eight-bit byte, while EBCDIC is an eight-bit

Floating Pt.	Scientific Notation	"e" notation
12.45	1.245×10^{1}	1.245e1
−211.0	-2.110×10^{2}	−2.110e2
0.0056	5.600×10^{-3}	5.600e−3
−0.000123	-1.230×10^{-4}	−1.230e−4

FIGURE 2.3 Examples of floating point notation and equivalent scientific and "e" notation.

```
main()
{
  float    f = 0.1245e2,
           g = -0.123e-3,
           h = 0.00013;

  double   d = 2.0,
           e = -371.2164982e17;

  printf("f: %f g: %f h: %f\n", f,g,h);      /* print f, g, h as floats */
  printf("d: %f e: %f\n", d,e);              /* print d, e as floats */
  printf("d: %e e: %e\n", d,e);              /* print d, e using "e" notation */
}
```

(a) Examples of declarations and use of floats *and* doubles

```
f: 12.450000 g: -0.000123 h: 0.000130
d: 2.000000 e: -37121649820000000000.000000
d: 2.000000e+00 e: -3.712165e+19
```

(b) Output from the program in part (a), run on a 32-bit machine

FIGURE 2.4 (*a*) Examples of declarations and use of floats and doubles; (*b*) Output from the program in part (*a*), run on a 32-bit machine.

set. There are 128 ASCII and 256 EBCDIC characters. They are shown in Appendixes 2 and 3, respectively.

A character variable is declared using the type identifier char:

```
char   c;
```

Single characters are indicated using single quotation marks. Here are examples of assigning to c, declared as a char:

```
c = 'A';           /* uppercase A */
c = 'a';           /* lowercase a */
c = '7';           /* the character code for the digit 7 */
```

Since all compilers store a char in an integer representation corresponding to the local character set, these assignments are machine independent. In ASCII, for example,

```
c = 'a';
printf("%d", c);
```

prints the number 97. To read or print a character as a *character*, use the %c format. The output of printf("%c", c) is the single character a.

Usually characters are stored in a single byte, the size that is appropriate for most machines.

Some character codes do not yield a printable character, and they are represented using escape sequences. An escape sequence is a backslash (\) followed by a code letter for the particular function. Figure 2.5 shows the character escape codes.

The last code in Figure 2.5 (`'\xxx'`) is provided because we need a more flexible mechanism to specify all the available characters, including nonprinting ones. Here **xxx** represents a (maximum) three-digit octal number. A leading zero is not needed because the value is always interpreted as octal. A maximum of three digits is permitted; if the number of bits is greater than that needed for a single character (such as `'\777'`), machine dependent results occur; usually the rightmost bits are used, but caution must be exercised.

For example, in ASCII, the code to ring the terminal bell on most terminals is a control-g, or seven. Therefore, we can define this as a constant BELL and use `putchar` to ring someone's bell:

```
#define BELL     '\007'              /* ASCII bell code */
    . . .
    putchar(BELL);                   /* ring terminal bell */
```

Figure 2.6 is a program that prints all the characters in a machine's character set (assuming a maximum of 128 characters), showing the decimal, octal, and character values. Caution is needed in running this program, though, because some of the nonprinting characters do strange things to a terminal (such as erase the screen) or to a printer (such as eject the paper to the top of the next page). For this reason, we have chosen the inelegant method of placing each character on a separate line.

`'\0'`	null character
`'\b'`	backspace
`'\f'`	form feed (top of next page)
`'\n'`	newline (as seen in Chapter 1)
`'\r'`	carriage return
`'\t'`	tab
`'\v'`	vertical tab
`'\''`	single quotation mark
`'\"'`	double quotation mark
`'\\'`	backslash
`'\xxx'`	octal value

FIGURE 2.5 Character codes using the backslash quoting mechanism.

```
/*
 *       Print character set in decimal, octal, and character form
 */
#define  MAXCHAR        128      /* change to 256 for EBCDIC machines */

main()
{
    int  c;

    for (c = 0; c < MAXCHAR; c++)
       printf ("%4d\t%4o\t%c\n", c, c, c);
}
```

FIGURE 2.6 Program that prints the local character set.

Characters versus Integers

Characters seem strange, because they are machine dependent and because there does not appear to be a strong distinction between them and integers. Characters give the first hint that C is not a strongly typed language, since we can often use characters and integers interchangeably; furthermore, unlike more strongly typed languages, C allows us to do arithmetic on characters and treat integers as if they were characters.

In a strongly typed language such as Pascal, built-in functions are needed to convert between characters and integers, and it is an error to try to convert an integer to a character if the integer is outside the local character set. In C, however, no explicit conversion from one to the other is needed. If c is a char and n is an int, the assignment

```
    n = c;                  /* assign char to int */
```

causes n to be an integer with the value of the local set's code for c. In ASCII, if c is 'a', this assigns 97 to n. Similarly, the assignment

```
    c = n;                  /* assign int to char */
```

causes the rightmost bits (depending on the character set and the machine) of c to be the same as the rightmost bits of n. A char can be safely converted to an int on any machine and will give the integer character code equivalent of the character. The reverse conversion, from int to char, is highly machine dependent and should be avoided when portability of code is desired.

It is useful to have a function to read characters and convert them to a single integer. Figure 2.7 is a program that illustrates how such a function might be written, reading characters representing a single number, converting them to an integer, which is then printed. It begins by scanning over leading spaces, tabs, and carriage returns (called *white space*) until a nonspace character is read. If the character is a + or a −, a flag is set appropriately and the remaining characters are assumed to be digits.

We use a `while` loop to convert the sequence of characters, reading and converting one character at a time, adding its value to a sum representing the value of the sequence. The loop stops when a nondigit is read. If the next character (c) is a digit (that is, a character greater than or equal to '0', and less than or equal to '9'), we add it to the sum representing the number. We do this by taking the current value of the sum and multiplying by 10, and then adding the digit that the new character represents:

```
sum = 10 * sum + (c - '0');
```

Note that to perform the conversion, we do not really need to know the machine representation of the character. We can convert a digit char-

```
/*
 *    Convert characters representing digits to a long integer.
 */

main()
{
    long    sum = 0;
    int     c,
            sign = 1;

    while ((c = getchar ()) == ' ' || c == '\t' || c == '\n')
        ;                              /* scan over "white space" */

    if (c == '-')
      sign = -1;
    if (c == '+' || c == '-')
      c = getchar ();                  /* skip over the '+' or '-' */

    while (c >= '0' && c <= '9')       /* accumulate sum */
    {
        sum = 10 * sum + (c - '0');
        c = getchar ();
    }
    if (sign == -1)                    /* is it neg? */
        sum = -sum;

    printf ("Integer value: %ld\n", sum);
}
```

FIGURE 2.7   A program that converts character input into a long integer.

acter to an integer by subtracting the character '0' from it. (This assumes that all digits are represented by contiguous codes, which is the case with both ASCII and EBCDIC.) For example, in ASCII the code for '7' is 55 and the code for '0' is 48; the subtraction yields the integer value 7. Trace out the conversion of a number such as 812 by hand to see the operation of the program clearly.

The idea of reading numerical data a character at a time and doing our own conversions may seem extreme when we already have scanf. However, scanf has several problems: it compiles into a large amount of runnable code, and it is slower than using our own conversions. More importantly, scanf makes it difficult for the programmer to handle errors because it tells us only how many values were correctly converted, giving us no information as to why any failure might have occurred. If a failure occurs (the number is less than expected), we still have to deal with the input a character at a time in order to provide suitable error messages or error recovery.

EXERCISES

2-5   Briefly discuss the advantages and disadvantages of explicit conversions between integers and characters (as in Pascal) and automatic conversions (as in C).   □

2-6   Write a program that reads a char and prints its integer equivalent in the local character set.   □

2-7   Write a program that reads an integer and prints the corresponding character. Be sure to do appropriate error/range checking.   □

2-8   The character-to-integer program, Figure 2.7, implements part of what scanf does – reading values from the input stream. printf performs the opposite function; it converts numbers to character strings and writes them. Write a program that converts an integer (perhaps defined by #define) to characters and writes them to the output.   □

2-9   Modify the character-to-integer program, Figure 2.7, so that it works for multiple numbers – one number per line, stopping on EOF.   □

2-10 Modify the function get_data from the program in Chapter 1 (Figure 1.13) so that it does its own character scanning and conversion to long's (as in Figure 2.7, eliminating scanf from the program. Compare the size and speed of the compiled code in both versions.   □

2-11 Modify the program in Figure 2.7 so that it reads and converts real numbers (that is, numbers containing a decimal point) as well as integers. □

2-12 Extend the program in the previous exercise so that it reads and converts numbers in scientific notation as well. □

2.2
OPERATORS

There are several classes of operators in C, distinguished by the number of operands they take and the types of values they return – numeric, logical, and so on. By now, the discussion of operators is somewhat repetitive, so we will quickly describe each of them and note any unusual requirements in the types of operands, in the values returned, or in the restrictions on ranges of values.

Many of the operators require operands to be a certain type. If an operand of an incorrect type is given, the operation may still be performed but the results may be different from those expected. It is the responsibility of the programmer to guarantee that operands are the correct type, in range, and that the result has not produced overflow or underflow. The alternative, as with languages such as Pascal, is for the compiler or run-time environment to capture incorrect operand types. When this is done at compile time, we can change the incorrect operation and recompile. When it occurs at run time, many languages do not provide tools for capturing errors and attempting to correct them. In using C, we must know our own code and monitor the operations ourselves. The benefit is that the need for run-time type checking is eliminated; our programs, if they run, will run more efficiently.

Table 2.2 summarizes the C operators, the types of operands expected, and their relative precedence. Parentheses can be used to override the default precedence, although the compiler is allowed to rearrange arbitrarily expressions involving only commutative operators (+, *, &, |, and ^), so temporary variables must be used to force the desired order of evaluation. The following sections elaborate on the table.

2.2.1 ARITHMETIC OPERATORS

The arithmetic operators are addition (+), subtraction (−), multiplication (*), division (/), and remaindering (%). All except % operate on integer, character, and floating point operands, as expected.

TABLE 2.2 C operators summarized in order of decreasing precedence.

Operator	Description
`x[i]`	Array subscripting.
`f(x)`	Function call.
`.`	Structure field selection.
`->`	Indirect structure field selection.
`++, --`	Postfix/prefix increment/decrement. If both occur in the same expression, postfix has higher precedence.
`sizeof`	Size of a variable or type (in bytes).
`(type)`	Cast to *type*.
`~`	Bitwise negation.
`!`	Logical NOT.
`-`	Unary minus.
`&`	Address of.
`*`	Indirection (dereferencing).
`*, /, %`	Multiply, divide, modulus. All are equal in precedence.
`+, -`	Addition, subtraction. Equal in precedence.
`<<, >>`	Left, right shift. Equal in precedence.
`<, >, <=, >=`	Test for inequality. Equal in precedence.
`==, !=`	Test for equality, inequality. Equal in precedence.
`&`	Bitwise AND.
`^`	Bitwise exclusive OR.
`|`	Bitwise OR.
`&&`	Logical AND.
`||`	Logical OR.
`? :`	Conditional operator.
`=, +=, -=, *=,` `/=, %=, <<=, >>=,` `&=, ^=, |=`	Assignment operators. All are equal in precedence.
`,`	The comma operator – sequential evaluation of expressions.

Integer addition (and subtraction) is carried out without regard to overflow. On most machines, adding one to the largest positive number yields the largest negative value. For unsigned integers, one added to the largest value yields zero. Integer arithmetic is always exact within the limits of the number of values that can be represented in the data type.

Multiplication, division, and remaindering are known as *multiplicative operators*. For integers, the results are exact if the result is representable in the data type. Problems can occur if the result of integer operations is assigned to a variable of a shorter type. Given the assignments

```
long    i = 10000,
        j = 10000;
short   answer;

answer = i * j;
```

the calculation of `answer` will correctly evaluate to 100,000,000. However, the assignment of the `long` result to a `short` produces machine-dependent results. Generally, the least significant bits are assigned. In the following illustration of the assignment

```
short s = -1691154500L;
```

notice that the `long` is a negative number (the sign bit is 1): −1,691,154,500; the truncated `short` (assuming that conversion from `long` to `short` uses the least significant bits) is a positive number: 1980. Conversion from a longer type to a shorter type leads to loss of significance or, worse, meaningless results.

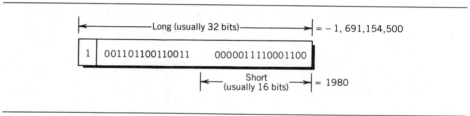

Floating point arithmetic is an approximation of the correct result, since floating point values are rounded to the number of significant digits allowable in the representation. Typically, this is 7 digits for `floats` and 14 digits for `doubles`. Adding to the largest possible `float` will produce overflow, and the results are machine dependent. The hardware of most machines traps floating point overflow, causing a run-time error and termination of the program.

All floating point arithmetic is carried out with double precision operands. This means that `floats` are always "widened" to `doubles` before the arithmetic occurs (at the expense of machine efficiency). After the expression is completely evaluated, the result is converted to the type of the left hand side of the assignment. This may involve loss of precision when converting back to a `float`, or overflow when converting to an `int`. Overflow and underflow can occur with real arithmetic; the action taken is machine dependent.

Division operates differently on floating point and integer operands. If both operands are integers with the same sign the result is *truncated* to an integer (towards zero). If only one of the operands is negative, the direction of truncation is not specified; it is implementation dependent.

Since integer division truncates toward zero, "fractional" division of integers always returns zero. Whether a and b are int's or floats,

```
a = 1/3;
b = 6/7;
```

assigns zero to both a and b.

However, if either operand of the division is a float, both operands are converted to double (for the purpose of the arithmetic) and the division is carried out in double precision. If x and y are floats,

```
x = 1.0/3.0;
y = 6.0/7.0;

w = 1.0/3;
z = 6/7.0;
```

assigns 0.333333 to both x and w and 0.857143 to both y and z.

The remaindering operator % takes two integer operands and returns the remainder when the first is divided by the second. If both are positive, this is the familiar modulus operation. The sign of the result is always the sign of the dividend (the first operand, or the one "upstairs"). Here are some examples:

```
 10 %   5  =   0
 10 %   7  =   3
  5 %  12  =   5
-20 %  12  =  -8
-20 % -12  =  -8        ← WATCH OUT - machine dependent
```

Regardless of the sign of a and b (a/b)*b+a%b will always equal a.

The arithmetic operators associate (are evaluated), as expected, left to right and follow the usual precedence rules. Table 2.3 shows the precedence of the arithmetic operators, from high to low, including assignment, which is also an operator. In this table, operations of equal precedence are applied left to right.

Operands should agree in type. If they do not, automatic conversions occur; these will be discussed in Section 2.3. After the expression on the

TABLE 2.3 Precedence of
C arithmetic operators

high	unary −, ++ −−
↓	*, /, %
v	+, −
low	= (assignment)

right side of the assignment is evaluated, it is converted to the type of the left (known as *assignment compatibility*) whenever that is possible.

Unary Minus

The minus sign in front of an expression is an operator. Since all constants are positive in C, the unary minus is equivalent to multiplying by minus one. This is straightforward with the `ints` and `floats`. With unsigned data, however, we must carefully consider the effect of multiplying by minus one and the effect on the bits. Consider the following small program that assigns negative values to unsigned variables.

```
main ()
{
    unsigned int a = -1;

    printf ("unsigned a: %u\n", a);
    printf ("signed a: %d\n", a);
}
```

The program was run on a 32-bit machine, and produced this output:

```
unsigned a: 4294967295
signed a: -1
```

To understand why this output occurs, recall that unsigned values are considered to be positive (or zero). Because minus one is represented as a word of all ones[2] and because minus one was interpreted as a signed integer (using the `%d` formatting in the second `printf`), we printed minus one. But a word of all ones is the largest positive value when interpreted as an `unsigned int`. In this example, using 32 bits for an `int`, 4,294,967,295 is printed.

2.2.2 RELATIONAL TESTS

The relational tests allow two values to be compared for equality (==), inequality (!=), greater than (>), less than (<), greater than or equal (>=), and less than or equal (<=). The result of a relational operator is an `int`, one (true) if the specified relation between the operands holds and zero (false) otherwise.

The inequality operators (>, >=, <, <=) all have the same precedence, which is higher than the precedence of == and !=. Since all of these have precedence higher than assignment, it is often necessary to use parentheses

---

[2]At least on two's complement machines.

in order to be certain that comparisons and assignments are made in the correct order, as in

```
if ((c = getchar()) == '\n')
```

(In fact, it is a good idea to parenthesize relational operators, since they are in the middle of the precedence hierarchy.)

2.2.3 LOGICAL OPERATORS

Logical operators perform the logical AND (`&&`), logical OR (`||`), or logical negation (`!`) of their operands. The logical operators take any numerical argument, including `char`, and return true or false (represented by one for true, zero for false) according to the truth table of Table 2.4. Nonzero values are interpreted as true and zero as false. Negation returns one if its operand is zero, and zero otherwise.

The logical operators associate (that is, are evaluated) left to right, and their precedence is low, so we rarely need to parenthesize. Figure 2.8 shows how expressions using `&&` and `||` are evaluated.

Evaluation Order

The operands of logical operations can be any expression and may have side effects that change the values of their parameters. To use logical operators correctly, we must understand the order of evaluation and the possibility that a clause might not be evaluated at all.

Without parentheses, logical operations are performed left to right, and evaluation stops as soon as the result can be determined. For logical AND, such as in the statement

TABLE 2.4 Truth table showing results of logical AND and logical OR

Operands		Result	
Op1	*Op2*	`&&`	`||`
Nonzero	Nonzero	1	1
Nonzero	Zero	0	1
Zero	Nonzero	0	1
Zero	Zero	0	0

Declarations and Initial Values

```
int     a = 1, b = 2, n = 1, m = 2;
char    c = 'm';
```

Expression	*Equivalent Expression*	*Value*
a && b && n	(a && b) && n	1
a || b || n	(a || b) || n	1
c >= 'a' && c<= 'z'	(c >= 'a') && (c<= 'z')	1
c >= 'A' && c<= 'Z'	(c >= 'A') && (c<= 'Z')	0

FIGURE 2.8   Examples of evaluation of logical operators.

```
while (i < MAX && scanf("%d", &value) != EOF)
    a[i] = value;
```

the clause i<MAX is evaluated first. If it is false, the value of the entire logical expression is false, regardless of how the second clause would evaluate, and therefore the second clause is *not* evaluated. More to the point, the call to scanf does not occur; no reading of or assignment to value occurs. If there are multiple clauses connected by logical AND, the first false one terminates the evaluation. In this example, only when i<MAX evaluates to true is the second clause, scanf("%d",&value)!=EOF evaluated.

In logical OR, the first true clause terminates evaluation of all succeeding clauses. In the following statement, the function scanf is not called if x is greater than zero:

```
while (x > 0 || scanf("%d", &x) == 1)
    ...
```

2.2.4 BITWISE OPERATORS

While the operators we have seen so far are common to most higher-level programming languages, C also provides bit manipulation operators for shifting bits left or right; for bitwise AND, OR, and exclusive OR of two operands; and for the bitwise inversion of a single operand. These operations are provided to allow us to deal with the details of the machine. They are used when the hardware requires individual bits within a machine word to be set or read and can also provide faster versions of some numerical operations. All these operators require their operands to be an integral type. (Some compilers, however, forbid their use on longs.)

Bit Shifts

The left and right bit shift operators shift an operand left or right by a specified number of bits. The form of the operator is

left shift:

    op << n

right shift:

    op >> n

As an example,

    a = val << 1;

assigns `val`, shifted one bit to the left, to `a`. The similar right shift operator,

    a = val >> 1;

shifts `val` one bit to the right, assigning the result to `a`. The first assignment is equivalent to multiplying `val` by two; the second divides `val` by two. If `val` is originally a four-bit quantity

    val

    0 1 1 0

here is what `val`, shifted left by one bit and shifted right by one bit, looks like:

    val << 1   val >> 1
    1 1 0 0   0 0 1 1

The number of bits to shift must be an `int` expression or an expression convertible to an `int` and should be positive. Bit shift operations are not defined for negative shifts. The number of bits to shift should also be less than or equal to the number of bits in an integer. The result of a large shift is machine dependent.

On *left* shifts, zeroes are always shifted into the vacated bits on the right. On *right* shifts, the bit shifted in depends on the variable's type. If the variable is `unsigned`, zeroes are shifted in; if the variable is `signed`, *usually* the sign bit is extended, but this operation is machine dependent. It is possible that on some machines zeroes are shifted in for signed values, which would have the (most likely undesired) effect of changing the sign of the value. Caution is the general rule when using right shifts on signed values.

TABLE 2.5 Result of bitwise AND, OR, and exclusive OR

Operands		Result		
Op1	Op2	&	|	^
1	1	1	1	0
1	0	0	1	1
0	1	0	1	1
0	0	0	0	0

Bitwise Logical Operators

There are three bitwise logical operators: bitwise AND (&), bitwise OR (|), and bitwise exclusive OR (^). These operators work on their operands bit by bit, setting each bit in the result, as shown in Table 2.5. The bitwise AND is one only when both bits are one; otherwise it is zero. The bitwise OR is one if either operand is one. The exclusive OR is one if exactly one of the bits is one.

As an example of the results of these bitwise operations, Figure 2.9 shows the result of AND, OR, and exclusive OR on two `ints`, assuming 16-bit integers. OR is sometimes called the "either" or "any" function, AND the "both" or "all" function, and exclusive OR the "odd" or "only one" function.

Bit operations are useful because they allow the selection of individual bits or groups of bits in a word. They are needed when special devices use individual bits as flags or controlling signals. We can use combinations of logical AND, logical OR, and bitwise negation to create a `mask` that allows selected bit fields to be manipulated. The following program fragment sets a particular bit (the second bit from the right) in a variable `flag`; the last piece tests whether the particular bit has been set. Parentheses are needed because the precedence of the test-for-equality operator (==) is higher than that of bitwisc AND (&).

```
#define  FLAGBIT1    01          /* equiv to 00..0001 */
#define  FLAGBIT2    02          /* equiv to 00..0010 */
     ...
  int   flag;
     ...

  flag = flag | FLAGBIT2;        /* turn on appropriate flag */
     ...
  if ((flag & FLAGBIT2) != 0)    /* test if flag is set */
     ...
```

Notice that the meaning and use of bitwise operators & and | are much different than those of the logical operators && and ||.

Exclusive OR is an operator that is useful in data encryption. Encrypting data in such a way that it takes a substantial amount of time (many weeks) to decipher an encrypted file, without knowing the encryption key, is obviously an important property of any secure encryption scheme. But there are some surprisingly simple methods that produce good results as long as the encrypting key is long enough.

Perhaps the simplest method is to take the exclusive OR of the text to be encrypted with the encryption key. If the text is larger than the key (which is usually the case), just cycle through the key repeatedly until the entire file has been encrypted. The nice aspect of this scheme is that the encrypted version of the file can be decrypted with the same key using the same method: take the exclusive OR with the key.

As an example, Figure 2.10 shows an eight-bit piece of data to be encrypted, and an eight-bit key. Taking the exclusive OR with the key produces the encrypted data. Taking the exclusive OR with the key again produces the original data.

A program used to encrypt or decrypt a file is shown in Figure 2.11; it is virtually identical to the character-copying program from Chapter 1 (Figure 1.9). Instead of copying each character directly to the output (via putchar), we take the exclusive OR of the current character with the next character of the key. To simplify the structure of the program, we built the key into the program. In a truly secure encryption program, the key would be provided independently by the user of the program. Notice the use of the remaindering operator % for cycling through the elements in the key.

There is one final bitwise operator, negation (~), which inverts each bit in its operand; that is, each one bit becomes zero, each zero becomes one. The operand must be an integral type (that is, int, short, long, or char, either signed or unsigned). If x is represented as eight bits, here is ~x:

```
x:    1 0 0 1 1 0 0 1
~x:   0 1 1 0 0 1 1 0
```

```
A:       1 0 0 1 0 1 1 0    1 1 1 0 0 0 0 1
B:       0 0 0 1 1 0 1 0    1 1 0 1 1 0 0 1
-------------------------------------------------
A | B:   1 0 0 1 1 1 1 0    1 1 1 1 1 0 0 1    /* bitwise OR */
A & B:   0 0 0 1 0 0 1 0    1 1 0 0 0 0 0 1    /* bitwise AND *
A ^ B:   1 0 0 0 1 1 0 0    0 0 1 1 1 0 0 0    /* bitwise exclusive OR */
```

FIGURE 2.9   AND, OR, and exclusive OR on two 16-bit integers.

```
0 1 0 1 0 0 0 0     DATA     (ASCII 'P')
0 0 0 1 0 0 1 0     KEY
```
```
0 1 0 0 0 0 1 0     DATA exclusive OR KEY = encrypted data
```
```
0 0 0 1 0 0 1 0     KEY
```
```
0 1 0 1 0 0 0 0     encrypted data exclusive OR KEY = DATA
```

FIGURE 2.10   Data encryption and decryption using the exclusive OR function.

2.2.5 CASE STUDY — BIT MANIPULATION FUNCTIONS

Routines that need to manipulate individual bits or strings of bits within a word can often be written in a portable way by appropriately combining C's shift, negation, ANDing, and ORing operators. We will examine short functions to determine the number of bits in various data types on a partic-

```
/*
 *   Encrypt the standard input using a built-in encryption key.
 *   The encryption key is "The encryption key."
 */

#include <stdio.h>
#define MAXKEY   19

main ()
{
    char    key[MAXKEY];
    int     c, j = 0;

    key[0]  = 'T';      key[1]  = 'h';   key[2]  = 'e';   key[3]  = ' ';
    key[4]  = 'e';      key[5]  = 'n';   key[6]  = 'c';   key[7]  = 'r';
    key[8]  = 'y';      key[9]  = 'p';   key[10] = 't';   key[11] = 'i';
    key[12] = 'o';      key[13] = 'n';   key[14] = ' ';   key[15] = 'k';
    key[16] = 'e';      key[17] = 'y';   key[18] = '.';

    while ((c = getchar ()) != EOF)
    {
        putchar (c ^ key[j % MAXKEY]);
        j++;
    }
}
```

FIGURE 2.11   Program to encrypt a file, using exclusive OR with a key. In this version the key is built into the program, but this would not be done in a "secure" encryption scheme.

```
/*
 * Returns the number of bits in a word.
 */
int wordlength ()
{
    unsigned int    word;                   /* used to find word length */
    int             bits = 0;               /* bits in the word */

    for (word = ~0; word != 0; word <<= 1)
        bits++;

    return bits;
}
```

FIGURE 2.12 A function to determine the number of bits in an `int`.

ular machine, to extract a given bit from a word, and to turn on or off (that is, to set to ones or zeroes) a specified string of bits in a word.

The first function, `wordlength` in Figure 2.12, returns the number of bits in an `int`. The function initializes `word` to all ones (by setting it to ~0) and then shifts left one bit at a time, until `word` is zero. A counter is kept of the number of shifts, and this is returned as the number of bits in the word.

The next function, `getbit` in Figure 2.13, gets the value of the nth bit in `word` (a zero or one), assuming that the *rightmost* bit in the word is bit number zero. Thus, the call `getbit(word, 2)`, where `word` looks like

```
bit:        3 2 1 0
      ┌─────────────┐
   0  ...   0 1 0 1 │
      └─────────────┘
```

```
/*
 * Gets the value of bit "n" in "word".  Assumes that the rightmost
 * bit of the word is bit zero, and that "n" will be between zero and the
 * word length of the machine, minus one.
 */
int getbit (word, n)
unsigned int    word;
int             n;
{
    return (word >> n) & 01;
}
```

FIGURE 2.13 A function to determine the nth bit in a word.

will return one. The function works by shifting `word` *right* n places and then ANDing the entire word with a mask consisting of all zeroes, except for the rightmost bit: `01`.

Lastly we review a method used to turn on a bit string in a single word. Specifically, we want to set n bits in a word to ones, starting with a position i from the right (again, the rightmost bit is zero). We can do so with the expression

```
word = word | ~(~0 << n) << i;
```

For example, if we have a word that looks like this,

```
bit:           7 6 5 4 3 2 1 0
0  0  ...    1 0 1 0 1 1 0 1
```

and we would like bits seven, six, and five to be ones (the rest unchanged), so that the word then looks like

```
bit:           7 6 5 4 3 2 1 0
0  0  ...    1 1 1 0 1 1 0 1
```

                        now all ones

we use an n of three and an i of five. Tracing the result of this expression by hand will help you see how it works.

EXERCISES

2-13 Write a program using the function `wordlength` of Figure 2.12 as a model that determines the number of bits in an `int`, `short`, and `char` on your machine. □

2-14 Write an expression that takes a word, a location, and the number of bits, and sets the bits, starting at the location from the right of the word (counting the rightmost bit as bit zero) to zero. All other bits remain the same. □

2-15 Write an expression that takes a word, a location, and the number of bits and inverts the bits, starting at the location from the right of the word (counting the rightmost bit as bit zero). All other bits remain the same. □

2-16 Write a function that takes a word (assumed to be an `unsigned int`) and prints its binary representation. Use the function `getbit` in Figure 2.13 to get the individual bits in the word. □

2-17 Show that `A^A` is zero. □

2-18 Show how the exclusive OR can be used to exchange two `int` variables without the use of an intermediate variable. Is this a reasonable method of exchanging variables? Why or why not? □

2.2.6 ASSIGNMENT OPERATORS

Assignment operators are used to assign the result of an expression to a variable. The type of the right-hand side of the assignment should match the type of the left. If it does not, the type of the right is converted to that of the left before the assignment is made (although no change is made in any variables on the right).

In C, assignment is an operator that returns a value — the value assigned. Thus, assignment operators may be used more than once in a single statement. To initialize more than one variable to `INITVAL`, enter

```
a = b = c = INITVAL;
```

The assignment operator is evaluated right to left, so this multiple assignment is equivalent to

```
a = (b = (c = INITVAL));
```

In addition to the usual assignment, `=`, there are shorthand assignment operators of the form

lhs *op* = rhs

where lhs is the left-hand side of the assignment, rhs is an expression, and *op* is a C binary operator. The shorthand form is equivalent to

lhs = lhs *op* (rhs)

with lhs evaluated once. *op* can be any of the arithmetic or bit-shift operators (but not `&&` or `||`). Like `=`, the shorthand assignment operators return the value assigned and can be used in other expressions.

We used a shorthand assignment operator in Chapter 1, in the second version of the interest rate program, Figure 1.4, with the statement

```
sum += sum * irate;
```

This statement is equivalent to

```
sum = sum + (sum * irate);
```

As another example, we can divide an integer variable `val` by two with `val /= 2`, which is interpreted as `val = val / 2`. This division can also be accomplished (if `val` is positive) with `val >>= 1`, the shorthand for `val = val >> 1`, which is a right shift of one bit.

The assignment operators are convenient and lead to more concise, more efficient, and perhaps surprisingly, more readable code. For example, consider the assignment

```
table[2 * i * j] = table[2 * i * j] + newval;
```

Using the assignment operator `+=`, this assignment can be written more concisely as

```
table[2 * i * j] += newval;
```

which is more efficient because the expression `2 * i * j` is evaluated only once. It is also more readable because it makes it clear that only one array element is involved in the computation. Lastly, it is less likely to be in error because we have to enter the subscripting expression only once.

Postfix and Prefix Assignment Operators

Two sets of shorthand operators are provided for incrementing and decrementing by one, `++` and `--`. As we saw in Chapter 1, they have the effect of adding one to or subtracting one from their operand. What we did not mention was that there are two forms of these operators, *postfix* and *prefix*.

As either a prefix or a postfix operator, `++` adds one to its operand. When used as a postfix operator, `++` first evaluates the operand, providing its value to the rest of the statement or expression and then adds one. When it is used as a prefix operator, the addition occurs first and then the new value of the variable is used in the expression.

As an example, if `n` has a value of five, then the postfix assignment `a = n++` assigns five to `a` and then increments `n`. After the assignment, `a` is five and `n` is six.

The corresponding prefix assignment, `a = ++n`, first increments `n` and then makes the assignment. After the assignment, both `a` and `n` are six. Both prefix and postfix `--` work similarly to `++`, except that they decrement their variable by one.

We will often use one form or the other when going through an array. Because an assignment using the `++` or `--` operator causes two assignments to occur, we can often save an instruction and produce more efficient code. The assignment `max = a[i++]` assigns the current `a[i]` to `max` and then increments `i`, equivalent to the two statements

```
max = a[i];
i++;
```

Similarly, `max = a[++i]` first increments `i`, then makes the assignment, and is equivalent to the two statements

```
i++;
max = a[i];
```

Notice that as a statement not involving other side effects,

```
i++;
```

is the same as

```
++i;
```

The choice of which form to use, as for example, the increment expression in a `for` loop, is yours.[3]

2.2.7 THE COMMA OPERATOR

The *comma operator* is used to link related expressions together as a single expression, making programs more compact. A comma-separated list of expressions is treated as a single expression and evaluated left to right, with the value of the rightmost expression returned as the expression's value. A program fragment to exchange the values of two variables `x` and `y` as shown here

```
temp = x;                    /* swap the values of "x" and "y" */
x = y;
y = temp;
```

can be written more compactly using the comma operator as

```
temp = x, x = y, y = temp;
```

We can also use the comma operator to rewrite tests with embedded assignments such as

---

[3] There can be differences in efficiency, however. On some machines there are post-increment and decrement operations that make `i++` more efficient than `++i`.

```
    while ((c = getchar()) != EOF)
```

as

```
    while (c = getchar(), c != EOF)
```

separating the reading of the character from testing for end of file. Because the comma operator evaluates left to right, the rightmost expression's value (here, the test for end of file) controls the `while`'s execution. Either method is acceptable; use the one that is easier for you to read.

The comma operator has the lowest precedence of any of C's operators, so it can safely be used to turn any list of expressions into a single statement. However, the comma used to separate the parameters in function calls is not a comma operator and does not guarantee left to right evaluation.

2.2.8 THE `SIZEOF` OPERATOR

One final operator we consider in this chapter is `sizeof`. It returns the number of bytes in its operand, which may be a constant, a variable, or a data type. A byte is somewhat loosely defined as the size of a character. On most but not all machines, this is eight bits. If the variable is an array or another constructed type (structure, union, or enumeration type; see Chapter 9), the value returned is the total number of bytes needed.

The syntax of `sizeof` requires parentheses around a type, but they are optional around a variable.

```
    sizeof(type)
```

```
    sizeof variable    OR    sizeof(variable)
```

If a variable `x` is of some type `T`, `sizeof (T)` returns the same as `sizeof x`.

For arrays, `sizeof` returns the size of the base type (whether it is a built-in or a constructed type) times the declared size of the array. If `a` is an array of 100 `int`s, `sizeof(a)` is 400, assuming 4-byte (32-bit) `int`s, and 200, assuming 2-byte (16-bit) `int`s.

The program in Figure 2.14a prints the size of several different data types, including the standard types `short`, `int`, `long`, and so on. (We did not print the size of a `char` since by definition that is one byte.) The output is shown in Figure 2.14b.

The `sizeof` operator is unique because it is evaluated at compile time, not when the program is running. The compiler replaces the call with a constant.

```
main ()
{
    int i;
    int a[100];

    printf ("Size of array a:\t %d \n", sizeof (a));
    printf ("Size of short: \t %d \n", sizeof (short));
    printf ("Size of int:   \t %d \n", sizeof (int));
    printf ("Size of long:  \t %d \n", sizeof (long));
    printf ("Size of float: \t %d \n", sizeof (float));
    printf ("Size of double: \t %d \n", sizeof (double));
}
```

(a) Program that prints the size of various data types

```
Size of array a:      400
Size of short:        2
Size of int:          4
Size of long:         4
Size of float:        4
Size of double:       8
```

(b) Output from part (a)

FIGURE 2.14 (*a*) Program that prints the size of various data types; (*b*) output from part (*a*).

2.3

CONVERSIONS AND CASTS

C performs some type conversions automatically. However, there are times when we want to force a type conversion in a way that is different from the automatic conversion. We call such a process *casting* a value. A cast is specified by giving the cast type in parentheses followed by the expression to be cast:

(*cast-type*) *expression*

As an example, to force the floating point number 17.7 to be an int, we use a cast:

```
a = (int) 17.7 * 2;
```

casts 17.7 (and only 17.7, not the entire expression) to an int by truncation. The result of this assignment using a cast is that a receives the value 34. Here 17.7 is cast to an int, 17, rather than the entire product, since the precedence of the cast operator is higher than that of most other operators.

We normally cast a variable to ensure that the arithmetic is carried out with the type of the left-hand side. We can round (rather than truncate) a variable to an integer by first adding 0.5 and then casting to an `int`, as we do here by again assigning to the integer variable `a`:

```
a = (int) (val + 0.5);
```

If `val` is 37.8, adding 0.5 to it yields 38.3; casting this to an `int` truncates the result to 38, the value that is then assigned to `a`. Of course, the variable or expression being cast is not changed; a cast simply returns a value of the cast type. Because of the high precedence of the cast operator, the expression to be cast must be parenthesized, as we did above. Contrast this to the effect of writing

```
a = (int) val + 0.5;
```

A typical use of a cast is in forcing division to return a real number when both operands are `ints`. For example, a program to average a series of integers might accumulate a total in an integer variable `sum` and a count of the number of values read in the integer `n`. To compute the average, we divide:

```
ave = (double) sum / n;
```

Casting `sum` to a `double` causes the division to be carried out as floating point division. Without the cast, truncated integer division is performed, since both `sum` and `n` are `ints`. Here are some other examples of casts and their results. Many of these are machine dependent and may seem unintuitive; they should therefore be used with caution.

```
(unsigned short)  -1        =            65535
(short)          65000      =             -536
(char)           65000      =              'h'
(double)             5      =             5.00
(unsigned long)   -1        =       4294967295
```

2.3.1 AUTOMATIC TYPE CONVERSION

The rules of automatic type conversion are reasonably natural, except when dealing with conversions involving `chars` and `unsigned ints`. Figure 2.15 gives the rules. A cast can always be used to force the conversion as appropriate, and it overrides the default conversions.

1. If both operands are the same type, no conversions are performed.
2. If one operand is a `double`, the other is converted to a `double`.
3. If one operand is an `unsigned long`, the other is converted to an `unsigned long`. (Note: this means that signed `ints` are converted to `unsigned ints`.)
4. If one operand is a (signed) `long int` and the other is an `unsigned int`, then *both* are converted to `unsigned long`. (Note: this means that signed `ints` are converted to `unsigned ints`.)
5. If one operand is an `unsigned int`, the other is converted to an `unsigned int`. (Note: this means that signed `ints` are converted to `unsigned ints`.)
6. Otherwise, both operands are of type `int`: no additional conversion takes place.

FIGURE 2.15 Automatic conversions between data types.

EXERCISES

2-19 What are the types and values of the following expressions?

```
float     average;
int       iaverage,
          sum = 1024;
double    total = 1024;

average = sum / 23;
iaverage = sum / 23;
average = total / 23;
iaverage = total / 23;  □
```

2-20 What are the types and values of the following expressions?

```
short  s1 = -154,
       s2 = 154,
       s3;
int    i;
long   l1 = 165000,
       l2 = -1234,
       l3;
```

```
s1 = 100L * s2;
s3 = 100L* s2;
l3 = l1 * (short) l1;
i = s1 + (unsigned) s2;   □
```

2-21 What are the types and values of the following expressions?

```
int           i;
unsigned int  j;

i = (unsigned)1 + -1;
i = (unsigned)1 + -5;
i = (unsigned)1 - 5;
j = (unsigned)1 + -1;
j = (unsigned)1 + -5;
j = (unsigned)1 - 5;   □
```

2.4

IDENTIFIERS AND NAMING CONVENTIONS

Variable and function names are known as *identifiers*. Not every combination of characters is a legal identifier, however. Identifiers are composed of any sequence of lowercase and uppercase letters, digits, and underscore (_) characters, with the restriction that the first character must not be a digit. To provide access to certain system functions, some compilers allow the dollar sign ($) to appear in identifiers. Case is significant in identifiers: count refers to a different identifier than Count.

Even though a dollar sign may be legal in an identifier, it is not portable, and the use of names with it may conflict with the use of names already defined at the systems level. In addition, some operating systems use identifiers with an underscore as the first character in their own internal names. Therefore, avoid using an underscore at the start of a name.

Certain identifiers are reserved as keywords and cannot be used as normal identifiers; these reserved identifiers are listed in Table 2.6. Other identifiers may be reserved by a particular compiler; among the more common ones are asm, entry and fortran.

The maximum number of characters in an identifier is unrestricted by the language, although most compilers place a limit on the number of significant characters. In the original definition of C, only the first eight characters were significant, implying that var_name1 and var_name2 refer to the same identifier. In most modern C compilers, the first 31 characters are significant, although to be truly portable to all current compilers, it may be necessary to restrict names to six, seven, or eight characters, a topic covered in Chapter 12.

TABLE 2.6 C reserved words

auto	break	case	char	continue
default	do	double	else	enum
extern	float	for	goto	if
int	long	register	return	short
sizeof	static	struct	switch	typedef
union	unsigned	void	while	

EXERCISES

2-22 Find out how many characters in an identifier are unique on your compiler. Is there a limit to the length of an identifier? □

2-23 What happens if you define a name in the preprocessor and later use it as an identifier? A type? □

WRITING EXPRESSIONS

Because of the large number of operators, and the not always intuitive precedence and implicit type conversion rules, it is the programmer's responsibility to make sure that an expression performs as expected. Here are some suggestions that make it is easier to write readable, efficient (and correct) expressions.

- Some of C's precedence rules are not intuitive. When in doubt, use parentheses to specify the order and priority of evaluation. Remember, however, that the compiler is free to rearrange the evaluation order of certain expressions (those involving only the operators &, |, ^, +, and *), even in the presence of parentheses. In these cases temporary variables may have to be used to guarantee a correct order of evaluation.
- Casts can usually be used to force conversions to the appropriate type. Since arithmetic involving different types includes automatic type conversions that are occasionally different from the expected, use a cast to get what you want.
- There is no performance penalty in the evaluation of constant expressions, because they are evaluated at compile time. For ex-

ample, the compiler converts the expression

```
a = 17.3 / 14.7 * PI / vals[i];
```

(assuming PI has been defined as 3.14159) into

```
a = 3.69724537 / vals[i];
```

- Some of C's operations can be performed in subtly different ways. For example, the logical AND of two clauses can sometimes be replaced by the bitwise AND, which may be faster to evaluate. This is appropriate, however, only when you want all of the clauses evaluated.
- Use the prefix and postfix additive operators ++ and –– carefully. In general, do not use more than one prefix or postfix operator in a single expression. What, for example, is the result of the following?

```
a[i++] = a[--i];
```

or

```
a[--i] = b[++i];
```

Notice how easy it is to write ambiguous expressions. Even if these examples can be clearly interpreted by the compiler, they will probably confuse most programmers. When in doubt, simplify it out.

CHAPTER 3

POINTERS, ARRAYS AND STRINGS

This chapter introduces pointers (addresses), discusses the relationship between pointers and arrays, and examines a special kind of array — an array of characters, called a string. In doing so, we examine two important uses of pointers: accessing specific memory locations, and traversing arrays efficiently. We also discuss the differences between arrays and strings, and present the standard library functions for manipulating strings. We conclude with a program that eliminates duplicate lines from its input, building a useful new program from small, existing functions.

3.1
POINTERS

Pointers are a fundamental data type in C. We cannot hope to use the complete capabilities of the language unless we are thoroughly familiar with them. Pointers are needed to take full advantage of parameter passing with functions; they are used in dynamic memory allocation for a wide range of data structures and algorithms, and they are intimately related to arrays. In addition to the fundamental importance of pointers in the language, their use often results in more compact, faster code compared to alternative methods.

A pointer is a value that indicates where another value is stored. These storage locations represent the address of a variable in memory. If a variable `val` is defined as an `int`, the compiler allocates an appropriate amount of storage at the time this definition occurs. For example, the compiler might allocate memory location 10000 for `val`. After the assignment

```
val = -15;
```

memory location 10000 will contain the integer value −15.

The address of `val`, indicated as `&val`, is 10000. We can print addresses (as well as the contents of addresses) with `printf`. To print the address of `val`, we use

```
printf("Address of val: %d\n", &val);
```

On some machines, addresses are long integers and the `%ld` form is necessary. Of course, we can be more portable and use a cast:

```
printf("Address of val: %ld\n", (long) &val);
```

The address-of operator (`&`) returns the location where its operand is stored. The operand must be a variable, but not an array or function name.

A variable can be declared as an address (or pointer) type. That is, it can contain the address (and thus a pointer to) another value. A pointer variable must have a type, just like an ordinary variable. Pointers are usually thought of as pointing only to an `int`, a `float`, a `char`, and so on. In addition, because the storage requirements for all pointer types need not be the same, we must be certain that a pointer variable of one type is not used to contain the address of a variable of another type.

We declare a variable as a pointer to a given type with

```
type    *name;
```

This declares that `name` is a pointer to *type*. The following declares `iptr` as a "pointer to `int`," `fptr` as a "pointer to `float`," `cptr` as a "pointer to `char`," and `dptr` as a "pointer to `double`."

```
int      *iptr;     /* iptr is "pointer to int" */
float    *fptr;     /* fptr is "pointer to float" */
char     *cptr;     /* cptr is "pointer to char" */
double   *dptr;     /* dptr is "pointer to double" */
```

Each of these declarations allocates space for the named pointer variable, but *not* for what it points to. Once a pointer variable has been declared, it must still be made to point to something. This can be done with an assignment such as

```
iptr = &val;
```

which causes `iptr` to point to `val`. That is, `iptr` now contains the address 10000, the location of `val`. Before a pointer is given an address, it should not be used, since pointer variables are not automatically initialized and therefore contain garbage values.

With this declaration of `iptr`, Figure 3.1 traces an assignment to `val` (the same `val` declared earlier) by assigning through `iptr`. Accessing the underlying storage location (in this case `val`, or 10000) through a pointer variable is called *dereferencing*. Dereferencing uses the indirection operator `*`, which returns the value pointed to by the pointer variable operand. The assignment

```
val = *iptr;
```

assigns to `val` whatever `iptr` points to, 10 in the case of Figure 3.1. Similarly, the assignment

```
*iptr = val;
```

assigns the current value of `val` to whatever `iptr` points to.

A dereferenced pointer can be used in any context in which the underlying type can occur. The assignment

```
val = *iptr + 10;
```

adds 10 to whatever `iptr` points to and assigns the result to `val`. Again, `iptr` is of type "pointer to `int`," and we can and should think of `*iptr` as if it were a single variable of type `int`. Therefore, this assignment is interpreted to mean that `val` is assigned some `int` variable plus 10.

We can (though we would probably not want to) initialize or assign a constant value to a pointer. Since a pointer must be the correct type, it is necessary to cast a constant correctly. The assignment

```
iptr = (int *) 100000;
```

although legal, is obviously machine dependent and likely to lead to memory violations. It is only when we must address specific memory locations, such as for device drivers, that such constructs are suitable. Even though in most systems pointers are integers (that is, they use the same amount of storage as an `int`), we should still cast the address to the type "pointer to `int`" or `(int *)` if `iptr` is a pointer to an `int`; a direct address assignment to a `float` pointer should be cast to `(float *)`, and so on.

```
fptr = (float *) 200000;
```

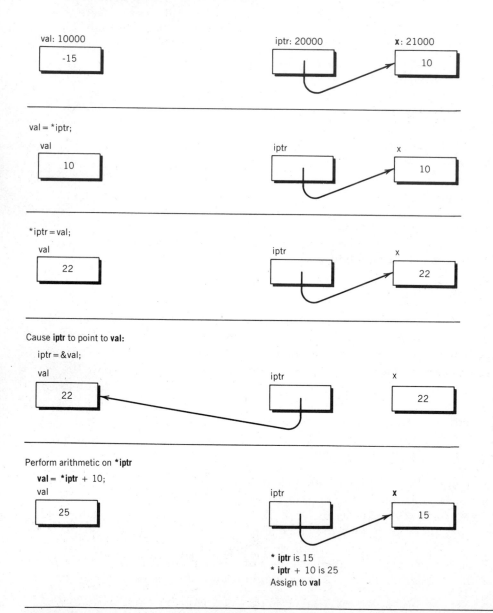

val: 10000

-15

iptr: 20000

x: 21000

10

val = *iptr;

val

10

iptr

x

10

*iptr = val;

val

22

iptr

x

22

Cause **iptr** to point to **val**:

iptr = &val;

val

22

iptr

x

22

Perform arithmetic on ***iptr**

val = ***iptr** + 10;

val

25

iptr

x

15

* iptr is 15
* iptr + 10 is 25
Assign to **val**

FIGURE 3.1 Referencing val through iptr.

```
/*
 * Examine the contents of a specific int memory location "where".
 * Assume addresses are longs.
 */
peek(where)
long  where;
{
   printf("%d\n", * (int *) where);
}
```

(a) Function to print the contents of a specific memory location

```
/*
 * Put a specific int "val" into memory location "where".
 * Assume addresses are longs.
 */
poke(val, where)
int   val;
long  where;
{
   * (int *) where = val;
}
```

(b) Function to place a value into a specific memory location

```
peek(100000L);                    /* Print the value in address 100000 */
poke(-32, 100000L);               /* Place -32 in that address */
```

(c) Example calls to peek *and* poke

FIGURE 3.2 *(a)* Function peek to print the contents of a specific memory location. *(b)* Function poke that assigns a value to a specific location. *(c)* Examples of the use of these functions.

These assignments and casts are used when we need to examine a specific memory location or assign it a value. Rather than code these instructions inline, we use functions. Two useful routines are called peek, to print the value in a location, and poke, to put a value into a location. These routines, shown in Figure 3.2, are machine dependent, and they must be given addresses that are reasonable, or the run-time system will cause a memory exception error and terminate the program.

It is permissible to assign one pointer to another, and it is also possible (although there can be difficulties on some machines) to assign a pointer of one type to that of another, using appropriate casts. We will examine such operations in later chapters.

There is a special pointer, NULL, that points to nowhere. More specifically, NULL is a guaranteed illegal address (the constant zero, which C guarantees to convert to the NULL pointer) that can be used for any pointer type. The constant NULL is defined in the include file *stdio.h*, so any program that uses the NULL pointer should have the preprocessor directive

```
#include <stdio.h>
```

Pointers are used extensively in three ways. First, they are necessary for parameter passing in functions. Second, as we will see in the next section, arrays and pointers are very similar objects. Third, pointers are an effective means of using dynamic storage allocation and linked data structures (see Chapter 9).

EXERCISES

3-1 What happens if you dereference the NULL pointer on your machine (try calling peek(NULL) or poke(val, NULL))? □

3-2 Use sizeof to determine the size of pointers to different objects. Are they two bytes or four? Are they all the same size? Will a long hold the largest pointer? □

3-3 Assuming that j is an int, what is the effect of *&j? □

3-4 What is the problem with the following statement, assuming that j is an int?

```
x = i /*j - iptr;   □
```

3-5 For each of the following, state whether it is legal, and if so, state its effect (assuming that iptr is a pointer to an int, and that a, b, and x are ints.)

```
(*iptr)++;
*iptr++;
x = a**b;
(&iptr)++   □
```

3.2
ARRAYS

As we saw in Chapter 1, arrays in C are similar to those in other programming languages. An array is declared by giving its underlying type (or "base type"), name, and size.

> *type*   name[*size*];

The size of an array tells the compiler how much storage to allocate for it. The actual amount of storage allocated depends on the base type; the amount of storage is at least *size* times the amount required for a single variable of *type*. *type* can be any type (except `void`, discussed in Chapter 5). Figure 3.3 shows examples of legal and illegal array declarations.

All arrays are indexed beginning at zero. That is, if we declare a to be an array of 100 `ints` by:

> int   a[100];

the compiler allocates 100 storage locations, each holding an `int`, and we can (legally) access elements of a by giving an index in the range of 0 to 99, which is done by specifying the index of the element in brackets. A common mistake is to assume that array subscripting begins at one, and thus to attempt to access a[100]. Accessing out-of-bounds elements is not required to be caught by the compiler and may not even cause a run-time error.

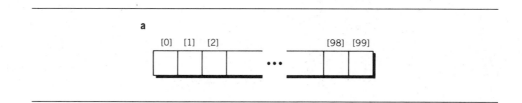

3.2.1 RELATION TO POINTERS

Why have we spent so much time on pointers? Because when we declare an array, the array name is associated with a pointer to the first (zeroth)

```
#define MAXLINE    80

char    line[MAXLINE];        /* legal — allocates an 80-character array */
char    line[2 * MAXLINE];    /* legal — allocates a 160-character array */
char    line[MAXLINE + 1];    /* legal — allocates an 81-character array */
char    line[-100];           /* illegal — should be a positive array size */
char    line[1];              /* legal — allocates a single storage location */
int     a[1.3 * 2.2];         /* NOT legal — must be an integer expression */
int     a[0];                 /* NOT legal — must be greater than 0 */
```

FIGURE 3.3 Examples of array declarations.

element of the array. The declaration

```
int     a[100];
```

in addition to allocating space for 100 integers, defines the name a as the address of the first element of the array; that is, a is a constant, the address of the zeroth element (equivalent to &a[0]). In Figure 3.4, a is the constant 1000, the location where a[0] is stored. Since a is a constant address, the assignment

```
int     a[100];
int     *iptr;

iptr = a;
```

is well defined and is shown in Figure 3.4. This assignment is equivalent to

```
iptr = &a[0];
```

Either assignment could be used to set iptr to point to a's first element (a[0]).

Instead of using array indexing, we can use pointers to access array elements. This is because pointer arithmetic (that is, adding integers to or subtracting integers from a pointer) is always done in units of the pointer's underlying base type. To illustrate, suppose we declare an integer pointer iptr and make it point to a's first element (a[0]) by

```
int     *iptr;                          int  *iptr = a;
        . . .          or equivalently
iptr = a;
```

Then iptr + 1 is the address of the second element (a[1]), iptr + 2 is the address of the third element (a[2]), and in general, iptr + i is the address of element a[i]. More specifically, given iptr declared as a pointer to a[0], we can assign the value 10 to a[3] either by array indexing or by pointer dereferencing. Thus, since iptr has been assigned a's address

```
a[3] = 10;     is equivalent to     *(iptr + 3) = 10;
```

and in our programs we can use either form:

```
iptr[3]    or    *(iptr + 3)    or    a[3]    or    *(a + 3)
```

In fact, the compiler translates all array subscripting into pointer dereferences:

```
a[i]     becomes     *(a + i)
```

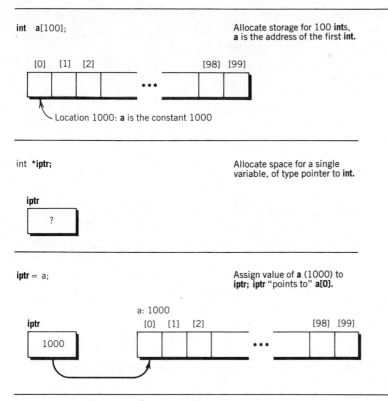

int a[100];

Allocate storage for 100 **ints**,
a is the address of the first **int**.

[0]   [1]   [2]   [98] [99]

Location 1000: **a** is the constant 1000

int *iptr;

Allocate space for a single
variable, of type pointer to **int**.

iptr

?

iptr = a;

Assign value of **a** (1000) to
iptr; **iptr** "points to" **a[0]**.

a: 1000

iptr   [0]   [1]   [2]   [98] [99]

1000

FIGURE 3.4   Trace of array allocation and pointer assignments.

In the pointer dereference, `*(a + i)`, the addition `a + i` is carried out in `sizeof(int)` increments. Selecting the ith element involves calculating the address of the element, given the base address (the location of `a[0]`). For example, to access `a[2]`, C computes

$$a[2] \longrightarrow address\ of\ a[0] + 2 \times sizeof(int)$$
$$\longrightarrow\ a + 2 \times sizeof(int)$$
$$\longrightarrow\ 1000 + 2 \times 4 = 1008$$

This calculation is based on the assumption that `a` is stored beginning at memory location 1000, with an integer size of four bytes.

The advantage of using a pointer is that we can simply increment it to go to the next element. Using this notion, we can traverse an array using a pointer, or proceed directly by array indexing. To increment `iptr` along `a`, we need only add one to `iptr`. All pointer arithmetic (on pointers to ints) is done in units of four (bytes) on a four-byte-per-int machine, and in units of two on a two-byte-per-int machine. To understand the use of pointers for array accessing, consider the following loop, which prints the first n values in an array of ints, one per line, using the usual array accessing and pointer accessing methods:

<table>
<tr><td>Array Accessing</td><td>Pointer Accessing</td></tr>
</table>

```
          . . .                    int  *iptr = a;
     i = 0;                              . . .
     while (n-- > 0)               while (n-- > 0)
     {                             {
       printf("%d\n", a[i]);       printf("%d\n",*iptr)
       i++;                          iptr++;
     }                             }
```

The pointer accessing method is often faster because, at the hardware instruction level, the pointer dereferencing and incrementing is done with a single machine instruction, avoiding the additional calculations needed in array subscript accesses.

Since pointer arithmetic is performed in units of the base type, we can use it to traverse any kind of array. If another array d is declared as an array of doubles,

```
     double    d[MAX];
```

then indexing through d involves arithmetic in units of eight (bytes). An assignment such as

```
     d[i] = 2.0e3;
```

is always converted to

```
     *(d + i) = 2.0e3;
```

and if d[0] is stored at location 2000 (equivalently, &d[0] is 2000 or equivalently, d is the constant value 2000), the assignment is made into location 2000 + 8i. As with a earlier, we can print an element of d directly using d[i] or indirectly using a pointer. If we want dptr to be a pointer to a double (that is, to point to an element of array d), we can declare and use it as in the following piece of code, which prints the first n elements of d:

```
     double    *dptr = d;
        . . .
     while (n-- > 0)
     {
       printf("%f\n", *dptr);
       dptr++;
     }
        . . .
```

C allows us to add integers to or subtract integers from pointers, as well as to subtract one pointer from another, yielding the number of elements between them (but only if they point to the same array). However, other arithmetic is not allowed (specifically, no multiplying or dividing pointers and no arithmetic involving reals).

The restrictions on pointer arithmetic are occasionally irritating, such as when we need to find the middle element in a subarray, bounded below by an index `L` and above by an index `H`. With array indexing, the middle element can be found at location `(H + L) / 2`. However, if `lp` is a pointer to `a[L]` and `hp` is a pointer to `a[H]`, we cannot find the middle element at `(bp + lp) / 2`, since pointer *addition* is illegal. However, pointer *subtraction* is legal and well defined, so we use an equivalent method, `lp + ((hp − lp) / 2)`. Although this looks like pointer addition, it is not. The difference between two pointers is an integer, and the division by two returns an integer. Adding an integer to a pointer is allowed. In summary, to obtain the value of an array's middle element, the following are equivalent:

```
int  value = a[(H + L) / 2];
```

is equivalent to

```
int  value;
int  *lp, *hp;
    . . .
lp = &a[L];
hp = &a[H];
    . . .
value = *(lp + (hp − lp) / 2);
```

3.2.2 ARRAY ADDRESS COMPARISONS USING POINTERS

In addition to participating in the arithmetic operations we have described previously, pointers can be compared for equality (`==`), inequality (`!=`), and less than, less than or equal, greater than, or greater than or equal (`<`, `<=`, `>`, `>=`). Table 3.1 summarizes the valid comparisons and operations on pointers. These comparisons are portable only if the pointers access the same array.

We illustrate the comparison operators using two simple array accessing functions – printing the elements in an array and printing them in reverse order (*traversing* an array). Because accessing arrays using pointers is often faster than accessing directly through indexes, we should be familiar with the use and restrictions of pointers for this purpose.

If `a` is an array of `MAX` ints, it is straightforward to print `a`'s ele-

TABLE 3.1 Pointer operations and their meanings

Pointer Operator	Operation	Return
p1 == p2	Test for equality	One if the two pointers point to the same location; zero if they do not.
p1 != p2	Test for inequality	Zero if the two pointers point to the same location; one if they do not.
p1 < p2, <=	Test for less than, less than or equal	One if p1 points to an array element with a lower (less than or equal) index; zero otherwise.
p1 > p2, >=	Test for greater than, greater than or equal	One if p1 points to an array element with a higher (greater than or equal) index; zero otherwise.
p1–p2	Pointer subtraction	If p1 and p2 point to the same array, it returns the number of elements between them (if p2 points to a higher indexed element, it returns the negative of the number of elements between them).

ments using a pointer. We declare iptr to point to a[0] and then use a for loop, stopping when iptr points to a[MAX − 1].

```
int     a[MAX];
int     *iptr;
    . . .
for (iptr = a; iptr <= &a[MAX − 1]; iptr++)
    printf ("%d\n", *iptr);
    . . .
```

We can print the array in reverse order by making appropriate changes in the for loop:

```
int     a[MAX];
int     *iptr;
    . . .
for (iptr = &a[MAX − 1]; iptr >= a; iptr—)
  printf ("%d\n", *iptr);
    . . .
```

Notice that in these examples we do not test a counter to determine when the array has been traversed; instead, we compare the indexing pointer with the address of the array's first (or last) element.

EXERCISES

3-6 Can the above program fragments be made more compact? How? □

3-7 Write a program that sums the elements in an array, using only pointers (no extra array indexing). □

3-8 Rewrite the insertion sort program from Chapter 1 (Figure 1.7), but use pointers rather than array indexes to perform the sorting. □

3-9 Rewrite the reverse printing program from Chapter 1 (Figure 1.13), using pointers rather than array indexes. □

3.3

PASSING ARRAYS AS PARAMETERS TO FUNCTIONS

The complete use of functions is covered in Chapter 5. However, we introduced them briefly in Chapter 1, and we should now discuss how arrays are passed to functions and how they are accessed within functions.

If we have a function that takes an array `x` as a parameter,

```
int f(x)
int x[];
{
    . . .
}
```

the name of the array `x` is in fact a pointer – the address of the first location in the array. That is, within functions, array parameters are specifically pointers. When we make the function call `f(a)`, the address of `a[0]` is copied and given to `f`, so the function is receiving an address, *not* an entire array. We call `f` with an actual array parameter `a` by `f(a)`.

No bounds are indicated on `x`, because we are not passing an array. What we are passing is a pointer to an `int`, the address of `a[0]`. With that information, the compiler can compute the correct address of any array access.

Because we are passing a pointer to an `int`, an equivalent specification for the parameter `x` is

```
int f(x)
int *x;
{
    . . .
}
```

and within the body of f, we can access x by using either the array (square bracket) form or the pointer form (using the dereferencing operator *). Within the body of f, the following two assignments are equivalent.

```
x[i] = 15;

*(x + i) = 15;
```

Pick your favorite, though it is customary to use the form corresponding to the way the object was defined – either a pointer or an array.

3.4

CHARACTER ARRAYS — STRINGS

In brief, a string is an array of characters. But to stop there neglects the interesting details of character string use. The most important property of a string in C is that constant strings are always terminated with an extra character, the null character, `'\0'`.

A constant string is one that is defined between double quotation marks. (Remember, a *character* constant is defined as a single `character` between single quotation marks, The string constant

```
"By the light of the silvery moon."
```

contains 34 characters: the 33 between the double quotation marks, and an additional one inserted by the compiler. Internally, the string looks like this:

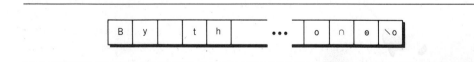

To place a double quotation mark in a string, precede it with a backslash:

```
"Have you seen \"Gone with the wind\"?"
```

We declare a string as a character array. In Chapter 6 we will consider how to declare and initialize an array of characters (it requires a knowledge of C storage classes). However, we can initialize a string as a pointer variable by specifying the type (`char *`) and the characters in the string:

```
char  *s = "By the light of the silvery moon.";
```

The C compiler allocates enough space for the string and causes s to point to the first character, B. In this case, there is room for 34 chars, the 34th being the null character, '\0'. Even though the string is constant, the pointer to it is not. However, it is bad practice to change the assignment, such as

```
char *T = "I love rock and roll"; S = T
```

since that leaves the space occupied by the old string dangling in memory.

When the compiler initializes a string constant, the trailing null ('\0') is supplied automatically, but when we build strings ourselves, we have to supply the terminating null. The reason for the terminating null is that C has a library of useful string functions, all of which expect a string to be null terminated, including printing a string using the %s format for printf. Figure 3.5 is a short function that reads a string of characters (up

```
/*
 *  Get a line, terminating on carriage return, or more than "max"
 *  chars entered.  DOES NOT include the ending new line.
 *
 *  RETURNS: EOF if end of input file detected; number of chars read otherwise
 *  (NOT counting the trailing null).
 */
int  get_line (line, max)
char line[];
int  max;
{
  int    c;                       /* current char being read */
  int    i = 0;                   /* number of chars read */

 /* Read until max chars; ignore all chars after max until CR. */

    while ((c = getchar ()) != '\n' && c != EOF)
       if (i < max - 1)
           line[i++] = c;

    line[i] = '\0';               /* always terminate with null */
    if (c == EOF)
      return EOF;
    else
      return i;
}
```

FIGURE 3.5 Function get_line gets a line and terminates with a null character.

to a maximum of `max`) into a string `line`. It then places a null at the end of the string. Since there must be room for the extra null character, we are careful to terminate reading when `max − 1` characters have been read. The function returns the number of characters read, not counting the added null character, or `EOF` on end of file.

This is a very useful function that we will use again and again in various forms. We read characters, placing them into the array `line`. Since there are two stopping conditions (too many characters or end of line reached), we must continue reading characters, even though we do not save them, until the end-of-line character (`'\n'`) is entered. This guarantees that the next time the function is called, it will begin reading characters from the start of a new line, not from the last character before `max` characters on the previous line.

We can always declare the elements in a string array in a similar way to other arrays − by specifying the individual elements. In this case, however, we must provide the trailing null ourselves.

```
char  error_msg[14];
    . . .
error_msg[0]  = 'I';
error_msg[1]  = 'l';
error_msg[2]  = 'l';
error_msg[3]  = 'e';
error_msg[4]  = 'g';
error_msg[5]  = 'a';
error_msg[6]  = 'l';
error_msg[7]  = ' ';
error_msg[8]  = 'V';
error_msg[9]  = 'a';
error_msg[10] = 'l';
error_msg[11] = 'u';
error_msg[12] = 'e';
error_msg[13] = '\0';
```

or

```
char * error_msg = "Illegal Value";
```

EXERCISES

3-10 Write a pointer version of `get_line`, Figure 3.5. Is it more efficient than the array accessing version? Why or why not?

3-11 Write a function, `stoi` (for *string* to *integer*), that takes a null terminated string (array of `char`) and converts the characters to an integer, using a method similar to that of Chapter 2. The function header is

```
int stoi(s)
char  s[];  □
```

3-12 Write a function, `itos`, that takes two parameters. The first is an integer, and the second is a character array. The function converts the integer into characters (null terminated) and places them into the array parameter. You should assume that the array is large enough to hold the necessary characters. The function header is

```
itos(val, s)
int    val;
char   s[];  □ ·
```

3.5

STRING FUNCTIONS FROM THE STANDARD LIBRARY

C does not provide operators that work on strings directly. If we do not initialize a string, assigning one string to another requires the assignment to be done on a character-by-character basis. This seems a bit strange at first, because strings are just arrays of characters, and arrays are in fact pointers to the first location. Although it seems as though the following set of declarations and assignments should work, they do not:

```
char  *s = "Hello out there.";
char  t[100];
   . . .
t = s;
```

The reason is that even though `t` is indeed a pointer to the first character location in the array, it is a *constant*. Its value (the address of `t[0]`) may not change. If we really want to copy the characters in `s` into `t`, we have to do so one at a time. Alternatively, we can use a built-in function called `strcpy` (for *string copy*) provided in the standard string library. The functions in the string library are used for copying one string to another, as we need to do here, for finding the length of a string, for concatenating two strings, and for comparing two strings.

The function used to copy one string array to another is `strcpy`. This function takes two arguments, both strings, and copies the second to the first. It is assumed that the second string is null terminated and that there is room in the first for all the characters. To copy string `s` to string `t`, as we tried to do above, we use

```
strcpy(t, s);
```

Notice that the order of the parameters mimics that of the assignment t = s.

It is instructive to examine how a function such as strcpy is written. The first thing to notice is that it is very short. The advantage of having the string functions provided for us is not that they implement hard-to-code routines, but precisely because they are already provided; our job of program construction is greatly simplified. Figure 3.6 shows us one way in which strcpy can be implemented. The actual code differs from one machine to another and a more compact example will be given at the end of the chapter.[1]

Other string functions concatenate two strings, compare two strings for equality, and compute the length of a string. These functions are declared in the system include file *strings.h*,[2] which can be included in any program that uses the built-in string functions. Use the preprocessor directive

```
#include <strings.h>
```

The string-handling functions provided with most C compilers are shown in Table 3.2.

One function that we will use in a case study at the end of the chapter is strcmp. This function takes two strings, s1 and s2, and returns a value that is less than zero if s1 is alphabetically less than s2, zero if they

---

```
/*
 *  Copy string "source" to string "dest".
 */
strcpy (dest, source)
char dest[], source[];
{
  int    i = 0;

  while ((dest[i] = source[i]) != '\0')
    i++;
}
```

FIGURE 3.6 One version of strcpy from the standard library.

[1] These versions are a slight simplification. Most versions of strcpy return a value, a pointer to the destination string. The details of the returned values of functions in the standard string library are shown in Appendix 7.

[2] This is a header file that declares the types of the standard string functions. On some systems the file is named *string.h*; other systems do not have the header file available at all. If the file is not available, the types of the functions must be declared in programs where they are used.

TABLE 3.2   String functions from the standard string library

Name	Function
strcat(s1,s2)	Concatenates s2 to the end of s1.
strncat(s1,s2,n)	Concatenates at most *n* characters from s2 to the end of s1.
strcpy(s1,s2)	Copies s2 to s1.
strncpy(s1,s2,n)	Copies *n* characters from s2 to s1.
strcmp(s1,s2)	Compares s1 and s2; return less than zero, zero or greater than zero, depending on whether s1 is less than, equal to, or greater than s2, respectively.
strncmp(s1,s2,n)	Compares at most *n* characters; returns the same as strcmp.
strlen(s)	Returns the number of characters in s, *not* counting the trailing null.
index(s,c)	Returns a pointer to the first occurrence of c in s, or NULL. It is sometimes called strchr.
rindex(s,c)	Returns a pointer to the last occurrence of c in s, or NULL. It is sometimes called strrchr.

are equal, and greater than zero if s1 is alphabetically greater than s2. As with strcpy, the function is short and quite simple to write. But because it is used so often, we see the value of having it provided in a standard library.

Figure 3.7 shows strcmp. It works by walking through the two strings, comparing corresponding characters (s1[i] and s2[i]). If the characters are the same and are also null, we are at the end of the string. Since we know the strings are equal, we return zero. However, if at any point in the comparison the characters differ we know that one of the strings is alphabetically less than the other and we return the difference between them:

```
return s1[i] - s2[i];
```

This returns a negative value when s1[i] is alphabetically less than s2[i] and a positive value when it is greater.

```
/*     Compare two strings; returning zero if they are the same, a negative
 *     value if the first is lexicographically less than the second, and
 *     a positive value if the first is lexicographically greater than the
 *     second.
 */
int  strcmp (sl, s2)
char sl[], s2[];                    /* strings to compare */
{
  int    i = 0;

  while (sl[i] == s2[i])            /* as long as they are the same */
    if (sl[i++] == '\0')            /* see if we hit the end of one */
      return 0;                     /*     and return equality */

  return sl[i] - s2[i];             /* otherwise return difference between characters */
}
```

FIGURE 3.7 A version of `strcmp` from the standard string library.

3.5.1 ADDITIONAL STRING FUNCTIONS

The standard I/O library provides two functions, extensions to `printf` and `scanf`, that allow output to and input from a string. These functions are `sprintf` and `sscanf` respectively. Each of these functions takes a string for input or output, followed by the formatting control string and the values to read or write, as with `printf` and `scanf`.

```
sprintf(string,  format,  var-list);
sscanf(string,  format,  var-list);
```

As with `scanf`, `sscanf` returns the number of values correctly converted, or `EOF` on end of file.

We can use `sscanf` together with `get_line` to avoid some of the problems associated with illegal input using `scanf`. We can read an entire input line using `get_line` and then use `sscanf` to extract the values of the variables, as outlined in the following code fragment:

```
    . . .
while ((n = get_line(line, MAX)) != EOF)
  if ((inpres = sscanf(line, "%d %f %f", &hours, &rate, &overtime)) == 3)
    process_data(. . .);                  /* process valid input */
  else
    printf("Bad line encountered\n");     /* report bad input data */
```

In this way, only those lines containing invalid or missing data items are ignored; we no longer have to quit the first time bad data is encountered.

Despite their usefulness, the string functions in the string and standard I/O libraries are not part of the language definition. These functions are now considered part of the entire environment, but are *not* guaranteed to be provided with every C compiler; some compilers provide only a few of these routines, and others provide them with slightly different names. If your compiler does not have them, they should be written and used whenever their capabilities are needed.

EXERCISES

3-13 Another useful string function from the standard library is the length function, `strlen`. `strlen` takes a string terminated by a null (`'\0'`) and returns the number of characters in the string, *not counting* the null. Write a function `strlen` using the following function header:

```
int     strlen (s)
char    s[];
```

The function requires s to be null terminated, so the length of the empty string (a string consisting of just a null) is zero. Test your function on a program using strings of various lengths, including the empty string. Use `get_line` from Figure 3.5 to get a line of input from the terminal. □

3-14 Write a version of `strlen` that uses pointers to access the array, rather than array indexes. Compare the running time on this version with that of an indexing version on a very long string. □

3-15 Write a version of `strcmp` that uses pointers to access the arrays. Compare its running time with that of an indexing version. □

3-16 Modify the insertion sort program in Chapter 1 to read its input with `get_line` and `sscanf`. □

3-17 Find out which string-handling functions are available on your system. Implement those, if any, that are missing. □

3.6

ARRAY ACCESSING WITH POINTERS – EFFICIENCY CONSIDERATIONS

Earlier, we wrote a version of `strcpy`, a function found in the standard C library, which copies one string to another (Figure 3.6). We saw that `strcpy` merely copied characters, one at a time, by accessing the arrays source and dest through the array index i. The work was done in a while loop:

```
while ((dest[i] = source[i]) != '\0')
    i++;
```

An alternative way to write the function is to treat source and dest as pointers (to the first element of the respective arrays) rather than as arrays. When we do this, we access the elements indirectly through pointers rather than directly through array indexes. If dptr is a pointer to the destination array and sptr is a pointer to the source array, declared by

```
char *dptr = dest,
     *sptr = source;
```

as in the following diagram

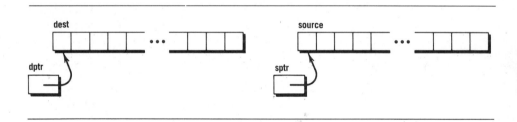

the previous while loop can be compactly and efficiently coded as:

```
while ((*dptr++ = *sptr++) != '\0')
    ; /* copy string */
```

Let us analyze this operation briefly and see why it is equivalent. First, notice that the increment operators (++) are postfix; they take effect after their operand is used. Thus, this single while statement operates similarly

```
while ((*dptr = *sptr) != '\0')
{
    dptr++;
    sptr++;
}
```

Now the action should be easy to trace. *sptr dereferences sptr; that is, it fetches the character that sptr points to and assigns that character to the location to which dptr points. Since assignment is an operator returning a value, the value of the entire expression is the character assigned, the character '\0' when the end of the string is reached. The while tests if the null character was assigned and the loop terminates if it was. If any other character is assigned, the loop body is entered; both dptr and sptr are incremented. Note that in this case there is no loop body so the null statement, a semicolon (;) is used. (See Chapter 4 for a complete discussion of the null statement.)

What advantage do we gain by accessing storage through pointers rather than through array indexing? The answer, in most computers, is speed. We ran both the original array version and the pointer version on a DEC VAX 11/750, copying a string of 15,000 characters. The array version, Figure 3.6, required about 0.32 seconds of CPU time. The pointer version, written using the modified while loop above, needed only 0.13 seconds, a saving of almost 60 percent! With time savings like this, it is worthwhile to spend some time studying the pointer version in order to understand the way the pointers access the various array elements, and the order in which the operations of dereferencing (*) and incrementing (++) occur.

Because of the precedence and evaluation order of * and ++, *sptr++ means "obtain the character that sptr points to (i.e., *sptr). After obtaining that character increment the pointer (i.e., perform sptr++ in terms of pointer arithmetic)." The following diagram illustrates the accessing of the array indirectly through a pointer.

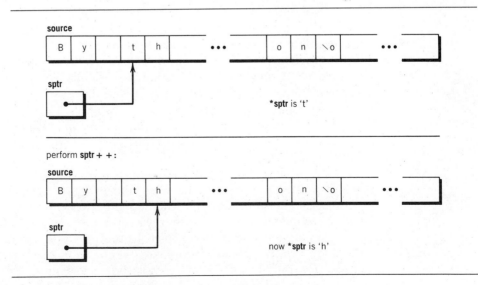

3.7

CASE STUDY – A PROGRAM TO ELIMINATE DUPLICATE LINES

To illustrate the use of arrays and the string functions from the standard string library, we will write a program (called *Uniq*) that takes a text file as its input and copies its input to its output, minus any lines that are the same as the line they follow. For example, if the input consists of the lines

```
There was a young lady from Norway
There was a young lady from Norway
There was a young lady from Norway
who hung by her heels in the doorway
she said to her man,
she said to her man,
           . . .
```

We want the output to be

```
There was a young lady from Norway
who hung by her heels in the doorway
she said to her man,
           . . .
```

The program has a number of uses, and a variation suggested in the exercises has been used to help remove duplicated words in large text files created with a text editor. The sentence *"I told him not to go and and he went anyway,"* contains two "and"s. We can eliminate one of them by running two programs over the text: first, a program that breaks the input into individual words, one per line, and second, a program that only prints the first line of any set of duplicated lines.

Importantly, this program illustrates how a useful function can be created from small, already existing pieces. The program uses `get_line`, `strcmp`, and `strcpy`, each of which we have already written or is provided for us as a library function.

The program processes its input a line at a time, storing both the current and previous lines (using `get_line`, Figure 3.5, and not repeated here). The current and previous lines are compared using the library function `strcmp` (see Figure 3.7), and if they are not the same, the current line is printed; if they are the same, the program continues. For this program, we are interested in whether the previous and current lines are equal: we test `strcmp` for a nonzero return.

The current line is then copied to the previous one using `strcpy`, and the loop continues. We terminate when `get_line` returns `EOF`. The entire program (minus `get_line`) is shown in Figure 3.8. Note the use of the two include files: *stdio.h*, which defines `EOF`, and *strings.h*, which declares the types of the string functions.

```
/*
 *  Uniq — A program to strip duplicate lines.
 */
#include <stdio.h>
#include <strings.h>                        /* declares types of strcpy, etc */

#define MAXLINE      256                     /* longest line program can handle */
#define FALSE          0
#define TRUE           1

main ()
{
  char    curr_line[MAXLINE + 1],           /* current line */
          prev_line[MAXLINE + 1];           /* previous line */
  int     first = TRUE;                      /* first time for this line? */

  while (get_line (curr_line, MAXLINE) != EOF)
  {
    if (first || strcmp (prev_line, curr_line) != 0)
    {
      printf ("%s\n", curr_line);
      first = FALSE;
    }
    strcpy (prev_line, curr_line);          /* copy curr_line to prev_line */
  }
}
```

"get_line" goes here

FIGURE 3.8   Uniq – A program to remove duplicate lines from its input.

EXERCISES

3-18 Write a variation of *Uniq* that prints only duplicated lines, and then only the first occurrence of each repetition.   □

3-19 Write a variation of *Uniq* that prints one instance of each line, preceded by a count of the number of times the line is repeated. If the input is

```
Now is the time
for all good men
for all good men
to come to the aid
of their party.
of their party.
of their party.
```

the output should look like this:

```
1               Now is the time
2               for all good men
1               to come to the aid
3               of their party.  □
```

3-20 Write a program that reads the input and breaks it up into individual words, which are then printed one per line. Words are strings of alphabetic or numeric characters separated by nonalphanumerics.   □

3-21 Write a function, `put_line`, that takes a string and writes it and a trailing newline. Use `putchar` in a loop, rather than `printf`, to do this. The standard I/O library defines a function, `puts`, that does just this. Compare the size and running time of a test program that uses your own `put_line` rather than `printf`.   □

3-22 Finish the limerick on page 90. Be creative.   □

ARRAYS, STRINGS, AND POINTERS

The relationship between arrays, strings, and pointers can be confusing. Here are some hints, suggestions, and reminders to help clarify these concepts.

- Remember that although an array name is a pointer, it is a constant pointer and cannot be used to traverse the array. When an array is defined, the compiler first allocates enough storage to contain the requested number of elements, and then makes the array's name a constant pointer to the first (zeroth) element of the array.

- Make sure any strings (arrays of characters) you create are terminated by a null character, since the built-in functions dealing with strings make that assumption and fail miserably if it does not hold. You also have to make sure any character array you declare has enough space for all input characters, plus the null, as shown in `get_line` in Figure 3.5. The compiler, however, automatically terminates any string defined within double quotation marks with the necessary null character.

- Use the common, useful string functions that are provided in the standard C environment. Do not write your own versions (other than for practice), because the standard string functions are coded efficiently, because they save the programmer the job of having to provide them (they are used frequently), and because they lead to more modular, more cleanly designed programs.

- When possible, use pointers to traverse arrays, rather than array subscripting. However, the clear purpose of a piece of code should never be sacrificed for the sake of efficiency until it can be shown through direct execution monitoring that substantial program speedup occurs as the result of fine tuning an individual piece. Chapter 12 covers efficiency issues in more detail, and discusses some of the ways that execution monitoring can be used.

CHAPTER 4

STATEMENTS

We have already introduced many of C's statements. However, our previous descriptions were brief, so we will now explain more fully the statements already used and give detailed descriptions of those we have ignored. We conclude by tying together the concepts covered so far in a program that produces a histogram of its input values. In this chapter we begin to combine language features to write larger programs, including a simple calculator and a palindrome checker.

4.1

EXPRESSION STATEMENTS

C's simplest statement is the *expression statement*, an expression followed by a semicolon.

    expression;

An expression statement can be used anywhere the language syntax requires a statement, and is executed by evaluating *expression* and ignoring its result. Both function calls and assignment statements are merely expression statements; they are not separate kinds of statements, as in FORTRAN or BASIC. Notice that the semicolon terminates statements instead of separating them, as in Pascal. Some examples are shown in Figure 4.1.

```
avg = sum / entries;          /* compute average */
sum += next;                  /* update sum */
entries++;                    /* one more entry */
entries--;                    /* one less entry */
printf("sum is %d\n", sum);   /* write out average (function call) */
sum / entries;                /* legal, but useless */
scanf("%d", &next);           /* get "next" ignoring return value */
```

FIGURE 4.1   Some examples of legal expression statements.

Any useful expression statement must have a side effect such as invoking a function, incrementing or decrementing a variable, or assigning a value to a variable. Expression statements with no side effects accomplish nothing and, although syntactically legal, should be avoided. In Figure 4.1 the legal but useless expression statement

```
sum / entries;
```

causes sum to be divided by entries, with the result ignored.[1]

EXERCISE

4-1 What does your compiler do with an expression statement that does nothing? Is this behavior reasonable? □

4.2

COMPOUND STATEMENTS

Any group of statements surrounded by braces is a *compound statement* or *block* and, like an expression statement, can be used wherever the language syntax requires a statement.

```
{
    declarations
    statements
}
```

Notice that a compound statement is not followed by a semicolon. Statements within a block can be preceded by variable declarations, a topic covered in detail in Chapter 6.

[1]Some compilers recognize useless expression statements and fail to generate code for them or give a warning.

A compound statement composed entirely of expression statements, such as a series of assignment statements, is often rewritten as a single more compact expression statement using the comma operator. For example, we can replace

```
{
    lineno = 0;
    pageno = 1;
    lastch = '\n';
}
```

with

```
lineno = 0, pageno = 1, lastch = '\n';
```

Changing a compound statement into a single expression statement can make the program more compact, although not necessarily more readable. Generally, compound statements should be left alone unless the expression statements contained in them are closely related or unless the lines saved make the function fit on a single page, aiding readability.

4.3

SIMPLE DECISION STATEMENTS — IF

Most decisions in C are made using the `if` statement, which is similar to the if statement of other languages. In its simplest form

```
if (expression)
    true-statement
```

expression is evaluated, and if it is not zero, *true-statement* is executed.[2] The behavior of the `if`'s more general form

```
if (expression)
    true-statement
else
    false-statement
```

is similar, with the exception that if *expression* evaluates to zero, *false-statement* is executed. After execution of either form, control passes to the statement following the `if`.

We illustrate both forms of `if` in Figure 4.2, a program that finds and

---

[2]Remember that the relational operators return zero if the condition fails and one if it holds.

```
/*
 * Find maximum value in input (includes error checking).
 */
#include <stdio.h>

main()
{
    int inpres,                 /* result of reading an input value */
        max,                    /* maximum value so far */
        value,                  /* current input value */
        valuecnt = 0;           /* number of values read so far */

    while ((inpres = scanf("%d", &value)) == 1)
        if (valuecnt++ == 0 || value > max)
            max = value;
    if (inpres == EOF)
        printf("Maximum: %d\n", max);
    else
        printf("Bad value found\n");
    printf("Values read in: %d\n", valuecnt);
}
```

FIGURE 4.2   Finding the largest input value.

prints the largest value in its input. The program's input is a series of
values; as each value is read, it is compared with the largest value previously read; if it is larger, it is saved as the new largest value. If an error is
encountered while the input is being read, an error message is written and
the program terminates.

Most of the program's work is done by the program fragment to
decide if the value read is the largest value so far:

```
if (valuecnt++ == 0 || value > max)
    max = value;
```

Although this fragment is executed once for every value read, the assignment occurs only if `value` is the first value read or if it is greater than the
largest value previously read. We take advantage of two of C's operators
to make this program more concise: ++ increments `valuecnt` *after* it is
used in the equality test; || does not evaluate the expression on the right
if the expression on the left evaluates to zero, guaranteeing that the
expression `value > max` will not be evaluated the first time it goes
through the `while` loop. Notice that == is used for equality testing, not
= (the assignment operator).

When the end of the input is reached or when an error occurs when
reading a value, control is passed to the program fragment

```
if (inpres == EOF)
  printf("Maximum: %d\n", max);
else
  printf("Bad value found\n");
printf("Values read in %d\n", valuecnt);
```

When all values have been read without error, `inpres` is equal to `EOF`, and the largest value in the input is written. Any error causes `inpres` to be zero and an error message to be written instead. After either case, the count of the values read is printed.

EXERCISE

4-2 What would be the result of the above program fragment if the test was accidentally changed to `inpres = EOF`? Would this be a difficult bug to find? □

4.3.1 THE NESTED IF

There is a bug in the program of Figure 4.2. If there is no input, an undefined value will be produced as the maximum value. This happens because `max` is not defined until the first value is read. We can correct this problem by writing a message that no values were read using the following *nested if*.

```
if (inpres == EOF)
  if (valuecnt != 0)
    printf("Maximum: %d\nValues: %d\n", max, valuecnt);
  else
    printf("No values given\n");
else
  printf("Bad value found after %d values\n", valuecnt);
```

The test for no values read (`valuecnt != 0`) is made only if the end of the file is reached without error.

Another way to correct this problem is to produce output only when at least one value has been read. At first glance, it may appear that the following accomplishes this purpose:

```
/* BUG: The following doesn't do what it is supposed to do */
/*      despite misleading indentation */

if (inpres == EOF)
  if (valuecnt != 0)
    printf("Maximum: %d\nValues: %d\n", max, valuecnt);
  else
    printf("Bad value found after %d values\n", valuecnt);
```

There is a subtle problem with this correction, however, caused by an ambiguity over which `if` the `else` belongs to. The ambiguity is resolved by arbitrarily assuming that any `else` is attached to the closest nonterminated `if`. Therefore, despite this program's indentation, the `else` is associated with the *inner* `if` and the error message is incorrectly written when there is no input. To avoid the association of an `else` with the closest `if`, that `if` must be placed in braces. The following produces the desired result:

```
if (inpres == EOF)
{
  if (valuecnt != 0)
    printf("Maximum: %d\nValues: %d\n", max, valuecnt);
}
else
  printf("Bad value found after %d values\n", valuecnt);
```

EXERCISES

4-3 Using nested `ifs`, write a function `min3` that returns the smallest of the three `int` values passed to it as parameters. Use the function declaration

```
min3(value1, value2, value3)
int value1, value2, value3;
```

Are there other reasonable ways to accomplish this?   □

4-4 Many programmers place braces around all their `if` statements. Comment on this style.   □

4.3.2 ASSIGNMENT DECISIONS — THE CONDITIONAL OPERATOR

When an `if` decides which one of two values a particular variable should be assigned, the conditional operator `?:` is a convenient shorthand. For example, using the conditional operator, the `if` that assigns `min` the smaller value of `x` and `y`

```
if (x < y)
  min = x;
else
  min = y;
```

can be rewritten as

```
min = (x < y) ? x : y
```

The conditional operator is C's only ternary operator; all three of its operands are expressions:

expression **?** *true-expression* **:** *false-expression*

The conditional operator is evaluated by first evaluating *expression*. If the result is not zero, *true-expression* is evaluated and returned as the conditional expression's value. Otherwise, *false-expression* is evaluated and returned. It is a good idea to parenthesize *expression*; even though it is not usually necessary, the parentheses help distinguish the test from the values returned.

More complex assignment decisions can be rewritten using the conditional operator. The following `if` converts military hours (`mhour`) to standard hours (`stdhour`)[3]

```
if (mhour != 0)
  if (mhour > 12)              /* afternoon */
    stdhour = mhour - 12;
  else                         /* morning (or noon) */
    stdhour = mhour;
else                           /* midnight */
  stdhour = 12;
```

and can be rewritten using the conditional operator as

```
stdhour = (mhour != 0) ? ((mhour > 12) ? mhour - 12 : mhour) : 12
```

In addition to parenthesizing the expressions tested by the conditional operators, we parenthesized the nested conditional operator. Again, although not strictly necessary, this is a good habit to get into, since it protects against possible precedence problems.

When the conditional operator is used, the code will be more concise and possibly more efficient, but not as readable. Anything with more than a single nested conditional operator is better written using `if`s.

EXERCISES

4-5 Using the conditional operator, write a function, `max`, that returns the larger of its two integer arguments. □

[3]Hours in military time range from 0 (midnight) to 23 (11 p.m.).

4-6 Rewrite the function `min3` (from Exercise 4-3) using the conditional operator instead of a nested `if` statement. Is this function as understandable as the version written using nested `if` statements?   □

4.4

MULTIWAY DECISIONS — ELSE-IF

There is one more form of `if` we have not discussed yet: the *multiway decision*. A multiway decision is a chain of `if`s in which the statement associated with each `else` happens to be an `if`:

```
if (first-expression)
    first-statement
else if (second-expression)
    second-statement
    . . .
else if (final-expression)
    final-statement
else
    default-statement
```

The final `else` and its associated *default-statement* are optional.

When a multiway `if` is executed, each of the expressions is evaluated in turn until one of them evaluates to something other than zero. Then the single statement associated with it is executed and the multiway `if` is exited. If all the expressions evaluate to zero and *default-statement* is present, it is executed. This is not really a new statement type; it is simply a common way of putting `if`s together.

Figure 4.3, a program to find the smallest and largest values in its input, contains two examples of the multiway `if`. The first multiway `if`, within the `while`, is executed once for each value read and updates the variables `min` and `max`. The first time through, `max = min = value` is executed. For subsequent values, the new value is compared with `max`; if it is larger, `max` is assigned `value`. Otherwise, the new value is compared with `min`; if it is smaller, `min` is set equal to `value`.

The second multiway `if` is used for error handling. When there are several error conditions to check, a multiway `if` is often convenient. The tests for the various errors come first, and the default statement (the final `else`) is executed when no errors are found.

```
/*
 *  Find maximum and minimum values in input.
 */
#include <stdio.h>
main()
{
  int inpres,               /* result of reading in input value */
      max, min,             /* maximum and minimum values so far */
      value,                /* next value in input */
      valuecnt = 0;         /* number of values so far */

  while ( (inpres = scanf("%d", &value)) == 1)
    if (valuecnt++ == 0)     /* first value? */
      max = min = value;
    else if (value > max)    /* new maximum? */
      max = value;
    else if (value < min)    /* new minimum? */
      min = value;
  if (inpres != EOF)
    printf("Error after %d values\n", valuecnt);
  else if (valuecnt == 0)
    printf("No values read\n");
  else
    printf("Maximum: %d\nMinimum: %d\nValues: %d\n", max, min, valuecnt);
}
```

FIGURE 4.3 Finding the smallest and largest input values.

EXERCISES

4-7 Write a program to read numeric scores and assign letter grades to them based on the traditional scale: 90-100 is an A, 80-89 is a B, 70-79 is a C, 60-69 is a D, and anything less is an F. Print an error message for any scores greater than 100 or less than 0. Do not forget to test for improper input data by checking the return value of scanf or by using get_line and sscanf. □

4-8 Write a program to find the two largest and the two smallest values in its input. Can you easily generalize your program to find the n largest and the n smallest? □

4.4.1 CONSTANT MULTIWAY DECISIONS — SWITCH

When each of the comparisons in a multiway if checks for different values of the same expression, we have a constant multiway decision. This occurs, for example, in programs that process single-letter commands; the user-entered command is compared with the program's legal commands to determine the appropriate action to be taken. The `switch` statement is often a more convenient, more efficient, and more readable way to make such decisions than a multiway `if`.

```
switch(expression)
{
    case first-constant-expression:
        statement-list
    case second-constant-expression:
        statement-list
            . . .
    case final-constant-expression:
        statement-list
    default:
        statement-list
}
```

`switch` is similar to the case and computed goto statements found in other languages. A `switch` can contain zero or more cases appearing in any order with an optional `default` case. Each of the case labels must be an expression evaluable at compile time to an integral constant, and all case labels within a single `switch` must be unique. A *statement-list* can contain zero or more statements; there is no need to put braces around them.

When `switch` is executed, *expression* is evaluated and control passes to the case labeled with the expression's value. When the case's statement list has been executed, control falls through to the next case label. Since this is almost always undesirable, a `break` statement is usually placed at the end of each case's statement list; `break` causes the enclosing `switch` to exit, passing control to the statement following the `switch`.

We illustrate the use of `switch` with a simple calculator program shown in Figure 4.4. The calculator's input is a series of operator-operand pairs. Each pair contains a single character operator (such as +, −, *, or /) followed by a floating point operand. A running total is updated as each pair is processed, and the total is printed when the end of input is reached. For example, given the input

```
+ 3.1415926
  * 30.56  * 30.56
  / 2.0
```

the calculator's output is

```
1466.988027
```

We use `scanf` to read both the operator and the operand. Because `scanf` skips white space before character strings but not before single characters, the operator is read as a string instead of as a character.

Allowing operators and operands to be surrounded by white space makes the calculator easier to use. Notice that when `scanf` is used to read a string, the string's name is passed and the `&` operator is not used.

A `switch` uses the string's first character to select the appropriate operator-labeled case. The default case prints an error message and is executed whenever there is an invalid operator. We have ended the actions for each case with a `break` statement; without it, control would automatically pass to the following case. Although we do not need the `break` after the `default`, we have used it as a defensive measure, preventing an accidental fall-through if additional case labels are added.

```
/*
 *  Simple calculator program.
 */
#include <stdio.h>

main()
{
    int     inpres;             /* return value when reading in value */
    char    operator[2];        /* read in operator: op followed by null */
    double  operand,            /* read in operand */
            result;             /* Result of computation */

    result = 0.0;
    while (inpres = scanf("%s%f", operator, &operand), inpres == 2)
      switch(operator[0])
      {
        case '+':   result += operand;
                    break;
        case '-':   result -= operand;
                    break;
        case '*':   result *= operand;
                    break;
        case '/':   if (operand != 0)
                       result /= operand;
                    else
                       printf("Division by zero, ignored.\n");
                    break;
        default:    printf("Unknown operator: %c\n", operator[0]);
                    break;
      }
    if (inpres == EOF)
      printf("%f\n", result);
    else
      printf("Error in input.\n");
}
```

FIGURE 4.4 A simple calculator program illustrating `switch`.

Although falling through cases automatically can lead to serious problems when `break` is forgotten, it is useful when we want numerous cases to select the same action. The program fragment

```
case 'a':                              /* fall through */
case '+':   result += operand;
            break;
```

makes `a` an operator equivalent to `+`. Since there are no actions for its case and no `break`, when the operator is an `a` its operand is added to the running total. Falling through should be used only when the same action occurs for many different constants, and should not be used to execute statements in one case followed by statements in another.[4] Even though we could combine the actions of the calculator's addition and subtraction operators,

```
case '-':   operand = -operand;    /* here we fall through, */
case '+':   result += operand;     /* but this is GROSS! */
            break;
```

it is not good style, since the program becomes less readable and more difficult to modify.

EXERCISES

4-9 Modify the calculator program to include various synonyms for the existing operators (such as `d` for `/`, `m` for `*`, `s` for `-`, and `a` for `+`), and to include the two additional operators `%` (remainder) and `^` (exponentiation). □

4-10 The calculator will print out incorrect results if any of the computations overflow. Modify the calculator to print an error message if overflow occurs. □

4-11 Rewrite the calculator to use a multiway `if` instead of a `switch`. Which form of multiway decision do you prefer? □

4-12 Write a simple program to aid in balancing a checkbook. The input to the program should be a single-letter command followed by an amount. The legal commands are `d` (deposit), `c` (check), `s` (service charge), `w` (withdrawal), and `b` (set starting balance). After each command, the account's new balance should be printed. □

[4]Falling through can occasionally simplify code, but these cases are rare, and any falling through should be well commented.

4.5

SIMPLE LOOPS — WHILE AND DO-WHILE

The simplest looping mechanisms in C are the `while` and `do-while` statements. We have used `while` in many of our programs.

```
while (expression)
    statement
```

When `while` is executed, a cycle of evaluating *expression* and executing *statement* is entered, the cycle ending when *expression* evaluates to zero.

Unlike the `while`, which tests before its body is executed, the `do-while` tests afterward.

```
do
    statement
while (expression);
```

When a `do-while` is executed, a cycle of executing *statement* and evaluating *expression* is entered. As with the `while`, the cycle ends when *expression* evaluates to zero. But unlike the `while`, *statement* is always executed at least once.

Although `do-while` is used much less often than `while`, it can be convenient. Figure 4.5*a* uses it in the function `yesorno`, which encapsulates the common operation of asking a yes-or-no question, verifying the response, and returning it. An example use of `yesorno` is shown in Figure 4.5*b*.

When `yesorno` is called, after the question is asked, a `do-while` is entered. Within the loop, a prompt is written, the first character typed is taken as the answer, and the remainder of the current input line is discarded. The loop terminates when an appropriate character is entered.[5] We use a `do-while` since at least one response will be entered, and we want to loop until we get a correct response.

When the body of a `do-while` consists of a single statement, it should be made into a compound statement by surrounding it with braces. The braces are not required by the language syntax, but their use clearly shows that the `do` and the `while` are associated. For example,

```
do   /* Ignore the rest of the line */
{
  c = getchar();
} while (c != '\n' && c != EOF);
```

[5]We are careful to test for end of file because on systems where a program's input can be redirected, this prevents an infinite loop if the end of file is hit before a correct response is entered. Our example use of `yesorno` simply treats EOF as a no.

```
/*
 * Write prompt, wait for 'y', 'n' or EOF as the user's answer
 * (include <stdio.h> before this function)
 */$
int yesorno(question)
char question[];
{
  int answer,                   /* user's response */
      junk;                     /* used to skip characters */

  printf("%s? ", question);
  do
  {
    printf(" (y for yes, n for no): ");
    junk = answer = getchar();  /* get user's answer */
    while (junk != EOF && junk != '\n')
      junk = getchar();         /* skip rest of line */
  } while (answer != 'y' && answer != 'n' && answer != EOF);
  return answer;
}
```

(a)   *Get a yes or no answer from the user*

```
if (yesorno("Are you smart") == 'y')
  printf("Me too.\n");
else
  printf("Too bad.\n");
```

(b)   *An example use of* yesorno

FIGURE 4.5   A function to get a yes or no answer from the user.

is preferred to the more compact but less readable

```
do   /* Ignore the rest of the line */
  c = getchar();
while (c != '\n' && c != EOF);
```

EXERCISES

4-13 What is the shortest infinite while loop? The shortest infinite do-while loop? □

4-14 Modify yesorno to accept uppercase as well as lowercase and to accept answers such as "yes," "no," and "ok." □

4.6

MORE GENERAL LOOPS — FOR

C's most general looping statement is the `for`, which is considerably more general than the iterative for loops of BASIC or Pascal.

```
for (Start; Test; Action)
    statement
```

`for` is executed by evaluating *Start*, discarding the result, and entering a cycle of evaluating *Test*, executing *statement*, and evaluating *Action*. The cycle terminates when *Test* evaluates to zero.

Usually, *Start* and *Action* are assignments or function calls and *Test* is a relational test. As we mentioned earlier, however, these expressions are all arbitrary and can be omitted. When *Start* is omitted, it is generally because any needed initializations have already been done. As an example, Figure 4.6 contains a function `init_table` to set the first *n* elements of an array to a given value. In `init_table` the index `i` is initialized to zero when it is declared, rather than in the loop.

A missing *Test* is assumed to evaluate to something other than zero; such a loop is infinite and will normally be exited by a `return` or other control flow altering statement. For example,

```
for (;;)
    printf("Reflex test - hit the terminal interrupt key\n");
```

repeatedly writes the same message until the terminal interrupt key is pressed. Notice that the semicolons remain even when the expressions are left out.

```
/*
 * Initialize each of the "nelems" elements in "x" to "value"
 */
init_table(x,nelems,value)
int x[],          /* table to initialize */
    nelems,       /* number of table elements */
    value;        /* value to initialize them with */
{
  int i = 0;      /* loop index */

  for (; i < nelems; i++)
    x[i] = value;
}
```

FIGURE 4.6   Initializing an array. The initialization part of the `for` is left empty, because the loop's index was initialized when it was declared.

Because the `for` is so general, we often write `for` loops with multiple index variables as well as index variables that are pointers instead of integers. Figure 4.7 shows examples of both in a program (called *Pal*) that checks to see if its input lines are palindromes. A palindrome is a group of characters that, excluding blanks, reads the same way forward or backward. For example, "able was I ere I saw elba" is a palindrome.

Most of *Pal* is built from existing functions. `get_line` (Chapter 3) reads each input line, and `strcpy` copies it. `ispalin` is new, however, returning whether a string is a palindrome after first removing the blanks from it. `main` simply calls these functions, echoing each line followed by a message stating whether it is a palindrome.

To simplify the later palindrome checking, the first `for` in `ispalin` removes any blanks from the string being checked.

```
for (r = f = test; *f != '\0'; f++)
  if (*f != ' ')
    *r++ = *f;
*r = '\0';
```

As the character pointer `f` walks through the string `test`, each nonblank character is copied into the character pointed to by `r` and `r` is incremented, as shown below. Since `r` starts by pointing to `test`'s first character, this effectively removes all of its blanks. If `test` contains no blanks, the string is simply copied onto itself.

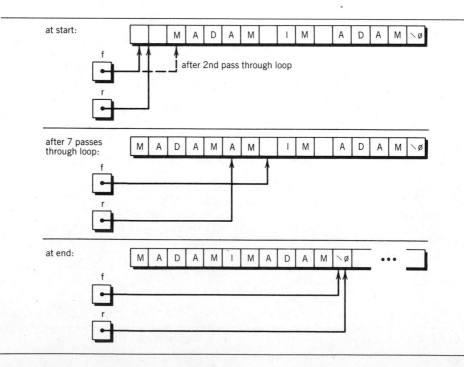

```
/*
 *  Palindrome checker (assumes get_line from Chapter 3)
 */
#include <stdio.h>

#define MAXLINE 81                      /* longest input line + ending null */
#define TRUE    1                       /* the usual booleans */
#define FALSE   0

main()
{
  char line[MAXLINE],                   /* user input line */
       copy[MAXLINE];                   /* copy of user input line */

  while (printf("line? "), get_line(line, MAXLINE) != EOF)
  {
    strcpy(copy, line);                 /* make copy of user line */
    printf("%s: %spalindrome.\n", line, ispalin(copy) ? "" : "not ");
  }
}
int ispalin(test)
char *test;                             /* string to check for palindrome */
{
  char *f,                              /* forward and reverse pointers into */
       *r;                              /*    test string */
  int palin;                            /* flag: do we have palindrome? */

  /* Remove any blanks from potential palindrome */

  for (r = f = test; *f != '\0'; f++)
    if (*f != ' ')
      *r++ = *f;
  *r = '\0';

  /* Walk pointers through string from both ends; mismatch means not
     palindrome and testing stops */

  palin = TRUE;
  for (f = test, r--; f < r && palin; f++, r--)
    if (*f != *r)
      palin = FALSE;

  return palin;
}
```

FIGURE 4.7 Palindrome checker.

The second for checks to see if the string is a palindrome. The comma operator allows the multiple initializations and reinitializations within the loop.

```
palin = TRUE;
for (f = test, r--; f < r && palin; f++, r--)
  if (*f != *r)
    palin = FALSE;
```

This `for` works by having a pointer `f` go forward from the start of the string and a pointer `r` go backward from its end, as shown below. As these pointers move along, the characters they point to are compared and the loop stops when the characters are different (it is not a palindrome) or the pointers cross (it is a palindrome). Because `r` points at the string-terminating null after the blanks are removed, it is decremented when the loop is initialized.

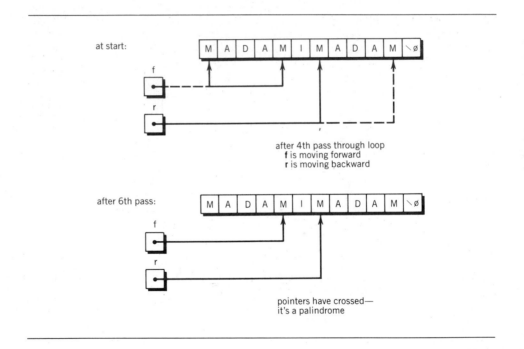

at start:

after 4th pass through loop
f is moving forward
r is moving backward

after 6th pass:

pointers have crossed—
it's a palindrome

It is a good idea to initialize index variables (here, pointers) within the loop; whether to initialize related variables in the loop (such as `palin`) is up to you.

Since the `for` is more general than the `while`, you may be wondering when each is appropriate. `for` is appropriate when the loop control statements are simple and related, and the same values are updated each time the loop is executed. `while` should be used when an equivalent `for` would contain unrelated computations or would omit both *Start* and *Action*. When in doubt, it often helps to write the code for both, using the one that appears to be more readable.

EXERCISES

4-15 Modify *Pal* to strip all punctuation, as well as any tabs, from the input string. □

4-16 Write a function, `strrev`, that takes its single character string argument and reverses it in place. □

4-17 How can `while` be simulated using `for`? Can `do-while` be simulated using `for`? □

4-18 Write a program that prints all the prime numbers between 1 and 1000. A prime number is one that is exactly divisible only by one and itself. □

4.7

THE NULL STATEMENT

Any semicolon not preceded by an expression is a *null statement*. A null statement does nothing and is used when no action is desired but the language syntax requires a statement. This occurs most frequently when side effects in a loop's control expression obviate any need for the loop's body. Using the null statement makes these loops more compact by allowing expression statements to be moved from the loop's body into its controlling expression. As an example, Figure 4.8 shows the standard I/O library function `strcat`, which concatenates (or appends) one null-terminated character string to another null-terminated character string. Assuming that `base` and `msg` are character strings, the call

```
strcat(base,msg)
```

replaces the trailing null in `base` with the character string `msg`, while `msg` remains unchanged. Chaos ensues if `base` does not have enough additional room for `msg`.

A null statement should never be placed on the same line as a `for` or a `while`, because it is easy to ignore a semicolon at the end of the line and mistake the following lines for the loop's body. As we have done in our examples, whenever the null statement is used, it should be placed on a line by itself, indented slightly, and followed by a comment.

Accidentally inserting a null statement following a loop's control expression is a common mistake with disastrous results. The loop

4.8
ALTERING CONTROL FLOW

Normally, statements are executed sequentially. We now describe statements that can be used to alter the normal sequential flow of control. Although it is easy to use these statements to violate some of the basic principles of structured programming, and although their use is never absolutely necessary, on occasion they are convenient and help to simplify our programs.

4.8.1 LEAVING LOOPS EARLY — BREAK

Sometimes leaving a loop from within its body simplifies the loop's control expression by separating tests for special cases or errors. In addition to its already described use in exiting a `switch`, break can be used to exit immediately from anywhere within the nearest enclosing `for`, `while`, or `do-while`, as shown below.

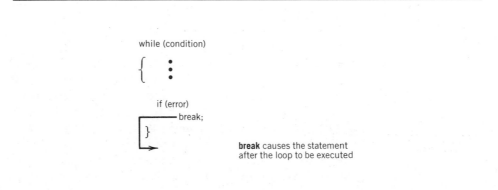

```
while (condition)
{      .
       .
       .

if (error)
        break;
}
```

break causes the statement
after the loop to be executed

As an example, a loop to find the first nonblank on an input line

```
while (c = getchar(), (c == ' ' || c == '\t') && c != EOF && c != '\n')
    ;      /* skip blanks and tabs until first nonblank on line */
```

is more readable when written using `break`:

```
while (c = getchar(), c == ' ' || c == '\t')   /* skip blanks and tabs */
   if (c == EOF || c == '\n')
      break;                     /* special cases: end of file and end of line */
```

```
/*
 * Get a single letter ('a', 'd', or 'q') command from the user
 * (#include <stdio.h> should precede this function).
 */
int getcommand()
{
  int command,                          /* user's command */
      junk;                             /* used to ignore rest of line */

  for (;;)
  {
    printf("Please enter a single letter command: ");
    if ((junk = command = getchar()) == EOF)
      break;                            /* EOF, no more commands */
    if (command == 'a' || command == 'd' || command == 'q')
      break;                            /* valid command */
    printf("Bad command given\n");
    while (command != EOF && junk != '\n')
      junk = getchar();                 /* skip rest of line */
  }
  if (command != EOF)
    printf("Valid command %c entered\n", command);
  else
    printf("End of file reached, treating as quit command.\n");
  return command;
}
```

FIGURE 4.9   Get a command from the user.

The break causes the while to exit and control to pass to whatever state-ment follows it. Using break simplifies the loop's control expression and makes it clearer that end of file and end of line are special cases.

It is common to use break to get out of infinite loops. We show this use in Figure 4.9, which contains the function getcommand. getcommand is used to get and return a valid command from the user. It prints a prompt, reads an input command, and if the command is not valid, skips over the rest of the characters on the input line. The infinite loop in getcommand indicates that the function forces the user to type in a valid command. break is used to exit the loop when a valid command or end of file is encountered.[6]

4.8.2 AVOIDING CODE IN LOOPS — CONTINUE

The continue statement can be used to skip the remaining part of a loop iteration and is usually used to avoid excessive nesting within the loop.

[6]We are assuming here that EOF is a reasonable way to exit a program (equivalent to a *quit* command).

```
/*
 * Process table of elements
 */
process(table, tabentries)
int table[], tabentries;
{
  int i;

  for (i = 0; i < tabentries; i++)
  {
    if (table[i] < MINVAL || table[i] > MAXVAL)
    {
      printf("Element #%d, value %d, is out of range\n", i, table[i]);
      continue;           /* skip processing if element in error */
    }

    processing of valid table elements
  }
}
```

FIGURE 4.10   Using `continue` to avoid the remainder of a loop.

After a `continue` within a `for`, the reinitializing expression is evaluated, then the loop's control expression. In a `while` or `do-while`, `continue` causes the control expression to be evaluated immediately.

The most common use of `continue` is to avoid an extra level of nesting by checking error conditions and skipping the rest of the loop if an error occurs. As an example, Figure 4.10 shows a function that does some unspecified but complicated processing on a table. Whenever an out-of-range element is encountered, an error message is written and `continue` is used to skip any further processing of the element. Since the `continue` is within a `for`, when it is executed the reinitialization expression `i++` is evaluated before the loop termination test occurs. Despite its occasional usefulness, `continue` can usually be avoided by rewriting the complex code as a separate function.

EXERCISE

4-23 Some programmers use `continue` or an empty compound statement to indicate a null loop body instead of the null statement. Discuss the advantages and disadvantages of these styles. □

4.8.3 UNCONDITIONAL BRANCHING — GOTO

The final way to alter control flow is the `goto` statement. A `goto` can be used to branch to a labeled statement within any statement group enclosing it. A *label* has the same syntax as an identifier and is visible only within the statement group in which it is defined.

```
goto label
   . . .
label: statement
```

A `goto` is executed by transferring control to the statement labeled by *label*. There must be a statement to which control can be transferred; the null statement must be used if control is to be transferred to the end of a compound statement or function body. It is not possible to go to a statement in another function, and although it is legal, it is terrible style to use a `goto` to jump into a loop or compound statement.

A reasonable use of `goto` is to exit from within nested loops when an error condition occurs:

```
while ( . . .)
  for ( . . .)
  {
     . . .
    if (error condition)
      goto error;
     . . .
  }
   . . .
error:
  printf("Serious error detected . . .time to go home!\n");
   . . .
```

When the error condition occurs, control is transferred to the label `error` and the error message is printed. Because `break` and `continue` exit only a single loop, avoiding a `goto` in a situation like this requires a boolean variable to note the error condition and additional tests of its value in the expressions controlling the loops. Another way to avoid using a `goto` is to make the code fragment containing the loops a function; `return` can then be used to exit the loops when the error condition occurs, returning a value indicating the error condition. (The complete use of functions and `return` is covered in the next chapter.)

There are many reasons to avoid using `goto`'s. When `goto` is used, most compilers generate less efficient code than with the structured loop constructs. In addition, using many of them quickly renders a program unreadable. Since there are several reasonable ways to avoid using `goto`, it is a good idea to do so whenever possible and to document any `goto` whose use is deemed necessary. The `goto` is used infrequently in most well-written programs, and we have found no need for it in any of the programs in this book.

4.9
CONCISE CONTROL EXPRESSIONS

As mentioned earlier, the control expressions of the `if`, `for`, `while`, and `do-while` statements are evaluated and compared with zero to determine the action to be taken. Therefore, explicit comparisons with zero in any control expression are unnecessary and can be eliminated. For example,

if (*expression* != 0)   *is equivalent to*   if (*expression*)

and

if (*expression* == 0)   *is equivalent to*   if (!*expression*)

Since zero is used both as the end-of-string character and as the null pointer, testing if the end of a string has been reached or if a pointer is null is often done implicitly. As an example, Figure 4.11 shows a concise version of the standard I/O library function `strlen`. `*end` is the entire control expression for the `for`. Its value is compared implicitly to zero and the loop stops when `end` points to the null character at the end of the string. We compute the string's length using the expression `end − string`.

The version of `strlen` shown in Figure 4.11 requires `string` to point to a valid character string, as does the `strlen` in the standard I/O library. If instead `string` is `NULL`, `strlen` will bomb at run time. We can make `strlen` verify that `string` is not `NULL` by adding the following before the `for`:

```
if (!string)      /* null pointer? */
    return −1;    /*   return impossible legal string length */
```

Only when `string` is the null pointer does `!string` evaluate to nonzero.

```
/*
 * Return number of characters in "string".
 */
int strlen(string)
char *string;
{
    char *end = string;     /* will point to string's end */

    for (; *end; end++)
        ;                   /* find string's end */
    return end − string;
}
```

FIGURE 4.11 Finding the length of a string.

Because of the implicit comparison with zero, using the assignment operator when the equality operator was desired can be disastrous. When

```
if (errorcnt = 0)
  printf("No errors");
```

is executed, the `printf` will never be executed, regardless of `errorcnt`'s value. This happens because every time the `if` is executed, `errorcnt` is set to zero, causing the implicit test to fail. The most likely correct form is

```
if (errorcnt == 0)
  printf("No errors");
```

Any time an assignment of a constant to a variable forms a control expression, it is likely to be in error.

EXERCISES

4-24 Rewrite `strcat` using pointers, taking advantage of the implicit tests against zero. □

4-25 Again, taking advantage of the implicit tests against zero, write a function `print_reverse` that prints an array of n elements in reverse order. □

4.10

CASE STUDY — A HISTOGRAM PROGRAM

We end this chapter with a program (called *Histo*) that produces a histogram of its input. A histogram is a visual representation of a frequency distribution that is composed of bars representing different ranges of values. Each bar's length represents the relative frequency of the group of values represented by that bar. Figure 4.12 shows some sample output from *Histo*.

Histograms are usually generated by maintaining an array whose elements count the values falling within each range. Once all input values have been read, the bars for each range of values are written by printing an asterisk (or whatever character is used to represent a value) for each of the values that fell within that range.

Histo is interesting because it is an example of a useful program, clearly and cleanly written in just under 100 lines of C, that uses many of the control structures discussed in this chapter. The following sections describe its input, internal processing, and output in more detail, followed by a listing of the program.

```
All 78 values in range

  0-  9 |
 10- 19 |***                                                            (3)
 20- 29 |*                                                              (1)
 30- 39 |
 40- 49 |*                                                              (1)
 50- 59 |*****                                                          (5)
 60- 69 |***********                                                    (11)
 70- 79 |*************************************                          (37)
 80- 89 |************                                                   (12)
 90- 99 |***                                                            (3)
100-100 |*****                                                          (5)
```

FIGURE 4.12 Sample Histogram Output.

4.10.1 THE HISTOGRAM PROGRAM — INPUT

Histo's input is a series of free-format integer values to be read using scanf. Figure 4.13 shows the histogram input used to produce the histogram output shown above. *Histo* terminates with an appropriate error message if there are any input errors, such as a nonnumeric character. Most users would probably prefer it to simply skip over or report all occurrences of bad input, but this is difficult to do with scanf. In Chapter 6 we develop an alternative to scanf that greatly simplifies input error handling.

All input values are checked to verify that they fall within the legal range (defined as constants within the program). After the input has been read, the number of out-of-range values is written.

4.10.2 THE HISTOGRAM PROGRAM — INTERNAL PROCESSING

Each valid data value must be counted into the correct data bucket. There is an array of these data buckets, one for each range of values; each bucket counts those values falling within the range of values it represents. Once

```
89  87  56  89  67  78  79  80  85  97 100 100  23
45  12  14  87  88  84  84  84  77  77  72  73  68
69  69 100 100  11  75  71  71  72  79  84  71  72
70  74  75  73  71  79  72  55  55  68  65  67  72
71  75  73  71  74  71  71  78  79  80 100  91  92
66  61  61  57  57  65  71  74  78  78  78  78  78
```

FIGURE 4.13 Sample Histogram Program Input.

all input values have been read, these counters are used to print the histogram.

When the program starts, the range of values in each bucket is easily computed from defined constants for the minimum and maximum legal data values and the desired number of buckets. Selecting an appropriate bucket is also straightforward, as shown below.

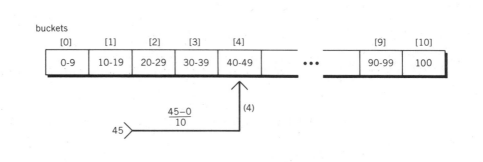

In this example, we assume that the minimum value is 0 and that each bucket holds 10 different values. Then for an input of 45, we can determine the correct bucket by subtracting the minimum value (0) from the data value (45) and dividing the result by the size of a bucket (10). The result (4) is the bucket in which the data value should be counted. (Remember, we are using integer division here.)

4.10.3 THE HISTOGRAM PROGRAM — OUTPUT

Histo's output is a horizontal bar chart like the one shown in Figure 4.12. Each bar is a row of asterisks, and each asterisk represents a single value. Each row of asterisks is preceded by the range of values the row represents and is followed by a count of the values falling in that range. If there are no values in the row, the count is suppressed.

If there are many input values, it is possible that more asterisks will be needed than there are columns available on the output device. Should this occur, the output is scaled so that the row with the most asterisks covers the available width and the other rows are proportionally shorter, allowing users to see the relationship between the various groups. To make sure that scaling doesn't make any row with proportionally few values appear to have none at all, at least one asterisk is written for each row that has one or more values. In any case, the exact count is still written at each row's end.

4.10.4 THE HISTOGRAM PROGRAM

The histogram program is broken into two functions other than `main`. `fill_ bkts` reads input values, checks their legality, and updates the appropriate bucket. It returns an `int` indicating whether any input errors were encountered. `print_histo` prints the histogram based on the counts in the buckets. `main` computes the bucket size, invokes `fill_ bkts` to update them, and then invokes `print_histo` only if no input errors are detected. Here is a skeletal version of the main program.

```
main()
{
    compute bucket size
    if (we can fill the buckets without error)
        print the histogram
}
```

At this point, *Histo* should be easily understandable. Glancing through the program, you will notice null statements, considerable use of the comma and conditional operators, and loops manipulating multiple indexes. Although *Histo* is a sizable program, it is worthwhile taking some time to study it in preparation for the larger programs we present in later chapters.

EXERCISES

4-26 Modify the constants for the minimum and maximum values and bucket count, and examine the effects on the output. ☐

4-27 Modify *Histo* to read the minimum and maximum values and bucket count. Obviously, there must be some internal maximum bucket count; the program should verify that the desired bucket count is not too large. ☐

4-28 Our histogram has a horizontal orientation; modify `print_histo` to print a histogram with a vertical orientation instead. ☐

4-29 Each bar in the histogram is a single row. Change *Histo* so that the number of rows used per bar is a program constant. ☐

4-30 Modify *Histo* to use pointers where appropriate. Does this have a noticeable effect on the program's speed? ☐

4-31 We have pointed out many of the problems with `scanf`. A simple solution is to write a function `getnum` that uses `scanf` to try to read a number. If

```
/*
 *   Produce nice histogram from input values.
 */
#include <stdio.h>

#define   MAXCOLS    50          /* columns available for markers */
#define   MARKER     '*'         /* character used to mark columns */
#define   MAXVAL     100         /* largest legal input value */
#define   MINVAL     0           /* smallest legal input value */
#define   NUMBKTS    11          /* number of buckets */

main()
{
  int buckets[NUMBKTS],          /* buckets to place values in */
      bktsize;                   /* range bucket represents */

  bktsize = (MAXVAL - MINVAL) / (NUMBKTS - 1);
  if (fill_bkts(buckets, bktsize))
    print_histo(buckets, bktsize);
  else
    printf("Illegal data value--no histogram printed\n");
}


/*
 * Read values, updating bucket counts.  Returns nonzero only
 * if EOF was reached without error.
 */

int fill_bkts(buckets, bktsize)
int buckets[],                   /* buckets to place values in */
    bktsize;                     /* range of values in bucket */
{
  int badcnt = 0,                /* count of out-of-range values */
      bkt,                       /* next bucket to initialize */
      inpres,                    /* result of reading in an input line */
      totalcnt = 0,              /* count of values */
      value;                     /* next input value */

  for (bkt = 0; bkt <= NUMBKTS; buckets[bkt++] = 0)
    ;                            /* initialize bucket counts */
  while (inpres = scanf("%d", &value), inpres == 1)
  {
    if (value >= MINVAL && value <= MAXVAL)
      buckets[(value - MINVAL) / bktsize]++;
    else
      badcnt++;
    totalcnt++;
  }
  if (!badcnt)
    printf("All %d values in range\n", totalcnt);
  else
    printf("Out of range %d, total %d\n", badcnt, totalcnt);
  return inpres == EOF;          /* did we get all the input? */
}
```

FIGURE 4.13   The Histogram Program.

```
/*
 * Print a nice histogram, first computing a scaling factor
 */
print_histo(buckets, bktsize)
int buckets[],                /* buckets to place values in */
    bktsize;                  /* range of values in bucket */
{
  int bottom,                 /* first value in current bucket */
      bkt,                    /* current bucket */
      markcnt,                /* number of marks written */
      most,                   /* values in largest bucket */
      values;                 /* number of values to write out */
  float scale;                /* scaling factor */

  /* compute scaling factor */

  for (bkt = most = 0; bkt < NUMBKTS; bkt++)
    if (most < buckets[bkt])
      most = buckets[bkt];
  scale = (most > MAXCOLS) ? (MAXCOLS / (float) most) : 1.0;

  /* print the histogram */

  putchar('\n');
  for (bkt = 0, bottom = MINVAL; bkt < NUMBKTS; bottom += bktsize, bkt++)
  {
    /* write range */

    printf("%3d-%3d |", bottom,
               (bkt == NUMBKTS - 1) ? MAXVAL : bottom + bktsize - 1);

    /* compute number of MARKERS to write, making sure that at least
       one is written if there are any values in the bucket */

    if (buckets[bkt] && !(values = buckets[bkt] * scale))
      values = 1;

    /* writes MARKERS and count of values */

    for (markcnt = 0; markcnt < MAXCOLS; markcnt++)
      putchar((markcnt < values) ? MARKER : ' ');
    if (buckets[bkt])
      printf(" (%d)", buckets[bkt]);
    putchar('\n');
  }
}
```

FIGURE 4.13   The Histogram Program.

scanf fails, getnum skips characters until a white space character is
reached. Write getnum and modify *Histo* to use it. What problems are
there with getnum? □

PROGRAM FORMATTING

Although we have not emphasized formatting and have written our programs in the style we are most comfortable with, a program's format has a considerable effect on its understandability. Here are some formatting guidelines that work for us and some common mistakes.

- While you are learning the language, format statements as we have done in this chapter. Although this is not necessarily the most compact style, it is readable.

- Separate declarations and statements with a blank line, even though this is not required by the compiler. Never be afraid to use extra blank lines.

- Avoid placing multiple statements on a line. Related expression statements can be tied together using the comma operator; unrelated expression statements deserve separate lines.

- Avoid placing the statement part of looping or decision statements on the same line as the loop's control expression. The more compact form is less readable and more prone to errors such as accidentally including a null statement.

- Remember to parenthesize control expressions. Also remember that there is no "do" following `while` and no "then" following `if`; inserting these keywords causes syntax errors.

- Do not terminate compound statements with a semicolon. The extra semicolon is an unnecessary and possibly harmful null statement.

- Lastly, avoid the tendency of many C programmers to see just how compact a program can be written. If you feel a need to do this, do it and then throw the program away, because it will be unreadable.

C H A P T E R 5

FUNCTIONS

One of C's strengths is that functions are easy to define and use. In this chapter we discuss functions in detail, concentrating on how they communicate with one another through parameter passing and return values. In addition, we examine pointers to functions, which are used to pass functions as parameters. We conclude with a discussion of recursive functions (functions that call themselves), presenting implementations of two interesting and useful recursive algorithms: binary search and quicksort.

5.1

PARAMETER PASSING

As we saw in Chapter 1, when a function is defined, we specify the type of its return value, the names and types of each of its parameters, and the function's body.

```
type function-name(parameter-1,...,parameter-n)
type parameter-1;
. . .
type parameter-n;
{
    declarations
    statements
}
```

The parameter names are given in a parenthesized list following the function name; this list is followed by their type declarations. Even though a parameter's type defaults to int if left unspecified, to aid readability the types of all parameters should be explicitly declared.

The values provided for a function's parameters when it is called are known as its *arguments*. The type of each argument should be the same as the type of its corresponding parameter. That is, if a function expects a parameter of a particular type, it should be passed one of that type or unpredictable results will occur.

All parameters are passed by value; every time a function is called, each parameter has space allocated for it and is then assigned the value of its corresponding argument. When the function exits, the space is deallocated. In effect, parameters can be treated as previously initialized local variables. Because modifying a parameter does not affect its corresponding argument, *a function cannot change the values it is passed*. This allows the use of arbitrary expressions as function arguments and prevents a function from accidentally modifying its arguments.

We take advantage of this call by value in the function sum, shown in Figure 5.1. sum computes the total of the first n elements of an array. Although its parameter n is decremented during each pass through the loop, n's corresponding argument remains unchanged, saving us the trouble of using an additional local variable to index the loop, resulting in a more compact function.

5.1.1 PASSING ARRAYS AS PARAMETERS

Arrays are *not* passed by value and array contents are *not* copied. Instead, only the address of the array's first element is passed. Array elements are then indexed through this address, either explicitly by subscripting or indirectly through a pointer. Since a pointer is passed, the parameter

```
/*
 * Return sum of first "n" array elements.
 */
int sum(a,n)
int a[], n;
{
  int total = 0;            /* running total */

  while (n-- > 0)
    total += a[n];
  return total;
}
```

FIGURE 5.1 Compactly sum elements in an array.

representing the array can be declared explicitly as an array or as a pointer to an array element. Thus, in parameter declarations

type `*name`

is equivalent to

type `name[ ]`

The form used should match the parameter's use in the function.

Notice that we do not explicitly declare an array parameter's size. Instead, any function passed an array should also be passed the number of elements in the array or should have some other way (such as the null character at the end of a string) to determine how many elements to process. Unfortunately, we cannot use `sizeof` for this purpose because the number of elements actually passed is not necessarily known at compile time. Instead, when `sizeof` is applied to an array parameter, it returns the size of a pointer to an array element. For both of the above declarations, `sizeof(name)` returns `sizeof(&name[0])`, which is equivalent to `sizeof(`*type* `*)`.

Because an array parameter is a pointer to the array's first element, it can be used to traverse the array. We illustrate this in Figure 5.2*a*, a function `print_table` that prints the elements in an array. Figure 5.2*b* shows an example call that prints a table named `scores` that contains `MAX-SCORES` elements.

```
/*
 * Print table of "num" integers
 */
print_table(tab_ptr, num)
int *tab_ptr,                        /* pointer to table's first element */
    num;                             /* number of elements to print */
{
  while (num-- > 0)
    printf("%d\n", *tab_ptr++);
}
```

(a)   Print an array's elements

```
{
  int scores[MAXSCORES];             /* table of scores */
  . . .
  print_table(scores, MAXSCORES);    /* print "scores" */
  . . .
}
```

(b)   Example use of `print_table`

FIGURE 5.2   Printing an array's elements using the parameter to traverse the array.

When `print_table` is called, `tab_ptr` is initialized with the address of the array's first element and then used to traverse the array, incremented after each element is printed. `scores` is a constant and is not affected by the call to `print_table`. An infrequently used but equivalent alternative to the call in Figure 5.2*b* is:

```
print_table(&scores[0], MAXSCORES);        /* print "scores" */
```

Because an array is passed as a pointer, we can pass the address of any array element, which effectively allows us to pass only part of an array. As an example, either

```
print_table(&scores[i], k);
```

or

```
print_table(scores + i, k);
```

prints `k` scores, starting with `scores[i]`. In both cases, the address of `scores[i]` is passed, and all elements of `scores` are still accessible to `print_table` through appropriate negative or positive offsets of `tab_ptr`.

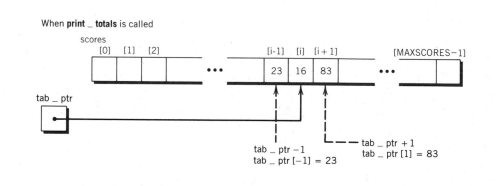

It is a common mistake to pass an array element instead of its address to a function expecting an array parameter. The call

```
print_table(scores[i], k);     /* incorrect: pointer not passed! */
```

is a serious mistake, since `print_table` is expecting a pointer and is instead receiving an `int`. A function expecting an array *must* be passed an array name or an element's address.

EXERCISES

5-1 When is a negative array subscript valid? Give an example. □

5-2 Write a function, `insert`, that takes a sorted array of `long`'s and a `long` value and inserts the value in its correct place in the table. Write both pointer and array versions. Which is more efficient? Which is more compact? □

5.1.2 STRINGS AND CALL BY VALUE

Many string-handling functions are made more concise by traversing the strings using the pointers they are passed. For instance, Figure 5.3a shows yet another version of `strcpy` and Figure 5.3b an example of its use. Even though the parameters `dest` and `source` are modified as the copy is performed, the pointers (`prev_line` and `curr_line`) passed to `strcpy` remain unchanged. However, the character string to which `prev_line` points becomes a copy of the character string pointed to by `curr_line`.

```
/*
 * Copy "source" string into "dest".
 */
strcpy(dest,source)
char *dest, *source;
{
  while ((*dest++ = *source++) != '\0')
    ;                    /* copy strings */
}
```

(a) Yet another version of `strcpy`

```
{
  char prev_line[MAXLINE], curr_line[MAXLINE];
  . . .
  strcpy(prev_line, curr_line);
  . . .
}
```

(b) An example call of `strcpy`

FIGURE 5.3 Copying two strings using the passed pointers to traverse them.

EXERCISES

5-3 Using pointers and avoiding unnecessary local variables, write a function, `rmchr`, that takes a string and a character as arguments, removing all occurrences of the character from the string. `rmchr` should not leave holes in the string. What should `rmchr` return?　□

5-4 Write a function, `rmstr`, that takes two strings as arguments, removing all occurrences of any characters in the second string from the first string. Like `rmchr`, `rmstr` should not leave holes in the string. What should `rmstr` return?　□

5-5 Can `strcpy` be made even more compact? How? Is this a good idea?　□

5-6 Write compact pointer versions of the standard string library functions. Are these more efficient than straightforward array versions?　□

5.2

USING POINTERS TO ALTER NONLOCAL VARIABLES

It is often useful to have a function alter the value of a variable in its calling function; `scanf` is one example. We cannot simply change its value, however, because changes to parameters are local to the function. Instead, we must use `&` to pass a pointer to it; the function can then dereference the pointer with `*` whenever the variable's value is to be accessed or modified.

We illustrate this technique with a function `swap` that exchanges the values of two integer variables. Because of call by value, the version of `swap` shown in Figure 5.4 does not do what we want: it swaps the values of its parameters `x` and `y` but does not affect the values of its arguments.

```
/*
 * Incorrect version of swap.
 */
swap(x,y)
int x,y;
{
  int temp = x;

  x = y, y = temp;
}
```

FIGURE 5.4 Incorrect version of swapping function.

For `swap` to exchange the values of variables in its calling function, it must be passed *pointers* to them; the values can then be swapped indirectly through these pointers. A corrected version of `swap` is shown in Figure 5.5*a* and an example call in Figure 5.5*b*.

The call to `swap` shown in Figure 5.5*b* is illustrated below, assuming that the addresses of `s` and `t` are 1000 and 2000, respectively, `s` is 5, and `t` is 10. When `swap` is called, `x_ptr` becomes 1000 and `y_ptr` becomes 2000, the addresses of their corresponding arguments. The assignment `temp = *x_ptr` causes the value in location 1000 (5) to be placed in `temp`. Similarly, `*x_ptr = *y_ptr` assigns location 1000 the value in location 2000 (10), and `*y_ptr = temp` completes the exchange by placing `temp`'s contents (5) in location 2000.

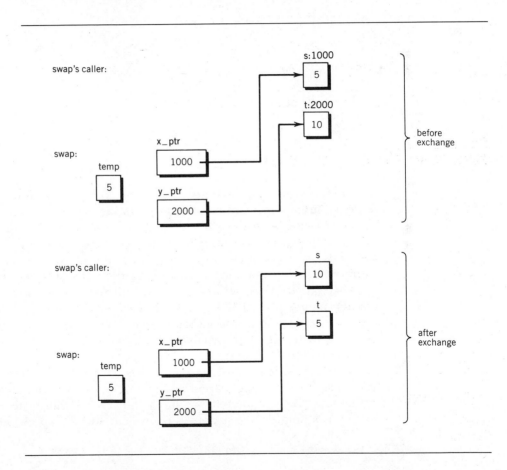

Remember that when we have a pointer parameter, its corresponding argument must also be a pointer. For `swap` to work correctly, it must be passed the addresses of the variables whose values are to be exchanged. Passing the variables themselves is likely to cause an addressing exception.

```
/*
 * Corrected version of swap — exchange two values.
 */
swap(x_ptr, y_ptr)
int *x_ptr, *y_ptr;
{
  int temp = *x_ptr;

  *x_ptr = *y_ptr, *y_ptr = temp;
}
```

(a) *Correctly exchange two values using pointers*

```
{
  int s,t;
  . . .
  swap(&s,&t);
}
```

(b) *Exchanging the values in* s *and* t

FIGURE 5.5   Corrected version of swap and example call. The values are exchanged through pointers.

Perhaps the most common mistake made when writing functions with pointer parameters is to use the pointers inconsistently. One way to avoid this problem is to first write the function without any pointer parameters, pretending that C has call by reference parameter passing. Once the function has been written this way, the appropriate parameters can be transformed into pointers by modifying their declarations, renaming them to reflect their new use, and replacing all their uses with the appropriate pointer name, preceded by a *. Indeed, this is how we got the correct version of swap from the incorrect one. We replaced the int variables x and y with the pointer variables x_ptr and y_ptr and preceded all uses of these pointers with *.

Although it is not necessary for swap, references through pointer variables may have to be parenthesized to guarantee the desired order of evaluation. As we pointed out in Chapter 3 and illustrate again below, if i_ptr is a pointer, *i_ptr++ is equivalent to the expression

```
old = *i_ptr, i_ptr++, old
```

returning what i_ptr points to as the expression's value and then incrementing i_ptr. In contrast, (*i_ptr)++ simply increments whatever i_ptr points to. Failing to correctly parenthesize expressions that involve pointer dereferences often leads to bugs that are difficult to locate.

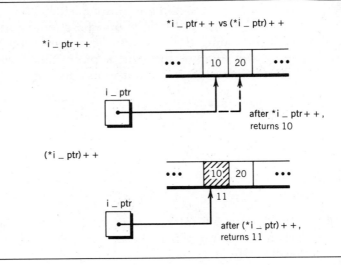

Another common mistake is to accidentally pass a pointer's address instead of the pointer itself. An example is shown in Figure 5.6. get_val is supposed to use scanf to read a single value, placing it in the location pointed to by x_ptr and returning whether the value read is between min

```
/*
 * Reads value, places it in "*x_ptr", and returns whether or not it is
 * between "max" and "min".  Warning, the surgeon general has determined
 * that there is a bug in this program!
 */
int get_val(x_ptr, min, max)
int *x_ptr, min, max;
{
  return (scanf("%d", &x_ptr) == 1)          /* BUG ALERT! */
          && (*x_ptr >= min) && (*x_ptr <= max);
}
```

(a) Reading a value and checking that it is in range

```
{
  int x;
  ...
  if (!get_val(&x, 1, 100))                  /* read legal value into x */
    printf("Bad value found...\n");
  ...
}
```

(b) An example call of get_val

FIGURE 5.6 An example of the incorrect use of pointer parameters.

and `max`. There is a bug in this implementation, however. Since `x_ptr` is already a pointer to the location where `scanf` should place the value read, `scanf` is reading its value into `x_ptr` instead of what it points to, invalidating later accesses through `x_ptr`. Since we already have the pointer we need, we do not want to take its address:

```
return (scanf("%d", x_ptr) == 1)          /* This is correct */
        && (*x_ptr >= min) && (*x_ptr <= max);
```

EXERCISES

5-7 Turn Figure 5.6 into a program and run it. What happens? Are there certain values for which the program appears to work? Fix Figure 5.6 so that it works as intended. ☐

5-8 Write a function, `maxmin`, that returns through its parameters the largest and smallest values in an array of floating point numbers. Use the declaration

```
maxmin(table, n, max_ptr, min_ptr)
float table[], *max_ptr, *min_ptr;
int n; ☐
```

5-9 Write the function `str_swap`, whose arguments are pointers to strings. The values of these pointers are swapped. When is `str_swap` useful? (Hint: this requires pointers to pointers. It helps to draw a picture in order to see what is going on.) ☐

5.3

PARAMETERS AND TYPE CHECKING

As we have repeatedly pointed out, the parameter-passing mechanism works correctly only when the type of each argument is the same as the type of its corresponding parameter. To avoid errors resulting from type mismatches, we must use a cast if their types differ.

Unfortunately, type mismatches are not always detected at compile time and can cause strange run-time behavior. We use the function `inrange`, shown in Figure 5.7a, as an example. `inrange` verifies that a given value is between two other values, returning zero only if it is out of range.

```
/*
 * Return one if "value" is between "min" and "max", zero if it isn't
 */
int inrange(min,max,value)
double min, max, value;
{
  return value >= min && value <= max;
}
```

(a) Function to check if a value is in a given range

```
int result;
. . .
if (!inrange(1, 100, result))
    printf("Error: %d is out of range\n", result);
```

(b) Example call of inrange *with a parameter type mismatch*

FIGURE 5.7 Example of parameter type mismatch.

Consider what happens when inrange is called, as shown in Figure 5.7*b*. Surprisingly, the error message is never printed, regardless of the value of result passed to inrange. This occurs because inrange expects its parameters to be doubles (two words in floating point representation) and instead receives ints (one word in two's complement representation). As a result, on a DEC-VAX, regardless of the values passed, min and max are always zero – clearly, not what was intended. Luckily, we can correct the call shown in Figure 5.7*b* by making sure that each of its arguments is a double:

```
if (!inrange(1.0, 100.0, (double) result))
```

All floating point constants are doubles, and the cast guarantees that a copy of result will be converted to a double before being passed as a parameter.

5.3.1 AUTOMATIC TYPE CONVERSIONS

Some parameter conversions are done automatically. Any char or short argument is implicitly cast to an int before it is passed; similarly, a float argument is cast to a double. In the following call to inrange, it is unnecessary to cast low_val, high_val, or result explicitly, because the necessary conversions are done automatically before they are passed.

```
float low_val, high_val, result;
. . .
if (!inrange(low_val, high_val, result))
    printf("Error: %f is out of range\n", result)
```

```
/*
 * Concatenate array "source" to array "dest"; "dest" needs enough room.
 */
strcat(dest, source)
char dest[], source[];
{
    int d, s;          /* destination and source indexes */

    for (d = 0; dest[d] != '\0'; d++)
        ;                       /* find end of destination */
    for (s = 0; (dest[d] = source[s]) != '\0'; s++, d++)
        ;                       /* append source to destination */
}
```

FIGURE 4.8 Concatenating two character strings.

```
for (sum = i = 0; i < N; i++);       /* sum first "N" scores */
    sum += score[i];                 /*   (but accidentally null loop body) */
```

was probably meant to add N scores together in the variable sum. However, the null statement following the loop's control expression forms the loop's body. Thus, the statement

```
    sum += score[i];
```

is executed only after the loop is terminated, when i is N+1 and is probably no longer a legal subscript.

EXERCISES

4-19 Rewrite strcat (in Figure 4.8) using pointers instead of subscripts. You should not have to change the function's general structure. □

4-20 Rewrite strcat to use while loops instead of for loops. Which version do you find more readable? Which version is more efficient? (Hint: Examine the machine code your compiler generates for both versions.) □

4-21 Write the standard I/O library function strncat, which behaves similarly to strcat, except that a maximum of n characters are concatenated. □

4-22 Write the standard I/O library function strncpy, which behaves similarly to strcpy, except that a maximum of n characters are copied. □

Within functions, `short` or `char` *parameters* (but not local variables) are automatically redeclared as `int`; `float` parameters become `double`s. Appropriate casts are inserted wherever the parameter is used; for example, when the compiler redeclares a `short` parameter as an `int`, it implicitly casts its value to `short` wherever it appears within the function. Thus, the definition of `inrange` in Figure 5.8a behaves as if it were written as in Figure 5.8b.

Since the compiler must insert code to do type conversions wherever `char`, `short`, and `float` parameters are used, it is significantly more efficient to pass `int`, `long`, and `double` parameters instead.

5.3.2 PARAMETERS AND PORTABILITY

C's lack of type checking, combined with programmer carelessness, leads to programs that work on one machine but fail on another. Consider the version of `inrange` shown in Figure 5.9a as invoked in Figure 5.9b.[1]

On a VAX, `int` and `long` happen to be the same size (32 bits), and the code works as expected. However, on the IBM-PC, where `int` is one word and `long` is two words, we get bizarre results. It is easy to make this program work correctly on all machines; we simply cast the arguments appropriately (here, `long` constants can be used instead of the cast):

```
if (!inrange(1L, 100L, (long) result))
```

```
int inrange(min,max,value)
short min, max, value;
{
  return value >= min && value <= max;
}
```

(a) A version of inrange *for* short *parameters*

```
int inrange(min,max,value)
int min, max, value;
{
  return (short) value >= (short) min && (short) value <= (short) max;
}
```

(b) inrange *after the compiler's automatic conversions*

FIGURE 5.8   An example of automatic type conversions.

[1]We know you are getting a little tired of `inrange`, but please bear with us; this is the last example using it.

```
int inrange(min,max,value)
long min, max, value;
{
  return value >= min && value <= max;
}
```

(a) *defining* inrange *with* long *arguments*

```
{
  int result;
  . . .
  if (!inrange(1, 100, result))
    printf("Error: %d is out of range\n", result);
}
```

(b) *calling* inrange incorrectly with int *arguments*

FIGURE 5.9   Still another version of our range checking function. The call isn't portable.

Portability problems can also occur when we pass NULL to a function expecting a pointer. If we do not cast NULL to the correct pointer type, our program will not be portable to machines where pointers and integers are not the same size. For example, suppose we have a function f that takes a single parameter, a pointer to a char. To see why the call

```
    f(NULL)
```

is *not* portable, consider an architecture that has two-word pointers and one-word ints. Since NULL is defined as the constant zero, we are passing a one-word integer when a two-word pointer is expected. It is easy to prevent this mistake by casting NULL appropriately. The call

```
    f((char *) NULL)
```

is portable.

Not only do we have to be careful that there are no type mismatches, we must also ensure that we pass the correct number of parameters. Functions ignore extra parameters; missing parameters contain undefined values. Although C's lack of type checking can be exploited to write functions that handle variable numbers of arguments such as printf or scanf, these functions are not portable. Indeed, they must contain knowledge about the underlying hardware.

EXERCISES

5-10 Try the various versions of inrange on your machine. Can you explain their output by examining the relative sizes of the data types on your machine? Which version produces the smallest amount of code? The largest? □

5-11 Write a function, `isvalid`, that is similar to `inrange`, except that it verifies whether a pointer is between two other pointers. Assume the pointers passed to `isvalid` are pointers to `long`. A null pointer for either range should disable that range check. What is `isvalid` useful for? □

5.4

RETURN VALUES — THE TYPE OF A FUNCTION

In addition to communicating through parameter passing, functions can communicate through return values. A function can return a single `short`, `int`, `long`, `char`, `float`, `double`, or pointer but cannot return an array. (We can get around this restriction by returning a pointer to its first element instead.) The type of the function's return value is specified when the function is declared and precedes the function's name, defaulting to `int` if left unspecified.

All of our previous functions have returned an `int` or nothing at all. We illustrate the use of a non-`int` return value in Figure 5.10, a program to compute x^y for integers `x` and `y`. Since the result can be fractional if `y` is negative, or large for small values of `x` and `y`, we define `power` to return a `double`.

When the compiler encounters a function call, if the type of the function's return value has not been declared, it is assumed to be `int`. The *declaration*

```
double power();          /* computes x to the y */
```

appears in `main`, before `power` is called, to inform the compiler that `power` returns a `double`, instead of the default `int`. Parentheses follow `power` to specify that `power` is a function instead of a variable. The types of a function's parameters are not specified in a declaration. Without this declaration, the compiler would incorrectly assume that `power` returns an `int`, and incorrect code to handle its return value would be generated. This assumption would be contradicted when `power`'s later definition occurs, causing most compilers to report an error. Not all compilers detect this inconsistency, however, particularly when separate compilation (which we will discuss in the next chapter) allows the function to be defined in another file.

Figure 5.11 shows an alternative way to guarantee that `power`'s type is declared before its use in `main`; we simply define `power` before we define

```
/*
 * Compute powers.
 */
main()
{
  int x,y;                  /* user inputs */
  double power();           /* computes x to the y */

  while (printf("Enter x,y: "), scanf("%d %d", &x, &y) == 2)
    printf("%d to the %d is % f\n", x, y, power(x,y));
}

/*
 * Return x to the y, works best for small integers.
 */
double power(x,y)
int x,y;
{
  double p = 1.0;           /* start off with x to the zero */

  if (y >= 0)
    while (y--)             /* compute positive powers */
      p *= x;
  else
    while (y++)             /* compute negative powers */
      p /= x;
  return p;
}
```

FIGURE 5.10 Computing x to the y for integers x and y.

main. power's type is then known from its definition, so we no longer need its type declaration in main. We prefer explicit declarations to relying on the default assumptions of the compiler or on the order in which the functions appear in the source file, since we can then determine the program's structure easily by scanning declarations.

EXERCISES

5-12 Write the function index, which takes a string and a character, and returns a pointer to the character's first occurrence within the string. □

5-13 Write the function rindex, which is similar to index, except that it returns a pointer to the character's last occurrence within the string. □

```
/*
 * Compute powers
 */

double power(x,y)          /* return x to the y */
int x,y;                   /*   (works best for small integers) */
{
  double p = 1.0;          /* start off with x to the zero */

  if (y >= 0)
    while (y--)            /* compute positive powers */
      p *= x;
  else
    while (y++)            /* compute negative powers */
      p /= x;
  return p;
}

main()
{
  int x,y;                 /* user inputs */

  while (printf("Enter x,y: "), scanf("%d %d", &x, &y) == 2)
    printf("%d to the %d is % f\n", x, y, power(x,y));
}
```

FIGURE 5.11 Defining a function before its use.

5.4.1 FUNCTIONS THAT RETURN A VALUE

As we have seen, `return` terminates a function, possibly returning a value to its caller. There are two forms of `return`:[2]

> `return` *expression*`;`

and

> `return;`

`return` without an expression does not return a value and is similar to simply dropping off the function's end. This form should not be used in a function that is supposed to return a value.

`return` can appear anywhere within the function body, and a function can contain more than one `return`. As an example, Figure 5.12*a* shows the function `search` that searches for a value in an array of integers, and Figure 5.12*b* is an example call.   `search` uses a pointer to traverse the

---

[2]Some compilers require parentheses around *expression* even though the language syntax doesn't require them.

array, using `return` to exit the function immediately when a match is found. If the entire table was searched and the value was not found, the `return` at the function's end returns a null pointer.

When a value is returned, it is automatically cast to the function's type. This automatic return value conversion is often useful; in `search` it means that we do not have to cast the returned `NULL` to a pointer. In functions that do computations using `doubles`, yet return an `int`, any `double` returned will be truncated into an `int` before being given to the caller.

EXERCISES

5-14 Improve the sequential search shown in Figure 5.12 by assuming a sorted table. □

5-15 Many programmers believe that more than one `return` in a function is bad style. Write a version of `search` with only one `return`. Which do you prefer? Why? □

```
/*
 * Search "num" element table for "value", returning a pointer to
 * the matching element, or the null pointer if it is not found.
 */
int *search(tab_ptr, num, value)
int *tab_ptr,                   /* pointer to table's first element */
    num,                        /* number of elements in table */
    value;                      /* value we're looking for */
{
  for (; num--; tab_ptr++)
    if (*tab_ptr == value)
      return tab_ptr;           /* found target, return pointer to it */
  return NULL;                  /* failure, return null pointer */
}
```

(a) Function to search an array sequentially

```
int scores[MAXSCORES],          /* table of scores */
    *search(),                  /* function doing searching */
    *fnd_ptr,                   /* pointer to found element */
    target;                     /* element searching for */
. . .
if (fnd_ptr = search(scores, MAXSCORES, target), fnd_ptr != NULL)
  printf("Found %d as element %d.\n", target, fnd_ptr - scores);
else
  printf("Didn't find %d.\n", target);
```

(b) An example call of `search`

FIGURE 5.12 Sequential search of an array using pointers.

5-16 Modify the function insert (Exercise 5-2) to return a pointer to the place in the table where the value was entered or NULL if the table was full. Rewrite insertion sort using this version of insert. □

5.4.2 FUNCTIONS THAT DO NOT RETURN A VALUE

In C all functions return a value, unlike languages such as Pascal, which distinguish between functions that return a value (functions) and those that do not (procedures). C does, however, provide a special type void for functions that do not return a useful value. void can be used only with functions; we cannot declare a variable to be void.

Normally, if a function returns a value, we can use it in an expression. But when we declare a function to return void, we explicitly state that the function's value cannot be used. Thus, a void function should not attempt to return anything.

Of course, as with all types other than int, before a function returning void can be called, its type must be known to the compiler. Figure 5.13 shows a new definition of print_table (Figure 5.2a). Since print_table does not return a value, we declare its return value as void. If print_table is not defined before it is called, the caller must include the declaration

```
void print_table();
```

to inform the compiler of the function's type.

The value returned by a function returning void is undefined and should not be used. An assignment such as

```
n = print_table(x,j)
```

will compile and execute, but print_table's actual return value is arbitrary and system dependent.

In our earlier programs, we left off the function's type on those functions that returned no value. It is better programming practice to declare the type of any function explicitly; declaring functions that do not return a value as void increases readability.[3]

We can ignore a function's return value by failing to use it in the expression where the function is called. For functions that return a value, the call should be explicitly cast to void if its value is to be ignored. The cast makes it clear to the program's reader that a conscious choice was made to ignore the return value and that it was not ignored by mistake.

[3]Some compilers do not support void. We examine ways to create a void type in Chapters 6 and 7.

```
/*
 * Print out table of "num" integers.
 */
void print_table(tab_ptr, num)
int *tab_ptr,                           /* pointer to table's first element */
    num;                                /* number of elements to print */
{
  while (num-- > 0)
    printf("%d\n", *tab_ptr++);
}
```

FIGURE 5.13   Print elements in an array.

For example,

```
(void) scanf("%d", &next);    /* get "next", ignoring return value */
```

explicitly ignores the normal integer status returned by scanf.

EXERCISE

5-17   Rewrite print_table so that it writes out the table in reverse order.   □

5.5

POINTERS TO FUNCTIONS

You may have wondered if there is a way to pass functions as parameters. This ability would be useful, for example, in writing a function to evaluate differing mathematical functions, such as sine and cosine, over a range of values, perhaps to generate plots of the functions. Unfortunately, functions cannot be passed as parameters or stored in variables. Instead, we must use *pointers* to functions, which can be thought of as the address of the code executed when a function is called or as a pointer to a block of internal information about the function. A pointer to a function is dereferenced to call the function to which it points.

When declaring a pointer to a function, we specify the pointed-to function's return type, but not its parameters. For example, the declaration

```
type (*func_ptr)();
```

declares `func_ptr` as a pointer to a function returning *type*. The parentheses around `*func_ptr` are required; without them we would instead be declaring it as a function returning a pointer to *type*.[4]

We do not apply the address operator (&) to a function to obtain a pointer to it. Instead, we simply use the function name without following it with a parenthesized parameter list. For example, assuming the declaration

```
double (*func_ptr)(), power();
```

we can make `func_ptr` point to the function `power` with the assignment

```
func_ptr = power    /* "funcptr" now points to the "power" function */
```

To call the function pointed to by `func_ptr`, we simply dereference it as we would any other pointer, following it with a list of parameters. After the previous assignment,

```
(*func_ptr)(2,5)
```

is equivalent to

```
power(2,5)
```

calling `power` to compute 2^5. The parentheses surrounding `*func_ptr` are necessary to guarantee a correct order of evaluation.

How do we use all this information? We illustrate pointers to functions with the function `gen_points`, shown in Figure 5.14a. `gen_points` fills a table of points by evaluating the function passed to it over a range of values. A main program that uses `gen_points` to compute tables of points for the `sin` and `cos` functions and a function to print these tables is shown in Figure 5.14b. `sin` and `cos` are defined as part of the math library available in most C implementations. Appendix 4 lists the math library functions and discusses how to compile programs using them.

Within `gen_points`, we declare the formal parameter `func_ptr` as a pointer to a function returning a double:

```
double (*func_ptr)();
```

When `gen_points` is called, its first parameter must be a pointer to a function returning a `double`. In the assignment we call the function pointed to by `func_ptr`, passing it the single parameter `nextval`.

```
*y_ptr++ = (*funcptr)(nextval)
```

[4]We agree that this syntax is gross, but we are stuck with it. We explain the rationale behind C's declaration syntax in Chapter 8. For now, memorize this form.

```
/*
 * Generate a table of points by evaluating a passed function at
 * different values.
 */
void gen_points(func_ptr, x_ptr, y_ptr, sval, eval, numpts)
double (*func_ptr)(),                       /* function to generate points */
       *x_ptr, *y_ptr,                      /* tables of x,y values */
       sval, eval;                          /* starting and ending points */
int numpts;                                 /* number of points to generate */
{
  double  inc = (eval - sval)/(numpts - 1), /* increment between values */
          nextval;                          /* next x value */

  for (nextval = sval; numpts--; nextval += inc)
  {
    *x_ptr++ = nextval;
    *y_ptr++ = (*func_ptr)(nextval);
  }
}
```

(a)   Generating a table of points by evaluating a function

```
#define PI      3.1415926                /* our favorite constant */
#define NUMPTS 100                        /* needed number of points */

main()
{
  double xtab[NUMPTS], ytab[NUMPTS],    /* stores the points */
         sin(), cos();                   /* some functions to plot */
  void gen_points(), pr_points();        /* generate, print points */

  gen_points(sin, xtab, ytab, 0.0, PI, NUMPTS);
  pr_points("sin", xtab, ytab, NUMPTS);
  gen_points(cos, xtab, ytab, 0.0, PI, NUMPTS);
  pr_points("cos", xtab, ytab, NUMPTS);
}

void pr_points(name, nxtx_ptr, nxty_ptr, numpts)
char *name;                               /* name of function to plot */
double *nxtx_ptr, *nxty_ptr;              /* table of points */
int numpts;                               /* number of points */
{
  printf("Points for %s function\n", name);
  while (numpts--)
    printf("%f, %f\n", *nxtx_ptr++, *nxty_ptr++);
}
```

(b) A main program that uses `gen_points`

FIGURE 5.14 Using pointers to functions.

The `double` returned from the function call is stored in the location pointed to by `y_ptr` and `y_ptr` is incremented.

We generate the table of points for `sin` with the call

```
gen_points(sin, xtab, ytab, 0.0, PI, NUMPTS);
```

Because `sin` is not followed by a parameter list, a pointer to it is passed as `gen_points`'s first parameter. Of course, had `sin` been followed by a parameter list, it would have been a function call whose return value was passed to `gen_points`. Similarly, we generate the table of points for `cos`:

```
gen_points(cos, xtab, ytab, 0.0, PI, NUMPTS);
```

In either case, the compiler must know the type of the function's return value before the function name appears. In this example, the compiler is informed with the declaration

```
double sin(), cos();
```

that appears before either name is used.

Using pointers to functions, we have made `gen_points` general enough to generate points for any single parameter function returning a `double`. We leave the function to plot the table of values generated by `gen_points` as an exercise for the reader.

EXERCISES

5-18 Try `gen_points` on other functions from the math library; good candidates are `tan` and `exp`. □

5-19 Write a function to plot (horizontally) the table generated by `gen_points`. □

5.6

RECURSION

Many algorithms and mathematical definitions are naturally described recursively, that is, partially in terms of themselves. One example is the mathematical definition of a factorial. The factorial of n (written $n!$) is the product of all integers between one and n and is defined only for non-negative n.

$$n! = \begin{cases} 1 & n=0 \\ n \times (n-1)! & n \geq 1 \end{cases}$$

Notice that to determine the factorial of any $n \geq 1$, the factorial of $n-1$ must also be determined. As with all recursive definitions, the function's value at one or more points is specified. Some example factorials are $2! = 2$, $3! = 6$, $4! = 24$, and $5! = 120$.

Functions are allowed to call themselves recursively; this makes it easy to translate the mathematical definition of a factorial into the function `fact` that can compute one shown in Figure 5.15a. A version of `fact` that prints additional information allowing us to trace the recursive calls is shown in Figure 5.15b, and a trace of the recursive calls to `fact` done to compute `fact(4)` is shown in Figure 5.15c.

```
/*
 * Compute n! for n >= 0.
 */
long fact(n)
int n;
{
  return (n <= 1) ? 1 : n * fact(n-1);
}
```

(a) Recursively computing n!

```
long fact(n)
int n
{
  long temp;

  printf("Computing %d factorial\n", n);
  temp = (n <= 1) ? 1 : n * fact(n-1);
  printf("Computed %d factorial = %d\n", n, temp);
  return temp;
}
```

(b) Recursively computing n! *with tracing information*

```
Computing 4 factorial
Computing 3 factorial
Computing 2 factorial
Computing 1 factorial
Computed 1 factorial = 1
Computed 2 factorial = 2
Computed 3 factorial = 6
Computed 4 factorial = 24
```

(c) Trace of `fact(4)`

FIGURE 5.15 Recursive computation of factorials.

EXERCISES

5-20 The Fibonacci numbers are a famous mathematical sequence that can be defined recursively:

$$
fib(n) = \begin{cases} 0 & n=0 \\ 1 & n=1 \\ fib(n-1)+fib(n-2) & n \geq 2 \end{cases}
$$

The first 10 Fibonacci numbers are 0, 1, 1, 2, 3, 5, 8, 13, 21, and 34. Write recursive and iterative functions to compute the nth Fibonacci number and print the 100th number in this sequence. Which version is faster? Which would you want to use if you wanted to print the first 100 Fibonacci numbers?   □

5.6.1 A RECURSIVE SEARCH ALGORITHM — BINARY SEARCH

The simplest method to use in searching a table for a target value is simply to compare the value with each table entry until the entire table has been examined or a match is found. This method is known as *sequential search* and, for the average successful search, will examine about half of the table's elements. In an unsuccessful search, every table element must be examined. Although this method is reasonable for searching small unordered tables, for large sorted tables we can do much better. Binary search is a much faster (indeed, optimal) algorithm for searching sorted tables that is easily expressed with a recursive algorithm.

In binary search, the target value is compared with the table's middle element. Since the table is sorted, if the target is larger, we know that all values smaller than the middle element (the values in the table's lower half) can be ignored, and we can apply binary search recursively to the table's upper half. Similarly, if the target is smaller, we know that all values larger than the middle element (the values in the table's upper half) can be ignored, and we need only apply binary search recursively to the table's lower half. Lastly, if the target is equal to the middle element, the desired element has been found and the search can stop. When there are no values left to search, we know that the target is not in the table and the search can terminate. Binary search is significantly faster than sequential search because every time we compare the target to a table element, we no longer have to consider half of the remaining values.

The function `bsearch` shown in Figure 5.16*a* uses binary search to search a sorted table of integers. Figure 5.16*b* shows a program fragment using `bsearch`. `bsearch` is passed the target value and pointers to the

```
/*
 *  Binary search function (for table of integers).
 */

int *bsearch(min_ptr, max_ptr, target)
int *min_ptr, *max_ptr;                     /* section of table to search */
int target;                                 /* value search for */
{
  int *mid_ptr = min_ptr + (max_ptr - min_ptr) / 2;  /* find midpoint */

  if (max_ptr < min_ptr)                            /* value not in table */
    return NULL;
  else if (target < *mid_ptr)                       /* adjust upper bound */
    return bsearch(min_ptr, mid_ptr - 1, target);   /*   and search again */
  else if (target > *mid_ptr)                       /* adjust lower bound */
    return bsearch(mid_ptr + 1, max_ptr, target);   /*   and search again */
  else
    return mid_ptr;                                 /* found it */
}
```

(a) Binary search

```
{
  int table[MAXVALS], target,      /* table to search and target value */
      n,                           /* elements in table */
      *tar_ptr,                    /* returned pointer to target element */
      *bsearch();                  /* binary searching function */
  . . .
  tar_ptr = bsearch(&table[0], &table[n - 1], target);
  . . .
}
```

(b) Using binary search

FIGURE 5.16 Binary search function and sample call.

table's first (`min_ptr`) and last (`max_ptr`) elements. For instance, we can search the first n elements of `table` for `target` with the call

```
tar_ptr = bsearch(&table[0], &table[n-1], target);
```

`bsearch` returns a pointer to the matching table element or the null pointer if no such element is found. Any variable saving `bsearch`'s return value must be a pointer to an `int`.

An illustration of a successful binary search on a 15-element table is shown in Figure 5.17*a*, and Figure 5.17*b* illustrates an unsuccessful search on the same table. With every recursive call to `bsearch`, the pointers `min_ptr` and `max_ptr` move toward each other, the search and recursive calls terminating when the pointers cross or the target value is found.

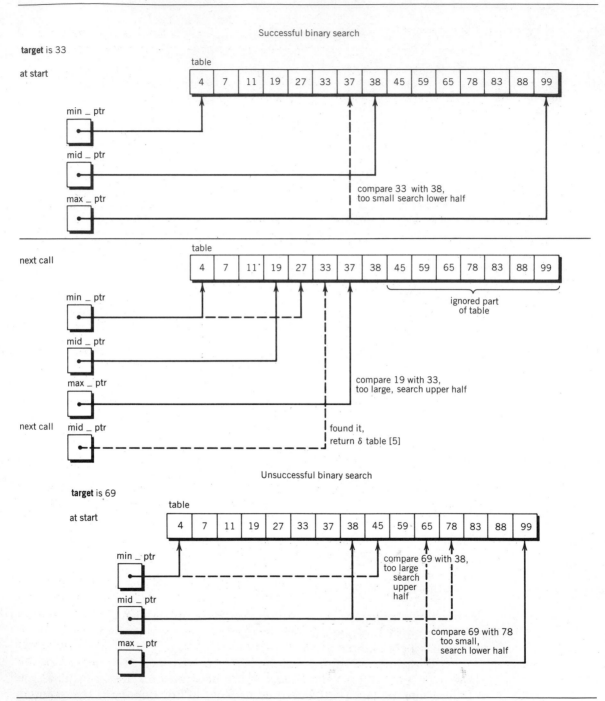

FIGURE 5.17 Illustration of binary search during both successful and unsuccessful searches.

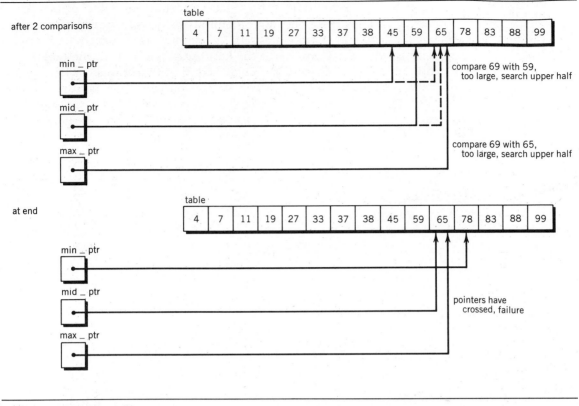

after 2 comparisons

compare 69 with 59,
too large, search upper half

compare 69 with 65,
too large, search upper half

at end

pointers have
crossed, failure

FIGURE 5.17 (continued)

When `bsearch` is called, it first calculates the address of the middle element in the unsearched portion of the table (the whole table when it is first called). Because addition or division of pointer types is not allowed, this calculation is done with the expression

```
mid_ptr = min_ptr + (max_ptr - min_ptr) / 2
```

instead of adding the two pointers together and dividing by two. Recall that the subtraction of the two pointers produces the number of elements between them (an integer), and both integer division and addition of an integer to a pointer are legal operations.

After `mid_ptr` has been computed, we test to determine if the search has failed. The target is not present when the pointers representing the endpoints of the unsearched portion of the table cross (`max_ptr < min_ptr`). This happens only when one element is left to search, and that element is not the target. If the search fails, the null pointer (automatically cast to a pointer to an `int`) is returned.

Once we are assured that there are unexamined table elements, we compare the target with the value pointed to by `mid_ptr`. If the values are equal, a pointer to the desired table entry is returned. Otherwise, `bsearch` is applied recursively to the appropriate section of the table.

Although functions such as `fact` and `bsearch` can be written more efficiently iteratively than recursively, recursion can often be used to make functions more compact or to make them reflect some high-level algorithm or mathematical definition more closely. Recursion is a powerful technique used often in the programs in the rest of this book.

EXERCISES

5-21 Add tracing information to `bsearch` that prints messages whenever the function is entered or exited, noting the values delimiting the area left to be searched. □

5-22 Rewrite the binary search algorithm nonrecursively. Is this version more efficient than the recursive version? Which version is more compact? □

5-23 Because of the overhead involved in calculating the midpoint, binary search is often slower than sequential search when searching small tables. Determine the point on your system where both functions take the same amount of time. Then write a single search function, called with the same arguments as `bsearch`, that does a sequential search if the table is small (less than the breakeven point) and otherwise calls `bsearch`. □

5.7

CASE STUDY — A RECURSIVE SORTING ALGORITHM

The insertion sort presented in Chapter 1 is a simple, easily implemented sorting technique that is reasonably efficient for sorting small sets of values. However, there are many sorting algorithms that are significantly better at sorting large sets of values; the fastest known sorting algorithm is called *quicksort*.[5] In the following sections, we implement a compact recursive version of the quicksort algorithm and compare its efficiency with that of the insertion sort program presented in Chapter 1.

---

[5]Quicksort was invented by C.A.R. Hoare in the early 1960's.

5.7.1 QUICKSORT

Quicksort works by partitioning the array to be sorted into two subarrays. In one, all elements are less than some value; in the other, all elements are greater than or equal to that value. The value used to divide the array into the two subarrays is known as the *pivot*. Because, after partitioning, every element in the first subarray is less than any element in the second subarray, we can recursively apply the quicksort algorithm to both subarrays, eventually sorting the entire array. Figure 5.18 illustrates quicksort, assuming that the array's middle element is used as the pivot.

Before the array can be partitioned, a pivot must be selected. The best possible pivot is the one that divides the array into two equal-sized subarrays: the median. However, finding the median of an array is time-consuming, so we will settle for a simpler method of pivot selection; we simply use the middle element of the array, a reasonable choice for most arrays. (The exercises suggest an alternative method of pivot selection.)

Once the pivot has been selected, the array can be partitioned into those values that are less than the pivot and those values that are greater than or equal to the pivot. Two pointers, starting at opposite ends of the array, are used to accomplish the partitioning. Both pointers move toward the center, stopping when they cross or when an out-of-place value is found. When both pointers are pointing at out-of-place values, these

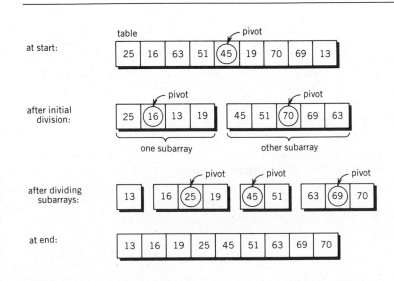

FIGURE 5.18 Illustration of the quicksort algorithm.

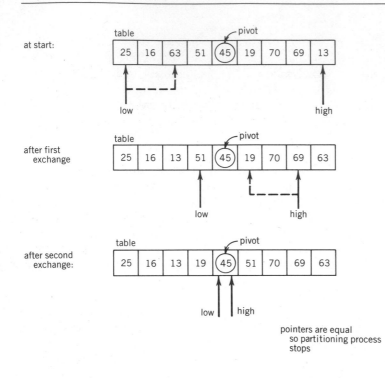

at start:

after first
exchange

after second
exchange:

pointers are equal
so partitioning process
stops

FIGURE 5.19 Partitioning the array.

values are exchanged and the pointers continue moving toward the middle. The partitioning process terminates when the pointers cross. Figure 5.19 illustrates this process.

Given the partitioning function, it is easy to code the function `quick_sort` shown in Figure 5.20. `quick_sort` sorts a table of `doubles`, expecting to be passed pointers to the beginning and end of the table. `partition` is assumed to return a pointer to the first element in the subarray that contains values greater than or equal to the pivot. After partitioning, `quick_sort` recursively calls itself to sort the two subarrays. When `quick_sort` is called and the top and bottom pointers have crossed or are equal, there is at most one element in the partition to sort and `quick_sort` simply returns.

The partitioning function shown in Figure 5.21 is a little trickier to write. `partition` is passed pointers to the bottom and top elements of the subarray to partition, and first selects the table's middle element (using the same technique as the binary search in Figure 5.16), assigning its value

```
/*
 * Sort a table using quicksort.
 */
void quick_sort(low_ptr, up_ptr)
double *low_ptr,                        /* pointer to bottom of array */
       *up_ptr;                         /* pointer to top of array */
{
  double *piv_ptr;                      /* pointer to point */
  double *partition();                  /* does the partitioning */

  if (low_ptr < up_ptr)                 /* if there is something to sort */
  {
    piv_ptr = partition(low_ptr, up_ptr);  /* divide into sections to sort */
    quick_sort(low_ptr, piv_ptr - 1);   /* sort lower half */
    quick_sort(piv_ptr, up_ptr);        /* sort upper half */
  }
}
```

FIGURE 5.20 Quicksort function.

to pivot. After the pivot has been selected, the previously described partitioning process occurs; and when the subarray has been partitioned, a pointer to the bottom of the upper subarray is returned.

To exchange values, partition uses the function swap shown in Figure 5.22. swap is a modified version of the swap shown earlier in the

```
/*
 * Partition the table around the pivot.
 */
double *partition(low_ptr, up_ptr)
double *low_ptr, *up_ptr;
{
  double pivot = *(low_ptr + (up_ptr - low_ptr) / 2);
  void swap();

  while (low_ptr <= up_ptr)             /* until the pointers cross */
  {
    while (*low_ptr < pivot)            /* find an out of place value in the */
      low_ptr++;                        /*   lower part of array */
    while (*up_ptr > pivot)             /* find an out of place value in the */
      up_ptr--;                         /*   upper part of array */
    if (low_ptr <= up_ptr)              /* found out of place values? */
      swap(low_ptr++, up_ptr--);        /* exchange out of place values */
  }
  return low_ptr;                       /* bottom of upper partition */
}
```

FIGURE 5.21 The partitioning function for quicksort.

```
/*
 * Swap values of two variables.
 */
void swap(x_ptr, y_ptr)
double *x_ptr, *y_ptr;                      /* pointers to values to swap */
{
  double temp = *x_ptr;

  *x_ptr = *y_ptr, *y_ptr = temp;
}
```

FIGURE 5.22   A version of swap that exchanges `doubles`.

chapter, changed to return type `void` and to swap `doubles` instead of `ints`. Since both `low_ptr` and `up_ptr` are already pointers, the `&` is not used when `swap` is called by `partition`:

```
swap(low_ptr++, up_ptr--)
```

5.7.2 QUICKSORT VERSUS INSERTION SORT

Comparing quicksort's performance with that of other sorting techniques helps us understand how efficient quicksort is. We measured the times needed to sort varying numbers of values for implementations of quicksort and insertion sort; the results are shown in Table 5.1. The insertion sort program was modified to sort the table in place. While the sorting times are about the same for small sets of values, quicksort is much faster than insertion sort for larger sets. For example, while insertion sort takes just over 13 minutes to sort a random collection of 6400 values, quicksort takes less than 4 seconds. Although quicksort is more complicated than insertion sort and perhaps somewhat less intuitive, the extra effort in its implementation pays off handsomely if large collections of data are sorted.

EXERCISES

5-24 Write a version of insertion sort that sorts a table in place. Its parameters should be pointers to the first and last table elements. □

5-25 Insertion sort is slightly more efficient than quicksort when sorting small sets of data (fewer than 25 elements). Modify the quicksort algorithm to use insertion sort whenever there are fewer than a constant `MIN` elements left to sort. □

TABLE 5.1 Comparison of sorting methods

Number of Values to Be sorted	Sorting Method	
	Insertion Sort (seconds)	Quicksort (seconds)
25	0.02	0.02
50	0.04	0.02
100	0.18	0.05
200	0.74	0.11
400	3.01	0.19
800	11.74	0.38
1600	46.33	0.82
3200	189.45	1.81
6400	785.64	3.89

5-26 The method used to select the pivot in our quicksort implementation is somewhat simplistic. Modify the quicksort program to choose three values (the first, middle, and last) in the set of values to sort and use their median as the pivot. □

5-27 What happens if quicksort is given an already sorted set of values to sort? How can this behavior be prevented? □

5-28 Using the quicksort partitioning approach, implement a program that finds the median of a set of values. Extend the program to find the kth largest value in a set of values. □

WRITING READABLE FUNCTIONS

We have discussed how functions communicate in some detail but have spent little time discussing what makes a good function. Here are some of the characteristics well-written functions should have:

- *Cohesiveness*: A function should perform only one task, and all statements in the function should be related to that task. If the actions of a function cannot be described in a single sentence, the function is trying to do too much.

- *Generality*: A function should perform its one task well. A sorting routine, for example, should work well for all sizes of input, handling error cases (such as being given no elements to sort) reasonably.

- *Simplicity*: A function should perform its task in the simplest manner possible; do not try to fine tune the code in order to save an instruction or two. Usually, changing the algorithm (for example, using quicksort instead of insertion sort) will contribute much more to efficiency than any amount of manipulation of the code.[6]

- *Small Size*: Functions that perform a single task in a simple manner are generally not lengthy. Limiting functions to a screen or page (about 25 to 50 lines) works well. Of course, too many small functions can also fragment a program and obscure program readability and efficiency. Most programmers, however, write functions that are too long rather than too short.

- *Documentation*: Every function deserves a comment describing its task. The function's parameters and local variables should also be commented. A single sentence description of the function or variable is often sufficient. Write the comments while writing the code; do not wait until after the function has been written.

---

[6]There are times when efficiency is important; Chapter 12 examines this issue.

C H A P T E R   6

PROGRAM STRUCTURE AND STORAGE CLASSES

So far, our programs have resided in a single source file and have communicated with each other solely through parameter passing and return values. However, we are not confined to such a simple program structure. We can build an executable program from multiple source files, with each file compiled separately and linked together, and we can write functions that communicate through globally accessible variables. In this chapter, we examine the mechanism (called *storage classes*) that supports these more complex program structures, and illustrate the usefulness of separate compilation with the implementation of a "set" data type and its associated operations.

6.1

AUTOMATIC VARIABLES

Along with its type, every variable and function has a storage class that specifies its visibility and lifetime. The storage class precedes the type in a declaration and can be any one of auto, register, extern, or static.[1] If the storage class is not specified, a default storage class is determined from the declaration's context.

We have already used variables with the storage class auto. Variables declared within function bodies and compound statements are called *automatic* variables and are given the storage class auto by default.[2] Although it is unnecessary and rarely done, the keyword auto can be used to make the storage class explicit:

```
{                                              {
    int x,y;                                       auto int x,y;
    . . .          is equivalent to                  . . .
}                                              }
```

Automatic variables are visible only from the point of their declaration until the block's end and cannot be directly accessed outside it.

An automatic variable exists only from block entry to block exit. Whenever a block is entered, space is allocated for its local variables; this space is then deallocated when the block is exited. As a result, the next time the block is entered, its local variables may not even use the same physical memory locations. Unfortunately, automatic variables are not automatically initialized to zero; instead, they start with whatever was previously in the memory space allocated for them — usually garbage. This means that to avoid hard-to-find problems, we have to be careful to initialize all variables before using them.

As we have seen, we can initialize a variable when we declare it by following its name with an equal sign and an arbitrary expression. This expression can include previously declared local variables, the function's formal parameters, and function calls. Each time the function is called, the initialization expression is evaluated and assigned to the declared variable. Unfortunately, automatic arrays cannot be initialized when they are declared, although later in the chapter we will see a way to avoid that restriction.

Initializing variables when they are declared leads to more concise functions. As an example, Figure 6.1 contains the function strrev, which takes a string and reverses it in place. We use two pointers to reverse the string; f_ptr starts out pointing to its first character, r_ptr to its last. The string is reversed by moving the pointers toward each other; as they move along, the characters they point to are switched, as shown below. The process stops when the pointers cross or point to the same character. Both f_ptr and r_ptr are initialized when they are declared. f_ptr is

---

[1] The order of the storage class and type is not really restricted by the language, but many compilers silently enforce the "storage class first" rule.
[2] The name comes from their *automatic* creation and deletion on block entry and exit.

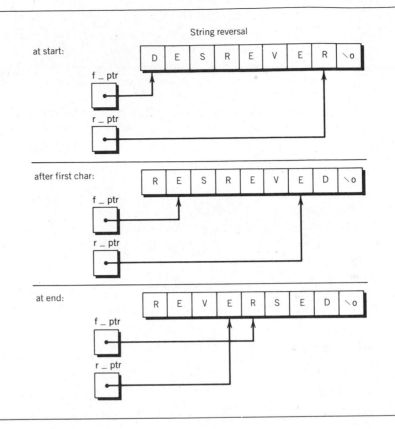

String reversal

at start:

| D | E | S | R | E | V | E | R | \o |

f _ ptr

r _ ptr

after first char:

| R | E | S | R | E | V | E | D | \o |

f _ ptr

r _ ptr

at end:

| R | E | V | E | R | S | E | D | \o |

f _ ptr

r _ ptr

initialized with the formal parameter `to_rev`'s value and `r_ptr` is initialized with its length, computed using both the function `strlen` and the local variable `f_ptr`. The order of the declarations is important; because `f_ptr`'s value is used in initializing `r_ptr`, it must be declared before `r_ptr`.

The ability to declare automatic variables local to any block is a convenience that aids modularity. As an example, Figure 6.2 contains a short program that first computes the average of its input and then prints any input values less than the average. First, the program reads scores into an array, accumulating the total score in `sum`. For speed, we use a pointer to traverse the array instead of explicit subscripting. Then, after the scores are read, the average score is computed and any below-average scores are printed. We do this within a nested block that contains two local variables, `avg` and `next_ptr`. They are declared there, instead of at the beginning of the function's body, to make it clear that they are needed only for this small section of code.

```
/*
 * Reverse a string in place.
 */
strrev(to_rev)
char *to_rev;                                    /* string to reverse */
{
  char *f_ptr = to_rev,                          /* pointer to string's first char */
       *r_ptr = f_ptr + strlen(f_ptr) - 1,       /* pointer to string's last char */
       tmp;                                      /* holds character during switch */

  while(f_ptr < r_ptr)
    tmp = *f_ptr, *f_ptr++ = *r_ptr, *r_ptr-- = tmp;
}
```

FIGURE 6.1   Reversing a string in place.

```
/*
 * Read scores, compute average, and print below average.
 */
#include <stdio.h>
#define MAX_STUDENTS 1000

main()
{
  int n,                          /* number of scores */
      scores[MAX_STUDENTS],       /* holds scores */
      *end_ptr = scores;          /* pointer to just beyond last score */
  float sum = 0.0;                /* total scores */

  /* Get input data and compute sum -- stop reading if no more room,
     end of file, or bad input data */

  for (n=0; n < MAX_STUDENTS && scanf("%d", end_ptr) == 1; n++)
    sum += *end_ptr++;

  /* Figure average and print out low scores */

  {
    int *next_ptr = scores;       /* pointer to next array element */
    float avg = sum / n;          /* average of scores */

    printf("Average: %.2f\nBelow Average Scores:\n", avg);
    for (; next_ptr < end_ptr; next_ptr++)
      if (*next_ptr < avg)
        printf("%d\n", *next_ptr);
  }
}
```

FIGURE 6.2   An example of nested blocks – printing below average scores.

Attempting to access a variable outside its declaring block causes a compile time error. For example, placing

```
printf("I told you, the average is: %.2f\n", avg);
```

outside the inner block but before main's end will cause the compiler to generate an "undefined variable" error. Be careful that any variable declared within a block is not needed outside it.

Carelessly chosen variable names can cause confusion when blocks are nested. When a variable is redeclared in an inner block, it becomes inaccessible to the rest of the inner block, and from the point of redeclaration the inner block accesses the locally declared variable. When the inner block exits, the variable's original declaration becomes visible again. Using the same name for variables within nested blocks can adversely affect readability and should be avoided.

EXERCISES

6-1 Modify the palindrome checking function in Chapter 4 to initialize its variables within their declarations. Is the function still readable? □

6-2 Would it ever make sense to have a block containing nothing but declarations? Why or why not? □

6.2
REGISTER VARIABLES

We can tell the compiler that an automatic variable should be kept in one of the machine's high-speed registers, instead of placed by default in memory, by giving it the storage class register. As an example,

```
register int sum;
```

declares sum as a register variable. Making frequently accessed variables register leads to faster and slightly smaller programs.

There are, however, some restrictions on the use of register variables. Most compilers allow only int, char, or pointer automatic variables and parameters to be placed in registers. Additionally, most machines have few registers available to user programs, usually two or three. If the variable is not the right type or not enough registers are

```
/*
 * Return the total of the first "n" elements of table pointed to by "tab_ptr".
 */
int sum(tab_ptr,n)
register int *tab_ptr;                          /* ptr to array's first element */
int n;                                          /* number of elements */
{
  register int *end_ptr = tab_ptr + n - 1,    /* ptr to array's last element*/
                total  = 0;                    /* running total */

  while (tab_ptr <= end_ptr)
    total += *tab_ptr++;
  return total;
}
```

FIGURE 6.3   Fast function to sum elements in an array.

available, the `register` declaration is ignored and the variable is placed in memory instead. Lastly, and perhaps obviously, since a `register` variable is not kept in memory, we cannot use & to take its address.

The function to sum the array shown in Figure 6.3 is about 20 percent faster, and contains 7 percent fewer machine language instructions than the same function without the `register` declarations.[3] Since there are usually few available registers, it is important to carefully select the variables placed in them. You need not declare variables as `register` until the program has been written and profiled. Then the most often used variables in the functions that take the most time can be put into registers.

EXERCISES

6-3 Profile the quicksort program of Chapter 5 to determine where most of its time is spent. Add `register` declarations in those places. Repeat the process until no more performance is gained by additional declarations.   □

6-4 Repeat the previous exercise with the Histogram program (Chapter 4).   □

6-5 Make the pointer version of `strcpy` (Chapter 5) into a function with `register` declarations. Is it more efficient that `strcpy` is implemented without using `register`?   □

6-6 How can you determine how many registers are available for user programs on your machine? Do so.   □

[3]Measurements taken with a program compiled by the standard 4.2bsd UNIX C compiler with the optimizing and profiling options turned on run on a lightly loaded system.

6-7 Can adding register declarations ever slow a program down? Test your hypothesis. □

6.3

EXTERNAL VARIABLES AND FUNCTIONS

In addition to declaring variables at the start of blocks, we can declare variables outside any function anywhere in the file. These variables (like the global variables of Pascal or the common variables of FORTRAN) are known as *externals* and can be accessed by other functions without being passed as parameters to them. Any function can access a previously declared external simply by referring to it by name. Besides having global visibility, externals differ from automatics in that space for externals is allocated once, is initialized to zero when the program starts, and remains allocated throughout the program's execution.

We illustrate one common use of external variables in Figure 6.4, a program that counts occurrences of each unique character in its input. As each character is read, it is used as an index in a table of counters (count) and the appropriate counter is updated.[4] Since count is declared outside any function, it is an external variable. The definitions of main and print_totals follow count's declaration and can use it by referring to it by name.

The default initialization of externals makes programs more concise because external counters do not have to be explicitly initialized. We did not bother to initialize count in Figure 6.4, since its elements are zero by default. Although this implicit initialization is convenient (and is taken advantage of by countless programs), programs are more readable when variables are explicitly initialized.

When using external variables, consider carefully the tradeoff between readability and convenience. The extra effort involved in using only automatic variables passed as parameters increases modularity, aiding readability. In longer programs, external variables obscure the connections between functions, decreasing readability and modular independence. An external variable's value is also easily changed by any of the program's functions, leading to subtle errors when the change is accidental. The most reasonable uses of external variables are for tables and for variables shared between routines when it is inconvenient to pass them as parameters.

---

[4]We actually use only the first seven bits of the character as the index; in ASCII the eighth bit is ignored.

```
/*
 *  Character-counting program (assumes seven-bit characters).
 */
#define MAXCHARS     128        /* first seven bits to determine char */
#define MASK         0177       /* used to remove any high order bits */

char count[MAXCHARS];           /* external--holds character counters */

main()
{
  int c;                        /* next character */
  void print_totals();          /* to write out totals */

  while (c=getchar(), c != EOF)
    count[c & MASK]++;          /* count character, stripping extra bits */
  print_totals();
}

void print_totals()             /* writes totals */
{
  int i;

  for (i = 0; i < MAXCHARS; i++)
    if (count[i])               /* only write total if nonzero */
      printf("\\%03o: %d\n", i, count[i]);
}
```

FIGURE 6.4 An example of externals – a character counting program.

EXERCISES

6-8 Rewrite the character-counting program (Figure 6.4) without any external variables. Which version is more readable? Which version is more compact? □

6-9 Rewrite the program in the previous exercise so that initialization of the table and its printing are done in-line in main. Use blocks to limit the scope of any index variables used. Which version do you prefer? Why? □

6.3.1 INITIALIZING EXTERNAL VARIABLES

We initialize external variables in the same way as their automatic counterparts. In addition, external arrays, unlike automatic arrays, can be initialized. We do this by supplying a brace-enclosed, comma-separated list of expressions as the initialization expression. The values in this list become the initial values of the corresponding array elements; missing values default to zero and extra values result in an error message. External initializations are done once, conceptually, before the program begins execution, so they cannot contain function calls.

As an example, we can initialize `days` to contain the days for each month with the declaration

```
int days[] = {31, 28, 31, 30, 31, 30, 31, 31, 30, 31, 30, 31};
```

If the subscript is omitted, the compiler allocates enough space for all initialized elements. The array's size can be supplied, but it must be large enough to hold the given elements. Unfortunately, there is no convenient way to initialize only selected array elements. Remember, we can initialize external but not automatic arrays.

Letting the compiler calculate the array's size is especially useful when initializing character strings, since it saves us the trouble of computing their length.

```
char message[] = {'h', 'i', ' ', 'm', 'o', 'm', '!', 'O'};
```

declares `message` to be an array of eight characters, initialized with the string "hi mom!". A convenient shorthand for the above

```
char message[] = {'h', 'i', ' ', 'm', 'o', 'm', '!', '\0'};
```

automatically places the null at the string's end.

Explicit initialization makes programs more readable. We improve Figure 6.4 by explicitly initializing `count`:

```
int count[MAXCHARS] = {0};
```

Instead of listing many zeroes, we explicitly initialize `count[0]` to zero; the other elements are zero by default. Initializing the array's first element to zero is an idiom that makes explicit the expectation that all array elements start with zero.

EXERCISES

6-10 Implement a simple random number generator using two functions, `rand` and `seed`. `seed` provides an initial value, used by `rand` to generate its first random number. □

6.3.2 EXTERNAL DECLARATIONS AND DEFINITIONS

In Figure 6.4 we conveniently defined count before the functions using it, allowing them to access it simply by referring to it by name. A function can, however, access any external variable (even those defined after it or in another source file) by declaring it with the storage class specifier extern. This external declaration specifies the variable's type and informs the compiler that space for the variable is defined somewhere else, but it does not allocate space for the variable. An external variable is defined (has space allocated for it) whenever it is declared outside any function without the extern storage class specifier. Since an external variable definition also declares the variable's type, an external declaration is not required if the external variable was defined earlier in the source file.

As an illustration, consider Figure 6.5. count is defined after the functions using it, so the *external declaration*

```
extern int count[];
```

must appear in each of the functions accessing count, as shown in Figure 6.5a or before any of them, as shown in Figure 6.5b. This declaration informs the compiler that count is an array of integers defined somewhere else in the program. In contrast, the *external definition*

```
int count[MAXCHARS] = {0};
```

allocates space for count, initializes its elements to zero, and makes its type known to the compiler. Since no space is allocated in external

```
main()
{
  extern int count[];
  void print_totals();
  int c;
  . . .
}

void print_totals()
{
  extern int count[];
  int i;
  . . .
}

int count[MAXCHARS] = {0};
```

(a) Local external declarations

```
extern int count[];

main()
{
  void print_totals();
    int c;
  . . .
}

void print_totals()
{
  int i;
    . . .
}

int count[MAXCHARS] = {0};
```

(b) Global external declarations

FIGURE 6.5 Using external declarations and definitions. An external must be declared before it can be referenced.

declarations, the number of elements `count` contains is specified only in its definition.

Both external declarations and definitions inform the compiler of the variable's type. However, a definition also allocates storage for the variable, while a declaration does not. Thus, an external variable should be *defined* only once, but should be *declared* by all functions that need to reference it or before any of them.

The distinction between definition and declaration also applies to functions. A function is defined when its parameters and function body are specified and is external by default. Functions are declared in the same way as variables, except that since all functions are external, `extern` can be left off their declarations. In Figure 6.5, since `main`'s call to `print_totals` precedes its definition, `main` must declare `print_totals`'s type, and does so with the declaration

```
void print_totals();
```

Because `print_totals` is a function, this declaration is equivalent to

```
extern void print_totals();
```

As we have observed, the compiler automatically assumes that any function that has not been declared when it is first used returns an `int`. This means that we do not need to write external declarations for these functions, and almost all C programs take advantage of this option. Nevertheless, including external declarations for all functions, even those returning `int`, leads to more readable programs.

EXERCISES

6-11 Remove `count`'s external *declarations* from Figure 6.5. What happens when you try to compile it?   □

6-12 Remove `count`'s external *definition* from Figure 6.5. What happens when you try to compile it? Is the error message from the compiler or the linker?   □

6.4

SEPARATE COMPILATION

Externals allow the functions and variables composing a C program to be spread out over multiple files. Figure 6.6 shows a diagram of the compila-

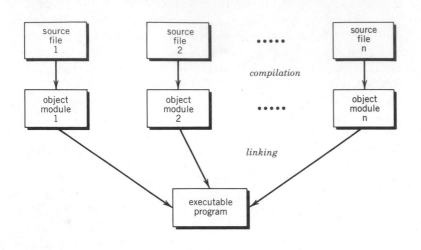

FIGURE 6.6 The process of compilation and linking.

tion process when multiple files are compiled. Each source file is compiled into an *object module* containing its machine language code, a list of the names and addresses of all external functions and variables defined in it, and a list of all of its external references to functions and variables defined in other source files. The *linker* resolves these external references, linking the object modules together to create an executable program.[5]

In effect, any external declaration or definition causes the external's name to be given to the linker. The linker then creates an executable file from the various object modules by turning all external references into the variable's or function's address.

While resolving external references, the linker adds any referenced library functions. A library is a group of object modules that have been compiled in advance and stored in a special format. Some linkers automatically include the entire library; others include only the referenced functions and any functions or variables they require. No special action is usually required to use certain libraries, such as the standard I/O, although to use other libraries, the library's name may have to be given to the linker. The details of library use and creation vary; once again, you should consult your local reference manual for details.

Both the compiler and the linker can detect errors. Syntax errors and

[5]The object modules given to the linker do not have to be generated by the C compiler; often the linker can be used to link together object modules generated by compilers for different programming languages. On UNIX, for example, a C program can call functions written in Pascal, FORTRAN and assembly language.

certain semantic errors can be detected by the compiler, and no object module is produced for a source file containing compiler-detectable errors. Errors such as failing to define a referenced external, defining a particular function or variable more than once, or failing to define `main` can be detected by the linker. Most linkers will not produce an executable program if any errors are detected.

6.4.1 ILLUSTRATING SEPARATE COMPILATION — CHARACTER TESTING

Many programs need to do simple testing to classify characters, for example, determining if a character is a digit, an upper- or lowercase letter, white space, or printable. The standard I/O library provides a set of functions to make these tests; a complete list can be found in Appendix 6.[6] These functions are useful because they are easier to use than the tests they replace, because they increase the readability of the programs that use them, and because they are both machine and character set independent. To illustrate separate compilation, we present an implementation of the character-testing functions listed in Table 6.1. Each function takes a character and returns nonzero only if the tested property holds for it.

We have divided the character-testing package into a header file containing constant definitions (*ctype.h*) and two files that include it. The first (*table.c*) contains a table describing the character set, and the second (*ctype.c*) contains the functions that use it. We chose this organization instead of using a single source file because it separates the portable from the nonportable code. The table is character set dependent, while the functions that use it are not.

Each property (such as printable, white space, and so on) is represented by a constant defined in *ctype.h*, shown in Figure 6.7.

To test if a character has a particular property, each of the functions

TABLE 6.1   Implemented character-testing functions

Function	Test
isalpha	Upper- or lowercase letter.
isdigit	Digit.
islower	Lowercase letter.
isprint	Printable.
isspace	White space.
isupper	Uppercase letter.

---

[6]For efficiency, in most standard I/O library implementations these predicates are implemented as macros, a topic discussed in the next chapter.

```
/*
 *  Character type flags.
 */
#define P          001             /* printing */
#define D          002             /* decimal digit */
#define L          010             /* lowercase letter */
#define U          020             /* uppercase letter */
#define S          040             /* white space character */
#define CHRMASK    0177            /* assume only lower seven bits matter */
```

FIGURE 6.7 *ctype.h* – Character type header file.

in *ctype.c* uses the character as an index into a table of unsigned integers (cprop) in *table.c*. Each property is represented by a single bit. If the bit is on, the character has that property, and if it is off, the character does not. For example, if the character is printable, bit zero is on; if it is a digit, bit one is on; and so forth. Because a character can have multiple properties, its description is created by ORing together the constants describing each of its properties. For example, the entry for the letter 'a' is P | L, indicating that it is both printable and a lowercase letter. If a character does not contain any of the properties we test for, its table entry is zero. Figure 6.8 shows *table.c*, which contains the table to describe the ASCII character set.

Given this table, it is easy to write the character-testing functions shown in Figure 6.9. Each function tests whether the bit or bits representing the desired property are on for the given character. The check is done by ORing together the constants for the properties to check. The result is then ANDed with the character's description in the table. For example, the expression cprop[c & CHRMASK] & (L|U) will be zero unless c is an upper- or lowercase letter. Only the low-order seven bits of the character are used as the index into the table; the other bits are masked off with CHRMASK.

Both *ctype.c* and *table.c* include *ctype.h* with

```
#include "ctype.h"
```

ctype.h is surrounded by quotation marks instead of by the angle brackets used for previous include files. The quotation marks specify that *ctype.h* is not a system include file and that the standard system locations should not be searched for it. Recall that including a file causes its contents to be processed as if they were in the file including it, in this case defining the needed constants.

Because cprop is defined in a different file from the functions using it, the external declaration

```
/*
 * Character description table.
 */
#include "ctype.h"

unsigned int cprop[] = {
/* nul */  0,          /* soh */  0,          /* stx */  0,          /* etx */  0,
/* eot */  0,          /* enq */  0,          /* ack */  0,          /* bel */  0,
/* \b  */  P | S,      /* \t  */  P | S,      /* \n  */  P | S,      /* vt  */  P | S,
/* \f  */  P | S,      /* \r  */  P | S,      /* so  */  0,          /* si  */  0,
/* dle */  0,          /* dcl */  0,          /* dc2 */  0,          /* dc3 */  0,
/* dc4 */  0,          /* nak */  0,          /* syn */  0,          /* etb */  0,
/* can */  0,          /* em  */  0,          /* sub */  0,          /* esc */  0,
/* fs  */  0,          /* gs  */  0,          /* rs  */  0,          /* us  */  0,
/* ' ' */  P | S,      /* '!' */  P,          /* '"' */  P,          /* '#' */  P,
/* '$' */  P,          /* '%' */  P,          /* '&' */  P,          /* ''' */  P,
/* '(' */  P,          /* ')' */  P,          /* '*' */  P,          /* '+' */  P,
/* ',' */  P,          /* '-' */  P,          /* '.' */  P,          /* '/' */  P,
/* '0' */  P | D,      /* '1' */  P | D,      /* '2' */  P | D,      /* '3' */  P | D,
/* '4' */  P | D,      /* '5' */  P | D,      /* '6' */  P | D,      /* '7' */  P | D,
/* '8' */  P | D,      /* '9' */  P | D,      /* ':' */  P,          /* ';' */  P | D,
/* '<' */  P,          /* '=' */  P,          /* '>' */  P,          /* '?' */  P,
/* '@' */  P,          /* 'A' */  P | U,      /* 'B' */  P | U,      /* 'C' */  P | U,
/* 'D' */  P | U,      /* 'E' */  P | U,      /* 'F' */  P | U,      /* 'G' */  P | U,
/* 'H' */  P | U,      /* 'I' */  P | U,      /* 'J' */  P | U,      /* 'K' */  P | U,
/* 'L' */  P | U,      /* 'M' */  P | U,      /* 'N' */  P | U,      /* 'O' */  P | U,
/* 'P' */  P | U,      /* 'Q' */  P | U,      /* 'R' */  P | U,      /* 'S' */  P | U,
/* 'T' */  P | U,      /* 'U' */  P | U,      /* 'V' */  P | U,      /* 'W' */  P | U,
/* 'X' */  P | U,      /* 'Y' */  P | U,      /* 'Z' */  P | U,      /* '[' */  P,
/* '\' */  P,          /* ']' */  P,          /* '^' */  P,          /* '_' */  P,
/* ''' */  P,          /* 'a' */  P | L,      /* 'b' */  P | L,      /* 'c' */  P | L,
/* 'd' */  P | L,      /* 'e' */  P | L,      /* 'f' */  P | L,      /* 'g' */  P | L,
/* 'h' */  P | L,      /* 'i' */  P | L,      /* 'j' */  P | L,      /* 'k' */  P | L,
/* 'l' */  P | L,      /* 'm' */  P | L,      /* 'n' */  P | L,      /* 'o' */  P | L,
/* 'p' */  P | L,      /* 'q' */  P | L,      /* 'r' */  P | L,      /* 's' */  P | L,
/* 't' */  P | L,      /* 'u' */  P | L,      /* 'v' */  P | L,      /* 'w' */  P | L,
/* 'x' */  P | L,      /* 'y' */  P | L,      /* 'z' */  P | L,      /* '{' */  P,
/* '|' */  P,          /* '}' */  P,          /* ' ' */  P,          /* del */  P
};
```

FIGURE 6.8 *table.c* – character description table.

```
        extern unsigned int cprop[];
```

precedes any of their definitions. Alternatively, we could have included the external declaration in all functions that need it; however, this increases the program's length without improving its readability.

To illustrate one use of the character-testing functions, Figure 6.10 contains a program (called *Vis*) that makes all characters in its input visible

```
/*
 *  Character type checkers - all of them take a single int parameter.
 */

#include "ctype.h"

extern unsigned int cprop[];                     /* table describing character set */

int isalpha(c)                                   /* is 'c' upper- or lowercase? */
int c;

{  return cprop[c & CHRMASK] & (L | U); }

int isdigit(c)                                   /* is 'c' digit? */
int c;
{  return cprop[c & CHRMASK] & D; }

int islower(c)                                   /* is 'c' lowercase? */
int c;
{  return cprop[c & CHRMASK] & L; }

int isprint(c)                                   /* is 'c' printable? */
int c;
{  return cprop[c & CHRMASK] & P; }

int isspace(c)                                   /* is 'c' white space? */
int c;
{  return cprop[c & CHRMASK] & S; }

int isupper(c)                                   /* is 'c' uppercase? */
int c;
{  return cprop[c & CHRMASK] & U; }
```

FIGURE 6.9   *ctype.c* – character type checking functions.

even if they are unprintable. We do this by writing the C escape sequence used to specify them, with unprintable characters written as a backslash followed by their octal character code. A newline is output after any newline character in the input.

Even though *Vis* uses some of the character-testing functions written in the previous section, their source and header files are unnecessary. Instead, we can compile *vis.c* separately and then link its object module with the object modules from the character-testing package, a process illustrated in Figure 6.11.

Separate compilation and linking allows us to break large programs into smaller, more manageable pieces that can be developed separately and then, when completed, linked together. This makes libraries easy to use because only their object modules must be available, not their source. It

```
/*
 *  Make unprintable characters visible
 *    (uses our previously defined testing functions).
 */
#include <stdio.h>

main()
{
  int  c;                                     /* next character */
  char name;                                  /* special character name */

  while (c = getchar(), c != EOF)
    if ((isspace(c) && c != ' '))
    {
      switch(c)                               /* its a special character */
      {
        case '\b' :  name = 'b';   break;
        case '\f' :  name = 'f';   break;
        case '\n' :  name = 'n';   break;
        case '\r' :  name = 'r';   break;
        case '\t' :  name = 't';   break;
        case '\v' :  name = 'v';   break;
        default   :  name = '?';   break; /* should never get here! */
      }
      printf("\\%c%s", name, c == '\n' ? "\n" : "    ");
    }
    else if (isprint(c))
      printf("%c    ", c);   /* normal printable character */
    else
      printf("\\%03o ", c);   /* unprintable and not special */
}
```

FIGURE 6.10 *vis.c* – make all characters visible.

also makes changes easier to implement, because we need only recompile the files affected by those changes, not the entire program.

When we compile files separately, however, we have to keep track of the files that must be recompiled. Forgetting to recompile a particular file can lead to confusing runtime behavior because the source and the executing program are inconsistent. We must also avoid certain errors, such as defining a function to return a particular type in one file and using it as if it returns a different type in another file, because these errors are not caught by either the compiler or the linker.[7]

[7]On UNIX the program verifier lint and the program maintainer make are reasonably successful attempts to correct these disadvantages. However, lint often finds errors that are not really errors, and misses true errors, and creating the program description file for make can be a confusing endeavor.

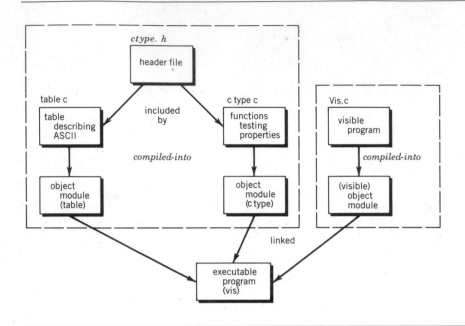

FIGURE 6.11 Compiling *Vis* – using the character test package.

EXERCISES

6-13 Add the functions `isxdig` (is hexadecimal digit), `isodig` (is octal digit), and `ispunct` (is punctuation character). If you are not using ASCII, you will have to set up the table appropriately for your own character set. ☐

6-14 What happens if the character-testing functions are called with `EOF`? Modify the character test package to do something more reasonable. ☐

6-15 Using the character-testing functions, write a program to count the words in its input. (A reasonable definition for a word is a group of upper- or lowercase characters terminated by non-white-space characters.) ☐

6-16 Using the character-testing functions, write a program that prints out the percentage of its input that is printable. How might such a program be used? ☐

6-17 Using the character-testing functions, write a function `dumpmem` to dump a specified piece of memory in a readable format, showing the contents of each memory location in octal, followed by its ASCII character if it is printable. Is `dumpmem` a useful function?   □

6-18 Add `register` declarations to *Vis*. Does its performance increase notice-ably? Why or why not?   □

6.5
STATIC VARIABLES AND FUNCTIONS

The final storage class, `static`, is used to hide information. `static` variables and functions are not made available to the linker, so they are visible only in the file in which they are defined. Like externals, all `stat-ics` are allocated and initialized to zero when the program starts, and the space remains allocated throughout the program's execution. This means that `static` variables retain their values between successive block entries. The rules for initializing `static` variables are the same as those for exter-nals, and `static` arrays can be initialized. A `static` external is initial-ized when the program begins, a `static` the first time the block contain-ing it is entered.

6.5.1 STATIC AUTOMATIC VARIABLES

We illustrate the use of `static` automatics with the function `out_line`, shown in Figure 6.12a. `out_line` writes a line of output, keeps track of the number of lines written, and writes a page number at the top of every new page. The idea behind `out_line` is to encapsulate all page handling in a single function. Figure 6.12b contains a sample call.

The page number and line number are kept as `static` variables (`pageno` and `lineno`, respectively), so that their values remain between successive calls to `out_line`. Their initialization occurs once, the first time `out_ line` is called.

6.5.2 STATIC EXTERNAL VARIABLES

We have noted that by default, external variables are made available to any file making an external reference to them. In contrast, `static` variables and functions are not made available to the linker and therefore cannot be accessed by other files. In fact, a `static` external variable or function is visible only to the part of the source file following its declaration.

```
/*
 *  Print lines with automatic numbering (uses get_line from Chapter 3).
 */
#define PAGELEN  20            /* length of page */

void out_line(line)
char *line;
{
  static int pageno = 0,        /* current page number */
         int lineno = PAGELEN;  /* lines on page */

  if (lineno == PAGELEN)
  {                             /* start new page, write page number */
    pageno++;
    printf("\fPage Number: %d\n\n", pageno);
    lineno = 0;
  }
  printf("%s", line);
  lineno++;
}
```

(a) Print a line with page numbering

```
# include <stdio.h> main()
{
char input[MAXLEN];                 /* input line */

while(get_line(input, MAXLEN) != EOF)
  out_line(input);
}
```

(b) A main program using out_line

FIGURE 6.12 An example of static variables – page numbering the input.

static external variables are most often used when a file contains functions accessing a common data structure that functions in other files should not be able to access. Figure 6.13 illustrates this use with a simple debugging package (*debug.c*) that provides functions to write variable names and values in a consistent, readable format, as well as a mechanism to turn debugging output on or off without making major changes in the source file.

The package contains four functions. The first two, on_debug and off_debug, turn debugging output on and off by setting the external variable debug appropriately. The other two, real_debug and string_debug, take a variable name and its value, examine debug, and, if debugging has been turned on, write a debugging message including the variable's name and value. real_debug is used with doubles, string_debug

```
/*
 * Useful debugging functions.
 */
#define TRUE    1
#define FALSE   0

static int debug = FALSE;                 /* are we debugging? */

void on_debug()                           /* turn debugging on */
{
  debug = TRUE;
}

void off_debug()                          /* turn debugging off */
{
  debug = FALSE;
}

void real_debug(name,value)               /* output float or double value */
char *name;
double value;
{
  if (debug)
    printf("DEBUG: %s=%f\n", name, value);
}

void string_debug(name,value)             /* output character string */
char *name, *value;
{
  if (debug)
  {
    printf("DEBUG: %s=", name);
    if (!value)                           /* check for null pointer */
      printf("a null pointer!\n");
    else
      printf("\n%s, length=%d\n", value, strlen(value));
  }
}
```

FIGURE 6.13 *debug.c* – a simple debugging package.

with strings. string_debug first tests if it is given a null pointer – a common bug when using strings. When the program has been debugged, debugging output is easily turned off by removing any calls to on_debug.

Since all functions in the debugging module must access debug, it is made external and precedes them in the source file. However, since no outside functions should be able to access or modify its value, debug is made static. This allows us to change the internal structure of the debugging package without breaking programs that use it. static vari-

```
/*
 *  Header file for debugging package.
 */
extern void on_debug(),                          /* turn debugging on */
            off_debug(),                         /* turn debugging off */
            real_debug(/* char *, double */),    /* output a real value */
            string_debug(/* char *, char * */);  /* output a string value */
```

FIGURE 6.14 *debug.h* – declarations of debugging functions.

ables provide another means of strengthening code from unexpected side effects and aid in producing correct, verifiable code.

The debugging functions return `void`, so they must be declared before they are used. We can make the debugging package easier to use by placing the external declarations for the debugging functions in the header file *debug.h*, shown in Figure 6.14. As additional documentation, we have placed comments within the function declarations that describe their parameters.

Any file using the debugging package should include *debug.h*. After it is compiled, the object module that results from compiling *debug.c* should be linked with it, as shown below.

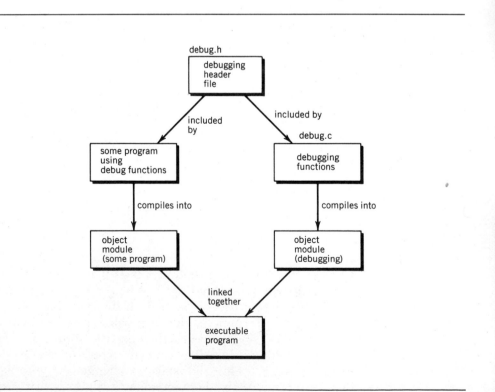

EXERCISES

6-19 Add the functions `int_debug`, `char_debug`, and `pointer_debug` to the debugging package. `char_debug` should make nonprinting characters visible. (*Hint*: link in the character testing functions.) What type of pointer should `pointer_debug` assume it is passed? Is this portable? How should pointers be printed? □

6-20 Use the debugging package to trace an earlier program. How can the package be improved? Make these improvements. □

6.5.3 STATIC FUNCTIONS

We declare a function as `static` when we do not want functions in other files to be able to access it. We do this most often when we have a package of functions that use some low-level functions that should not be used by the rest of the program.

As an example, Figure 6.15a (*getnum.c*) contains an implementation of an alternative to `scanf` for input handling. The package contains two globally accessible functions. The first, `getnum`, skips over white space, reads an integer from its input a character at a time, and places it in the `long` pointed to by its parameter. It returns `EOF` if the end of file is reached, zero if it does not find a number, and one otherwise. The second, `skip_garbage`, skips over any nonnumeric, non-white-space characters in the input.

With these functions, we can recover easily from input errors. When we need to read an integer, we call `getnum`. If an error occurs, we write an error message and call `skip_garbage` to skip over the troublesome characters, as illustrated in Figure 6.15b.

getnum.c contains two `static` functions, `fetch` and `unfetch`. `fetch` reads a possibly pushed-back character from the input, and `unfetch` returns a single character to the input. To understand why these functions are useful, consider `skip_garbage`. We do not know if all unwanted characters have been ignored until a nonblank character has been read. That is, we have to read one character too many. This problem is not unique to `skip_garbage`; getnum, for instance, does not know if it has finished reading a number until a nondigit has been read. Returning the extra character with `unfetch` allows the functions to pretend that the character was not read, simplifying our programs.

The variables `savechar` and `pushed` manage push back. `savechar` holds a pushed-back character, and `pushed` specifies whether anything has been pushed back. `fetch` and `unfetch` are straightforward. If there is no pushback, `fetch` calls `getchar` to read a character; otherwise, it

```
/*
 *  Getting a number - a way around scanf.
 */
#include <stdio.h>

static int savechar;              /* character pushed back */
static int pushed = 0;            /* is anything pushed back? */

static int fetch()                /* read character with push back */
{
  return pushed ? pushed--, savechar : getchar();
}

static void unfetch(c)            /* push back character */
int c;
{
  pushed++, savechar = c;
}

int getnum(num_ptr)               /* read a number (ascii only)
long *num_ptr;                    /* place to put number */
{
  int gotnum,                     /* did we get a number? */
      sign = 1,                   /* number's sign: 1 or -1 */
      c;                          /* next character */
  while (isspace(c))
    ;                             /* skip over white space */
  if ((gotnum = c) != EOF)
  {
    if (c == '-')                 /* set sign */
      sign = -1;
    else if (c != '+')            /* put back if not sign */
      unfetch(c);
    *num_ptr = 0;
    c = fetch();
    if ((gotnum = isdigit(c)) != 0)
      do                          /* build sum */
      {
        *num_ptr = *num_ptr * 10 + c - '0';
        c =fetch()
      } while (isdigit(c));
    unfetch(c);                   /* put back - not digit */
    *num_ptr *= sign;
  }
  return gotnum;                  /* number was valid? */
}
```

FIGURE 6.15 Getting a number from the input – an alternative to scanf for input handling.

```
void skip_garbage()              /* skip until digit, blank, or EOF */
{
  int c;

  while (c = fetch(), ! isdigit(c) && isspace(c))
    ;            /* skip over junk */
  unfetch(c);
}
```

(a) getnum.c - a partial alternative to scanf

```
long num, getnum();
int inpres;
void skip_garbage();
  ...
while (inpres = getnum(&num), inpres != EOF)
  if (!inpres)
  {
    printf("Bad input encountered\n");      /* input error found */
    skip_garbage();                         /* skip unwanted characters */
  }
  else                                      /* handle valid input */
    normal_processing();
```

(b) An example use of get_num *and* skip_garbage

FIGURE 6.15 (continued)

pushed back. unfetch simply sets the pushed-back character. By making
these variables and functions static, we keep the details of the implementation of getnum and skip_garbage hidden from their callers. Note
that these functions make use of the character testing functions described
earlier.

EXERCISES

6-21 Using fetch and unfetch, write the function get_double that reads in
a floating point value, storing it in a double, write the function
ignore_line that skips the characters remaining on the current line, and
modify get_line (Chapter 3) to work with the package. What other
functions would be useful if this package was a complete replacement for
scanf? Write them. Are programs written using these functions more
compact or more efficient than if they were written using scanf. □

6-22 Can anything unexpected happen if calls to getchar are are intermixed
with calls to getnum and skip_garbage? Why or why not? □

6-23 Modify the histogram program in Chapter 4 to use getnum and
skip_garbage instead of scanf. Is the program more efficient? □

6.6

SETS — IMPLEMENTING AN ABSTRACT DATA TYPE

When Pascal and C are compared, a frequent criticism of C is its lack of the "set" data type. A set is an unordered collection of values with certain operations defined on it. Some of the more common operations are adding and deleting values, testing to determine if a value is in a set, and taking the union and intersection of two sets. In this section, we show an implementation of these set operations and present an interesting application of their use.

We implement sets as an *abstract data type* by providing a SET data type and functions for the various set operations. The implementation details of an abstract data type are kept hidden from its users. Programs using sets know only the names of the functions implementing the various operations, certain restrictions on their use, and the order and expected type of parameters. To ensure this, we package the set operations in a single module that is compiled separately. This also allows us to change their implementation or add operations without having to rewrite the programs using them. The concept of an abstract data type should not seem strange. We have been using floats and doubles without knowing either their internal representation or the implementation details of operators such as + or /.

6.6.1 IMPLEMENTING SETS

We implement sets of small positive integers, allowing set elements in the range 0 to 2047. These sets are large enough to be useful without their representation taking up excessive space. As usual, the set size is defined as a constant so that it can be easily changed.

A reasonable representation for sets is a bit array, one bit for each set element. C does not provide bit arrays, but we can simulate them using an array of unsigned ints, with the number of bits in an int determining the number of set elements the array can represent. To access the bit corresponding to a given set element, its location (the array element containing the bit and the bit's position within that array element) must be determined. We do so by dividing the set element by the number of bits in an int; the remainder is the bit's position within the array element. A sample computation is shown in Figure 6.16.

Given our representation, implementing the various set operations is straightforward. We add an element to the set by turning on the bit it indexes and delete it by turning the bit off. We check membership by examining the bit's value. Lastly, we implement set union by ORing together

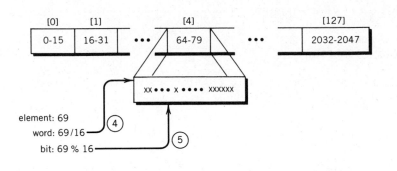

FIGURE 6.16 Locating the bit representing a set element. First we select
the array element, then the bit within it.

each of the array elements and set intersection by ANDing. Figure 6.17
illustrates each of these operations on a sample set.

There is no reason for the programs using sets to know that they are
implemented as a bit array. In fact, we would like the programs to be able
to declare a SET type as if the language provided one. To do so, we need
a new C facility, typedef, which allows us to define synonyms for existing
types. A typedef can appear outside any function, and its syntax resem-

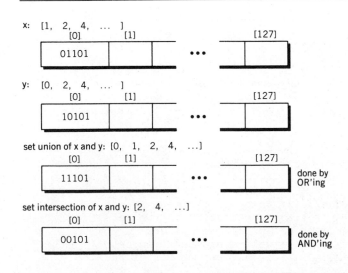

FIGURE 6.17   Illustration of the various set operations.

bles that of a variable declaration, with the type's name placed where the variable usually occurs. For example,

```
typedef int ELEMENT;
typedef char *CHARPTR;
```

makes `ELEMENT` a synonym for `int` and `CHARPTR` a synonym for `char *`.

We can use these types as if they were basic types. For instance, the declaration

```
ELEMENT x;
CHARPTR y;
```

declares `x` as an `int` and `y` as a pointer to a character. Types created with `typedef` are in effect from the `typedef` until the end of the file. We will examine additional examples of `typedef`'s usefulness in later chapters.

The `SET` type is a `typedef` to an array of `unsigned ints` and is defined in the header file *sets.h* (Figure 6.18). *sets.h* also defines constants for the minimum and maximum legal set elements (`SET_MIN` and `SET_MAX`), for the number of array elements needed to represent a `SET` (`_SET_WORDS`), and for the minimum size `int` required (`_WORD_SIZE`). In addition, *sets.h* defines the type `ELEMENT` (a synonym for `int`) and includes external declarations for the various set operations. `_SET_WORDS` and `_WORD_SIZE` are implementation constants and should not be used by programs using sets; their names begin with an underscore, so they will be less likely to conflict with other defined names. As expected, *sets.h* must be included by all files using sets.

```
/*
 *  Definitions to use "sets" of characters.
 */

#define SET_MIN          0              /* smallest set element */
#define SET_MAX          2047           /* largest set element */
#define _WORD_SIZE       16             /* assume at least 16 bit ints */
#define _SET_WORDS       128            /* set elements (2048/16) */

typedef unsigned int SET[_SET_WORDS];   /* representation of a set */
typedef int ELEMENT;                    /* set elements are ints */

extern void set_Empty(/* SET */),       /* initialize set to empty */
            set_Union(/* SET, SET, SET */), /* union of two sets */
            set_Inter(/* SET, SET, SET */), /* intersection of two sets */
            set_Add(/* SET, ELEMENT */),    /* add element to set */
            set_Del(/* SET, ELEMENT */);    /* delete element from set */
extern int  set_Mem(/* SET, ELEMENT */);    /* is element member of set? */
```

FIGURE 6.18 *sets.c* – implementing the set operations.

sets.c contains the set operations and is shown in Figure 6.19. It also contains the functions `get_bit`, `set_bit` and `get_bit_pos`. `set_bit` and `get_bit` use `get_bit_pos` to compute the location of a given set element's bit and then set or return that bit's value. These functions are internal to the abstract data type `SET`'s implementation, and we keep them hidden by declaring them as `static`.

`set_Add` (add an element), `set_Del`, and `set_Mem` (test membership) are trivial when built on top of these bit accessing functions. The other operations, `set_Union` (union of two sets), `set_Inter` (intersection of two sets), and `set_Empty` (initialize a set), deal with sets as a whole and do not use the internal functions. `set_Empty`, for example, initializes a set by setting each of its array elements to zero. We show how these functions are used in the next section.

6.6.2 USING SETS

Figure 6.20 shows a simple example of the use of sets with a program that partitions its input into values that appear once and those that appear many times. This program could be used, for example, to verify that no identification number is used more than once.

The program uses two sets. `unique` contains the values appearing once, `dup` the duplicates. When the program starts, `set_Empty` initializes these sets to empty. Values are read using `get_num` and any unexpected characters skipped with `skip_garbage`. As each value is read, it is checked for membership in `unique`. If it is a member, it is removed from `unique` and added to `dup`. If not, it is added to `unique`. After the input has been read, we print the input values in `unique` and then print the members of `dup`. To print a set, we iterate through all possible values in the set, printing out those values that are set members.

Programs using our `SET` data type must include the file *sets.h* to obtain the type definition and the definitions of the operations on it. To create an executable program from Figure 6.20, we need to link in the object module containing the implementation of the data type (compiled from *sets.c*). In addition, since we are using `getnum`, we need to include its object module. The compilation process for our sample program is shown in Figure 6.21.

We are trying to illustrate two important points with this example. The first point is that we should separate the details of a function or data type's implementation from those of its use. The program in Figure 6.20 would be considerably more complex and consequently harder to understand if it also contained the definitions of `getnum`, `skip_garbage`, and all the set operations. We can understand how it works without knowing that sets are implemented as bit arrays or that certain characters are pushed back on the input.

```
/*
 *   Routines to handle sets.
 */
#include "sets.h"

static int get_bit_pos(word_ptr, bit_ptr, elem)    /* find element's position */
int *word_ptr, *bit_ptr;                            /* filled with position */
ELEMENT elem;
{
  *word_ptr = elem / _WORD_SIZE;
  *bit_ptr = elem % _WORD_SIZE;
  return elem >= SET_MIN && elem <= SET_MAX;
}

static void set_bit(s, elem, inset)                 /* set element's bit */
SET s;
ELEMENT elem;
int inset;
{
  int word, bit;                                    /* element's position */

  if (get_bit_pos(&word, &bit, elem))
    inset ? s[word] |= (01 << bit) : s[word] &= ~(01 << bit);
}

static int get_bit(s, elem)                         /* get element's bit */
SET s;
ELEMENT elem;
{
  int word, bit;                                    /* element's position */

  return get_bit_pos(&word, &bit, elem) ? (s[word] >> bit) & 01 : 0;
}

void set_Add(s, elem)                               /* add element to set */
SET s;
ELEMENT elem;
{
  set_bit(s, elem, 1);
}

void set_Del(s, elem)                               /* delete element from set */
SET s;
ELEMENT elem;
{
  set_bit(s, elem, 0);
}

int set_Mem(s, elem)                                /* is element in set? */
SET s;
ELEMENT elem;
{
  return get_bit(s, elem);
}
```

FIGURE 6.19 *sets.c* – implementing the set operations.

```
void set_Empty(s)                              /* initialize set */
SET s;
{
  int i;

  for (i = 0; i < _SET_WORDS; s[i++] = 0)
    ;
}

void set_Union(x, y, res)                      /* union of two sets */
SET x, y, res;
{
  int i;

  for (i = 0; i < _SET_WORDS; i++)
    res[i] = x[i] | y[i];
}

void set_Inter(x, y, res)                      /* intersect two sets */
SET x, y, res;
{
  int i;

  for (i = 0; i < _SET_WORDS; i++)
    res[i] = x[i] & y[i];
}
```

FIGURE 6.19 (continued)

The second point is that wherever possible, we should build our programs on top of functions we have already written. We should create modules, like our sets, that can easily be used by new programs. Doing so effectively adds features to the language, allowing us to build programs much faster than we could if we had to start from scratch each time.

EXERCISES

6-24 The difference of two sets is the elements in the first set that are not also present in the second set. Write a function set_Diff, that places the difference of two sets into a third set. When might it be useful? □

6-25 Write a function, print_set, that prints out the elements of a set in traditional set notation. For example, a set containing the elements 3, 7 and 14, should print as {3, 7, 14}. Can this be implemented without adding set operations? □

```
/*
 * Identify duplicates in the input.
 */
#include <stdio.h>
#include "sets.h"

main()
{
  SET unique, dup;                    /* unique and duplicate elements */
  ELEMENT elem;                       /* next element */
  long inpval                         /* next input value
  int inpres;                         /* return value from getnum */
  void print_set(),                   /* to print out sets */
       skip_garbage();                /* to skip over garbage */

  set_Empty(unique), set_Empty(dup);
  while (inpres = getnum(&inpval), inpres != EOF)
    if (!inpres)
    {
      printf("Bad input, skipping...\n");
      skip_garbage();
    }
    else if (inpval < SET_MIN || inpval > SET_MAX)
      printf("Out of range: %ld\n", inpval);
    else
    {
      elem = inpval;
      if (set_Mem(unique, elem))         /* is element a duplicate? */
        set_Del(unique, elem), set_Add(dup, elem);
      else if (!set_Mem(dup, elem))      /* is element unique? */
        set_Add(unique, elem);
    }
  print_set(unique, "Unique Values");   /* print the sets */
  print_set(dup, "Duplicate Values");
}

void print_set(set, name)              /* print out set and its name */
SET set;
char *name;
{
  ELEMENT i;                           /* next potential element */

  printf("%s\n", name);
  for (i = SET_MIN; i <= SET_MAX; i++)
    if (set_Mem(set, i))
      printf("%d\n", i);
}
```

FIGURE 6.20 A program to check for duplicate input values.

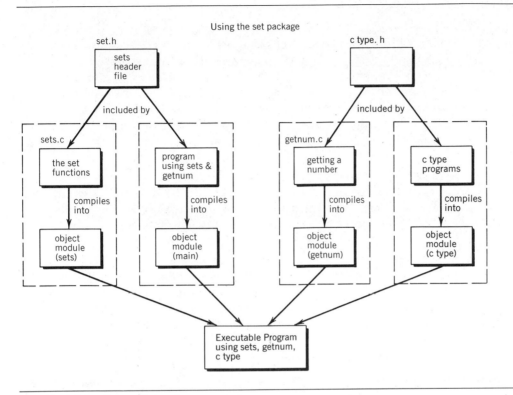

FIGURE 6.21 Compiling the set package.

ORGANIZING PROGRAMS AROUND THEIR DATA TYPES

When writing large programs, careful attention must be paid to their structure if they are to be understandable. By structuring programs around the abstract data types they use, such as sets, tables, and various other data structures, we can increase readability of our programs. Here are some suggestions for implementing abstract data types:

- Place the code implementing each data type in its own file and compile it separately. Information needed to use the data type is placed in a header file and included by those files using it. Wherever possible, keep the details of the data type's implementation out of the header file.

- Do not use functions other than the operations defined on a data type to manipulate it. If additional operations are required, add them to the module that defines the data type. However, add only those operations that are generally useful. Adding an operation to determine whether there are fewer than 10 elements in a set is foolish. Adding an operation to count set elements is reasonable.

- In implementing the data type, hide the details of the internal data structure. Make any externals necessary for communication among the operations implementing the data type `static` to prevent unintended access to them. Users of the data type should be able to change the internal data structure only through the operations defined on it – not by modifying globally accessible external variables.

- When using the data type, do not take advantage of details of its implementation that are not hidden. For example, we can determine the internal set representation by examining the header file, and we can write functions that take advantage of it. Doing so, however, defeats the purpose of an abstract data type, since the code will be less readable and later changes to the data type's implementation will be more difficult.

CHAPTER 7

THE PREPROCESSOR

Many useful features of C are not implemented by the compiler, but instead by a program that processes C source files before they are given to the compiler. This program, the C preprocessor, can be used to define constants and macros, include source files, and perform conditional compilation. In this chapter we describe the preprocessor, showing how we can use it to increase the readability, efficiency, and portability of our programs, as well as to make them easier to write and debug.

7.1

PREPROCESSOR DIRECTIVES

The preprocessor reads a source file, performs various actions on it, and gives the resulting output to the C compiler.[1] The preprocessor's actions are determined by directives placed in the source file; source files containing no preprocessor directives are simply passed on to the C compiler unchanged. These directives are differentiated from normal C source because they begin with a # and start in column 1. Table 7.1 lists the various preprocessor directives and their uses. Some of these directives should be familiar; many of our programs have used #include and #define.

---

[1]In some implementations the functionality of the preprocessor is built into the compiler, and the preprocessor is not a separate program. In most implementations, however, we can invoke the preprocessor without invoking the compiler.

TABLE 7.1 C preprocessor directives and their uses

Directive	Use
#include	Include text from a file.
#define	Define a macro.
#undef	Undefine a macro.
#line	Give a line number for compiler messages.
#if	Test if a compile-time condition holds.
#ifdef	Test if a symbol is defined.
#ifndef	Test if a symbol is not defined.
#else	Indicate alternatives if a test fails.
#elif	Combination of #if and #else.
#endif	End a preprocessor conditional.

Lines containing a preprocessor directive, called *preprocessor command lines*, are processed by the preprocessor and never seen by the compiler. Their syntax is somewhat different from that of the language itself. For example, end of line terminates a preprocessor command line instead of the semicolon used to terminate statements. In the following sections, we discuss each of the various directives and their uses.

7.2
SIMPLE MACRO SUBSTITUTION

We have used #define to define various symbolic constants, such as the number of elements in an array, the number of rows and columns on a terminal, the end-of-file character and the value of pi. The preprocessor command line

> #define *name   replacement-text*

instructs the preprocessor to replace all unquoted occurrences of *name* with *replacement-text* throughout the remainder of the source file. White space is required between the directive and *name* and between *name* and *replacement-text*. We write defined names in uppercase to distinguish them from variable and function names handled by the compiler. A defined name is often called a *macro*, and the process of substituting its replacement text is called *macro substitution*.

As an example, Figure 7.1a contains a program to compute the first 15 powers of 2. We use #define to define the two symbolic constants MAX-POWER (the highest power to compute) and BASE (the number we are rais-

```
/*
 *  Print a table of powers.
 */
#define MAXPOWER  15          /* highest power to compute */
#define BASE       2          /* number being raised */

main ()
{
  long sum = 1;               /* previous power */
  int  i;                     /* power to compute */

  printf("USING BASE %d\n\nPOWER\tVALUE\n", BASE);
  for (i = 0; i <= MAXPOWER; i++, sum *= BASE)
    printf("%d\t%d\n", i, sum);
}
```

(a)   Simple example of constant definition

```
main ()
{
  long sum = 1;
  int i;

  printf("USING BASE %d\n\nPOWER\tVALUE\n", 2);
  for (i = 0; i <= 15; i++, sum *= 2)
    printf("%d\t%d\n", i, sum);
}
```

(b)   The resulting output passed to the compiler

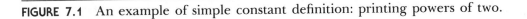

FIGURE 7.1   An example of simple constant definition: printing powers of two.

ing).   The output from the preprocessor's substitutions is shown in Figure 7.1*b*.[2] Except in quoted strings, whenever MAXPOWER appears, the preprocessor substitutes its value of 15. Similarly, BASE is replaced by its defined value two, except within the printf's control string, where it is quoted.[3]

Using #define to give symbolic names to constants aids readability and modifiability, especially in larger programs. When a numeric value appears in a program, its use is not always easy to determine, especially when the same value means different things in different places. For exam-

[2]Most compilers have an option to show the result of preprocessor substitutions. (On UNIX, for example, cc -E shows the preprocessor output.) Since some preprocessors substitute white space along with the replacement text, the resulting output may differ from that shown in our examples. Even though the output differs, the results should be equivalent.

[3]Unfortunately, many preprocessors will substitute for macro names within quoted strings, even though they are not supposed to. Run Figure 7.1*a* through your preprocessor to determine whether or not it behaves appropriately.

ple, 10 may be an interest rate, the size of an array, or a base for number conversion. A descriptive name for each unique use of a constant makes its use clearer, while making it possible to change the constant's value throughout the program simply by changing the line defining its name.

7.2.1 SYMBOLIC NAMES FOR STRINGS AND EXPRESSIONS

Symbolic names can also be given to string constants. For example,

```
#define  DIGITS   "0123456789"
```

causes each occurrence of DIGITS to be replaced with the string constant "0123456789" throughout the remainder of the source file. Because space is allocated for each occurrence of a string constant, space may be unnecessarily wasted if DIGITS appears many times. To save space, an external variable can be defined, initialized with the constant, and used in its place.

```
char *digits = "0123456789";    /* use digits to save space */
```

Remember, the external variable is necessary only if the constant is used in many places and space is an issue.

In addition to giving symbolic names to constants, we can give them to arbitrary expressions. The preprocessor simply substitutes the expression for its defined name *without evaluating it*. For example, following the definition

```
#define TWO_PI      (3.1415926 * 2.0)
```

the preprocessor replaces

```
circumf = radius * TWO_PI;
```

with

```
circumf = radius * (3.1415926 * 2.0);
```

No macro substitution takes place when a name is defined; the preprocessor simply remembers the name and its replacement text. Later, when the name is used, the preprocessor substitutes its replacement text and performs macro substitution on any defined names it contains. This allows us to define names in terms of other names and to define them in any order. As an example, Figure 7.2 shows constant definitions that determine the number of array elements needed to hold a bit map representing a set of

```
#define MIN_VAL        0                          /* smallest value */
#define MAX_VAL        2047                       /* largest value */
#define _SET_VALUES    (MAX_VAL - MIN_VAL + 1)    /* bits we need */
#define _WORD_SIZE     (sizeof(int) * 8)          /* bits in a long */
#define _SET_WORDS     (_SET_VALUES / _WORD_SIZE) /* words for bit map */
```

FIGURE 7.2 An example of defining constants in terms of other constants.

values, instead of simply defining precomputed constants for them, as we did in Chapter 6.

The size of the array (_SET_WORDS) is computed from the number of bits needed (_SET_VALUES) and the number of bits in an array element (_WORD_SIZE). _SET_VALUES, in turn, is computed from the largest (MAX_VAL) and smallest (MIN_VAL) values; WORD_SIZE is computed from the size of an array element and the number of bits in a byte. Figure 7.3 illustrates the replacement process for the expression n < _SET_WORDS.

Whenever the replacement text is an expression, it should be parenthesized to prevent an unexpected order of evaluation when the name it replaces is used. For example, if the expression to compute the number of words needed

```
_SET_VALUES / _WORD_SIZE
```

follows the unparenthesized definitions

```
#define _SET_VALUES    MAX_VAL - MIN_VAL + 1    /* bits we need */
#define _WORD_SIZE     sizeof(int) * 8          /* bits in a long */
```

the result of the preprocessor's substitutions for _SET_VALUES and WORD_SIZE is:

```
MAX_VAL - MIN_VAL + 1 / sizeof(int) * 8
```

This is certainly different from the desired expression

```
(MAX_VAL - MIN_VAL + 1) / (sizeof(int) * 8
```

resulting from the parenthesized definitions in Figure 7.2.

Because the preprocessor simply substitutes expressions without evaluating them, it is reasonable to wonder whether a program is less efficient when an often used defined name is replaced with an expression. Luckily, most C compilers compute the value of expressions involving only constants at compile time, instead of at run time, allowing us to use defined names freely in the definitions of other names without worrying too much

$$n < \_SET\_WORDS$$

Substituting for _ SET _ WORDS

$$n < (\_SET\_VALUES/\_WORD\_SIZE)$$

Substituting for _ SET _ VALUES and _ WORD _ SIZE

$$n < ((MAX\_VAL\_MIN\_VAL + 1)/(size\ of\ (int) \times 8))$$

substituting for MAX _ VAL and MIN _ VAL

$$n < ((2047 - 0 + 1)/(size\ of\ (int) \times 8))$$

FIGURE 7.3 Replacing defined names with defined names. All macro replacement takes place when the name is used, not when it is defined.

about efficiency. With a compiler that does not evaluate all constant expressions at compile time, an external variable can be initialized with the expression and used in its place.

EXERCISES

7-1 Write constant definitions for the maximum and minimum values of the types `short`, `int`, and `long` on your machine. Assuming a two's complement machine, can you write expressions to compute these values? □

7-2 Repeat the previous exercise for their unsigned counterparts. □

7-3 What does your preprocessor do with a name defined in terms of itself? For example,

```
#define TONY TONY              /* recursive definition */
```

Is this reasonable? □

7-4 Examine the output of your preprocessor's constant substitutions for Figure 7.1*a* Is the output the same as that shown in Figure 7.1*b*. If not, why not? □

7-5 Some preprocessors have a limit to the number of names that can be defined at any one time. Is there a way to avoid this problem using external variables? What is the drawback to this approach? □

7-6 Reorder the definitions in Figure 7.2. Does this affect subsequent uses of the names? □

7.2.2 SYNTACTIC REPLACEMENT

A defined name can be replaced with arbitrary text, not just expressions. We can use the preprocessor's ability to do arbitrary text replacement in order to hide parts of C's syntax that can be confusing or error prone. For example, the definitions

```
#define    FOREVER      for(;;)        /* infinite loop */
#define    IS           ==             /* equality test */
#define    ISNOT        !=             /* inequality test */
```

can be used to make infinite loops more explicit and to prevent the common mistake of using = instead of == for equality tests.

These definitions are used in Figure 7.4, a new version of the function `getcommand` (Figure 4.9). Following the definitions, the preprocessor replaces occurrences of FOREVER with `for(;;)`, occurrences of IS with ==, and occurences of ISNOT with !=.

An interesting use of these definitions is to create an extended syntax for C that resembles another language's syntax. We can use the definitions in Figure 7.5*a* to write C programs in a Pascal-like syntax, letting the preprocessor translate them into the form the compiler expects. We use these definitions in Figure 7.5*b*, a function `insert` that inserts a value into its correct place in a sorted table.

There are some drawbacks to major syntactic replacement. Since defined names have the same syntax as identifiers, operators and other nonalphabetic tokens such as comment delimiters cannot be redefined, limiting the amount of C's syntax that can be hidden. In addition, when the defined names are used incorrectly, the resulting error messages are likely to be less understandable because they correspond to C's syntax instead of the extended syntax. Lastly, maintaining these programs can be difficult for those unfamiliar with the extended syntax used.[4]

Because the replacement text in any definition is arbitrary, no syntax checking can be performed on it by the preprocessor. Syntax errors are detected when the compiler processes lines where the name is used, not the line where the name is defined. For example, the incorrect definition

```
#define  PI = 3.1415926;    /* incorrect: don't want "=" or ";" */
```

---

[4]Despite these limitations, some large programs (including a command interpreter and a object code debugger) have been written in an Algol-like syntax defined using the preprocessor.

```
/*
 * Get a single letter ('a', 'd', or 'q') command from the user
 * (#include <stdio.h> should precede this function).
 */
#define    FOREVER       for(;;)           /* infinite loop */
#define    IS            ==                /* equality test */
#define    ISNOT         !=                /* inequality test */

int getcommand()
{
  int command,                            /* user's command */
      junk;                               /* used to ignore rest of line */

  FOREVER
  {
    printf("Please enter a single letter command: ");
    if ((junk = command = getchar()) IS EOF)
      break;                              /* EOF, no more commands */
    if (command IS 'a' || command IS 'd' || command IS 'q')
      break;                              /* valid command */
    printf("Bad command given\n");
    while (command ISNOT EOF && junk ISNOT '\n')
      junk = getchar();                   /* skip rest of line */
  }
  if (command ISNOT EOF)
    printf("Valid command %c entered\n", command);
  else
    printf("End of file reached, treating as quit command.\n");
  return command;
}
```

FIGURE 7.4 Get a command from the user. The use of syntactic definitions aids readability.

contains the two most common syntax errors: terminating a definition with a semicolon and following the name with an assignment operator. If the definition is followed by

        circumf = 2 * PI * radius;

most compilers will report errors from the two incorrect statements

        circumf = 2 * = 3.1415926; * radius;

that result from the preprocessor's substitutions. When using #define, remember that the preprocessor does not know C; it blindly replaces names with replacement text.

```
#define    INTEGER      int
#define    REAL         double
#define    IF           if (
#define    THEN         )
#define    ELSE         else
#define    WHILE        while (
#define    DO           )
#define    BEGIN        {
#define    END          }
#define    PROCEDURE    void
#define    FUNCTION
#define    AND          &&
#define    OR           ||
#define    MOD          %
```

(a) Definitions used to create a Pascal-like syntax

```
PROCEDURE INSERT(table,value)          /* insert value in correct position */
REAL table[], value;


BEGIN
  INTEGER pos;                         /* temporary position in table */

  IF numvals < MAXVALS THEN BEGIN
    pos = numvals;
    WHILE pos > 0 AND value < table[pos - 1] DO BEGIN
      table[pos] = table[pos - 1];
      pos = pos - 1;
    END;
    table[pos] = value;
  END;
END
```

(b) Table insertion written using Pascal-like syntax.

FIGURE 7.5   Some definitions that allow us to write programs in a Pascal-like syntax, and a function that illustrates their use.

EXERCISES

7-7 If the compiler doesn't support void, is it possible to write a macro definition that simulates it? Does it work with your compiler? Why or why not? □

7-8 Rewrite the binary search from Chapter 5 using the definitions of a Pascal-like syntax. Is it easier or harder to debug? □

7-9 Are there C constructs other than those mentioned in this chapter that you think should be hidden? Write definitions to hide them. Do these make it easier or more difficult to write programs?   ☐

7-10 Most preprocessors do syntax checking, such as checking for unusual characters in the source file or unterminated quoted strings. Add some simple syntax errors to an existing source file. Are any errors detected by the preprocessors?   ☐

7.3
MACRO SUBSTITUTION WITH PARAMETERS

We can vary a macro's replacement text by defining a macro with parameters. Subsequent occurrences of the macro name are known as *macro calls*. When a macro is called, the preprocessor performs *macro expansion*, substituting the macro's replacement text for the call and replacing any occurrences of the macro's parameters with its arguments. Macro substitution with parameters is an extension of simple macro substitution, in which the replacement text is a template.

A macro is defined with a preprocessor command line of the form

```
#define   macro-name(parameter-name, ... ,parameter-name)   replacement-text
```

There can be no white space between the *macro-name* and the left parenthesis introducing the macro's parameter list. (When white space follows the *macro-name* it is a macro definition with no parameters: the simpler form of #define we encountered earlier.) The parameter list can contain zero or more parameters; these are analogous to the formal parameters in a function definition. For example,

```
#define CONVRT(temp)  ((5.0 / 9.0) * ((temp) - 32))
```

defines a macro named CONVRT with a single parameter temp. CONVRT converts a Fahrenheit temperature into its equivalent Celsius temperature. To prevent order-of-evaluation problems when CONVRT is expanded, we are careful to parenthesize all occurrences of its formal parameters in its replacement text, as well as the replacement text itself.

A macro call has a syntax similar to that of a function call and occurs whenever an unquoted expression of the form

```
macro-name(text,  text,  ... ,text)
```

appears. When a macro is called, the preprocessor replaces the call with

```
/*
 *  Reads in pairs of Fahrenheit temperatures and converts them to Celsius.
 */
#define CONVRT(temp) ((5.0 / 9.0) * ((temp) - 32)) /* Fahrenheit to Celsius */

main ()
{
  int minfahr,           /* minimum and maximum temperatures */
      maxfahr;           /*    (in Fahrenheit) */

  while (scanf("%d %d", &minfahr, &maxfahr) == 2)
    printf ("%f\t%f\n", CONVRT(minfahr), CONVRT(maxfahr));
}
```

FIGURE 7.6 Using a macro to do temperature conversion.

the replacement text and then replaces every occurrence of a parameter with its corresponding argument. Following CONVRT's definition, for example, the expression CONVRT(x) is a macro call the preprocessor replaces with

$$(5.0 \ / \ 9.0) \ * \ ((x) \ - \ 32))$$

substituting x for temp in CONVRT's replacement text.

A complete program using CONVRT is shown in Figure 7.6. The program reads pairs of Fahrenheit temperatures representing the high and low temperature for various cities, converts them into the corresponding Celsius temperatures, and prints them.

We could have written CONVRT as a function, as in Figure 7.7. We did not, however, because it is much less work to write CONVRT as a macro. Of course, we did not have to write either a macro or a function to do the temperature conversion; we could have written the program using the conversion formula directly. However, using the macro CONVRT makes the program more readable (without decreasing its efficiency), making it obvious that the same conversion formula is applied to both input temperatures.

```
/*
 * Convert Fahrenheit temperature to Celsius
 */
double convrt(temp)
int temp;                              /* temperature to convert */
{
  return (5.0 / 9.0) * (temp - 32);
}
```

FIGURE 7.7 Equivalent function to Figure 7.6 to do temperature conversion.

7.3.1 USEFUL MACROS

Macros can do things that functions cannot do. As an example, consider the macro `min`, which returns the minimum value of its parameters.

```
#define MIN(x,y) ( (x) < (y) ? (x) : (y) )   /* minimum of two values */
```

If the macro call

```
MIN(a + b,c + d)
```

appears after this definition, it is replaced with

```
( (a + b) < (c + d) ? (a + b) : (c + d) )
```

an expression that returns the minimum value of the expressions `(a + b)` and `(c + d)`. The parameter `x` has been replaced with `a + b`, the parameter `y` with `c + d`.

Because `MIN` is a macro and not a function, we can use it to find the minimum of any pair of values of the same data type. If we wrote `MIN` as a function, we would have to cast its arguments if their type differed from that of its parameters or we would have to have different versions of `MIN` for each data type. We also gain efficiency by writing `MIN` as a macro, since macro calls are done during preprocessing instead of at run time, and the overhead of a function call (argument passing, variable allocation, calling and returning from the function) is eliminated. There are some problems, however, with using macros; these will be discussed shortly.

Our macros so far have expanded into expressions; however, macros can also expand into arbitrary text, including statements or parts of statements. The macro `SWAP` defined by

```
#define SWAP(type,x,y)   /* swap contents of x and y */ \
        { type temp = (x); (x) = (y), (y) = temp; }
```

is useful for many programs, especially those that do sorting. (The definition's first line ends with a backslash to allow it to continue on to the next line.) `SWAP` expands into a compound statement declaring a temporary variable with the same type as the variable being swapped, using this variable to do the exchange. Whenever a macro expands into more than one statement, a compound statement should be used so that calls to the macro are similar to function calls.

The macro call

```
SWAP(double, old, new)
```

is replaced with the statement block

```
{ double temp = old; old = new, new = temp; }
```

that exchanges the values of old and new. Since SWAP is expanded into a compound statement, calls to it should not be terminated by a semicolon. SWAP can exchange values of arbitrary data types. Since there is no way to pass a type specifier to a function, this cannot be done with a function.

Macros can also be used to hide certain idioms of the language, improving the readability of programs with no loss of efficiency. For example, the macros STREQ, STRLT, and STRGT

```
#define STREQ(x,y)  (strcmp((x),(y)) == 0)    /* strings equal? */
#define STRLT(x,y)  (strcmp((x),(y)) < 0)     /* is string x < string y? */
#define STRGT(x,y)  (strcmp((x),(y)) > 0)     /* is string x > string y? */
```

test whether one string is lexicographically equal to, less than, or greater than another string. Their names clarify the string equality test strcmp is being used for, hiding the details of its return value. If these macros are not used, the program's reader is forced to remember the meaning of the various return values of strcmp in order to understand the string comparison being performed.

EXERCISES

7-11 Write a macro, PRINT_INT, that takes an integer parameter and writes it to the standard output using printf. Can you write a macro to print a value of an arbitrary type appropriately? Why or why not? □

7-12 Write a macro, GET_BITS, that takes a value, a starting bit, and the number of bits to return and returns the value of those bits. What other bit-oriented operations can easily be written as macros? □

7-13 Write a macro, INDEX, that expands into a for loop that indexes a variable from a minimum to a maximum. For example,

```
INDEX(i, 1, 100) printf("This is %d\n", i);
```

should expand into

```
for (i = 1; i <= 100; i++) printf("This is %d\n", i);  □
```

7.3.2 USING MACROS IN MACRO DEFINITIONS

We can also use macros with parameters in defining other macros. Figure 7.8 shows the definition of a macro AREA to compute the area of a circle, along with the definitions from which it is built.

```
#define  PI        3.1415926          /* famous friend */
#define  SQUARE(x) ((x) * (x))        /* square of number */
#define  AREA(r)   (PI * SQUARE(r))   /* area of circle */
```

FIGURE 7.8 Computing a circle's area—defining macros in terms of macros.

Because `PI` is a useful constant and `SQUARE` is a useful macro, we provide definitions for them instead of simply inserting their values in `AREA`'s definition. Following this definition, the preprocessor first replaces a macro call such as `AREA(distance)` with

```
(PI * SQUARE(distance))
```

Then it expands the defined names `PI` and `SQUARE`, resulting in the desired expression:

```
(3.1415926 * ( (distance) * (distance) ))
```

We can also use macros as the arguments of macro calls. For example, given the definition of `SQUARE`, n^4 can be computed using the expression

```
SQUARE(SQUARE(n))     /* quadruple a value */
```

The preprocessor first expands this expression into

```
((SQUARE(n)) * (SQUARE(n)))
```

replacing `SQUARE`'s parameter `x` with `SQUARE(n)`. Since there are still defined names in this expression, the preprocessor applies macro substitution to them, eventually generating the expression

```
((((n) * (n)) ) * (((n) * (n))))
```

Despite all the parentheses, this correctly computes n^4.

7.3.3 POTENTIAL PROBLEMS

Although macros are useful, there are some pitfalls, most of which can be avoided by remembering that macros are not functions. One drawback is that a macro's code appears in every place the macro is called, while a function's code appears only once, regardless of how many times the function is called. When minimal program size is important, large, often-used macros should be written as functions.

Another drawback is that a macro argument, unlike a function argument, may be evaluated more than once if its corresponding parameter appears in many places in the replacement text. For example:

```
#define CUBE(x) ((x) * (x) * (x))    /* x to the third power */
```

defines a macro that computes the cube of its parameter. The call
CUBE(x + y) expands to

```
((x + y) * (x + y) * (x + y))
```

causing three evaluations of (x + y).

The possibility of multiple evaluation is particularly troublesome when
arguments have side effects. CUBE(a++), a macro call intended to increment a after returning its cube, is expanded into the expression

```
((a++) * (a++) * (a++))
```

which does something different. Expressions appearing as arguments to
macros should be used sparingly and should be avoided entirely when they
contain side effects.

Forgetting to put parentheses around a macro's parameters within its
replacement text can lead to incorrect orders of evaluation. Leaving them
off in the following definition of CUBE

```
#define CUBE(x) (x * x * x)       /* sloppily parenthesized definition */
```

causes the call CUBE(a + 2) to expand into the expression

```
(a + 2 * a + 2 * a + 2)
```

which does not return the cube of a + 2.

Lastly, when a macro expands into a compound statement, poorly
chosen names can cause scoping problems. For example, the call
SWAP(double, old, temp) expands into the compound statement

```
{ double temp = (old); (old) = (temp), (temp) = (temp); }
```

which does not do the expected exchange. When a compound statement is
part of a macro's replacement text, its local variables must be chosen so
that they do not conflict with any variable name passed as an argument.

EXERCISES

7-14 Write the macros DIV and DIV_MOD. DIV(x,y) returns the value of
(x / y) for nonzero values of y, otherwise returning zero.

DIV_MOD(d,r,x,y) divides x by y, storing the result in d and the remainder in r. □

7-15 Write a macro, MSG(flag,msg), that writes the string msg only if flag is not zero. □

7-16 Write a macro, NULL_PTR(type), that returns a null pointer correctly cast to the passed type. When is this macro useful? □

7-17 Write a macro, DEREF(ptr, type), that dereferences ptr only if it is not null. If ptr is null the macro prints an error message and returns zero, cast to the appropriate type. □

7.4

UNDEFINING NAMES

Once a name is defined, all of its later occurrences are replaced with its defined replacement text. Occasionally it is desirable to define a name in only part of the file, either to show that the name is used only in a small section or to allow the name to be redefined. The directive

```
#undef name
```

undefines a defined name, stopping macro substitution for it. We can then use #define to redefine the name. Most preprocessors issue a warning if we try to redefine a name without first undefining it.[5]

We can use #undef to define a name for only a single function, giving it the same visibility as a local variable. For example, if we have a function that needs a null pointer to a character, perhaps to pass as a parameter to another function, we can define a constant NIL with

```
#define NIL (char *) 0          /* NULL pointer to character */
```

and use it wherever we need a null pointer, avoiding the explicit casting that would otherwise be required. This definition of NIL can be limited to the function by placing

```
#undef NIL
```

---

[5]Some preprocessors allow multiple definitions of names, storing them in reverse order of definition. Undefining a multiply defined name causes the previous definition to be used as the name's definition. It is best not to rely on this type of preprocessor behavior.

at the function's end. A later function using pointers to `doubles` can define `NIL` with

```
#define NIL (double *) 0        /* NULL pointer to double */
```

to define the appropriate null pointer.

EXERCISE

7-18 What happens if a name is undefined before an expression that uses it? □

7.5

FILE INCLUSION

Definitions useful to functions appearing in different source files can be placed in a single file and the file included when needed, preventing unnecessary repetition of definitions. Should it become necessary to change one of these definitions, only the file containing them must be modified and the programs that include it recompiled. The files containing these definitions are called *header files* or *include files*; by convention their names end with the suffix `.h`.

We include a file with the preprocessor directive `#include`. The preprocessor replaces `#include` lines with the entire contents of the specified file. If an incompletely specified file name is given, the preprocessor tries to search for the file in various locations determined by the form of `#include` used. The form

```
#include <filename>
```

instructs the preprocessor to look in only certain system-dependent locations to find *filename* and is usually reserved to include system header files such as *stdio.h*.[6] The alternative form

```
#include "filename"
```

instructs the preprocessor first to look locally for the file, searching the standard locations only if the file is not found locally. This form is used with local include files and files with completely specified names. Some

---

[6]On UNIX the standard header files are in the directory */usr/include* or one of its subdirectories.

preprocessors have an option whereby additional locations can be specified; check your preprocessor documentation to find out the specific locations that are searched. If an include file cannot be found, an error is reported and preprocessing stops.

Included files can include other files; most preprocessors allow at least five levels of nesting. (Of course, an included file should not include itself or any file that includes it.) In addition, macros can be defined that generate the file name and its surrounding delimiters. The sequence

```
#define  MATHHDR    <math.h>
 . . .
#include MATHHDR
```

is equivalent to the preprocessor command line

```
#include <math.h>
```

Defined names that expand into include file specifications can be used to aid readability when the file names are cryptic or when the file to be included is determined by other files.

One use of file inclusion, in addition to those we have already reviewed, is that it allows us to create a file of definitions that we find useful and to include it in all the programs we write. These definitions can extend C in a useful way while requiring little effort on our part. An example is shown in Figure 7.9. Most of these definitions and macros were explained in earlier sections. We have, however, added the macros MAX, which returns the maximum value of its arguments; ABS, which returns the absolute value of its argument; and INRANGE, which returns nonzero if its first parameter is between its other parameters. We also include a slightly different version of SWAP that is passed the temporary variable, along with the variables to be exchanged. This prevents the scoping problem mentioned earlier.

7.5.1 INCLUDING DATA TYPE DEFINITIONS

In addition to holding generally useful macro and constant definitions, include files are often used to provide data type definitions. In the previous chapter, the definitions of the set data type were placed in a file that was included by all functions using the set data type. With our implementation of sets, however, it is necessary to compile and link an additional file containing the functions that implemented the set operations. It is often possible to define a seemingly new data type completely within a header file. As an example, Figure 7.10 shows the include file *boolean.h*, which contains definitions that make it appear as though C has a boolean data

```
/*
 *  Generally useful definitions.
 */
#include <stdio.h>

#define TAB             '\t'                    /* common characters */
#define PAGE            '\f'
#define BELL            '\007'
#define EOS             '\0'
#define CR              '\n'

#define FOREVER         for(;;)                 /* syntactic extensions */
#define IS              ==
#define ISNOT           !=

#define MIN(x,y)        ((x) < (y) ? (x) : (y)) /* minimum of x and y */
#define MAX(x,y)        ((x) < (y) ? (y) : (x)) /* maximum of x and y */
#define ABS(x)          ((x) < 0) ? -(x) : (x)) /* absolute value */
#define INRANGE(x,y,z)  ((x) >= (y) && (x) <= (z)) /* is x < y and > z? */

#define SWAP(tmp, x, y) (tmp = x, x = y, y = tmp)  /* swap x and y */

#define INDEX(var,start,end)                    /* iterate from start */ \
        for ((var) = (start); (var) <= (end); (var)++)  /* to end */

#define STREQ(x,y)      (strcmp(x,y) == 0)      /* hide strcmp ugliness */
#define STRLT(x,y)      (strcmp(x,y) < 0)
#define STRGT(x,y)      (strcmp(x,y) > 0)
```

FIGURE 7.9   Generally useful definitions found in many programs.

type. These definitions are helpful in writing more readable code, as well
as making it easier to translate programs written in a language that has a
boolean type.

```
/*
 *  Boolean data type definitions.
 */
typedef char            BOOLEAN;                /* the data type */

#define TRUE            1                       /* possible boolean values */
#define FALSE           0                       /*   (TRUE and FALSE)   */

#define NOT             !                       /* boolean operators */
#define AND             &&                      /*   (for readability) */
#define OR              ||

#define BOOL_VAL(x)     ((x) ? "TRUE" : "FALSE")  /* string from boolean value */
```

FIGURE 7.10   *boolean.h* – defining a BOOLEAN data type.

```
/*
 *  Is character in string?
 */
#include "boolean.h"

BOOLEAN instr(string,ch)
char *string, ch;
{
  BOOLEAN found = FALSE;        /* have we found it yet? */

  for (; *string != '\0' AND NOT found; string++)
    if (*string == ch)
      found = TRUE;
  return found;
}
```

FIGURE 7.11 Using the boolean definitions.

The type BOOLEAN is appropriately represented by char because only the values zero and one are needed to represent the two possible states of a boolean variable. For consistency with other languages, the constants NOT, AND, and OR are defined as an alternative to the equivalent C logical operators. Lastly, BOOL_VAL returns a string representing the boolean's value and is useful when debugging.

Any program can pretend that C has BOOLEANs by including *boolean.h* and using these definitions. We use them in Figure 7.11, a function, instr, that determines whether a given character is in a particular string. Using BOOLEAN makes instr more readable but less concise.

EXERCISES

7-19 Examine some of the C programs you have written. Are there complicated expressions that could be greatly simplified by using macros? Write these macros. □

7-20 Define a function and include it in two files that are linked together to form a single object module. What happens and why? Try the same thing with a variable. Are the results similar? Why or why not? □

7-21 Rewrite the character-testing functions from Chapter 6 as macros. Are the macro versions more efficient? □

7-22 Define a macro package to do the set operations implemented in Chapter 6 for small sets – sets with no more elements that fit in a long. □

7.6

CONDITIONAL COMPILATION

Based on the values of various compile-time conditions, such as name definition, the preprocessor can be used to control the source file lines given to the compiler. This process is known as *conditional compilation* and can be used to make our programs more portable and easier to debug. Conditional compilation allows a program's source to compile into different versions depending on our needs.

7.6.1 TESTING NAME DEFINITION

Defined names are often used as flags that control conditional compilation. We can determine the lines to be processed by using the directives #ifdef, #else, and #endif to test if a name is defined. Any set of preprocessor commands of the form

```
#ifdef name
    first-group-of-lines
#else
    second-group-of-lines
#endif
```

causes *first-group-of-lines* to be processed by the preprocessor and compiled if *name* is defined, or *second-group-of-lines* to be processed if it is not. The #else is optional, and if it is omitted and the tested name is undefined, the lines up to the matching #endif are ignored.

As an example of their use, Figure 7.12 shows a new version of the insertion sort program from Chapter 1 that conditionally includes statements that provide debugging output. The debugging statements are included only if the name DEBUG is defined when the program is compiled.

In Figure 7.12, because DEBUG has been defined, when the preprocessor examines the lines

```
#ifdef DEBUG
    {
        printf("Moving value %d to position %d\n", table[pos − 1], pos);
        table[pos] = table[pos − 1];
    }
#else
    table[pos] = table[pos − 1];
#endif
```

it processes and gives to the compiler only the lines

```
/*
 * Read a table of values and sort them using insertion sort.
 */
#include <stdio.h>

#define  DEBUG                       /* turns debugging on - remove to turn it off */
#define  MAXVALS       100           /* maximum number of values to sort */


main()
{
  int  numvals = 0,                  /* number of values in table */
       pos,                          /* index into table */
       table[MAXVALS],               /* table of values */
       value;                        /* current value */

  while (numvals < MAXVALS && scanf("%d", &value) != EOF)
  {
    /* Insert new element in correct place. */

    for (pos = numvals; pos > 0 && value < table[pos - 1]; pos--)
#ifdef DEBUG
    {
       printf("Moving value %d to position %d\n", table[pos - 1], pos);
       table[pos] = table[pos - 1];
    }
#else
       table[pos] = table[pos - 1];
#endif
       table[pos] = value;
       numvals++;                    /* increment "numvals" after inserting */
#ifdef DEBUG
       printf("- Inserted value %d in position %d\n", value, pos);
#endif
  }
  /* Reached end of input file-print in order */

  for (pos = 0; pos < numvals; pos++)
    printf("%d\n", table[pos]);
}
```

FIGURE 7.12 Insertion sort with debugging statements compiled in when needed using conditional compilation.

```
    {
       printf("Moving value %d to position %d\n", table[pos - 1], pos);
       table[pos] = table[pos - 1];
    }
```

Had DEBUG not been defined, the single line

```
                table[pos] = table[pos - 1];
```

would be processed and the others ignored.

Using the preprocessor to decide if debugging output should be produced is more efficient than using the debugging package in Chapter 6, because the decision is made at compile time instead of run time. Also, the resulting object module is smaller, since the debugging statements no longer appear in the program's object module. Because of the many preprocessor tests, however, the source is likely to be be less readable and the debugging output less consistent. Since the debugging statements remain available when later changes are made to the program, either alternative is preferable to adding output statements wherever debugging output is desired and then removing these statements once the program has been debugged.

We have been using #ifdef to test if a name is defined. A similar preprocessor directive, #ifndef, can be used instead to test if a name is undefined. #ifndef appears most often in include files to ensure that even if the file has been included more than once, any definitions it contains will not be redefined.

#ifndef appears in Figure 7.13, a modified version of *boolean.h* (Figure 7.10) that defines the boolean data type only if it has not already been defined. The file's first line

```
                #ifndef BOOL_HDR
```

```
/*
 *  Boolean data type definitions.
 */
#ifndef BOOL_HDR

#define BOOL_HDR

typedef char            BOOLEAN;                    /* the data type */
#define TRUE            1                           /* possible boolean values */
#define FALSE           0                           /*   (TRUE and FALSE)   */

#define NOT             !                           /* boolean operators */
#define AND             &&                          /*   (for readability) */
#define OR              ||

#define BOOL_VAL(x)     ((x) ? "TRUE" : "FALSE")    /* string from boolean value */

#endif
```

FIGURE 7.13 *boolean.h* – A new version of the boolean include file.

causes the various names contained in the file to be defined only if BOOL_HDR is undefined. We cannot simply test whether BOOLEAN is defined because it is has been defined using `typedef` instead of `#define`. If BOOL_HDR is already defined, we assume that *boolean.h* has already been included and that the header file's definitions can be ignored. Remember that both `#ifdef` and `#ifndef` test only whether the name is defined in the preprocessor; they do not test whether the name of an identifier, function, or type has been declared.

7.6.2 USING NAME DEFINITIONS TO CONTROL MACRO DEFINITION

By writing a short sequence of characters (called an *escape sequence*), it is possible to clear a terminal screen or move the cursor to a specific screen location. Unfortunately, the escape sequence for a particular task varies from terminal to terminal. One way to remedy this situation is to have the program read the appropriate escape sequences from a file. This is especially useful if the program has to run on many different terminals.

As an alternative, if a program runs only on a particular terminal, the escape sequences can be determined at compile time, saving file accessing overhead. We can use the include file *cursor.h*, shown in Figure 7.14, to accomplish this. Two useful macros are made available when this file is included: CLEAR_SCREEN and MOVE_CURSOR. CLEAR_SCREEN clears the terminal's screen and MOVE_CURSOR moves to a specified row, column position on the screen. The file itself simply contains `#ifdefs` to check for a

```
/*
 * Define macros to clear screen and move cursor.
 */

#ifdef  WYSE
#define CLEAR_SCREEN()    putchar('\032')     /* control Z */
#define MOVE_CURSOR(r,c)  \
        printf("%c%c%c%c", '\033', '=', (r) + '\040', (c) + '\040')
#endif

#ifdef  TVI910
Definitions for a TVI910
#endif
#ifdef  GT101
Definitions for a GT101
#endif
    . . .
```

FIGURE 7.14 An include file to define useful cursor control macros.

specific constant identifying a terminal. Each `#ifdef` is followed by the appropriate macro definitions for that terminal.

For example, a program running on a Wyse terminal can obtain the appropriate macro definitions with

```
#define WYSE
#include "cursor.h"
```

Of course, the macro definitions will be provided only if there is an `#ifdef WYSE` in *cursor.h*.

7.6.3 PREDEFINED NAMES

In addition to the names we have explicitly defined and tested with `#ifdef` and `#ifndef`, most preprocessors predefine names such as the name of the machine the program is running on, its host operating system, and the name of the compiler being used. Table 7.2 contains some of the predefined names defined by various C compilers. Not all preprocessors predefine all these names; only those names relevant to the particular preprocessor are defined by it. When a name is defined, however, the program can assume the environment associated with it. For example, the names `UNIX` and `VAX` are defined only when the program is being compiled on a `VAX` running the `UNIX` operating system. Some systems may require that these names be lowercase.

By testing if various potential predefined names are actually defined, a program can determine its environment and adjust any environmental

TABLE 7.2   Various predefined preprocessor names.

Name	Environment
UNIX	UNIX operating system.
OS	IBM 360/370 operating system.
TSS	IBM Time Sharing System.
VMS	DEC's operating system.
CPM	CPM operating System.
PDP11	PDP-11 computer.
INTERDATA	Interdata computer.
VAX	VAX computer.
DECUS	Decus C compiler.
VAX11C	VAX 11 C compiler for VMS.
__LINE__	Current line number.
__FILE__	Current file name.

dependencies, increasing its portability. For example, if we determine the number of bits in an `unsigned int` with the expression

```
(sizeof(int) * 8)
```

we are assuming that a byte contains eight bits. Unfortunately, many machines have smaller or larger byte sizes, and programs relying on this assumption will either fail or work less efficiently.

A more portable way to determine the machine's byte size is to define a constant `BYTESIZ` with the number of bits in a byte on the particular machine the program is running on. Figure 7.15 shows how its value is set. During compilation, the program first checks for predefined names representing machines whose byte size is known to be unusual, defining `BYTESIZ` appropriately for those machines. If none of these names are defined, a default of eight is used for `BYTESIZ`. Of course, the program still will not behave correctly if it is compiled on a machine with an unusual byte size that has either no name predefined for it or a name for which testing is not done.

Most preprocessors predefine the names `__LINE__` and `__FILE__` as the current line number and current source file name. We illustrate one use of these definitions in the definition of the macro `ASSERT`, shown in Figure 7.16.   `ASSERT`'s arguments are an expression, representing an assumption of the programmer (something the programmer believes, or *asserts* to be true, which is not otherwise tested) and a string to print if this assumption does not hold when the macro's expansion is executed. Whenever a function makes an assumption whose failure would cause the function to behave incorrectly, a call to `ASSERT` can be inserted, documenting the assumption and indicating it when it fails. Invariably, our programs fail because an assumption we made turns out not to hold; `ASSERT` helps us find such assumptions.

The predefined names `__LINE__` and `__FILE__` are expanded into the line number and file name of the macro call, and their values are

```
#ifdef INTERDATA
#define BYTESIZ  9          /* 9 bit bytes */
#else
#ifdef CYBER
#define BYTESIZ 10          /* 10 bit bytes */
#else
#define BYTESIZ  8          /* 8 bit bytes are the default */
#endif
#endif
```

FIGURE 7.15 Setting up a constant containing the number of bits in a byte. Only those machines that differ from the norm are tested.

```
#define  ASSERT(cond,desc)                         \
         (!)cond) ? printf("Assertion failed: %s (line %d of %s).\n", \
                    (desc), __LINE__, __FILE__), 0 : 1 )
```

FIGURE 7.16 Assertion macro to write an error message if an assumption fails.

included in the error message written when an assertion fails. ASSERT is written as an expression in order to allow functions to test assertions and exit when they fail.

To illustrate ASSERT's usefulness, Figure 7.17 contains a new version of instr in which its assumption that it is passed a non-null string pointer is made explicit with a call to ASSERT. If instr is accidentally passed a null pointer, the useful error message

```
Assertion Failed: Null pointer parameter (line 11 of instr.c)
```

is printed.[7] Although the program will still die with a run-time error when the pointer is used, with ASSERT at least some indication of the problem is given first. It is certainly more difficult to locate bugs when starting with a potentially cryptic system message instead of an error message from a failed assertion.

```
/*
 *  Is character in string?
 */
#include "boolean.h"

BOOLEAN instr(string,ch)
char *string, ch;
{
  BOOLEAN found = FALSE;       /* have we found it yet? */

  ASSERT(string != NULL, "Null pointer parameter");
  for (; *string != '\0' AND NOT found; string++)
    if (*string == ch)
      found = TRUE;
  return found;
}
```

FIGURE 7.17 Making an assumption explicit with the ASSERT macro.

[7]On some systems, when a program dies abruptly there may be buffered output that has not been written. To remedy this situation, the appropriate library call to force out the remaining output should be added to ASSERT.

7.6.4 MORE GENERAL COMPILE-TIME TESTS

The preprocessor can test conditions more general than name definition. The directive

```
#if constant-expression
```

causes *constant-expression* to be evaluated and its value to be compared with zero (instead of being tested for definition) to determine the group of lines to process. Unlike testing for name definition, macro substitution can occur in the *constant-expression*.

One use of the simple form of this construction is to "comment out" sections of code that contain comments when the C compiler does not allow nested comments.

```
#if 0                       /* begin ignored section */
  lines-to-be-commented  out  /* (lines that can contain comments) */
#endif                      /* end ignored section */
```

The *constant-expression* in this example is always zero, so the *lines-to-be-commented-out* are ignored.

Another common use of #if is to allow for different levels of debugging, with more output at each level. To do this, we define DEBUG as the desired integer level of debugging and use #ifs to test its value in order to choose the particular debugging statements to include. For example,

```
#if DEBUG >= 5
    printf("Debugging level %d: x = %s", DEBUG, x);
#endif
```

causes the printf to be included only if the debugging level is five or higher.

7.6.5 OTHER USEFUL PREPROCESSOR FEATURES

Two other features provided by some preprocessors are likely to become part of the language standard. The first, #elif, transforms preprocessor conditionals of the form shown in Figure 7.18*a* into the form shown in Figure 7.18*b*.
Any #else immediately followed by an #if can be replaced with #elif and their associated #endif removed.

The other feature is the preprocessor function defined, which takes a *name* and returns zero only if *name* is undefined. defined is appropriate when a piece of code should be processed if any name in a group of names is defined. Figure 7.19 illustrates how defined and #elif can be com-

```
#if constant-expression-1          #if constant-expression-1
   . . .                              . . .
#else                              #elif constant-expression-2
#if constant-expression-2            . . .
   . . .                           #endif
#endif
#endif
```

(a) Without `elif`   *(b)* With `elif`

FIGURE 7.18 Simplifying conditionals with `#elif`

bined by defining `WORDLEN` as the number of bits in a word. Despite their usefulness, only a few preprocessors support `#elif` and `defined`, and their use is nonportable.

EXERCISES

7-23 Does your preprocessor have `#elif` and `defined`? If so, rewrite the program fragment that determines the number of bits in a word (Figure 7.15) using them. □

7.7

PRE-PREPROCESSING

Many C programs are generated or modified by other programs (called *pre-processors*) before they are seen by the preprocessor or compiler. Because these programs can transform their input, the line number referred to in a preprocessor or compiler error message may not correspond exactly to the line where the error occurred in the original source file. To cause these error messages to refer to the correct lines in the original source file, these programs can use the preprocessor (actually, the compiler) directive

> `#line` *line-number "filename"*

to tell the C preprocessor the file name and line number where a line in its input came from. If the file name is omitted from a `#line`, the current file name is assumed.

```
#if defined(PDP11)
#define WORDLEN 16              /* 16 bit words */
#elif defined(VAX) | defined(IBM370)
#define WORDLEN 32              /* 32 bit words */
#elif defined(INTERDATA)
#define WORDLEN 36              /* 36 bit words */
#endif
```

FIGURE 7.19 Defining the number of bits in a word – simplified using `#elif` and `defined`

A sample pre-preprocessor that lets us write C programs using an "at-sign" (@) to indicate comment lines is shown in Figure 7.20. The program simply removes all these pseudo-comment lines, allowing programs to be commented in a style similar to the line-oriented commenting styles of other languages. To ensure that line numbers for any C error messages correspond to the correct lines in the original program, when the lines

```
/*
 *  Remove any line in input that begins with @ .
 */
#include <stdio.h>

define COMCHAR '@'                      /* comment-indicating character */

main()
{
  int c,                                /* next input character */
      in_comment = 0,                   /* in a group of comment lines? */
      lastch = '\n',                    /* fake starting line */
      lineno = 1;                       /* first line number */

  while (c = getchar(), c != EOF)
  {
    if (lastch == '\n')
    {
      if (in_comment && c != COMCHAR)   /* output #line after last line in */
        printf("#line %d\n", lineno);   /*   comment group */
      in_comment = (c == COMCHAR);      /* record in/out of comment group */
      lineno++;                         /* remember on next line */
    }
    if (!in_comment)                    /* echo characters that are not in */
      putchar(c);                       /*   comment group */
    lastch = c;
  }
}
```

FIGURE 7.20 A simple pre-preprocessor that removes lines starting with an at-sign.

starting with an at-sign are removed, they are replaced with a `#line` whose line number is the line number of the original source file line following the removed at-sign comments.

Even in its limited form (it does not handle comments in include files, multiple input files, or at-sign comments in the middle of lines), this allows program commenting in an alternative style. Figure 7.21(a) shows the temperature conversion program from Figure 7.6 written using at-sign comments, and Figure 7.21(b) shows the pre-preprocessor's output. After the program in Figure 7.21(a) is run through the pre-preprocessor, it can be compiled in the usual way.

EXERCISES

7-24 Modify the example pre-preprocessor to allow comments beginning anywhere on a line. □

```
@
@  Temperature converter written using @ as the comment indicator.
@

    #define CONVRT(temp) ((5.0 / 9.0) * ((temp) - 32))

    main ()
@  Convert and output temperatures.
    {
      int minfahr, maxfahr;

      while (scanf ("%d %d", &minfahr, &maxfahr) == 2)
        printf ("%f\t%f\n", CONVRT(minfahr), CONVRT(maxfahr));
    }
```

(a) Temperature conversion program with a different commenting style

```
#line 4
#define CONVRT(temp) ((5.0 / 9.0) * ((temp) - 32))

main()
#line 8
{
   int minfahr,maxfahr;

while (scanf("%d%d", &minfahr, &maxfahr) == 2)
- printf("%f\t%f\n", CONVRT(minfahr), CONVRT(maxfahr));
}
```

(b) Output of comment remover

FIGURE 7.21 Using at-sign comments. (a) A program written with at-sign comments. (b) The output of the pre-preprocessor that removes these comments.

7-25 Write another pre-proprocessor to allow the pseudo-directive `#defexp`, that takes a name and an expression and generates a `#define` for the name, making sure that the expression is parenthesized.   □

WRITING MACROS

Macro substitution is the most often used preprocessor capability. Here are some guidelines for deciding when to write macros, and some stylistic suggestions for making them easier to use:

- For efficiency replace simple functions with macros. Be careful, however, not to try to do too much in a macro. It does not pay to rewrite a function as a macro when the function's calling overhead is small relative to the work it does.

- To simplify code, replace complicated or confusing expressions with a macro. The macro gives the expression a name, aiding readability. This is especially important if the expression appears in many places.

- Write macros that expand into expressions instead of statements. This allows the macro call to be used anywhere a function call can be used. When this is not possible, surround the text in the macro definition with braces, and do not terminate the macro call with a semicolon.

- Do not use side effects in macro calls, do not assume that an argument is only evaluated once, and do not make any assumptions about the order in which the arguments are evaluated. These rules also apply to functions, since it may not be possible to determine if a call is to a function or a macro.

- Parenthesize expressions within macro replacement text to protect against unexpected results when the macro is expanded. The text of macros that expand into expressions should also be parenthesized. Don't be afraid to overparenthesize; doing so rarely affects readability, but can prevent endless hours tracking down problems due to order of evaluation or incorrect macro expansion.

ARRAYS AND POINTERS REVISITED

So far, our programs have needed only simple, one-dimensional arrays with integer, character, and real elements. In this chapter we introduce multidimensional arrays and arrays of pointers, concentrating on the use of pointers to gain performance improvements. The chapter concludes with a look at C's declaration syntax — how variables and functions are declared to take advantage of the rich combinations of arrays, pointers, and functions available as data types in the language. This chapter is rather detailed, but study of it will result in program efficiency and in a thorough understanding of important fine points of the language.

8.1

TWO-DIMENSIONAL ARRAYS

Multidimensional arrays are declared by enclosing the bounds of each dimension separately in brackets. The declaration

```
int   scores[20][10];
```

declares scores to be a two-dimensional array of ints containing a total of 200 elements. As with one-dimensional arrays, the array name is a pointer to the first element of the array, or, more correctly for two-dimensional arrays, a pointer to the first *row* of the array.

It is conventional to think of the first dimension as representing the rows of a matrix and the second as the columns, so scores has been declared to contain 20 rows of 10 columns each. One use of scores is to contain the test scores for students in a class, with each row corresponding to the test scores for a particular student and each column corresponding to the scores for a particular test.

Figure 8.1 shows the indexing scheme used to access the elements of scores. As with one-dimensional arrays, each dimension of the array is indexed from zero to its maximum size minus one; the first index selects the row, and the second index selects the column within that row. Thus, the legal indexes for scores range from scores[0][0] to scores[19][9].

Two-dimensional arrays are accessed in a conventional way using double sets of brackets. As an example, Figure 8.2 contains a function, print_scores, that prints scores' elements, one row per line. Each output line, therefore, contains the test scores for a particular student. print_scores assumes that MAX_STUDENTS and MAX_TESTS are defined as the number of students (or rows) and the number of tests (or columns), respectively. Two variables, student and test, are used to index the array; student selects the row and test the element within that row.

Notice in Figure 8.2 that two-dimensional arrays as function parameters are declared in a different way from their one-dimensional counterparts. Because the compiler must know the number of columns in each row to subscript the array's elements correctly, the number of columns (the second dimension) must be specified in the array's parameter declaration. But as with one-dimensional arrays, when a two-dimensional array is passed as a parameter, only a pointer is passed (a pointer to the first *row*), and this is used in accessing array elements.

EXERCISES

8-1 Write a function, read_scores, that reads in a student identification number, followed by the student's test scores. The student number should be used to select the row in the array. Implement an appropriate error-testing and flagging mechanism. □

8-2 Write a function, print_tests, that prints out the elements of scores, one column per line. Each line of output should contain all of the scores for a particular test. □

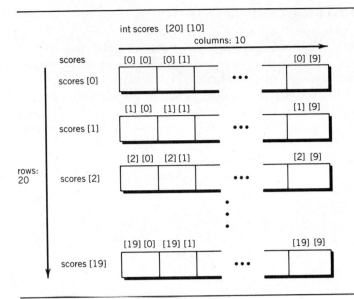

int scores [20] [10]

FIGURE 8.1 Elements of a two-dimensional array viewed as a matrix.

```
/*
 *  Print scores, one student per line.
 */
void print_scores(scores)
int   scores[][MAX_TESTS];
{
  int     student, test;

  for (student = 0; student < MAX_STUDENTS; putchar('\n'), student++)
    for (test = 0; test < MAX_TESTS; test++)
      printf("%d  ", scores[student][test]);
}
```

FIGURE 8.2 Print test scores using conventional array subscripting.

8.1.1 INTERNAL REPRESENTATION OF TWO-DIMENSIONAL ARRAYS

To understand why the second dimension is needed but the first is not when a two-dimensional array is passed to a function, we need to understand the internal representation of two-dimensional arrays. The values of these arrays are stored in "row major" order. That is, the elements of row zero are stored consecutively in memory, then the elements of row one, and so on, as shown in Figure 8.3. In a reference to a two-dimensional array element, such as `scores[10][5]`, the compiler calculates the element's position from the two subscripts and its knowledge of the number of columns in each row. With `scores` declared as

```
int  scores[20][10];
```

we find `scores[10][5]` at `&scores[0][0]` plus all the elements in rows zero through nine, plus five; that is, at

```
&scores[0][0] + 10 × 10 × sizeof(int) + 5
```

Therefore, if `scores[0][0]` is at location 1000 and we are using a four-byte-per-int machine, this is $1000 + 10 \times 10 \times 4 + 5 = 1405$. Generalizing, `scores[i][j]` is found at

```
&scores[0][0] + i × 10 × sizeof(int) + j = 1000 + 40i + j.
```

EXERCISES

8-3 Since the elements of any two-dimensional array are stored consecutively, how can the sum of `scores`' elements be computed without using two-dimensional subscripting (*Hint*: Remember that `scores` is stored as a one-dimensional array, with `&scores[0][0]` pointing to its first element and `&scores[19][9]` pointing to its last one.) Write a function to do this task. How much faster is it than the corresponding two-subscript version? □

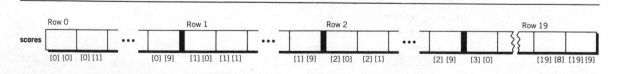

FIGURE 8.3 Internal storage structure in row major order for a two-dimensional array.

8.1.2 INITIALIZING TWO-DIMENSIONAL ARRAYS

Like their one-dimensional counterparts, static and external multidimensional arrays may be initialized by following their declaration with a list of values enclosed in braces. For example,

```
static int  board[3][3] = { 1, 1, 1, 2, 2, 2, 3, 3, 3 };
```

initializes the elements in board's first row to one, those in its second row to two, and those in its third row to three. By surrounding the elements in the row with braces, two-dimensional arrays can also be initialized row by row, making the declaration

```
static int  board[3][3] = { {1,1,1}, {2,2,2}, {3,3,3} };
```

equivalent to the previous one.

Because we often think of two-dimensional arrays as a matrix, we usually format array initializers to show the two-dimensional structure. Also, since the size and structure of the array can be determined from the values in the initializer, the first dimension of the array (that is, the number of rows) need not be specified. The previous declaration and initialization of board can also be written as

```
static int  board[][3] =
  { {1, 1, 1},
    {2, 2, 2},
    {3, 3, 3} };
```

If values are missing in an initializer, they are set to zero, so there is no need to supply values for all elements in the array. The declaration

```
static int  board[3][3] = { {1,1}, {1} };
```

initializes the first two elements of the first row and the first element in the second row to one, initializing all other elements to zero. Unfortunately, there is no way to initialize only selected rows. The simplest way to initialize rows that do not require initialization themselves, but precede rows that do, is to initialize their first element to zero.

EXERCISES

8-4 Write a function to determine whether a particular square two-dimensional array is a magic square (all rows, columns, and diagonals add up to the same value). □

8-5 Write a function to determine whether a particular square two-dimensional array is an identity matrix (ones on the diagonal, zeroes everywhere else). □

8.2

POINTERS AND TWO-DIMENSIONAL ARRAYS

As we discovered in Chapter 3, all array accesses are automatically converted to an equivalent pointer expression. Whenever an element in a two-dimensional array is referenced with two subscripts, C converts the array access into an equivalent pointer expression. The expression `scores[i][j]`, for example, is converted into the equivalent pointer expression

```
*(*(scores + i) + j)
```

Figure 8.4 illustrates how this somewhat bizarre-looking expression obtains the value of `scores[i][j]` and the rest of this section should clarify why that expression works.

Two-dimensional arrays give us an opportunity to explore further how pointers work and the power of pointer arithmetic. Since the name of a two-dimensional array is a pointer to the array's first row, in addition to declaring a two-dimensional array, a declaration such as

```
int scores[MAX_STUDENTS][MAX_TESTS];
```

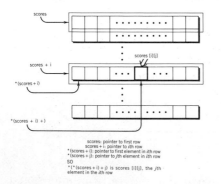

scores: pointer to first row
scores + i: pointer to ith row
*(scores + i): pointer to first element in ith row
*(scores + j): pointer to jth element in ith row
SO
((scores + i) + j) is scores [i][j], the jth element in the ith row

FIGURE 8.4   Using `*(*(scores + i) + j)` to access `scores[i][j]`

defines `scores` as a (constant) pointer to the array's first row, that is, a pointer to an array of `MAX_TESTS` elements, as we first noted in Figure 8.1. The previous figure, Figure 8.3, emphasizes the concept of a two-dimensional array as an array of arrays.

Because `scores` is a constant, we cannot use it to traverse the array. Instead, we can declare and initialize a pointer to a row, which can then be used to do the traversal. To do this, we declare a new variable `row_ptr` to be a pointer to a *row* of a matrix. More specifically, we want `row_ptr` to be a pointer to a single row of `scores`. Since each row of `scores` is a one-dimensional array of `MAX_TESTS` ints, `row_ptr` is declared as a pointer to an array of `MAX_TESTS` ints and initialized to point to the first row in `scores`:

```
int (*row_ptr)[MAX_TESTS] = scores;     /* pointer to first row of SCORES */
```

The parentheses around `*row_ptr` are necessary because `*` has lower precedence than `[ ]`. Without the parentheses, as in

```
int *row_ptr[MAX_TESTS];
```

we would be declaring `row_ptr` as an array of `MAX_TESTS` elements, each a pointer to an `int`.

Because pointer arithmetic is always conducted in units of the base type, and because `row_ptr` is declared as a pointer to an array of `MAX_TESTS` ints (or, in other words, a pointer to a block of storage large enough to contain an array of `MAX_TEST` ints), incrementing `row_ptr` causes it to point to the next *row* in `scores`. Similarly, decrementing `row_ptr` causes it to point to the previous row. That is the nice thing about pointer addition – it works in chunks that are appropriate to the way they are defined. All the normal operations on pointers are allowed on `row_ptr` and, as expected, are done in terms of rows (see Figure 8.5).

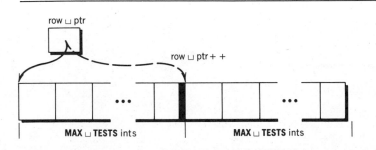

FIGURE 8.5   Using pointer arithmetic to traverse two-dimensional arrays.

row_ptr points to an array, thus dereferencing it (*row_ptr) gives the pointed-to array, or, more precisely, the address of its first element. Although row_ptr and *row_ptr point to the same address, their types are very different. row_ptr is a pointer to an array, *row_ptr is a pointer to an array element. Adding one to row_ptr gives a pointer to the next row, adding one to *row_ptr gives a pointer to the next element in a row. This allows us to subscript *rowptr in order to access elements in the row. For example, the *i*th element (counting from zero) in the row pointed to by row_ptr can be accessed with the expression

$$(\text{*row\_ptr})[i] \quad \textit{or equivalently} \quad \text{*(*(row\_ptr) + i)}$$

The parentheses around *row_ptr are necessary, since the expression *row_ptr[i] returns a pointer to the first element in the ith row. Figure 8.6 illustrates the element accessing in more detail.

Let us use this bit of arcane knowledge and compare subscripting with the use of pointers for two-dimensional array accesses. Figure 8.7 is a routine, test_avg, that computes the average of the values in a given column of the array, called by

```
test_avg (scores, MAX_STUDENTS, n);
```

int scores [MAX _ STUDENTS] [MAX _ TESTS];
int (*row _ ptr) [Max _ Tests] = scores;

scores				
97	15	41		16
83	12	52		18

row _ ptr

row _ ptr + +

(*row _ ptr) [1] is 97
(*row _ ptr) [2] is 15

Perform row _ ptr + +
(*row _ ptr) [1] is 83
(*row _ ptr) [2] is 12

FIGURE 8.6 Accessing elements through a pointer to a row.

```
/*
 *   Compute the average of the values in a given column of a 2D array.
 */
double test_avg (scores, max, n)
int  scores[][MAX_TESTS],              /* 2D array with "MAX_TESTS" columns */
     max,                              /* number of rows in "scores" */
     n;                                /* column we want to average */
{
    long  sum = 0;                     /* column total */
    int   i;                           /* row index */

    for (i = 0; i < max; i++)
      sum += scores[i][n];
    return (double) sum / max;
}
```

FIGURE 8.7 Computing the average of a given *column* of a two-dimensional array using conventional array subscripting.

where n is the column we wish to sum (n must be less than MAX_TESTS, but for generality and clarity of the presentation, we do no bounds checking on it) and MAX_STUDENTS is the number of rows (the first dimension) in the array. The function returns a double, the average of the nth column.   test_avg accesses the elements of the array conventionally by using double subscripting.

Perhaps surprisingly we can rewrite test_avg to run substantially faster, using pointers and pointer incrementing to access the elements in a given column of the array. To understand how to use a pointer for this purpose, we need to review pointer arithmetic. Suppose, as before, row_ptr is declared as a pointer to a specific row of scores. When we increment row_ptr (by rowptr++), the incrementing is done in units of the size of each row of scores, making rowptr point to the next row. Since row_ptr points to a particular row, (*row_ptr)[n] chooses the nth element in the row, as shown in Figure 8.8. All we need to do is initialize row_ptr to point to the first row, then loop by incrementing row_ptr.

test_avg has been rewritten in Figure 8.9 to take advantage of pointer indexing, and it runs substantially faster than the original version in Figure 8.7. We compiled and ran both of these versions on a DEC VAX 11/750 using an array with 10,000 rows. The direct array indexing version took 0.57 seconds and the pointer version took 0.42 seconds, a savings of 26 percent.

We can use pointers to process the rows as well as the columns, and Figure 8.10 is a routine that computes the average of each *row*. Its operation is even simpler than that of Figure 8.9. Again we declare the argu-

```
int scores [MAX _ STUDENTS][MAX TESTS]
int (*row-ptr)[MAX-TESTS] = scores;
```

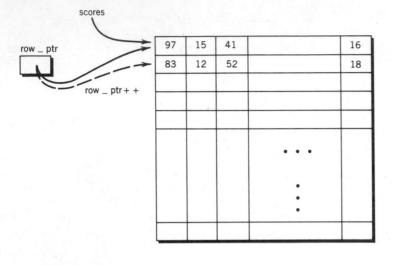

```
Let n = 2
sum + = (*row _ ptr + +) [h]
(1) INCREMENT sum by 15
(2) THEN increment row _ ptr
```

FIGURE 8.8 `row_ptr` initialized to column `n` of `scores`. Incrementing `row_ptr` causes it to point to the next row.

```
/*
 *  Compute the average of the scores on a given test - POINTER VERSION.
 */
double test_avg (scores, max, n)
int     scores[][MAX_TESTS],              /* pointer to first row of array */
        max,                              /* number of rows in the array */
        n;                                /* column to sum */
{
    long  sum = 0;                        /* column total */
    int   i,                              /* row index */
          (*row_ptr)[MAX_TESTS] = scores; /* pointer to first row */

    for (i = 0; i < max; i++)
      sum += (*row_ptr++)[n];
    return (double) sum / max;
}
```

FIGURE 8.9 Computing the average of a column of a two-dimensional array using a pointer to access the array elements.

```
/*
 *  Compute the average score of a student (row) using a pointer
 *  to the given row.
 */
double student_avg (scores, n)
int     scores[][MAX_TESTS],           /* 2D array of student scores */
        n;                             /* the row to average */
{
   int     *col_ptr = &scores[n][0];   /* pointer to first element */
   long    sum = 0;                     /* total so far */
   int     i;                           /* row index */

   for (i = 0; i < MAX_TESTS; i++)
     sum += *col_ptr++;
   return (double) sum / MAX_TESTS;
}
```

FIGURE 8.10 Compute the average of a row using a pointer to access the individual row values.

ment scores to be a two-dimensional array, and again we do not need to specify the size of the first dimension. Within the function, we use a pointer (called col_ptr) that points to the individual items (columns) in each *row*. Since it is pointing to individual ints, we declare it as a pointer to int and initialize it to point to the first element in row n of scores:

```
int     *col_ptr = &scores[n][0];
```

Then we march col_ptr through the elements of the given row, summing by adding the pointed-to value to sum:

```
sum += *col_ptr++;
```

In Figure 8.10 col_ptr is declared and initialized by

```
int *col_ptr = &scores[n][0];
```

We want col_ptr to point to the first element in the nth row of scores, and we could have done this equally well with the declaration

```
int     *col_ptr = scores[n];
```

At first, this seems a strange way to access a two-dimensional array such as scores, since we are using only a single array subscript. But the name of a two-dimensional array used with a single subscript is a pointer to the first element of the given *row*: scores[n] is a pointer to scores[n][0]. The forms are equivalent, and you can use whichever you prefer.

EXERCISES

8-6 Write a function, `reverse_print`, that prints the values in an array in reverse order, last row first and first row last. First, write it using the usual array subscripting; then rewrite it so that the rows are indexed with a pointer. Finally, rewrite it so that all elements are indexed with pointers. Which of the three versions is the fastest? □

8-7 Write a function, `sort_scores`, that takes two arguments: `scores`, a two-dimensional array of `int`s, and `n`, the column to sort on. The array should be sorted so that the `n`th column is sorted from low to high. □

8-8 [*Tricky!*] The function in Figure 8.9 initializes `row_ptr` to point to the first column of `scores` and uses `(*row_ptr)[n]` to get to the correct column. We can eliminate this indexing by initializing `row_ptr` to point directly to the specified column. Incrementing `row_ptr` using `row_ptr++` causes it to point to the row beginning with that column. (Remember, we are incrementing by `MAX_TESTS`.) The following declaration/initialization almost works. Fix it so that it does, and rewrite the function `test_avg` (Figure 8.9) in order to use it to traverse the elements in the column. (*Hint:* Cast the address so that it is the same type as `row_ptr`.)

```
int  (*row_ptr)[MAX_STUDENTS] = &scores[0][n];   /* pointer to nth col */
```

How much faster is this version? □

8.3

N-DIMENSIONAL ARRAYS

Three and higher dimensional arrays are generalizations of two-dimensional arrays. All multidimensional arrays can be declared, initialized, and subscripted in a similar way. For example,

```
int boards[3][4][5];
```

declares a three-dimensional array holding 60 elements organized into 3 two-dimensional arrays of 4 rows and 5 columns. In addition, `boards` is declared as a (constant) pointer to its first two-dimensional array. We can access the elements of `boards` using three subscripts; `boards[0][1][2]` refers to the third column of the second row of the first two-dimensional array.

Any multidimensional array can be initialized by giving a brace-enclosed list of elements. If any of these elements are arrays, their values can also be enclosed in braces. For example:

```
int class[2][3][2] =
    {  {  /* 1st 2D */
        {0, 1},             /* class[0][0][0],  class[0][0][1] */
        {2, 3},             /* class[0][1][0],  class[0][1][1] */
        {4, 5}  },          /* class[0][2][0],  class[0][2][1] */
    {  /* 2nd 2D */
        {6, 7},             /* class[1][0][0],  class[1][0][1] */
        {8, 9},             /* class[1][1][0],  class[1][1][1] */
        {10, 11} } };       /* class[1][2][0],  class[1][2][1] */
```

As with any array, the elements can also be provided in a list. The following initialization has the same effect as the previous one:

```
int class[2][3][2] = {0, 1, 2, 3, 4, 5, 6, 7, 8, 9, 10, 11};
```

When we pass an N-dimensional array to a function, we must supply all dimensions except the first. This is because when we pass an N-dimensional array as a parameter, we really pass a pointer to the first $N - 1$ dimensional array it contains. For example, we can declare a function print_it that expects to be passed boards using array indexing notation or using pointer notation:

```
void print_it(boards)                    void print_it(board_ptr)
int boards[][4][5];                      int (*board_ptr)[4][5];
{                                        {
    . . .              OR                    . . .
}                                        }
```

EXERCISE

8-9 Write a function to print the elements of a three-dimensional array. The elements should be grouped by the two-dimensional array they are contained in when they are printed. For example, the class array we initialized earlier would be printed as

```
0   1
2   3
4   5

6   7
8   9
10  11
```
□

8.3.1 N-DIMENSIONAL ARRAYS AND POINTERS

In C, any N-dimensional array is treated as if it is an array of $N-1$ dimensional arrays. A two-dimensional array, for example, is treated as an array of one-dimensional arrays, a three- or higher dimensional array is treated as an array of two-dimensional arrays, and so on. Regardless of the number of dimensions in it, however, the array is stored as a single one-dimensional array. The internal storage of `boards` is shown in Figure 8.11.

This internal organization makes it possible to traverse any multidimensional array using pointers, although the code can be confusing and hard to read when three-dimensional arrays or higher are traversed. As might be expected, pointer arithmetic involving a pointer to any N-dimensional array is done in terms of $N-1$-dimensional arrays. For example, we can initialize `board_ptr` as a pointer to the first two-dimensional array in `boards` with

```
int (*board_ptr)[4][5] = boards;
```

Subsequently incrementing `board_ptr` causes it to point to the next two-dimensional array in `boards`, as shown in Figure 8.12.

Since dereferencing a pointer to an array gives a pointer to the array's first element, and since `board_ptr` is a pointer to a two-dimensional array, `*board_ptr` refers to that two-dimensional array (really a pointer to its first row). For the same reason, `**board_ptr` refers to the first row in that array (really a pointer to its first element). This allows us to traverse three- and higher dimensional arrays using the same techniques we used to traverse two-dimensional arrays.

As with all array references, any N-dimensional array access is translated into a sequence of pointer additions and dereferences, with one addition and dereference for each dimension of the array. For example,

```
boards[1][2][2]
```

is translated by the compiler into the equivalent (and possibly a bit ominous) expression

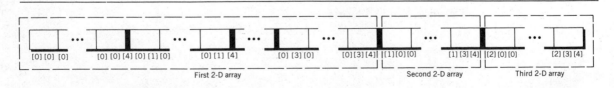

FIGURE 8.11 Storage layout for a three-dimensional array.

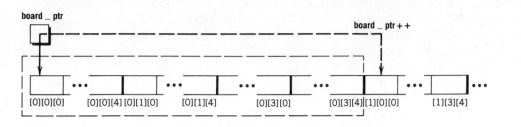

FIGURE 8.12 Incrementing a pointer to a two-dimensional array

```
*( * (*(boards + 1) + 2) + 2)
```

Try tracing through this by hand to see what is going on.

EXERCISES

8-10 Write a function that sums the elements in a three-dimensional array using a single pointer to traverse the array. How much faster is this than using three-dimensional subscripting? □

8-11 Repeat the previous exercise for a higher dimensioned array (choosing its dimensions yourself). Explain why the function is substantially faster when pointers are used. Can you generalize your function to work on any *N*-dimensional array? □

8-12 Write a function to print the total values of each of the two-dimensional arrays contained in `class`. There should be one value output for each two-dimensional array in `class`. □

8-13 Repeat the previous exercise using pointer subscripting. Is this version significantly faster? Why or why not? □

8.4

ARRAYS OF POINTERS — RAGGED ARRAYS

In two-dimensional arrays, the same number of elements is contained in each row. But if we use arrays of pointers, we can create arrays with rows of varying lengths, called *ragged arrays*.

One common and important use of ragged arrays is in defining a table of strings. Instead of making each entry in the table a fixed number of characters, we can make it a pointer to a string of varying length. By supplying a list of character strings, the compiler initializes the elements of an array of pointers. For example,

```
static char *days[] =
            {
                        "monday",
                        "tuesday",
                        "wednesday",
                        "thursday",
                        "friday",
                        "saturday",
                        "sunday"
            };
```

declares days to be an array of seven pointers to characters, allocates space for each of the listed string constants, and assigns to each element of days a pointer to the corresponding string. The result of this declaration is shown in Figure 8.13. The compiler determines the number of elements in days, allocating enough space for the required number of pointers and allowing us to omit the subscript from the declaration.

The elements of an array of pointers are accessed in the same way as elements of an array of any other type. Figure 8.14 contains a function that is passed a table of character strings, along with the number of entries in the table, and prints the pointed-to strings, one per line. The printing is done by passing printf the next table entry, table[i], a pointer to a character string.

An element in an array of pointers can be used as if it were a pointer to the first element in a row of a two-dimensional array, allowing us to use two-dimensional array subscripting even though table was declared to be a one-dimensional array. The type of table is "array of pointers to char." table[0] is the first character pointer in the array. Adding one to table[0] gives a pointer to the second element in the row. More generally, table[i]+j is a pointer to the jth character in the string pointed to by table[i]. To access the jth character, we write either *(table[i] + j) or the equivalent, table[i][j], as shown in Figure 8.15. For example, since table[0] is a pointer to monday we can access the 'n' by table[0][2].

EXERCISES

8-14 Write a function, print_sub_tab, that prints the ith thru jth characters in each row of a table of character strings. What might such a function be useful for? □

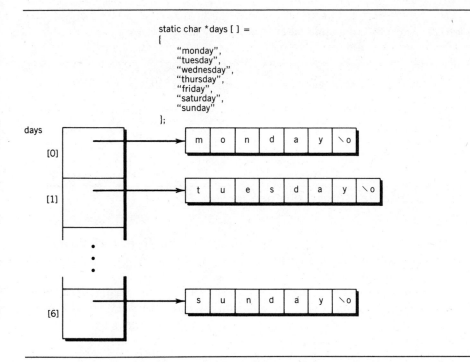

FIGURE 8.13 Compile-time initialization of an array of character strings.

```
/*
 *  Print a table of character strings, one per line.
 */
void print_tab(table, n)
char    *table[];                   /* table of pointers to strings */
int     n;                          /* number of elements in the table */
{
  int   i;

  for (i = 0; i < n; i++)
    printf(" %s\n", table [i]);
}
```

FIGURE 8.14 Print a table of n character strings, one per line.

8-15 Write a function, print_tab_len, that prints the length of each character string in a table of character stirngs. □

8-16 Write a function, reverse_tab, that reverses each of the strings in a table of character strings. (*Hint*: use strrev from Chapter 6 to reverse the individual strings.) □

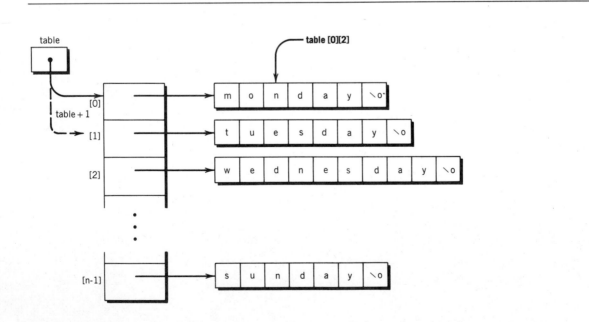

FIGURE 8.15 Accessing an individual character using an array of pointers to character strings.

8.4.1 USING POINTERS TO TRAVERSE RAGGED ARRAYS

As with all arrays, the name of an array of pointers is a pointer to the array's first element. When we pass an array of pointers as a parameter to a function, we are really passing a pointer to the array's first element, in this case, a pointer to a pointer. We can use this pointer to traverse the array in the same way we have used pointers to traverse any other array.

As an illustration of the use of pointers for traversing a ragged array, Figure 8.16 contains a version of `print_tab` (see Figure 8.14) that uses a pointer to traverse the array.

To simplify the constructions, we use the `typedef` mechanism, first mentioned in Chapter 6, to define a new type, `CHARPTR`, a pointer to the first character in a string:

```
typedef char * CHARPTR;
```

Figure 8.17 illustrates how this version of `print_tab` works. When `print_tab` is called, `tab_ptr` is initialized to point to the first element in the passed array. We also initialize a local pointer, `endptr`, to point to the last item in the table, using the assignment

```
CHARPTR *endptr = tab_ptr + (n-1); /* pointer to last table entry*/
```

```
/*
 *  Print a table of strings, one row per line - POINTER VERSION.
 */
void print_tab(tab_ptr, n)
CHARPTR    *tab_ptr;                      /* pointer to table of strings */
int        n;                             /* number of elements in table */
{
   CHARPTR  *end_ptr = tab_ptr + (n-1);   /* pointer to last table entry */

   while (tab_ptr <= end_ptr)
     printf("%s\n", *tab_ptr++);
}
```

FIGURE 8.16 Print an array of character strings, using a pointer to traverse the array.

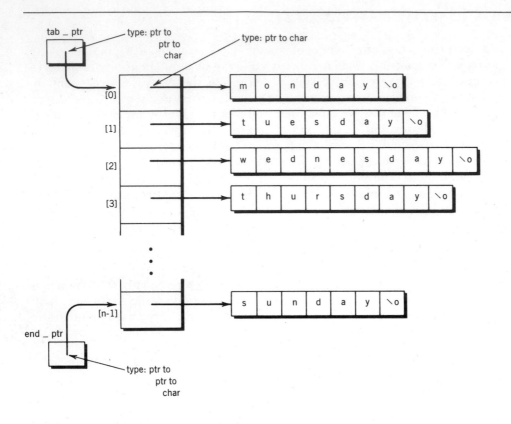

FIGURE 8.17 `tab_ptr` points to the first element in the string table, and `end_ptr` to the last. Printing continues while `tab_ptr` is less than or equal to `end_ptr`.

Printing is controlled by a `while` loop that exits after `tab_ptr` has reached `end_ptr`. `tab_ptr` is incremented as each of the array elements is accessed. The expression

```
printf("%s\n", *tab_ptr++);
```

is equivalent to

```
printf("%s\n", *tab_ptr);
tab_ptr++;                      /* because ++ binds tighter than *  */
```

This expression prints a string (using the `%s` format), the string pointed to by `*tab_ptr`. It is a common mistake to try printing using

```
printf("%s\n", tab_ptr);
```

that is, the string pointed to by `tab_ptr`. This does not work because `tab_ptr` does not point to a string. Rather, its type is "pointer to pointer to char" (that is, `CHARPTR`) so we must dereference `tab_ptr` to get the string.

The code in Figure 8.16 deserves special study, and you should try tracing it out by hand. Drawing your own diagrams of the actions of the pointers and how they are incremented is very helpful in understanding a piece of code and in writing your own functions.

EXERCISES

8-17 Using normal array subscripting, write a function,

```
search_tab (char_tab, target)
```

that takes two arguments — a table of character strings, `char_tab`, and a character string, `target`. The function searches the `char_tab` for `target` and returns a pointer to the matching string in the table. If `target` is not in the table, a null pointer (`NULL`) is returned. □

8-18 Rewrite the previous exercise using a pointer to index the string table. □

8-19 Could the `printf` statement in Figure 8.16 be replaced by the following statements?

```
printf("%s\n", **tab_ptr);        /* note the DOUBLE dereferencing */
tab_ptr++;
```

Why or why not? □

8-20 Write a function, `month_name`, that takes a single integer argument and returns a pointer to the associated month name. The month names should be kept in a `static` table of character strings local to the function. □

8-21 Write a function, `tab_size`, that computes the number of bytes a table of character strings is using. □

8.5

DYNAMIC STRING ALLOCATION

In the arrays of pointers used so far, each array element was initialized to point to a character string at compile time. The task of allocating space for the pointed-to string was left to the compiler when all the strings were known at compile time, such as for tables containing strings for the days of the week (as in Figure 8.13). In contrast, if the table's entries are not known at compile time, we have to make some assumptions about the maximum size of a string.

Extending the idea of storing varying length static strings (those that are defined at compile time), we want to write a program that allows us to read and store the strings by placing a pointer to the string into the next location in an array of string pointers. One way to do this is to define a two-dimensional array of `chars` and copy the newly-entered string into the next location. If `nxt_string` is a pointer to the next row in the array and `line` is an array of characters, we can read the line using `get_line` (from Chapter 3) and then use `strcpy` from the standard string library to copy the string, somewhat like this:

```
char line[MAXLINE],                    /* the input line */
     strtbl [NLINES][MAXLINE],         /* array of NLINES by MAXLINE */
     (*nxt_string)[MAXLINE] = strtbl;  /* ptr to an array of MAXLINE chars */
int  nchars;                           /* returned from "get_line" */
     . . .
nchars = get_line (line, MAXLINE);
strcpy (*nxt_string++, line);
     . . .
```

But this is unsatisfactory for one important reason: *each* row of the array is the same length, large enough to hold the maximum-length string. Since most strings are shorter than the maximum, we waste space in each row.

strtbl

MAXLINE

m	o	n	d	a	y	\o				
t	u	e	s	d	a	y	\o			
w	e	d	n	e	s	d	a	y	\o	
f	r	i	d	a	y	\o				
s	a	t	u	r	d	a	y	\o		
s	u	n	d	a	y	\o				

NLINES

Instead, we use a technique similar to that shown in Figure 8.13. strtbl will be an array of pointers to char, and each string will be the exact length needed. We perform this feat by using a predefined function from the standard library – that is, we ask the operating system to give us a block of storage large enough to hold the string.

The function used to do this is malloc (for memory allocation). malloc takes a single argument, the number of characters of storage needed (type unsigned int), and returns a pointer (type char *) to a block at least as big as requested, with all alignment constraints satisfied. If there is not enough space, malloc returns the NULL pointer, defined in the include file *stdio.h*.

We can use malloc because get_line returns the number of characters entered, and this is the amount of space we need (we need to add one because get_line does not count the trailing null). Figure 8.18 shows how we call malloc and the block of storage returned.

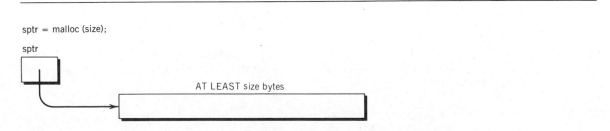

```
sptr = malloc (size);
```
sptr

AT LEAST size bytes

FIGURE 8.18   A call to malloc returns a block of at least the requested size.

Using `malloc` is simple. We read the line, request the needed size, assign the pointer to the newly allocated storage returned by `malloc` to a character pointer, and then copy the input line to the pointed-to space. We also want to be sure that we declare `malloc` properly; it is a function returning `char *`.

```
char *malloc(),                        /* always declare malloc */
     *sptr,                            /* ptr to block returned from malloc */
     *strtbl[NLINES];                  /* table of pointers to strings */
int  i = 0, nchars;
    . . .
nchars = get_line(line, MAXLINE);      /* get a line, return chars read */
sptr = malloc((unsigned) nchars + 1);
if (sptr != NULL)                      /* test return from malloc */
{
  strcpy (sptr, line);                 /* copy to space pointed to by "sptr" */
  strtbl[i++] = sptr;                  /* put pointer into the array */
}
     . . .                             /* continue */
```

If `malloc` fails (which can certainly occur in small microcomputers but is unlikely in large address-space machines), we have to decide what to do on a case-by-case basis. Figure 8.19 is a program that reads strings (until end of file), allocating space using `malloc`. The string is copied into the newly allocated space, and a pointer to the string is placed in the next location in the string table, building on the program fragment above. In this program, when `malloc` fails, we stop reading input, print a warning, and then print the contents of the string table.[1] We have coded the test of the return from `malloc` a little more compactly than in the previous example, doing the `malloc` within the `while` loop's condition, but the result is the same: if we run out of dynamic space, we stop what we are doing and print what we have.

EXERCISES

8-22 Modify the insertion sort program of Chapter 1 to work with strings instead of integers. □

8-23 Modify the quicksort program of Chapter 5 to work with strings instead of numbers. □

8-24 Write a program, *tail*, that prints the last *n* lines of its input, using the pro-

---

[1] `malloc` is usually written on top of an operating system utility; in UNIX this is `sbrk`. Managing pools of dynamic memory is an important topic in computer science practice, which we cannot hope to go in detail here. In Chapter 12, we will suggest some other techniques for managing free storage and for returning unneeded space to the free storage pool.

```
/*
 *  Read strings and keep a pointer to them in a string table.
 */
#include <stdio.h>
#include <strings.h>              /* may be differently named */

#define  MAXLINE      80         /* chars per line */
#define  NLINES      100         /* lines to store */

main ()
{
 int    i = 0, j,                /* indexes into "strtbl" array */
        nchars;                  /* number of chars read */
 char   line[MAXLINE],           /* current input line */
        *malloc(),               /* always declare malloc */
        *sptr,                   /* pointer to block returned from malloc */
        *strtbl[NLINES];         /* string table - array of pointers to strings */


/* Get a line at a time, terminating on EOF, or malloc failing. */

    while ( (nchars = get_line (line, MAXLINE))  != EOF &&
            (sptr = malloc ((unsigned) nchars + 1)) != NULL )
    {
        strcpy (sptr, line);        /* copy to space pointed to by "sptr" */
        strtbl[i++] = sptr;         /* copy pointer into the array */
    }

/* Print the table, one line per line. */

    if (sptr == NULL)               /* malloc has failed */
      printf("\nOut of internal storage.  Here's what you've got so far:\n");
    putchar('\n');
    for (j = 0; j < i; j++)
        printf ("%s\n", strtbl[j]);
}
```

FIGURE 8.19 A program that uses dynamically allocated space for arbitrary length strings (up to MAXLINE characters).

gram in Figure 8.19 as a model (*n* is a program constant). Make reasonable assumptions about the maximum line length and the maximum number of lines in the input (using the constants MAXLINE and NLINES, respectively). Be sure to test the return from malloc and decide on a suitable policy should it fail. □

8-25 Write a program, *reverse*, that prints out its input in reverse order; the first lines read are the last lines printed. Make sure that *reverse* does something reasonable if there are more lines in the input than were expected or if the program runs out of memory. How might this program be used? □

8.6

TYPE DECLARATIONS

We have introduced several new data types in this chapter (pointers to arrays, arrays of pointers, and pointers to pointers), and have showed how to declare variables of these types. We conclude this chapter by explaining the rationale behind C's declaration syntax and showing how to declare even more complex data types.

8.6.1 DECLARATORS

The types of variables, parameters, and function return values are declared with type declarations that consist of a basic type followed by a *declarator*. For example, in the declaration

```
char (*funcptr)();
```

char is the basic type and (*funcptr)() is the declarator. A type declaration specifies the type of the identifier contained in the declarator. Here, funcptr is the identifier contained in the declarator, and it is declared as a pointer to a function returning a character.

The simplest possible declarator is an identifier and is used to declare a variable of one of the basic types.

```
char x;                /*  a character */
```

Prefacing the identifier with * declares a pointer; following the identifier with () declares a function; and following the identifier with [] declares an array.

```
char *ptr;             /* a pointer to a char */
char tab[MAX];         /* an array of chars */
char func();           /* a function returning a char */
```

We can declare more complex types, such as pointers to functions and arrays of pointers, by combining the pieces used to form the previous declarators. For example,

```
char *tab[MAX];      /* an array of pointers to char */
char *func();        /* a function returning pointer to char */
char (*func_ptr)();  /* pointer to function returning char */
char (*row_ptr)[10]; /* pointer to an array of 10 characters */
```

When declarators are combined, * has lower precedence than either () or [], so to declare a pointer to an array or function, parentheses must be used to override the normal precedence.

Sometimes more complex declarations are needed. For example, suppose we want to plot each of the math library functions over the same range. One way to do this is to have a table of pointers to these functions and iterate through this table, generating points (using `gen_points` from Chapter 5) and then plotting them. The table must be declared as an array of pointers to functions returning `doubles`. If we used a pointer to index the table, its type would be even more complex (a pointer to a pointer to a function returning a `double`). Fortunately, arbitrarily complex declarations can be composed from the simpler declarations shown above. As an illustration, we will write a program that does what we have just described — create a table of pointers to functions from the math library and then index through this table, calling `gen_points` on each function in turn.

The table is an array of pointers to functions returning `doubles`. That is, each element in the array is a pointer to a function that returns a `double`. Here is the correct declaration for this table:

```
static double (*funcptr[])() =    /* table of function pointers */
{
   sin, cos, log, tan
};
```

To declare complex types, it is often helpful to think of the English description of an identifier's type as being composed of several pieces. Each piece of the description is either a basic type, "an array of," "a pointer to," or "a function returning." For example, our table is

an array of   *pointers to*   *functions returning*   *doubles*

The base type of the identifier is the final piece of the description. To compose the declarator, we work through the description from left to right, finding the C declarator for each piece. When we have declarators for each piece, we again go from left to right, substituting each declarator for the identifier in the declarator to its right, finishing when only a single declarator remains. Figure 8.20 illustrates the process for several different type declarations. Because the precedence of `*` is less than that of either `()` or `[]`, pointer declarators must be parenthesized when they are substituted in another declarator.

Assuming we have declared and initialized `funcptr` correctly, `gen_points` can be used to generate points for the various functions. The call to `gen_points` is in a loop and looks like this:

```
gen_points( *funcptr[i], xvals, yvals, 0.1, XMAX, MAXPTS);
```

where `xvals` and `yvals` are arrays of `doubles`, `XMAX` is the maximum *x* value to be plotted (0.1 is the minimum), and `MAXPTS` is the number of points to be plotted. Since `funcptr[i]` is a pointer to a function, dere-

(a) *an array of pointers to* character

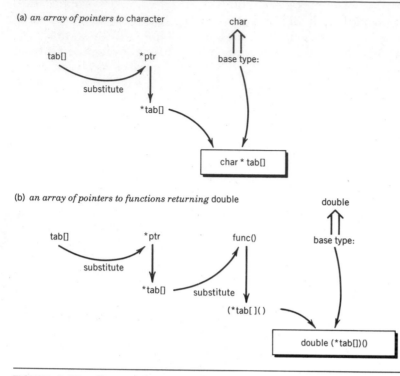

(b) *an array of pointers to functions returning* double

FIGURE 8.20 Composing complex declarations.

ferencing it with `*funcptr[i]` calls the pointed-to function. The entire program is shown in Figure 8.21.

Since we can compose arbitrarily complex type declarations, we should also be able to read and understand them. The process used for generating an English description from a declarator is illustrated in Figure 8.22. The type of a declarator is determined by finding the type of its innermost declarator, substituting a new identifier for the innermost declarator, and repeating the process for the declarator resulting from the substitution. The identifier's type is determined when the resulting declarator is a single identifier. The innermost declarator is the identifier and an immediately following `[]` or `()`, or, if neither of these is present, an immediately preceding `*`. Any parentheses around the innermost declarator can be ignored once its type is determined.

Although the compiler can process arbitrarily complex declarations, most people cannot. To keep declarations readable, it is a good idea to use `typedef` when declaring types more complex than arrays of pointers and pointers to arrays. The following is a more readable way to declare our

```
/*
 *  Generate a table of function values using pointers to functions.
 */
#include <stdio.h>
#include <math.h>

#define   MAXPTS        100            /* max points to plot */
#define   XMAX          10.0           /* max value of X */
#define   MAXFUNCTS       4

main()
{
  static double (*funcptr[])() =       /* table of function names */
    {
      sin, cos, log, tan
    };
  double   xvals[MAXPTS], yvals[MAXPTS];   /* function vals */
  void     gen_points();                   /* Chapter 5 */
  int      i, j;                           /* table/array indexes */

  for (i=0; i<MAXFUNCTS; i++)
  {
    gen_points( funcptr[i], xvals, yvals, 0.1, XMAX, MAXPTS);
    printf("Function: %d\n\n", i);          /* print vals for this function */
    for (j=0; j<MAXPTS; j++)
      printf("%8.4 f\t%8.4 f\n",xvals[j], yvals[j]);
  }
}
```

FIGURE 8.21   A program that generates points from a table of function names.

table of pointers to functions returning doubles.

```
typedef double (*PFD)();  /* PFD - ptr to function returning a double */
  . . .
static PFD funcptr[] =     /* a table of pointers to functions */
{
  sin, cos, log, tan
};
```

EXERCISES

8-26 Modify the plotting program to use a pointer to traverse funcptr. That pointer is a pointer to a pointer to a function returning a double. □

8-27 Write a function that walks through a table of pointers to functions, exe-

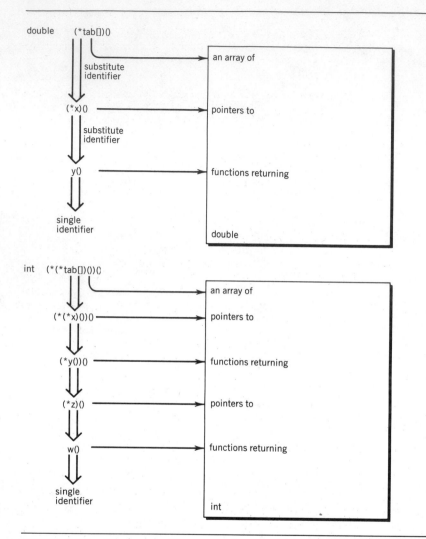

FIGURE 8.22 Understanding complex declarations.

cuting each function in turn, until one of them returns zero or all of the functions have been executed. □

8-28 How do you declare a pointer to a pointer to a function returning a pointer to an `int`. An array of pointers to pointers to characters? □

8-29 The program in Figure 8.21 declared a `funcptr` to be an array, with each element a pointer to a function returning a `double`. Write the declaration for a function `df` that returns a pointer to an array of `doubles` (it is not possible for a function to return an array; instead, it must be written to return a pointer to an array). □

8-30 For each of the following, state whether it is a legal declaration; if so, state the type of the variable or function.

```
int     (*intptr)()[100];
void    (*funcptr[100])();
void    *funcptr[100]();
float   *funcptr[]();  □
```

8.6.2 SPECIFYING TYPES IN CASTS

We have learned that when casting a value from one type to another, the type to cast to must be specified. Specifying a type in a cast is done similarly to specifying a type in a declaration, except that the identifier is omitted. For example,

```
(int *) x;
```

casts `x` into a pointer to an integer because

```
int  *name;
```

declares a pointer to an integer.

As a more complex example, consider passing a null pointer to a function that expects a pointer to a function returning `int`. For the parameter-passing mechanism to work correctly, the null pointer must be cast to a pointer to a function returning `int`. The cast is obtained by writing the declaration for a pointer to a function returning `int`:

```
int (*func_ptr)();
```

removing the identifier, and enclosing the type specifier that is left in parentheses:

```
(int (*)()) NULL
```

Type specifiers for casts, such as the one shown above, can be difficult to read, so it is more understandable to use `typedef`:

```
typedef int (*PFI)();
   . . .
(PFI) NULL
```

EXERCISE

8-31 How would you cast an integer into a pointer to an array of pointers to functions? Why would anyone want to do this?   □

POINTERS AND ARRAYS

We have covered several new topics in this chapter. It is easy to be overwhelmed by the complexity and subtleties of arrays, pointers, arrays of pointers, pointers to rows of an array, pointers to columns of an array, and pointers to pointers. Here are some suggestions to keep you "pointed" in the right direction.

- Use normal array subscripting when working with arrays for the first time. Then, if your program is not as speedy as you would like it to be, you can switch to pointer indexing. The overriding purpose of using pointers for array indexing is speed. You should be able to understand their use in existing programs, however, so you cannot expect to avoid them entirely.

- Use arrays of pointers to strings instead of two-dimensional arrays when the strings vary in length. `malloc` should be used to allocate space for the strings, saving a bit of otherwise wasted space for each string. Remember that when you declare an array of pointers, space is not allocated automatically for what those pointers will point to.

- Always test the return from `malloc`. Failing to do so can create serious problems, usually causing the operating system to terminate your program when you attempt to assign to space using a pointer to NULL. It is possible that you cannot do anything reasonable when the system has no dynamic space remaining, but the choice of terminating the program ought to be yours. The general rule is that lower-level routines, those that call `malloc`, should signal the caller that there is a problem. The calling party then handles the error.

- Use `typedef` to keep declarations and casts readable. Even if you can understand a complex declaration, many of your program's readers will not be able to.

CHAPTER 9

CONSTRUCTED DATA TYPES

We have already extensively used one type of programmer-constructed data type — arrays. However, a limitation of arrays is that all of the elements must be the same underlying type (or at least each must be a type that requires the same amount of storage). In this chapter we examine three new ways of representing collections of values — enumeration types, structures, and unions. We use structures to build a small data base of employee names, numbers, and addresses. The chapter concludes by using all of C's constructed data types in the implementation of a lexical scanner, a collection of functions that can be used to help parse a program's input.

9.1

ENUMERATION TYPES

When a variable can have only one of a set of values, we may use the *enumeration type* facility to specify the possible values of the variable.[1] We define an enumeration type by giving the keyword enum followed by an optional *type designator* and a brace-enclosed list of values.

[1] Enumerated types are a late addition to the language, and are not supported by many compilers, especially those available on small, personal computers. They are still worth studying, however, as this situation is changing rapidly.

An enumeration type that allows only the days of the week is defined by

```
enum Days
{
    sunday, monday, tuesday, wednesday, thursday, friday, saturday
};
```

Internally, these are defined as constants with an integer value equal to their position in the list: sunday is zero, monday is one, and so on. Of course, these can also be defined with #defines, but enum is an easier, more compact method.

The values of an enumeration type may not be numerical; they follow the rules for identifiers. We can, however, associate a specific integer value with a value of an enumeration type by following the type value with an equal sign and an integer:

```
enum Days
{
    tuesday = 2, wednesday, monday = 1, thursday = 4,
    friday, saturday, sunday
};
```

The associated integer values continue from the assignment. The previous declaration associates tuesday with two, wednesday with three, friday with five, and so on.

This declaration of an enumeration type defines a new programmer-constructed type called enum Days. To declare values of this type, we follow the type designator (enum Days) with the variable names.

```
enum Days  day1, day2, all_days[7];
```

After this declaration, day1 and day2 are type enum Days and all_days is an array of seven enum Days. They may take on only the values in the definition of the type. The following assignments are legal:

```
day1 = monday; day2 = tuesday; all_days[0] = sunday;
```

while assignments such as

```
day1 = 1.0; day2 = 5; all_days[0] = 'A';
```

are considered illegal.

Enumerated types are not integers; to use them as integers, we must first cast them to int. Figure 9.1 is a program illustrating the declaration and use of an enumeration type. The main program assigns an initial value to day1, the day after it to day2, and the day before it to day3. We use two functions to determine the day after and the day before. The first function, day_after, takes an argument of type enum Days and returns the day after (modulo the number of days). For example, the `day_after(saturday)` is `sunday` and the `day_after(sunday)` is monday. We compute the next day by converting the current day to an `int` and then adding one, modulo the number of days in a week. We then cast this result back to the appropriate type, `enum Days`. The cast converts the integer zero back to `sunday`, one back to `monday`, and so on.

The other function, `day_before`, is similar, returning the day before its argument. We have to be careful, however, that we do not take the modulus of a negative number. The only time a negative number occurs is when we find the predecessor of `sunday` (zero), in which case we should return the `enum Days` cast of six, or `saturday`. We can do this by testing specifically for `sunday` or by testing the sign of the result of the arithmetic. We chose the latter for no strong reason.

We use enumeration types because they allow for more descriptive names and for even greater separation of functionality from the underlying implementation than defined constants. Although they do not have the full range of uses that enumerated types in other languages have, they are still quite useful. One useful application of enumeration types is in error returns from functions. A function can return a value that indicates the nature of an error. One specific example is an input validator which can return an enumeration type, indicating such errors as values less than some minimum, values greater than some maximum, and so on, as the following program fragment shows. Another function translates the enumerated value into an error message, as in `print_day` in Figure 9.1.

```
enum Errors
{
  vallow, valhigh, valok, . . .
};
    . . .
enum Errors verify(value, min, max)        /* validate "value" */
long  value, min, max;
{
    . . .
  if (value < min)
    return vallow;
  if (value > max)
    return valhigh;
  else
    return valok;
}
```

EXERCISES

9-1 The functions `day_after` and `day_before` in Figure 9.1 are quite short. Rewrite them as macros. □

```
/*
 * Illustrate use of enumeration types.
 */
#define  NUMDAYS     7

enum Days
{
    sunday, monday, tuesday, wednesday, thursday, friday, saturday
};

main ()
{
  enum Days      day1, day2, day3,
                 day_before (), day_after ();
  void           print_day();

  day1 = sunday;
  day2 = day_after (day1);
  day3 = day_before (day1);

  printf ("The day after "), print_day (day1);
  printf (" is: "), print_day (day2);
  printf ("\nAnd the day before is: "), print_day (day3);
  putchar ('\n');
}


/* Return the successor of the given day. */

enum Days day_after (day)
enum Days day;
{
    return (enum Days) (((int) day + 1) % NUMDAYS);
}


/* Return the predecessor of the given day */

enum Days day_before (day)
enum Days day;
{
  int prev;

  prev = ((int) day - 1) % NUMDAYS;
  return (prev < 0) ? (enum Days) (NUMDAYS - 1) : (enum Days) prev;
}
```

FIGURE 9.1 Sample program illustrating enumeration types.

```
/* Print the string corresponding to the day */

void print_day (day)
enum Days     day;
{
  int           day_index = (int) day;
  static char  * days[] =
  {
    "sunday", "monday", "tuesday", "wednesday",
    "thursday", "friday", "saturday"
  };

 if (day_index < 0 || day_index >= NUMDAYS)
   printf ("**ERROR**");
 else
   printf ("%s", days[day_index]);
}
```

FIGURE 9.1 (continued)

9-2 Extend the macros of the previous exercise into more general predecessor and successor macros of any enumerated type (assuming that the values of the enumeration type represent the integers continuously from 0 to $n-1$. □

9-3 Write an input validator for a payroll program. The validator should check for hours and rate of pay within bounds. This requires writing a variation of `print_day` from Figure 9.1 to print an appropriate message for out-of-range values. □

9-4 How can we define a `boolean` enumerated type? Is an enumerated `boolean` type preferrable to using `typedef` or `#define`? Why or why not? □

9.2

STRUCTURES

If we need to combine data of different types into a single object, we cannot use an array. Instead, we use the data-packaging mechanisms of structures. We introduce and define structures here, and discuss their use more thoroughly in the next chapter. Structures are one way of making a programming language *extensible*. That is, defining complex data objects by packaging them together and giving them a new type name allows the language to operate on data types other than those originally defined in the language. It is a modern and powerful development in language and program design that we use extensively throughout this book.

9.2.1 STRUCTURE DEFINITION

If we have different pieces of information that must be kept together as a single data record, we do this with a structure (similar, for example, to Pascal's records). A structure consists of the keyword `struct` and the declarations of the names and data types that are part of the structure. In addition, we can give the structure a name and declare variables to be of the structure type.

As an example, a single data record in a personnel data base might consist of an employee number, name, and address. We can define a structure to hold this information by first declaring a new type, `struct p_record`, consisting of the three fields `emp_number` (an `int`), `name`, and `address` (character arrays)

```
struct p_record
{
   int    emp_number;
   char   name [MAX];
   char   address [MAX];
};
```

This looks like the following diagram:

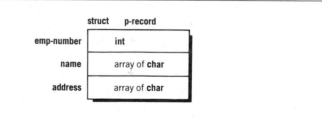

Now that the type `struct p_record` has been defined, we can declare variables that have that type:

```
struct p_record   next_person, old_person;
```

The name of the structure, `p_record` in this case, is called the *structure tag*. Remember, after these declarations `struct p_record` is a type and `next_person` and `old_person` are variables. The type of `next_person` and `old_person` is "struct p_record."

9.2.2 FIELD SELECTION

Variables of a structure type are used as if they were an ordinary type; that is, we can read their value, assign to them, pass them as parameters to functions, and return them as values of a function.[2] Since there are multiple fields in a structure, we need a means of selecting the appropriate one. To do this, we use the field selection operator '.'. We access the various fields by giving the variable name, the dot operator, and the appropriate field. Using the earlier declaration of the variable `next_person`, here is how we would assign values to the fields:

```
next_person.emp_number = 15263;
strcpy (next_person.name, "smallberg, dave");
strcpy (next_person.address, "1449 N. Capri Dr. Nerd City, USA 07886");
```

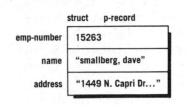

A field of a structure can be any type a variable can be, including other structures and arrays. Interestingly, the field names are in a separate "name class" from those of variables, so that a field name can be the same as an existing variable name. The declaration

```
struct point
{
    long x, y;
} x;
```

is valid. We select the `x` field of `struct point` `x` in the normal way:

```
x.x = 1234;
```

9.2.3 ASSIGNING, INITIALIZING, AND COMPARING STRUCTURES

For assignment and comparison purposes, structures behave virtually the same as ordinary variables. That is, in addition to assigning to an individual field, we may assign to the entire structure. If `p1` and `p2` have both been declared as variables of the same structure type, the following operations are valid:

[2] Some compilers do not allow structures to be passed as arguments to functions or as the value of a function. In this case, we can use a pointer to the structure instead.

Statement	Meaning
p1 = p2	Assign p2 to p1.
p1 == p2	Compare all fields of p1 and p2.
	Return one if they are equal, zero otherwise
p1 != p2	Compare all fields of p1 and p2.
	Return one if they are not equal, zero otherwise

Structures may be initialized at the time they are declared, with the same restrictions as for arrays; automatic structures may not be initialized, but statics and externals can be. If a structure is not specifically initialized, its fields are initialized in the same manner as if they were separately declared variables. That is, they may be initialized to zero (for statics and externals) or they may contain unknown random values for automatics. As always, we should initialize any variable before it is used.

To initialize the fields of a structure, specify each field's value in brackets after a variable of the structure type is declared. In this example, we have declared next_person to be a static struct p_record.

```
static struct p_record next_person =
{
    1234,                                 /* emp_number */
    "swenson, marcy",                     /* name */
    "7953 Jupiter Ave. L.A., CA. 90035"   /* address */
};
```

The emp_number field is initialized to 1234, the name field to "swenson, marcy", and the address field to "7953 Jupiter Ave. L.A., CA. 90035." Since these are string constants, they are automatically terminated with a null character.

9.2.4 STRUCTURES AS FUNCTION ARGUMENTS

Structures may be passed as arguments to functions. Unlike array names, which are always pointers to the start of the array, structure names are not pointer types. They are passed to functions by the usual parameter-passing mechanism: the entire structure is copied to the function. As a result, changes to a structure argument within a function are not reflected in changes in the actual parameter from the calling routine. This mechanism can be overriden, as with single-value parameters, by passing an address.

Some compilers do not allow us to pass structures as parameters. In this case, a pointer to a structure may always be passed, so that structures may still be used as function arguments or function values. It is faster to pass a pointer (since the structure does not have to be copied), so this is often done even when the compiler supports passing entire structures to functions. Figure 9.2 shows two versions of a small function that prints the fields of a `struct p_record`. The first version passes an entire structure and is called by

```
print_struct(next_record);
```

The second passes a pointer to the structure and is called by passing the address of the structure.

```
print_struct(&next_record);
```

Parentheses are needed when dereferencing the pointer to the structure because the dot field selection operator binds tighter than dereferencing.

The three `printf` statements in Figure 9.2b dereference the pointer to the structure, and then select the appropriate field. Dereferencing a pointer and then selecting a field of the pointed-to structure are so common that another shorthand notation is provided, a right arrow, made up of a minus sign and a "greater than" symbol: ->. The three `printf` statements in Figure 9.2b could also have been written

```
printf("Employee:\t%d\n", person_ptr->emp_number);
printf("Name:\t%s\n",     person_ptr->name);
printf("Address:\t%s\n",  person_ptr->address);
```

```
void print_struct (person)
struct p_record     person;
{
    printf("Employee:\t%d\n", person.emp_number);
    printf("Name:\t%s\n",     person.name);
    printf("Address:\t%s\n",  person.address);
}
```

(a) Function `print_struct` *that works on a copy of the structure*

```
void print_struct (person_ptr)
struct p_record     * person_ptr;
{
    printf("Employee:\t%d\n", (* person_ptr).emp_number);
    printf("Name:\t%s\n",     (* person_ptr).name);
    printf("Address:\t%s\n",  (* person_ptr).address);
}
```

(b) Function `print_struct` *that uses a pointer to a structure*

FIGURE 9.2 Two versions of a function that prints the fields of a structure. (*a*) The structure is copied to the function. (*b*) A pointer to the structure is passed to the function.

The two forms are equivalent:

```
person_ptr->emp_number     is equivalent to     (* person_ptr).emp_number
```

EXERCISES

9-5 Complex numbers are defined as having a real and an imaginary part. Write a structure definition for a type `struct complex`, and write functions for the four mathematical operations add, subtract, multiply, and divide. □

9-6 Define a structure type, `struct point`, for two-dimensional space coordinates (consisting of real values of x and y). Write a function, `distance`, that computes the distance between two `struct points`. □

9-7 Define a structure type, `struct date`, that describes a date. It should have integer fields for month, day, and year. Write functions to print a date in a nice format, to determine if a date is valid, and to determine the number of days between two `struct dates`. □

9.2.5 ARRAYS OF STRUCTURES

From Chapters 3 and 8, we know that we can have arrays of any type. Specifically, we can have arrays of structures and use them as we would any other array type. They may be initialized if they are external or static, but not if they are automatic.

We illustrate arrays of structures by defining a table of the personnel records in the previous section. Each element in the array is a `struct p_record` containing an `emp_number`, `name`, and `address` field. The array is declared just as we would any other array. We can declare `p_list` as an array of `SIZE` `struct p_records` with

```
struct p_record    p_list[SIZE];
```

Here is what `p-list` looks like:

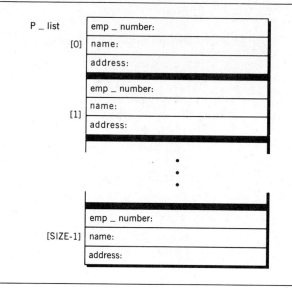

Since `p_list` is an array, we use the usual array-accessing methods to reach individual records and then the dot field selection operator to reach fields. For example, to assign to the fields of `p_list[2]`, we write

```
p_list[2].emp_number = 1234;
strcpy (p_list[2].name,  "seagull, jonathan livingston");
strcpy (p_list[2].address,  "pylon 87a, santa monica pier, california");
```

We can also initialize an array of structures at declaration time. The following declares an array of `struct p_records` and initializes its values. Because no size is given for the array, it is determined by the compiler based on the number of items in the declaration, six in this case. Note that each element in the array is enclosed in braces.

```
static struct p_record    strange_people [] =
{       {111, "bear, smokey",    "rocky mountains, u.s.a."},
        {112, "hood, robin",     "sherwood forest, england"},
        {113, "reagan, ronald",  "washington, d.c."},
        {114, "kay, david g.",   "tokyo, japan"},
        {115, "fairy, tooth",    "san francisco, ca."}
        {116, "quilici, tony",   "davis, ca."}
};
```

We choose an individual element in the array by indexing on the array name, such as

```
strange_people[1]
```

and we select an individual field using the dot selection operator:

```
strange_people[1].name
```

If the entire array is passed to a function, we still select individual elements and fields in the usual way. To call a function `print_all` that prints the name field of the first `n` elements (indexed from 0 to `n - 1`) of an array of `p_records`, we invoke the function by

```
print_all(strange_people, n);
```

with `print_all` as follows:

```
void print_all(parray, n)
struct p_record  parray[];
int  n;
{
  int  i;

  for (i = 0; i < n; i++)
    printf("Name: %s\n", parray[i].name);
}
```

Arrays of structures are commonly used in data base applications. Information is stored on the basis of some key or identification field, but this is only for ease of accessing. Relevant data are stored in other fields of the record. The beginnings of a mini-data base can be created by using the pieces we now develop. In Chapter 11 we will build on these ideas to create a more useful data base that keeps records on external files and uses an index to access individual records. For now, the data base is just an array of records. After it is built, we will query it interactively by entering employee identifications and returning the name and address.

`lookup` is a function that does this. It takes three arguments: the identification number we are looking for (`id`), the number of elements in the table (`size`), and the table itself (`table`). `lookup` returns a pointer to the desired record, or `NULL` if `id` is not in `table`.

We search `table` sequentially until we either go past the array's end or `id` matches the `emp_number` field of the array element. If there is a match, we return a pointer to the record. The complete function is shown in Figure 9.3.

For more general use of the `struct p_record` data type, we change the data type definition slightly so that the `name` and `address` fields are pointers to `char` rather than arrays of `char` (and we use `malloc` to get the space we need). That way we can have arbitrarily long names and addresses:

```
/*
 *  Look up an id in an array of personnel records, returning a pointer
 *  to the record, if found, or NULL if it is not found.
 */
struct p_record *lookup(id, size, table)
int     id,                             /* the i.d. we're looking for */
        size;                           /* the number of records in the array */
struct p_record  table[];               /* array of records */
{
  int   i;                              /* index for searching "table" */

  for (i=0; i<size && table[i].emp_number != id; i++)
      ;                                 /* scan until too many, or a match */

  return (i == size) ? NULL : &table[i];
}
```

FIGURE 9.3   Function `lookup` that searches a data base for a given id

```
struct p_record
{
    int     emp_number;
    char    *name;
    char    *address;
};
```

Figure 9.5 uses earlier pieces, including `lookup`, to illustrate how such a simple data base is built and how the various array and structure elements are defined. The program is interesting because we are using dynamic storage allocation to get the space we need for the `name` and `address` fields of the next record. Using the new definition of a `struct p_record`, notice that the `name` and `address` fields are pointers to `char`, not fixed-size character arrays. Therefore, when a new name is entered (using `get_line` from Chapter 3), we copy it into the space allocated by `malloc` and then place the pointer to this space into the `name` field of the record. Then we do the same for the `address` field. Figure 9.4 shows

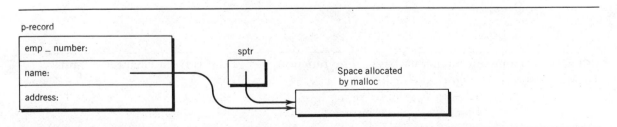

FIGURE 9.4   The `name` field of a new record points to the space allocated by `malloc`.

```
/*
 *  Program that initializes a data base (an array of structs), then
 *  interactively requests i.d.s, returning the record with the given i.d.
 */
#include <stdio.h>
#include <strings.h>

#define ENDOFINPUT  -1
#define MAX     80                      /* max chars in a string */
#define SIZE    100                     /* max entries in the data base */

struct p_record                         /* individual personnel record */
{
    int     emp_number;
    char    *name;
    char    *address;
};

main ()
{
    struct p_record     personnel[SIZE],
                        *lookup(),
                        *nextptr;
    int                 id;
    int                 inpres,
    char                line[MAX];

    while (init_record(&personnel[number++]))       /* get records */
        ;
    while (printf("\nID: "), get_line(line,MAX) != EOF)
      if (sscanf(line, "%d", &id) != 1)
        printf("Bad ID...skipping\n");
      else if ((nextptr=lookup(id, number, personnel)) != NULL)
        printf("\nName: %s\nAddress: %s\n", nextptr->name, nextptr->address);
      else
        printf("\nID %d not in data base.\n", id);
    }

/* Initialize a record to values from the terminal. */

int init_record(rptr)
struct p_record  *rptr;
{
    int     inpres, temp;
    char    *get_field();
    char    line[MAX];
```

FIGURE 9.5 Complete mini-data base. The function `get_line` is from Chapter 3, and `lookup` is shown in Figure 9.3.

```
      printf("Employee Number: ");
      if (get_line(line, MAX) != EOF && sscanf(line, "%d", &temp) == 1
               && temp != ENDOFINPUT)
      {
        rptr->emp_number = temp;
        rptr->name = get_field("Name: ");
        rptr->address = get_field("Address: ");
        return rptr->name && rptr->address;
      }
      return 0;
}
/*
 *  Get a line of input, first writing out a prompt.
 */
char *get_field(prompt)
char *prompt;
{
      char    line[MAX],                     /* next input line */
              *malloc(),
              *sptr;                         /* ptr to block from malloc */
      int     get_line(),
              length;                        /* returned from get_line */

      printf(prompt);
      if ((length = get_line(line, MAX)) != EOF &&
          (sptr = malloc((unsigned) length) + 1)) != NULL)
        strcpy (sptr, line);
      return sptr;
}
```

FIGURE 9.5 (continued)

how we place the pointer to the space and how we must code the reading of the line, requesting the space, copying the name into the space, and assigning the pointer.

9.2.6 SIZE OF STRUCTURES

A structure is a user-defined data type, but the space allocated when a structure variable is declared is known at compile time. The compile-time function `sizeof` returns the size in bytes of the structure type or structure variable. The *original* declaration of `struct p_record` consisted of three fields: an integer employee number and two fixed size `MAX` character arrays. The expression

```
    sizeof (struct p_record)
```

evaluates to a minimum of `sizeof(int)` plus the number of characters in the two arrays: $2 \times$ `MAX`. On a four-byte-per-int machine using 24 for

```
/*
 * Print the "emp_number" field of each record in "people" array.
 */
void print_emp_number (people, n)
struct p_record  people[];
int  n;
{
  struct p_record  *people_ptr = people,          /* ptr to next record */
                   *end_ptr = &people[n-1];        /* ptr to last record */

  for (; people_ptr <= end_ptr; people_ptr++)
    printf("I.D.: %d\n", people_ptr -> emp_number);
}
```

FIGURE 9.6 A function that prints a single field of an array of structures. `people_ptr` is incremented in units of the size of each record.

MAX, this is at least 52. We say "at least" because the compiler rounds up the space to force alignment as required by the underlying hardware.[3]

Since pointers are always incremented in units of the pointed-to type, declaring a pointer to (an array) of structures and incrementing it to traverse the array works as expected. In Figure 9.6 we use a pointer to print the `emp_number` field of the first n elements (indexed from 0 to n − 1) of an array of `struct p_records`. Notice that the function `print_emp_number` is passed two arguments, an array of structures and the number of elements to print. Earlier we declared an array of `struct p_records` called `strange_people`. If we want to use `print_emp_number`, we can define a constant that gives the number of elements in the array or we can use `sizeof`:

```
sizeof(strange_people) / sizeof(struct p_record)
```

This works because the size of `strange_people` is the total number of bytes the array requires. Each element in the array is `sizeof(struct p_record)` bytes.

EXERCISES

9-8 Modify `lookup` to use pointers in searching the table. □

9-9 Modify `gen_points` from Chapter 5 to use one array of `points` rather than two arrays of `ints`. Write both pointer array and indexing versions. □

---

[3] Alignment requires ints, longs, and other data types on most machines to begin on whole word boundaries rather than on individual byte boundaries.

9-10 Modify the histogram program in Chapter 4 to use a structure to pass its parameters. □

9-11 Modify `lookup` to do binary search instead of sequential search. Use insertion sort to keep the table sorted. □

9-12 Modify quicksort to sort a table of `struct p_records`, using the `name` field as the key. □

9-13 Generalize quicksort and binary search to work with any data type. (*Hint*: Pass them comparison functions and an offset within the structures to begin comparing.) Make sure to cast pointers appropriately. □

9.3

UNIONS

Structures allow packaging together different types of values as a single unit. Another similar concept is the the ability to store, in a single location, values of different types. Such a capability is called a *union*. A union may contain one of many different types of values (as long as only one is stored at a time!).

We define a union by giving the keyword `union`, an optional union name, and the alternative names and types in the union. For example, we can declare a variable `value` to be a union type, called `Data`, which may contain either an `int` or a `double` with:

```
union Data
{
    int     i;
    double  d;
} value;
```

We say that `value` is of type `union Data`. As with structures, we assign to an individual field of `value` by using the dot operator. To assign to the `int` field of `value`, we use `.i` and to the `double` field `.d`:

```
value.i = 1234;
value.d = -123.345;
```

Although a union contains enough storage for the largest type, it may contain only one value (here, either an `int` or a `double`) at a time; it is incorrect to assign to one field and then use another. A series of operations such as

```
    value.d = -123.345;                /* assign to "d" field */
    printf("%d\n", value.i);           /* print "i" field */
```

will produce anomalous results. Internally, unions are allocated storage to allow room for the largest field in the union. value, a union Data, will be allocated space sufficient for a double at all times.

EXERCISES

9-14 Create a union with one field for each of C's basic data types. Store various values in the union and print each of the fields. □

9.4

CASE STUDY — A LEXICAL SCANNER FOR A CALCULATOR

We use a combination of structures, enumeration types, and unions in a lexical scanner designed to scan an input line and extract meaningful units (known as lexical units or tokens, and hence the name *lexical scanner*). In a text passage, tokens are individual words, punctuation marks, and so on. In a C program, tokens are identifiers, keywords, numbers, operators, and special symbols ({, (, etc.). In a simple calculator the tokens are operands (numbers), operators, and parentheses.

We want the scanner to pick tokens from an input line and return the token type (either an *operator*, *operand*, *right-parenthesis*, or *left-parenthesis*) and its value (if an operator, the particular one, and if an operand, the numerical value). The scanner should also tell us if the next token is *not* one of the tokens that we expect; that is, it is *illegal*.

A natural representation for a token is to use a structure with two fields: one describing the token's type, the other giving its value. If the token is an operator, the value should be a character, '+', '−', '*', or whatever; if it is an operand, it should be a double. For parentheses, the token's type is enough and we don't need to store its value. Since a token is only one of these at a time, its value can be contained in a union. The token's type will be an enumeration type, either operator, operand, left_paren, or right_paren. In Figure 9.7 we define the data structures. We will assume that these definitions are kept in an include file *token.h* to be included in any program that uses tokens.

We use unions when data could be one of many types. Since we need to know which field of the union has a valid value (to avoid the problem of accessing the wrong union field), we often package a union in a structure, in which another field indicates the currently "active" union member. In this case, our structure is a `struct token`, and it has two fields. The `val` field is a union and may be either a `char` or a `double`. The `type` field is an enumerated type used to determine what field of the `val` field contains a valid value.

`get_nxt_token` is our tokenizer, and is shown in Figure 9.8, along with a main program that uses it to tokenize its input. Each time `get_nxt_token` is called, it gets a character and examines it to determine the type of token it is processing. If the character is in a table of operators, `get_nxt_token` sets the token's type to `operator` and remembers the character as its value. If the character is a digit, the token's type is `operand` and the character and any digits following it are converted to an integer, which is stored as the token's value. If the character is `EOF` or a right or left parenthesis, the token's type is set appropriately, but is not given a value. Otherwise, the token's type is assumed to be `illegal`.

We have reused pieces of earlier programs in building `get_nxt_token`. `fetch` and `unfetch` (Chapter 6) are used to read and unread characters. For efficiency they have been rewritten as macros. We have borrowed code from `getnum` (Chapter 6) to convert characters to integers. Finally, searching for an operator is a simple sequential table search that is similiar to the one in Chapter 5.

```
/*
 *      token.h: data type definitions for the calculator.
 */

enum token_type                     /* token types */
{
    operator, operand, illegal, endoffile, left_paren, right_paren, semicolon
};

union item                          /* operators are chars, operands are doubles */
{
    char        operator;
    double      operand;
};

struct token                        /* token type and its value */
{
    enum token_type type;           /* "operator" or "operand" */
    union item      val;            /* operator: char; operand: double */
};
```

FIGURE 9.7 Data structures for a calculator lexical scanner.

```
/*
 * Main program using lexical scanner.
 */
#include "token.h"

main()
{
  struct token *nxt_token, *get_nxt_token();

  while ((nxt_token = get_nxt_token()( && nxt_token->type != endoffile)
    switch(nxt_token->type)
    {
      case illegal:     printf("Illegal input\n");
                        break;
      case operand:     printf("Operand: %lf\n", nxt_token->val.operand);
                        break;
      case operator:    printf("Operator: %c\n", nxt_token->val.operator);
                        break;
      case left_paren:  printf("Left parenthesis\n");
                        break;
      case right_paren: printf("Right parenthesis\n");
                        break;
    }
}
```

(a) A main program using the scanner to break its input into tokens

```
/*
 * The tokenizer.
 */
#include <stdio.h>
#include <ctype.h>
#include "token.h"

static int savechar;          /* character pushed back */
static int pushed = 0;        /* is anything pushed back? */

#define fetch()    (pushed ? pushed--, savechar : getchar())
#define unfetch(c) (pushed++, savechar = c)

static int is_op(c)
int c;
{
  char *ptr = "+-*/%";        /* operators */

  while (*ptr && c != *ptr)   /* search for operator */
    ptr++;
  return *ptr;
}
```

FIGURE 9.8 The tokenizer and a program that uses it to tokenize its input.

```
struct token *get_nxt_token()
{
  char *malloc();
  struct token *t = (struct token *) malloc(sizeof(struct token));
  int c;
  long num = 0;

  if (t)                                /* if we could allocate a token */
  {
    while ((c = fetch()) != EOF && isspace(c))
      ;                                  /* skip over white space */
    if (c == EOF)                        /* End of file */
      t->type = endoffile;
    else if (c == '(')                   /* Left paren */
      t->type = left_paren;
    else if (c == ')')                   /* Right paren */
      t->type = right_paren;
    else if (c == ';')                   /* Semicolon */
      t->type = semicolon;
    else if (is_op(c))                   /* Operator */
      t->type = operator, t->val.operator = c;
    else if (isdigit(c))                 /* Number */
    {
      do
      {
        num = num * 10 + c - '0';
      } while (c = fetch(), isdigit(c));
      unfetch(c);
      t->type = operand, t->val.operand = num;
    }
    else                                 /* Illegal character */
      t->type = illegal;
  }
  return t;
}
```

(b)   The tokenizer

FIGURE 9.8 (continued)

EXERCISES

9-15 Write a program that takes a text file as input, and produces as output each word of the text on a separate line. Suggest reasons why such a program might be useful, either by itself or as a preprocessor that transforms its input into a form that another program might then act on, such as a word sorter program. □

9-16 The lexical scanner (Figure 9.8) can be adapted to the task of reading tokens for purposes other than calculation. Modify or extend the scanner so that it performs a function similar to that of `scanf`. It takes a *single* formatting string, and the address of a variable, and reads the next token on the input corresponding to the type in the format string. If the input cannot be accomplished, the function returns zero, and causes the input pointer to point to the first character *after* the one that caused the input to fail. □

9-17 Modify `get_nxt_token` to handle identifier names as tokens, as well as floating point numbers. □

9-18 Write a simple calculator program that uses `get_nxt_token` in parsing its input. □

USING CONSTRUCTED TYPES

Using C's constructed types correctly leads to more readable programs. Here are some suggestions about their use.

- Use enumerated types whenever a variable can have one of a set of values. They provide a convenient way to define constants, aid readability, and allow the compiler to provide additional type checking. Remember, however, that enumerated types are not integers and must be cast appropriately if they are to be used as integers.

- Use structures to store closely related pieces of data. Structures are yet another way to hide information, since they can be processed as a whole without worrying about the contents of their fields. Use a union when one location will contain different types.

- Remember that the difference between structures and unions is that space is allocated for every member of a structure, but only for the largest member of a union. You cannot store values for more than one field of a union at one time.

- Do not assume the fields within a structure are stored contiguously. Structures are often padded to satisfy alignment restrictions. Assuming that they are not padded leads to unportable code.

CHAPTER 10

LINKED DATA STRUCTURES

Arrays are data structures that require a fixed amount of storage to be specified and allocated at compile time, preventing us from increasing their size during run time. In addition, as we observed in the insertion sort in Chapter 1, putting data into the middle of an array or deleting data from the middle requires us to shift values to make room for the new or to close up the space used by the old. In this chapter we examine more dynamic data structures such as linked lists and trees, and we finish with a useful case study involving several data structures — a C program cross-referencer.

10.1

LINKED LISTS

The diagram in Figure 10.1 shows a linked list of five integers. Each element of the list, called a *node*, has two fields: one containing data, the other a pointer to the next element in the list.

The advantage of the linked list is that we can insert an element without shifting all elements that follow. All we need do is adjust pointers appropriately, as shown in Figure 10.2.

To illustrate linked lists, we will write an insertion sort routine in sec-

FIGURE 10.1 Diagram of a five-node linked list with values 2, 4, 6, 15, and 97.

tion 10.1.2 that inserts each new input value into an already sorted list, as shown in Figure 10.2. To do this, we need a way of representing a node. Since each node requires at least two fields, we can conveniently package an entire node as a structure.

```
struct node
{
    long        data;      /* or whatever is needed */
    struct node  *next;     /* "next" is a pointer to another node */
};
```

We can clarify the notation and encapsulate the complete data definitions in one place by using typedefs. A typedef such as

```
typedef   struct node    *NODEPTR;
```

causes NODEPTR to be a new type name, a pointer to a struct node. Then the earlier structure definition becomes

```
struct node
{
    long      data;
    NODEPTR   next;
};
```

To help hide the representation, we put the definitions for struct node and NODEPTR into a header file called *lists.h*. Then we include it in programs that manipulate linked lists.

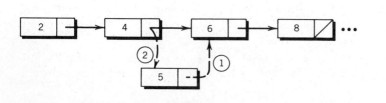

FIGURE 10.2 A linked list with a new node inserted into the middle.

10.1.1 BASIC LINKED LIST OPERATIONS

As we did with sets in Chapter 6, we can treat a list as an abstract data type, with certain allowable operations:

- Initialize a list to the empty list (init_list).
- Find a value in a list (search_list).
- Insert a value into a list (insert_list).
- Delete a value from a list (delete_list).
- Print a list (print_list).

By carefully constructing these primitive operations, we hide the underlying representation from other functions that need to use lists but do not care how they are implemented. At some later time, if changes to the representation are required (circular or two-way lists), only the accessing functions need to be changed.

Making a Node

The function make_node in Figure 10.3 creates a new node using malloc. We request enough space for a struct node; once we have the space, we insert the value and initialize the next field to NULL (used to

```
/*
 *  Make a new node, inserting "value".  Return a pointer to the node.
 *  Returns NULL when out of dynamic storage space. Assumes the definitions in "lists.h".
 */

NODEPTR  make_node(value)
long  value;
{
  NODEPTR    newptr;                 /* ptr. to allocated space */
  char       *malloc();

  if ((newptr = (NODEPTR) malloc(sizeof(struct node))) != NULL)
  {
    newptr->data = value;            /* fill in "data" field */
    newptr->next = NULL;             /* "next" field is always NULL */
  }
  return newptr;                     /* returns NULL if malloc fails */
}
```

FIGURE 10.3   A routine that gets a new node, inserting a value. The routine returns a pointer to the node (or NULL if malloc fails).

indicate the end of the list). Because `malloc` returns a pointer to `char`, we must cast it to a `NODEPTR`. As usual, we declare the type of `malloc`. The function returns a pointer to the node, or `NULL` if `malloc` fails.

Inserting at the Start of a Linked List

Before we show how to insert in the correct place in insertion sort, we'll look at a simpler case: inserting an element at the front of a list. A program to do this is shown in Figure 10.4. It uses `getnum` from Chapter 6 and `make_node` from Figure 10.3.

To do the insertion, two statements are required, performed in the indicated order:

```
newptr->next = list;          (1)
list = newptr;                (2)
```

The effect of these assignments is shown below.

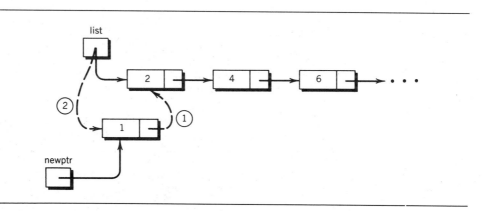

Printing the Values in a Linked List

The program in Figure 10.4 calls a function `print_list` to write the values in the list. This function, shown in Figure 10.5, *traverses* the list, printing the `data` field in each node, until the list pointer is `NULL`. Traversing a list means moving through a list in order, "visiting" (or performing some action on) each node in turn. In Figure 10.5 we print the `data` field when we visit the node. We use `L` itself to go through the list, until `L` is `NULL`, at which point we are at the end of the list. To get to the next node in the list, we write

```
L = L->next;
```

```
/*
 *  Read values and place at start of a linked list.
 */
#include <stdio.h>
#include "lists.h"                    /* data structure definitions */

main ()
{
  NODEPTR     list = NULL,            /* the linked list (initially empty) */
              newptr,                 /* next node in the list */
              make_node();            /* gets space for new node */
  long        val;                    /* next input value */
  void        print_list();           /* print values in a list */

  while (getnum(&val) == 1 && (newptr = make_node(val)) != NULL)
  {
    newptr->next = list;
    list = newptr;
  }
  print_list(list);
}
```

FIGURE 10.4 Program that builds a linked list by inserting new values at the start, and then prints the list. Calls on functions `make_node` and `print_list`.

10.1.2 INSERTION SORTING USING LINKED LISTS

Now we can combine these ideas to write an insertion sort program using linked lists. The advantage of sorting with a linked list is that we can sort an unlimited number of values (with the array version, we had to predeclare the maximum number of values to be sorted), and we can insert the new value into a linked list without shifting. The insertion sort program is

```
/*
 *  Print a list pointed to by "L".
 */
void print_list(L)
NODEPTR L;
{
  for ( ; L != NULL; L = L->next)
    printf("%ld\n", L->data);
}
```

FIGURE 10.5 The function `print_list` that prints the data fields of the nodes in the list pointed to by L.

written to read longs and insert them in order into a linked list. On end of input we print the list using print_list. The main program is trivial because we built the list access routines in small, functional pieces. Figure 10.6 shows the complete main program, with the data definitions in the include file *lists.h*.

There is one function to write that illustrates many of the uses of linked lists: insert_list. The function finds the correct place to insert the value so that the list remains sorted, as in Figure 10.7. We write this as a function (Figure 10.8) with two arguments, a value to be inserted and a pointer to a linked list.

To insert in the list, we must find the place where the node goes, make a node, and hook it into the list. We use two pointers, curr and prev, to do the traversing. We initialize curr to the list's first node and prev to NULL.

curr and prev move down the list, one in trail of the other. This is necessary because we find the correct place to insert by comparing with the value in a node, but we must insert *before* that node. Since our list contains

```
/*
 *  Sort integer (long) input using linked lists.
 */
#include <stdio.h>
#include "lists.h"                      /* data structure defs. */

main ()
{
  NODEPTR    L = NULL;                  /* the sorted linked list */
  long       val;                       /* input value */
  void       print_list(), skip_garbage();
  int        inpres;

  while((inpres = getnum(&val)) != EOF)
    if (!inpres)                        /* skip over rest of line */
      skip_garbage();                   /* Chapter 6 */
    else
      if (!insert_list(val, &L))        /* insert "val" into "L" */
      {
        printf("\nOut of internal memory space.\n");
        break;                          /* exit the while loop */
      }
  print_list(L);
  Functions called from the main program go here.
}
```

FIGURE 10.6 Main program structure for linked list insertion sort.

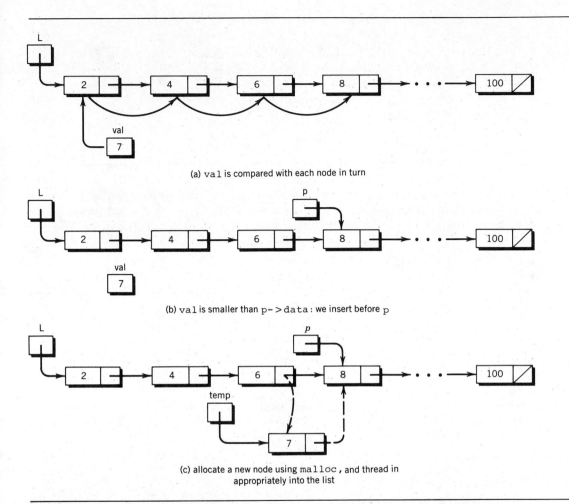

(a) `val` is compared with each node in turn

(b) `val` is smaller than `p->data`: we insert before `p`

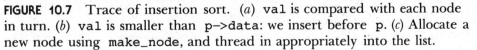

(c) allocate a new node using `malloc`, and thread in
appropriately into the list

FIGURE 10.7 Trace of insertion sort. (*a*) `val` is compared with each node
in turn. (*b*) `val` is smaller than `p->data`: we insert before `p`. (*c*) Allocate a
new node using `make_node`, and thread in appropriately into the list.

only pointers to the next node we keep this "trailing link pointer" one
node behind `curr` and we always insert after `prev`. The notion of a trailing pointer, one that points to the predecessor of a node, is a common
technique with linked structures. Once we find the place for the new
value, we create a new node with `make_node` and insert it by appropriate
manipulation of pointers.

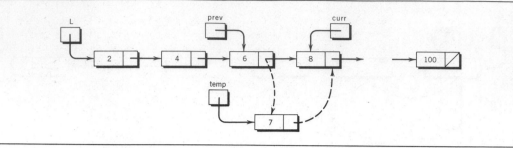

Although linked list insertion sort avoids the time-consuming process of shifting data to make room for a new item, it is still not substantially faster than the array-based insertion sort. For each new value to be inserted,

```
/*
 *  Insert "val" into already sorted linked list "L." Returns nonzero
 *  if space is available, zero otherwise.  Uses make_node to create node.
 */
int insert_list(val, L)
long       val;
NODEPTR    *L;
{
  NODEPTR    curr = *L,              /* current node in list */
             prev = NULL,            /* node before "curr" */
             make_node(),            /* get a new node */
             temp;                   /* pointer to new node */

/* March until correct place, or until end of list. */

  for ( ; curr != NULL && val > curr->data ; curr = curr->next)
    prev = curr;

/* Get new node and insert into proper place (if space is available). */

  if ((temp = make_node(val)) != NULL)
  {
    temp->next = curr;
    if (prev == NULL)              /* insert at start of list */
      *L = temp;
    else
      prev->next = temp;
  }
  return temp != NULL;             /* "temp" is NULL if malloc failed */
}
```

FIGURE 10.8 insert_list function used in the linked list version of insertion sort.

we still have to search the list for the correct place to insert, an operation that takes time proportional to m, if there are m values in the list or array. For all n input values, this takes a total amount of time proportional to n^2. If n doubles, sorting time goes up by a factor of four; if n triples, it goes up nine times. However, the total sorting time for the same n inputs will be about twice as fast for linked lists as for array insertion. In Section 10.3 we look at another dynamic data structure, a binary tree, which allows a sorting routine with time complexity proportional to $n \log_2 n$, a substantial improvement for large n, as we shall see.

EXERCISES

10-1 Write a function that takes a pointer to a linked list, and reverses the order of the nodes. If the list contains nodes with 1, 2, 5, and 7, the list will point to the node with 7, which points to 5, and so on. No data movement should occur, only appropriate alteration of pointers. □

10-2 Write a function, `length_list`, that returns the number of elements in a list. □

10-3 Write functions that implement the abstract data type *stack* using linked lists. A stack is a restricted access list: insertions and deletions may occur only at one end, the *top* of the stack. The operations are traditionally called *pushing* and *popping*. □

10-4 Add the operations `count`, `top`, and `isempty` to the stack data type created in the previous exercise. `count` returns the number of elements on the stack, `top` returns the top element without popping the stack, and `isempty` returns zero only if there are elements on the stack. □

10-5 Most of the list functions we have written in this chapter can be rewritten more compactly. Do so. Are the functions still as readable? □

10-6 Write a function, `search_list`, that finds the first location of a given value in a list, and returns a pointer to it. If the value is not in the list, the function should return `NULL`. The function header should be

```
NODEPTR   search_list(val, list);
long      val;
NODEPTR   list;  □
```

10-7 Write a function, `delete_list`, that removes the first node in a linked list with a given value. If the value is not in the list, the function should do nothing. The function header should be

```
void delete_list(val, list)
long     val;
NODEPTR  *list;
```

delete_list should make use of search_list of the previous exercise. What changes in search_list are necessary for this to be reasonable? □

10-8 Write a function, sort_list, that sorts a linked list in place. Can you modify quicksort (Chapter 5) to do this? □

10.1.3 RETURNING SPACE TO THE FREE STORAGE POOL

Calls to malloc consume space from the storage pool (FSP). If a list is serving a temporary function, we can return space to the free storage pool by calls to free. free takes a pointer to a contiguous block of storage (type char *) and returns the storage to the FSP. In theory, this storage is no longer accessible to the program. Eventually, the space may be doled out again by malloc as part of a larger or smaller block. Since only the space is returned – the name of the pointer is still available in the current block at least – problems occur when accessing a freed block of storage through its pointer.

```
/*
 *  Return each element in "L" to the FSP, then set "L" to the empty list.
 */
void free_list(L)
NODEPTR  *L;
{
  NODEPTR    curr = *L,
             temp;

  for (; curr != NULL ; curr = temp)
  {
    temp = curr->next;
    free ((char *) curr);
  }
  *L = NULL;
}
```

FIGURE 10.9 Function free_list returns the entire linked list pointed to by L, and sets L to the empty list.

Since `free` returns only the space pointed to by the pointer argument, it is necessary to traverse an entire list in order to return all its nodes. A slight variant on `print_list` whereby "visit the node" becomes a call to `free` accomplishes the job, as in Figure 10.9. We cast the argument to `free` to avoid illegal type combinations. We should avoid accessing a freed node outside the block where it is freed or if a call to `malloc` intervenes.

EXERCISES

10-9 Write functions that implement the abstract data type *queue*. A queue is another restricted list; additions are made to the end and deletions take place from the front. You should have functions to create the queue, to destroy the queue, to add to the queue's end, and to remove from the queue's front. □

10-10 What happens if you `free` space that was not allocated by `malloc`? What happens if you access storage that was previously freed? □

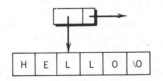

10.2

SORTING STRINGS USING DYNAMICALLY ALLOCATED ARRAYS

We now modify the insertion sort routines slightly so that input consists of character strings (or words), one word per line of input; in the original version, the input was integers. Since integers always take up a fixed amount of storage, each node was always the same size – room for the integer (`data` field) plus room for the pointer to the next node (the `next` field).

Using the technique from Chapter 8, each node will contain a *pointer* to a string rather than the string itself, using `malloc` to allocate the needed space. In this case, the space for each node is a fixed small amount: room for the string pointer plus room for the pointer to the next node.

The insertion sort algorithm is identical: compare the new word with each in turn, until it is smaller than the current word, and then insert before the current word. Figure 10.10 shows the situation for the list of

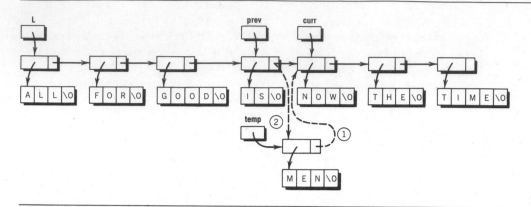

FIGURE 10.10 Linked list of nodes with pointers to a character string. The new word MEN is inserted just before NOW.

words NOW, IS, THE, TIME, FOR, ALL, GOOD, MEN, just before inserting MEN. Figure 10.11 is the new version of `insert_list` for string sorting. We use `strcmp` to compare the strings.

Figure 10.12 shows what is going on. We allocate space for the node with `malloc`. We also need to allocate room for the string `s`. We do this with another call to `malloc`, using `strlen` to compute the length of `s`. Since `strlen` does not count the trailing `'\0'`, we add one to the length in the call to `malloc`. `malloc` returns type `char *`, so no cast is needed. `sptr` is a pointer to the newly allocated block.

Finally, we copy `s` into the new block pointed to by `sptr` (using `strcpy`) and put the pointer (not the string) into the `data` field of the new node. Then links are adjusted as before.

Since the type of the `data` field of a node in the list has changed, we also need to change the declarations in `lists.h` and rewrite the function `print_list`, as well as the driver program from Figure 10.6 . These are shown in Figure 10.13.

EXERCISES

10-11 Generalize lists so that any data type can be held within the node. (*Hint:* Have the caller provide functions to create a node and to compare two nodes.) ☐

10-12 Modify the program of Figure 10.6 to use quicksort rather than insertion sort to sort the list. ☐

```
/*
 *  Insert "S" into already sorted list "L."   Returns nonzero if there is
 *  space and zero otherwise.
 */
#include <strings.h>              /* declares types of strcpy and strcmp */

int insert_list (S, L)
char       S[];                   /* before, we inserted longs */
NODEPTR    *L;
{
    NODEPTR     curr = *L,
                prev = NULL,
                temp;             /* returned from malloc */
    char        *malloc(),
                *sptr;            /* pointer from malloc */

/* March until correct place, or end of list. */

    for ( ; curr != NULL && strcmp(S, curr->data) > 0; curr = curr->next)
      prev = curr;

/* Get new node and insert into proper place, if space available. */

    if (temp = (NODEPTR) malloc (sizeof (struct node)) &&
        sptr = malloc ((unsigned) strlen (S) + 1))
    {
      strcpy (sptr, S);           /* copy "S" */
      temp->data = sptr;          /* "data" field points to string */
      temp->next = curr;
      if (prev == NULL)           /* insert at start of list */
        *L = temp;
      else
        prev->next = temp;
    }
    return temp && sptr;          /* one is NULL if malloc failed */
}
```

FIGURE 10.11 Revised version of `insert_list` that takes a string and inserts it into the proper place in a sorted linked list.

10-13 Write a function, `size_list`, that determines the total number of bytes used to store a linked list. When is `size_list` useful? □

10-14 Can the string sorting program be written more compactly? Do so. Is it still as readable? Is it more efficient? □

10-15 Modify the definition of a `struct node` and the linked list functions so that we have a two-way linked list. Each node in the list has two pointers:

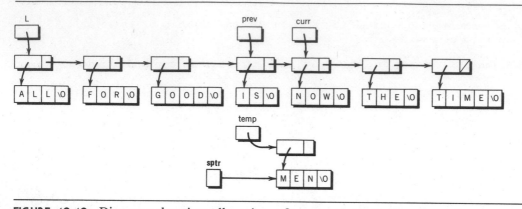
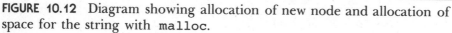

FIGURE 10.12 Diagram showing allocation of new node and allocation of space for the string with `malloc`.

one to the next node in the list, the other to the previous node. Use these modified functions to reimplement insertion sorting. ☐

10.2.1 LONG STRINGS

In the string-sorting example, we were limited to 80-character strings because we preallocated an array into which they could then be read. However, we can combine the notion of a string as a sequence of characters with the notion of arbitrary-length structures if we free ourselves from the idea that all characters in a given string must be in a single contiguous array. Instead, we use linked lists of characters, each node containing a pointer to an array of fixed size, and when a string being entered exceeds the maximum size of the array, we link in a new node, as illustrated in Figure 10.14.

Now our linked list is no longer viewed as a collection of separate strings, as was the case with word sorting in Figure 10.13, but rather as one large arbitrary-length string. The changes to the program in Figure 10.13 are small and a complete program is shown in Figure 10.15. This program reads arbitrary-length strings and stores them in a linked list, using **MAX** characters per node (**MAX** is 20 in this version). When we need more space, we get a new node with `malloc` and use `strcpy` to copy additional characters to new array space provided by an additional call to `malloc`. We have also renamed some of the data structures to reflect their use more accurately (**NODEPTR** becomes **STRINGPTR**, for example).

```
typedef   struct node   *NODEPTR;

struct node
{
    char        *data;                       /* only change is in "data" field */
    NODEPTR     next;
};
```

(a) New include file lists.h with new type for the data *field*

```
/*
 * Print a list pointed to by "L."
 */
void print_list (L)
NODEPTR  L;
{
  for ( ; L != NULL; L = L->next)
    printf("%s\n", L->data);               /* only change is to printf */
}
```

(b) New version of print_list. *Note that only the format specification in the* printf *statement has changed.*

```
/*
 * Read strings, one per line, and sort using linked list insertion.
 */
#include <stdio.h>
#include "lists.h"
#define   MAXSTRING      80

main()
{
  NODEPTR    L = NULL;                   /* the sorted linked lists */
  char       word[MAXSTRING];            /* input string */
  void       print_list();

  while (get_line(word, MAXSTRING) != EOF)
    if (!insert_list(word, &L))          /* insert "word" into "L" */
    {
      printf("\nOut of internal memory space.");
      break;                             /* exit the while loop */
    }
  print_list(L);
}
```

(c) New main program. The input format now specifies string input

FIGURE 10.13 New versions of lists.h, print_list and the main program, showing changes needed to handle character strings as input.

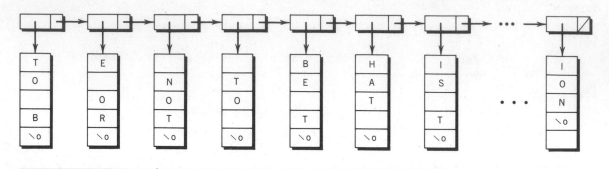

FIGURE 10.14 Arbitrary length string made up of a linked list of fixed-length strings.

10.3

TREES

We can generalize linked lists to structures of arbitrary complexity; each node may contain data (which itself may be a pointer, as we saw with the string-based insertion sort), as well as pointers to many other nodes. One type of multi-linked structure of great utility is the *binary tree*, a special linked structure in which each node contains two pointers. Formally, a binary tree contains:

- One special node, known as the root.
- Nodes containing two distinguished subtrees, the left and the right subtrees, each of which is a binary tree.

Figure 10.16 shows a particularly useful type of binary tree, a binary search tree (BST). A BST is a tree in which the data value at each node partitions all of the data in its subtrees into two subsets. Every data value in the left subtree is less than the current node, and every data value in the right subtree is greater than the current node. In this section, we see how such a tree is constructed and why it is useful. We will use such a tree to construct another sorting algorithm with a very beneficial time property: unlike insertion sorting, whose time is proportional to n^2, binary tree sorting will take time proportional to $n \log_2 n$.

Although the techniques we use to construct and manipulate trees are just extensions of those used for linear linked lists, binary trees are worthy of special attention for at least three reasons: they allow us to combine most of the full power of the C language; they illustrate the power and

```c
/*
 *  Read and store arbitrary-length strings.
 */
#include <stdio.h>

#define  MAX      20                    /* max chars per node */

typedef  struct node  *STRINGPTR;

struct node                             /* a node in the string */
{
    char        *word;                  /* pointer to the word */
    STRINGPTR   next;                   /* pointer to rest of word */
};

main ()
{
  int        c,i,
  STRINGPTR  S,last;                    /* the long string, pointers to its end */
  char       word[MAX];                 /* the input string */
  void       print_string();
  STRINGPTR  insert_string;

  while (c = getchar(), c != EOF)
  {
    for (S = last = NULL, i = 0; c != '\n' && c != EOF; c=getchar())
    {
      word[i++] = c;
      if (i >= MAX - 1)
      {
        word[i] = '\0';                 /* EACH substr ends with '\0' */
        if ((last = insert_string (word, &S, last)) == NULL)
          break;                        /* out of memory - exit loop */
        i = 0;                          /* reset for next node */
      }
    }
    if (last)
    {                                   /* make last node */
    word{i++} = '\n';
    word[i] = '\0';
      (void)insert_string (word, &S, last); /* can't do anything if no memory */
    }
      printf ("\nString:\n");           /* print what we have of the string */
      print_string (S);
  }
}
```

(a) The main program for reading, storing, and printing long strings

---

FIGURE 10.15 Program for reading storing and printing arbitrarily long strings.

```
/*
 *  Insert string "S" at end of string "L" (possibly empty).
 *  Returns 0 if "malloc" fails.
 */
STRINGPTR insert_string (S, L, last)
char       *S;
STRINGPTR  *L, last;
{
  STRINGPTR   temp; NULL;           /* returned from allocating a node */
  char *malloc(), *strcpy(),
      *sptr;                        /* returned from allocating a string */

  if ((temp = (STRINGPTR) malloc (sizeof (struct node))) != NULL &&
      (sptr = malloc ((unsigned) strlen (S) + 1)) != NULL)
  {
    (void) strcpy (sptr, S);            /* copy "S" */
    temp->word = sptr;                  /* "word" field points to string */
    temp->next = NULL;
    if (last == NULL)
      *L = temp;                        /* insert at start of string */
    else
      last->next = temp;
    last = temp;                        /* "last" points to last node */
  }
  return sptr ? last : NULL;            /* NULL if malloc fails */
}

/* Print the string pointed to by "S" */

void print_string (S)
STRINGPTR S;
{
  for ( ; S != NULL; S = S->next)
    printf ("%s", S->word);
  putchar('\n');
}
```

(b) The routines called from the main program: `insert_string` *and* `print_string`

FIGURE 10.15 Program for reading storing and printing arbitrarily long strings.

simplicity of recursion; and they further emphasize good program construction techniques through abstract data types (ADTs).

As with linear lists, we need to define the basic data type for a binary tree node and the basic abstract tree manipulation routines – create a tree, insert a new value into a tree, and print the data values in a tree. If a node in a binary tree looks like this:

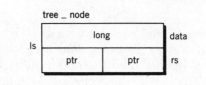

we define the fields using the structure definitions:

```
typedef struct tree_node    *TREEPTR;

struct tree_node
{
    long     data;
    TREEPTR  ls, rs;
};
```

We put these definitions in an include file *trees.h*, so that it may be included in any program that uses binary trees. In this example, the `data` field of a node contains a `long`; there are two pointer fields, `ls` and `rs`, each a pointer to another `struct tree_node`. Again, to make the programs easer to read, we use a `typedef` to define a `TREEPTR` as a pointer to a `struct tree_node`.

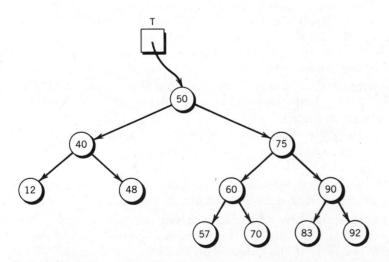

FIGURE 10.16 A binary search tree (BST), with the property that for every node, every node in the left subtree is less than the node, and every node in the right subtree is greater than the node.

10.3.1 BINARY SEARCH TREES

Figure 10.16 showed that a BST is a tree with the property that any node partitions its subtrees into two classes. The left subtree contains only values smaller than the node, the right only values greater than or equal to the node. We now write a function, `insert_tree`, that constructs such a tree. More correctly, `insert_tree` takes two arguments, a value and a pointer to an existing BST, and inserts the value into the tree so that the BST property is maintained. If the tree is empty, we insert the new value as the root of the tree.

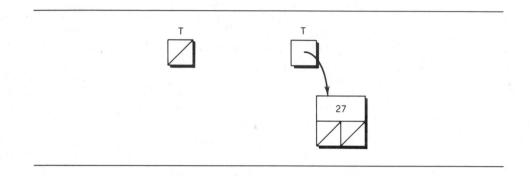

To insert a value into a nonempty tree is not much harder. As an example, Figure 10.17*a* shows an existing tree with integer values at the nodes, and we want to insert the new value 27 into the tree. In Figure 10.17*b* we compare 27 with the value at the root; since 27 is less than 40, we move to the left. In Figure 10.17*c* we compare 27 with 19, finding that 27 is greater; now we move right. Finally, we compare 27 with 23 and again find that it is greater. We cannot move right (the right subtree of 23 is `NULL`). We get a new node and attach 27 as the right subtree of 23. The final tree is shown in Figure 10.17*d*.

The algorithm for inserting a value into a BST is a simple three-step process:

1. Set the current node to the root of the tree. If the current node is empty, install the current value as the root of the tree.

2. Otherwise, compare the new value with the value at the current node. If the value is less than the current node, set the current node to its *left* subtree. If the value is greater than or equal to the current node, set the current node to its *right* subtree.

3. If the current node is now `NULL`, install the new node as the left or right subtree of the parent node, as appropriate. Otherwise, go back to step 2.

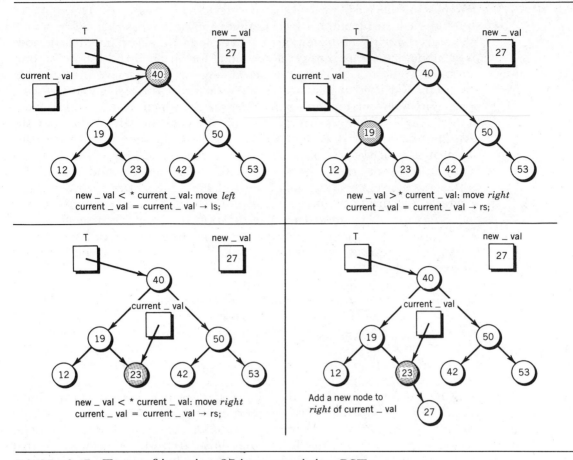

FIGURE 10.17   Trace of inserting 27 into an existing BST.

This algorithm is easy to code. We first get a new node (by calling `make_treenode`, a variation on `make_node` of Figure 10.3) and fill in the fields; the `data` field gets the value, while the `ls` and `rs` fields are NULL. If the tree is empty, we set the tree pointer to point to this new node; otherwise, we compare the value with the `data` field of the current node, moving left or right as appropriate, until the current node is NULL. Then we attach the new node to the parent.

In order to keep track of parent nodes, we use a trailing link pointer (called `prev`), just as we did with linear linked lists. When it is time to attach the new node to the appropriate field of `prev`, we do an extra comparison with the `data` field. If the value is less than the `data` field, we attach the new node as the left subtree of `prev`; otherwise, we attach it as the right subtree. We have to be careful when installing the node as the new root of the tree; we make a specific test for this case. Figure 10.18 shows the entire function, which assumes the data types defined in *trees.h*. We also show the function `make_treenode`, a slight modification to `make_node` that we used to get a new node for linear linked lists.

Once we have a BST, it is not clear how we can retrieve the values in any useful way, but in fact we can. We do so by traversing the tree in a systematic way, corresponding to the way in which it was constructed. Since the BST has the property that all values to the left of the root are less than the root, and all values to the right of the root are greater than or equal to it, if we first print all values in the left subtree, then print the value at the root, then all values in the right subtree, and repeat this process recursively for all nodes, we will have the values in order. The recursive tree-printing function in Figure 10.19 takes a pointer to a tree and prints the values in order. The function calls itself recursively on the left subtree (that is, it prints all the values in the left subtree), then prints the value at the root, and finally calls itself recursively again on the right subtree.

Now we can construct a program to sort using a BST as an internal storage mechanism for the values. The program's structure is virtually identical to that of the linked list insertion sort program (Figure 10.6), but it has rather surprising timing characteristics, as we shall soon see; Figure 10.20 is the main program. Once again, we use `getnum`, our alternative to `scanf`, to read the input values. `main` also calls the functions `insert_tree`, and `print_tree`.

Given a list of integers, this binary tree-sorting program prints them sorted from low to high, just as insertion sort did. However, we should examine the algorithm and the code carefully to see why this is substantially faster. If we are very lucky, the binary tree will be complete — that is, each node will have exactly two non-`NULL` subtrees, except for nodes at the last two levels. If we are unlucky (for example, if the input is already sorted), the tree will degenerate into a list; each node will have, at most, one non-`NULL` subtree, and it will take as long as insertion sort. Examples of both are shown in Figure 10.21.

For random input values, however, the BST will be nearly complete, and as a result, each comparison of an input value to a tree node reduces the search space by half. Therefore, we only have to do a few ($\log_2 n$) comparisons to determine where to put the new node. With insertion sort we look at half of the list ($n/2$) on the average. For a BST, sorting time for all n values averages about $n \log_2 n$ versus n^2 for insertion sort. For large values of n these differences are very large, as Table 10.1 shows. This table compares the sorting times for n randomly distributed integers; as n becomes large, the differences become quite noticeable. At 800 values, binary tree sort is more than seven times faster than insertion sort.[1] The

---

[1] The programs were compiled and run using the UNIX C compiler on a DEC VAX 11/780.

```
/*
 *  Insert "value" into an existing tree "T".  Return zero if out of memory space.
 */
int     insert_tree (value, T)
long    value;
TREEPTR *T;
{
  TREEPTR curr = *T,                    /* ptr. to node */
          prev = *T,                    /* ptr. to parent of curr node */
          temp,                         /* returned from malloc */
          make_treenode();             /* get space for new node */

 /* Get a new node and set fields and install. */

  if ((temp = make_treenode (value)) != NULL)
    if (*T == NULL)                     /* insert into empty tree */
      *T = temp;
    else
    {                                   /* general case, find insert place */
      while (curr != NULL)
      {
        prev = curr;
        curr = (value < curr->data) ?
          curr->ls :                    /* move left */
          curr->rs;                     /* move right */
      }
  /* "curr" is "NULL", "prev" points to its parent. */

      if (value < prev->data)           /* insert at left */
        prev->ls = temp;
      else
        prev->rs = temp;                /* insert at right */
    }

  return temp != NULL;
}

/*
 *  Make a new node, inserting "value".  Return a pointer to the node or NULL
 *  if out of space.
 */
TREEPTR make_treenode (value)
long    value;
{
  TREEPTR  newptr;
  char     *malloc();

  if ((newptr = (TREEPTR) malloc (sizeof (struct tree_node))) != NULL)
  {
    newptr->data = value;
    newptr->ls = newptr->rs = NULL;
  }
  return newptr;
}
```

FIGURE 10.18 Function to insert a value into the correct place in a binary search tree.

TABLE 10.1 Sorting time comparisons for insertion sort and binary tree sort

	Time (seconds)	
n	*Insertion Sort*	*Binary Tree Sort*
100	0.10	0.10
200	0.40	0.18
400	1.60	0.40
800	6.40	0.90

times do not include input and output, since they are required by both sorts.

EXERCISES

10-16 Can `insert_tree` be written more compactly? Do so. ☐

10-17 Write a *recursive* function to insert a value into a BST. ☐

10-18 Write a *recursive* function to delete a node from a BST. There are three cases to worry about: the node has no children, the node has one child, and the node has two children. ☐

10-19 Write both recursive and iterative versions of a function, `search_tree`,

```
/*
 *  Print the "data" values in "root" in order.
 */
void print_tree (root)
TREEPTR   root;
{
  if (root != NULL)
  {
    print_tree(root->ls);
    printf("%ld\n", root->data);
    print_tree(root->rs);
  }
}
```

FIGURE 10.19 Function `print_tree` prints the `data` fields of a tree in order.

```
/*
 *  Sort long integers using a BST.
 */
#include    <stdio.h>
#include    "trees.h"                          /* tree data structure defs. */

main ()
{
    TREEPTR     root = NULL;
    long        val;
    int         inpres;
    void        print_tree();

    while ((inpres = getnum(&val)) != EOF)
        if (inpres != 1)                        /* ignore bad data */
            skip_garbage();
        else
            if (!insert_tree(val, &root))       /* insert "val" into tree */
            {
                printf("\nOut of internal memory space.\n");
                break;                          /* exit the while loop */
            }
    print_tree(root);
}
```

FIGURE 10.20   Complete main program for performing binary tree sorting.

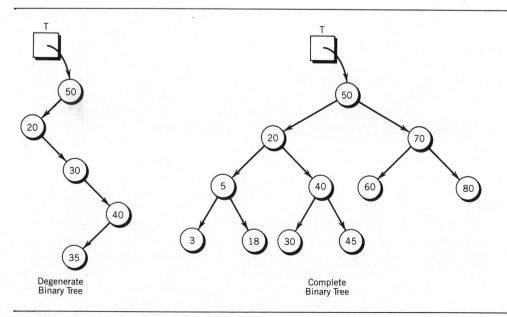

Degenerate
Binary Tree

Complete
Binary Tree

FIGURE 10.21   Examples of degenerate and complete binary trees.

that searches a BST for a node with a given value. `search_tree` should return a pointer to the node or `NULL` if the node cannot be found. □

10-20 Write a *recursive* function that computes the number of nodes in a binary tree. (*Hint*: Look at the function `print_tree`.) □

10-21 Write a *recursive* function that computes the height of a binary tree. The height of a binary tree is defined as the length of the longest path from the root to a leaf node (one with `NULL` subtrees). The height of an empty tree is zero; the height of a tree with a single node is one. Do not write your program to compute all path lengths. Use recursion instead. □

10-22 Modify the string-based insertion sort routine (Figure 10.13) so that it works with a BST. That is, write a binary tree-based sorting program that sorts strings rather than `longs`. As with the linked list version, a node should contain a pointer to the string. The space needed for the string should be allocated using `malloc`. □

10-23 Generalize the tree processing functions to allow any data type within the node. □

10.4

CASE STUDY — A CROSS-REFERENCE PROGRAM

When we write programs, debugging is often aided by having a separate listing of the identifiers in a program and the line numbers where they appear. Such a listing is called a *cross-reference*, and a program to produce it is called a *cross-referencer*. We will build one that can be used for any file of words and, in particular, can be easily adapted for use with C or other programming languages. To give you an idea of what such a program should produce, Figure 10.22*a* is the first C program (from Chapter 1) and Figure 10.22*b* is the output of a program cross-referencer run on this program.

The top-level structure of a program to do this is simple. The interesting aspects of the program are its data structures and the way the program is organized. For this program, we pay careful attention to selecting a reasonable representation for the table of words and line numbers, but we define the table in such a way that later changes can be made transparent to the rest of the program.

```
/*
 *    Generate a table showing interest accumulation.
 */

#define PRINCIPAL      1000.00          /* start with $1000 */
#define IRATE          0.10             /* interest rate of 10% */
#define PERIOD         10               /* over 10 year period */

main ()
{
  int       year;                       /* year of period */
  float     sum;                        /* total amount */

  sum = PRINCIPAL;
  year = 0;
  printf ("Year        Total at %.2f%%\n\n", IRATE * 100.0);
  while (year <= PERIOD) {
  {
    printf ("%d      $ %.2f\n", year, sum);
    sum = sum * IRATE + sum;
    year = year + 1;
  }
}
```

(a) A short C program

```
Generate       :  2
IRATE          :  5,   15,   19
PERIOD         :  6,   16
PRINCIPAL      :  4,   13
Total          :  15
Year           :  15
a              :  2
accumulation   :  2
amount         :  11
at             :  15
d              :  18
define         :  4,   5,   6
f              :  15,  18
float          :  11
int            :  10
interest       :  2,   5
main           :  8
n              :  15 (2),   18
of             :  5,   10
over           :  6
period         :  6,   10
printf         :  15,  18
```

FIGURE 10.22 (*a*) A short C program. (*b*) The output of a cross-referencer run on this program. Numbers in parenthesis are repetition counts if a word occurs more than once on the same line. The output continues on the next page.

```
rate        :  5
showing     :  2
start       :  4
sum         :  11,  13,  18,  19 (3)
table       :  2
total       :  11
while       :  16
with        :  4
year        :  6,  10 (2),  14,  16,  18,  20 (2)
```

(b) The output of a cross-referencer run on this program

FIGURE 10.22 (continued)

10.4.1 PROGRAM AND DATA STRUCTURES

A simple data flow model of the program is shown below. This model of a program's operation shows the separate functions that we need and the data that flows between them. The functions themselves are viewed as black boxes that take a set of inputs, perform some transformation, and produce a set of outputs.

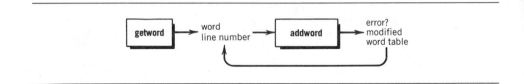

The program reads a word at a time in a function called `getword` and then passes the word and the current line number to a function called `addword`. This function adds the word and the line number to the table of words and line numbers. This table is itself one of the inputs to `addword`. The program's structure is so simple that we can begin designing the program by coding the main program immediately. Then we can add the pieces in a top-down way as they are built. Figure 10.23 is the entire main program. It is just a `while` loop that runs until there are no more words, with a `break` if the word table becomes full. At the end of the program, the word table is printed by the function `writewords`.

Note that the main program includes a header file *xref_tab.h*. This file contains the data structure definitions for the word table and declarations for any globals. Since we have not yet decided on a representation for the word table, we cannot fill in the details of the header file. There already are a few assumptions in the program, however. One is that adding a new word to the table could fail, and we specifically include an error return

```
/*
 *  XREF.C - A cross reference program.
 */
#include <stdio.h>
#include "xref_tab.h"

main ()
{
  char  word[MAXWORD + 1];              /* next input word */
  int   error = 0,                      /* indicates error when nonzero */
        lineno;                         /* line word is on */
  WTPTR wordtab;                        /* the word table */
  void  init_tab();

  init_tab(&wordtab);                   /* initialize to empty table */
  while (getword (word, MAXWORD, &lineno))
    if (wordtab = addword (wordtab, word, lineno, &error), error != 0)
    {
       printf ("Out of memory: processing word %s on line %d\n", word, lineno);
       break;                           /* no point in going on */
    }
  writewords (wordtab, MAXWORD);        /* write table, even if out of memory */
}
```

FIGURE 10.23   The main cross-referencer program.

from `addword` telling us if the table is full. The table might be full because it is represented as an array and we have run out of space, or it might fail because it is dynamically allocated and we have no more dynamic memory space. Either way, the underlying table is hidden from the main program. We have defined the table to be a variable called `wordtab`, of type `WTPTR` (for word table pointer), that hints at its type, but the actual definition of the type is in the include file *xref_tab.h*. Any changes in the table representation will require only a change in the data structure definitions in *xref_tab.h* and the access routines in `addword` and `init_tab`.

How should the word table be represented? Since there are several possibilities, we will list the characteristics that the table ought to have, so that we can make a choice in a more informed way.

- The table contains an arbitrary number of words of arbitrary size.
- Since we have to search the table for each word to see if the word is already there, table searches must be fast. We also need to be able to determine quickly if the word has already occurred on the current line.
- It should be easy to print the table alphabetically by word, and for each word, in line number order.

The first point suggests that the word itself should not be stored in the table. Instead, each table entry should contain a pointer to the (arbitrarily long) word. It also suggests that the table should consist of dynamically allocated records. The next point suggests that there should be a list associated with each entry in the table: the lines on which the word appears. Therefore, each record in the table must contain at least a pointer to the word and a pointer to the line numbers where the word occurs.

Since the words in the table will be printed out alphabetically at the end, and since we want searches to be fast, it seems reasonable to try to keep the table in word order. An alternative arrangement is to add the new word to the end of the table, along with the current line number, and

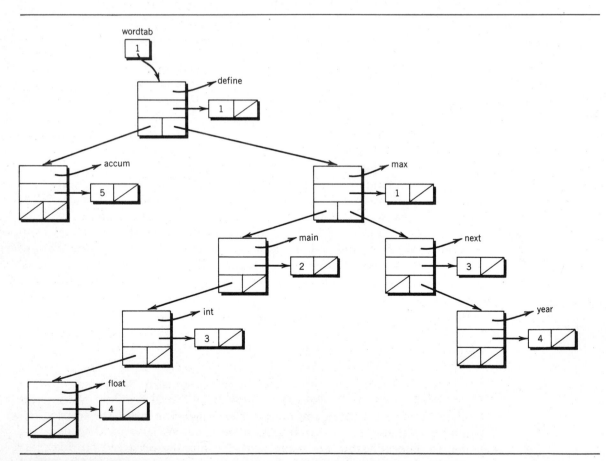

FIGURE 10.24 Binary tree representation for the cross-referencer word table.

then sort the table by word just before printing. However, in this case, searches will not be fast. A reasonable representation for the word table is a *binary tree*, using the word as the key field. All words less than the root word are in the left subtree, and all words greater than the root word are in the right subtree. A node in the tree must also contain pointers to the left and right subtrees.

With this representation for a node, a word table for a few entries from a program might look like that in Figure 10.24.

We need a little more information in each node to complete the representation. Rather than use multiple nodes when a word occurs more than once in a single line, we include a `count` field to hold the number of times a word appears on a given line.

Finally, we perform two actions on the line list in each node: adding new nodes at the end and printing the line list from the front. A list structure with the property that additions are made only at the rear while removals, or traversals, occur only from the front, is called a *queue*. Each tree node must contain two pointers to be able to maintain the queue in proper order — `first`, a pointer to the start of the line list, and `last`, a pointer to the end. Therefore, the word table is a BST, and the line numbers and counters for each word are simple linked lists organized as queues.

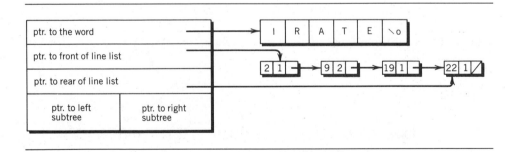

With these representation ideas, we can formally define the data structures for a `struct wordnode` that was used in Figure 10.24. They are defined in the include file *xref_tab.h*, shown in Figure 10.25.

With these concepts, the entire code is a series of routines that parse the input, selecting individual words; routines to put the word into the word table and update the line numbers; and routines for printing the table at the end. The rest of the program is shown in Figure 10.26. The listing of the code is broken into three files: *xref_in.c*, *xref_tab.c*, and *xref_out.c*. These three files, along with the main program in file *xref.c*, are compiled and linked together to produce the runnable cross-referencer. Note the `extern` declaration for `addword` in Figure 10.25.

```
/*
 *  XREF_TAB.H
 *
 *      Definitions of the internal structure of the word table, and the
 *      functions that use them.
 */

#define  MAXWORD    20                  /* longest word */

typedef struct linenode  *LINEPTR;      /* ptr to a struct linenode */

struct linenode                         /* node containing a line number */
{
  int      lineno,                      /* line word appears on */
           count;                       /* number of times it appears */
  LINEPTR  next;                        /* next line number for word */
};

typedef struct wordnode  *WTPTR;        /* ptr to a struct wordnode */

struct wordnode                         /* node containing a word */
{
  char     *word;                       /* word (has to be allocated) */
  WTPTR    left, right;                 /* tree children pointers */
  LINEPTR  first, last;                 /* line number list pointers */
};

extern WTPTR  addword(  /* WTPTR, WORD, LINENO, ERRPTR */  );
```

FIGURE 10.25 The include file *xref_tab.h*, where the binary tree data structures are defined.

EXERCISES

10-24 Extend the cross-referencer so that it works specifically for C programs. In order not to clutter the output with C reserved words, have the program check each word in a table of reserved words. Only those words not in the table are included in the cross-reference. □

10-25 Modify the cross-referencer so that it works for Pascal programs. What is the best form of the reserved word table? □

10-26 Profile the cross-referencer and find out where it is spending most of its time. Can you improve its performance without hurting readability? □

10-27 Change the representation of the cross-reference table to a hash table Aho, Hopcroft and Ullman, *The Design and Analysis of Computer Algorithms* for references on hash tables). Since a hash table is unsorted, perform a quicksort (see Chapter 5) on the words before printing. □

```
/*
 *   XREF_IN.C
 *
 *       Handles breaking up the input into words for XREF.  All decisions
 *       about what is a word, and where line breaks go, are made here.
 */
#include <stdio.h>
#include <ctype.h>

static int   lineno = 1;                    /* current line number */

/*
 *  Return the next character in the input, updating
 *  the line number count when new lines are hit.
 */
static int getachar()
{
  int    ch;                                /* current character */

  if ((ch = getchar()) == '\n')
      lineno++;
  return ch;
}


/*
 *  Get the next word from the input, filling in "linenoptr" with the
 *  line number this word is on, and returning zero if there are no
 *  more words; otherwise returns the length of the word.
 */
int getword (word, wordsize, linenoptr)
char    word[];                             /* place to store word */
int     wordsize,                           /* size of place */
        *linenoptr;                         /* line number to update */
{
  int   ch,                                 /* next character */
        wordlen = 0;                        /* length of word */

  while ((ch = getachar()) != EOF && !isalpha(ch))
     ;                                      /* skip nonletters */
  /* Once word is found, save it.  Ends with first nonalphanumeric. */

  while (ch != EOF && isalnum(ch))
  {
    *linenoptr = lineno;
    if (wordlen < wordsize)                 /* make sure there is room */
      word[wordlen++] = ch;
    ch = getachar();
  }
  word[wordlen] = '\0';
  return wordlen;                           /* return word length: zero if no word */
}
```

(a) xref_in.c: *The file of routines for handling input*

FIGURE 10.26 The routines called from the main cross-referencer program, and the routines they call.

```
/*
 *   XREF_TAB.C—Handles the table of words and line number references.
 */
#include <stdio.h>
#include "xref_tab.h"

#define  DOALLOC(type)   ((type *) malloc(sizeof(type)))

/* Initialize the word table "tabptr" to the empty table. */

void init_tab(tabptr)
WTPTR    *tabptr;
{
 *tabptr = NULL;
}


/*
 *  Allocate enough room for the string, and copy it, returning a pointer to
 *  the newly allocated string, or NULL if we can't allocate it.
 */
static char *strsave(str)
char     *str;
{
  char   *malloc(), *strcpy();              /* returns ptr to first string */
  char   *newstr = malloc( (unsigned) strlen(str) + 1);

  return (newstr != NULL) ? strcpy(newstr, str) : NULL;
                                            /* strcpy returns ptr to "newstr" */
}


/*
 *  Allocate a new word node, and fill it appropriately.
 */
static WTPTR  make_wordnode(word)
char     *word;
{
  char   *malloc(),
         *strcpy();
  WTPTR wnptr;

  if ((wnptr = DOALLOC(struct wordnode)) != NULL)
  {
    wnptr->left = wnptr->right = NULL;       /* no children */
    wnptr->first = wnptr->last = NULL;       /* no lines yet */
    if ((wnptr->word = strsave(word)) == NULL)
      free((char *) wnptr), wnptr = NULL;    /* can't alloc word, fail */
  }
  return wnptr;
}
```

FIGURE 10.26 (continued)

```
/*
 *   Allocate new line node, and save line number inside it.
 */
static LINEPTR  make_linenode(lineno)
int    lineno;
{
  char      *malloc();
  LINEPTR    lnptr;

  if ((lnptr = DOALLOC(struct linenode)) != NULL)
  {              /* Allocate new line number node, hook into list. */
    lnptr->lineno = lineno;
    lnptr->count = 1;
    lnptr->next = NULL;
  }
  return lnptr;
}
/*
 *   Add a new line number for the given node; check to see if word
 *   appears on the same line as the previous one.
 */
static LINEPTR  add_lineno(wnptr,lineno)
WTPTR   wnptr;                          /* word to add line to */
int     lineno;                         /* line number */
{
  LINEPTR  lnptr = wnptr->last;         /* new line node pointer */

  if (lnptr && lnptr->lineno == lineno)
    lnptr->count++;                     /* already occurs on this line */
  else
    if (lnptr = make_linenode(lineno))
    {                                   /* allocated new node, hook into list */
      if (wnptr->first == NULL)         /* empty list, place at front */
        wnptr->first = lnptr;
      else                              /* nonempty, place at back */
        wnptr->last->next = lnptr;
      wnptr->last = lnptr;              /* regardless it's the end of the list */
    }
  return lnptr;                         /* NULL if we can't allocate new node */
}

/*
 *   Add new word to tree, returning pointer to tree. "errptr" will be
 *   zero if no errors, and nonzero otherwise.
 */
WTPTR   addword(wnptr,word,lineno,errptr)
WTPTR   wnptr;                          /* base of tree */
char    *word;                          /* word to add */
int     lineno,                         /* line number word appears on */
        *errptr;                        /* were there errors? */
```

FIGURE 10.26 (continued)

```
{
    int    cmpres;                             /* result of comparing words */

    if (wnptr == NULL)
      if (wnptr = make_wordnode(word))          /* create word */
        *errptr = add_lineno(wnptr,lineno) == NULL;   /* add line no */
      else
        *errptr++;                              /* failed */
    else if ((cmpres = strcmp(word,wnptr->word)) < 0)
      wnptr->left = addword(wnptr->left, word, lineno, errptr);
    else if (cmpres > 0)
      wnptr->right = addword(wnptr->right, word, lineno, errptr);
    else
      *errptr = add_lineno(wnptr,lineno) == NULL;
    return wnptr;
}
```

(b) xref_tab.c: *the file of routines for manipulating the word table*

```
/*
 *  XREF_OUT.C
 *
 *      Writes the table.  If the internal data structure changes,
 *      then changes may need to be made here.
 */

#include <stdio.h>
#include "xref_tab.h"

#define   MAXLINENO       7          /* allow seven line numbers per line */

writewords (wnptr, maxword)
WTPTR   wnptr;                        /* the table of words */
int.    maxword;                      /* maximum word length */
{
  LINEPTR    lnptr;                   /* the lines for the given word */
  int        count = 0;               /* count of line numbers for this word */

  if (wnptr)
  {
    writewords(wnptr->left, MAXWORD);
    printf("%-*s", maxword, wnptr->word);
    for (lnptr = wnptr->first; lnptr != NULL; lnptr = lnptr->next)
    {
      if (count == MAXLINENO)              /* next line */
        printf("\n%-*s ", maxword, " "), count = 0;
      printf(" %d" , lnptr->lineno);       /* write line and count */
      if (lnptr->count > 1)
        printf(" (%d)", lnptr->count);
      if (lnptr->next)                     /* not last */
        putchar(',');
      count++;
    }
    putchar('\n');
    writewords(wnptr->right, MAXWORD);
  }
}
```

(c) xref_out.c: *the file of routines for printing the word table*

FIGURE 10.26 (continued)

DYNAMIC DATA STRUCTURES

In this chapter we have introduced the concept of dynamic data structures and have provided many examples of their power. We now want to emphasize several points about these data structures:

- Dynamic data structures make efficient use of programmer time. They also have the nice property of providing storage for arbitrary collections of values, while only requiring storage for those values actually stored. Finally, a large set of algorithms are easiest to implement when dynamically allocated space is available.

- Dynamic data structures are not necessarily more efficient at run time, however, as we shall learn in Chapter 12. The operating system and C run-time environment must usually manage the free storage pool in such a way that nodes of any size may be requested and freed in arbitrary order. With fixed-size arrays, we take a burden off the system at run time, at the price of having to specify in advance the amount of storage needed.

- Allocating storage for dynamic data structures can fail, so we must test `malloc`'s return value. This function will fail (returning NULL) when the system is out of space, which can certainly happen on machines with small amounts of memory, such as small microcomputers. Often there is little we can do if `malloc` does fail, but it is better for the program to maintain control and die gracefully than for the run-time system to terminate with an error as we attempt to store through the NULL pointer.

C H A P T E R   11

C AND THE OUTSIDE WORLD

Up to this point, our programs have interacted with their environment solely through the standard input and the standard output. In this chapter, we discuss two alternatives: command line arguments and external files. As part of this discussion, we introduce the remaining standard I/O library functions and provide examples of their use. We conclude with the implementation of a small indexed data base for storing names, addresses, and phone numbers, an extension of the version in Chapter 9.

11.1
COMMAND LINE ARGUMENTS

We have been hiding something all this time: main is a function that takes arguments. When main is called, it is passed two parameters that together describe the command line that invoked the program. The first is the number of arguments on the command line. The second is an array of pointers to strings containing the various arguments. Traditionally, these are called argc and argv, respectively. We declare main's parameters in the same way as those of any other function:

```
main(argc, argv)
int argc;                        /* command line argument count */
char *argv[];                    /* command line arguments */
```

By convention, the program's name is accessed through `argv[0]`, so `argc` is always at least one. The other arguments are used most often to specify various program options, as well as the external files the program should process.[1]

We illustrate command line argument processing with a program (called *echo*) that prints each of its arguments (minus the program name) to the standard output. If, for example, the command line is

```
echo programming in c is fun
```

echo's output is

```
programming in c is fun
```

For this command line, when `main` is called, `argc` is six and `argv` is an array of six pointers to strings, as shown below.

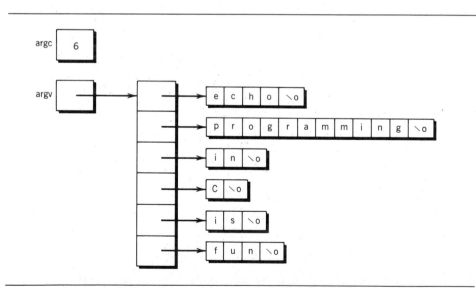

Figure 11.1 contains two implementations of *echo*. The first version is straightforward, using array indexing to traverse `argv` and printing each of the entries except the first (the program name). When written, the

[1]The precise definition of a command line argument varies from system to system; however, white space is usually used to delimit the arguments. An argument containing white space is placed within quotation marks.

arguments are separated by spaces with the last argument followed by a newline.

The second version is trickier, using `argv` as a pointer to traverse the array. We can do this because `argv`, like any other array parameter, is really a pointer to the array's first element.[2] Note that `argv` is incremented before the comparison with the table's end, allowing us to skip conveniently over the program's name, which is stored as the table's first entry.

Using a pointer to traverse command line arguments is usually more efficient than using array indexing, but it is also usually harder to read and understand. Thus, either method of command line argument processing is acceptable. However, the pointer method should be mastered, even if it is not the method of choice, because it is used frequently in existing programs.

```
/*
 * Echo arguments (using array indexing).
 */
main(argc, argv)
int argc;                          /* argument count */
char *argv[];                      /* list of arguments */
{
  int next;                        /* index to next argument */

  for (next = 1; next < argc; next++)
    printf("%s%c", argv[next], (next < argc - 1) ? ' ' : '\n');
}
```

(a) Echo the program's arguments using array indexing

```
/*
 * Echo arguments (using pointer indexing)
 */
main(argc, argv)
int argc;                          /* argument count */
char **argv;                       /* list of arguments */
{
  char **last_ptr = argv + argc - 1;   /* pointer to last argument */

  while(++argv <= last_ptr)
    printf("%s%c", *argv, (argv < last_ptr) ? ' ' : '\n');
}
```

(b) Echo the program's arguments using pointers

FIGURE 11.1 Two implementations of echo. The first using array subscripting, the second using pointers.

[2]See Section 8.4 if the reasons for this are not clear.

EXERCISES

11-1 Rewrite echo to print out its arguments in reverse order, first using array indexing, then using pointers. ☐

11-2 Write a program to print only those lines in its input that contain its argument. This is a simplified version of the UNIX *fgrep* utility. Can you easily extend your program to handle multiple arguments? ☐

11.2

EXTERNAL FILES

Programs are more useful if they access external files directly, with the file names supplied as the program's arguments. Files are declared using the `FILE` data type defined in *stdio.h* and are accessed through standard I/O library functions. `FILE` is not one of C's basic data types. Instead, `FILE` is usually a structure containing information useful to the library routines that process files.

Before we can access a file, we must "open" it, associating the file's name with the file's contents. The standard I/O function `fopen` opens a file, allocating the necessary `FILE` structure and returning a pointer to it. Once a file has been opened, this file pointer refers to the file and is passed to other standard I/O library functions instead of the file's name.

`fopen` is passed two strings: the name of the file to open and a "mode" specifying how the file will be used. The mode specifies where the initial reads and writes on the file will take place, as well as what to do if the file does not already exist, and can be either "r" (read), "w" (write), or "a" (append). Remember, the mode is a string and not a character. As an example use of `fopen`,

```
#include <stdio.h>                        /* defines the FILE data type */
   . . .
FILE *fp;
   . . .
fp = fopen("phone-numbers", "r");        /* open phone number file */
```

opens the file *phone-numbers* for reading.

A file must already exist to be opened for reading, but when it is opened for writing or appending it will be created if it does not already exist. If a file does exist, opening it for writing causes its old contents to be discarded. Opening it for appending causes new writes to take place at the file's end. If there is an error and the file cannot be opened, `fopen` returns `NULL`.

Once a file has been opened, there are a variety of ways to access it. The simplest file-accessing functions are getc and putc, which are analogous to getchar and putchar. getc takes a file pointer, returning the next character in the file, or EOF when end of file is encountered. As with getchar, getc's return value is an integer to allow EOF to be a value outside the character set. putc takes a character and a file pointer, writing the character to the specified file. Both functions return EOF if an error occurs.

When we have finished processing the file, we use fclose to "close" it. Closing a file causes any buffered output to be forced out and frees the file's FILE structure. fclose has a single file pointer argument, and returns EOF if there is an error in closing the file. Since most systems have a maximum number of files that can be open at any one time (usually about twenty per program), closing a file as soon as it is no longer needed should become a habit.

```
/*
 *  Copy "source" to "dest".
 */
#include <stdio.h>

int file_copy(dest, source)
char *dest,                             /* source file name */
     *source;                           /* destination file name */
{
  FILE *sfp,                            /* source file pointer */
       *dfp;                            /* destination file pointer */

  if ((sfp = fopen(source,"r")) == NULL)
    printf("Couldn't open %s for reading\n", source);
  else
  {
    if ((dfp = fopen(dest,"w")) == NULL)
      printf("Couldn't open %s for writing\n", dest);
    else
    {
      while ((c = getc(sfp)) != EOF)    /* do the copy */
        putc(c, dfp);
      (void) fclose(dfp);
    }
    (void) fclose(sfp);
  }
  return sfp && dfp;
}
```

FIGURE 11.2 Copying one file into another – an example of external files.

We now have the pieces to write a useful utility function to copy files. file_copy, shown in Figure 11.2, is passed two file names and copies the contents of one file into another, one character at a time. For example,

```
file_copy("paper.old", "paper");
```

copies the contents of the file *paper* into the file *paper.old*.

Because file_copy is given file names and not file pointers, it has to open the files before accessing them. We are careful to check whether the opening of either file fails, performing the copy only if both opens are successful. Since opening a file for writing destroys the file's contents, we are also careful to do the open for writing only after the open for reading has succeeded. In this way, we destroy the previous contents of the destination file only if there is something to copy.

file_copy's return value indicates whether the files can be opened, with zero indicating a failed open. We have ignored the possibility of other errors and have cast the value returned by fclose to void. (We will soon discuss when it is important to examine its return value.)

11.2.1 COMBINING EXTERNAL FILES AND COMMAND LINE ARGUMENTS

Given the function file_copy, it is easy to write a program to copy one file into another with the names supplied as its arguments. This program (called *cp*) is shown in Figure 11.3. *cp*'s first argument is the file to copy into and its second argument is the file we are copying. For example,

> *cp datebook.backup datebook*

```
/*
 * Copy two files.  Usage:  cp dest src.
 */
main(argc, argv)
int argc;
char *argv[];
{
  if (argc != 3)                             /* make sure it is: cp dest source */
    printf("Usage is: %s dest source\n", argv[0]);
  else if (!file_copy(argv[1], argv[2]))   /* make sure copy worked */
    printf("Copy failed.\n");
}
```

FIGURE 11.3 Copying one file into another – the arguments provide the file names.

makes the file *datebook.backup* a copy of the file *datebook*. *cp* is a simplified version of the *cp* utility found on most UNIX systems. *cp* verifies that there are three arguments (the program name and the two file names) and then uses `file_copy` to do the copying. Any error in invoking the command, such as providing too many or too few arguments, results in an error message. In addition, the user is notified if the copy fails because a file cannot be opened.

EXERCISES

11-3 Write a function, `file_append`, that appends one file to the end of another. Can `file_copy` and `file_append` be combined into one function? Is this a good idea? □

11-4 Write a function, `tail_file`, that prints the last *n* lines of a file. How might this function be used? □

11-5 Write a function, `fget_line`, to read a line of input from a file. This can be done easily by modifying `get_line` (Chapter 3). □

11.2.2 FORMATTED I/O TO FILES

As you might have guessed, both `printf` and `scanf` have counterparts that do formatted I/O on files. `fprintf` is like `printf`, with an additional file pointer argument that specifies the file to which we write. For example,

```
fprintf(fp, "BMW 320i's are great cars!\n");
```

writes a single line onto the file specified by `fp`. `fscanf` is like `scanf`, with an additional file pointer argument that specifies the file from which we read. As an example,

```
inpres = fscanf(fp, "%d", &value);
```

reads a single integer from the file specified by `fp`, places it in `value`, and returns the number of values read. Like `scanf`, `fscanf` returns EOF when end of file is reached or an error occurs. Because of their similarity to `printf` and `scanf`, forgetting to pass a file pointer to `fprintf` or `fscanf` is a common mistake.

EXERCISES

11-6 Modify the histogram program from Chapter 4 to read its data values from a file passed on the command line, while getting the histogram's parameters from the the standard input. □

11-7 Modify the debugging package of Chapter 6 to place all debugging output into a file. What should the package do if the debugging file cannot be opened? □

11.2.3 HANDLING I/O ERRORS

Although it is unlikely, a file read or write can fail. Usually such failures are caused by hardware errors, but write errors can also occur when a device becomes full and there is no room for the newly written characters. All the standard I/O output functions return `EOF` if a write error occurs, allowing us to check for these errors. We can, for example, make `file_copy` (Figure 11.3) more robust by checking `putc`'s return value and printing an error message if it is `EOF`. We should also check `fclose`'s return value, because output is usually buffered and it is possible that the last characters written are not really written to the file until the file is closed.

Detecting read errors is more difficult, since `EOF` can indicate either an error or end of file. We can use two new library functions, `feof` and `ferror`, to distinguish between the two meanings. `feof` takes a file pointer and returns nonzero only if the end of the file has been reached. `ferror` is similar, taking a file pointer and returning nonzero only if an error has occurred in processing that file. After any input function has returned `EOF`, one of these tests can be made and, if necessary, an appropriate error message printed.

To keep our examples simple, we have avoided the added complication of file I/O error handling. Unfortunately, when we fail to check for read and write errors and an error occurs, our program may behave abnormally, with no indication of any error. An unchecked input error is treated as `EOF`, prematurely terminating input processing. An unchecked output error can result in incorrect output. Production quality programs should check the values returned by the standard input and output library functions.

EXERCISES

11-8 Make `file_copy` check for both read and write errors. How much does this change complicate the code? □

11.2.4 THE STANDARD FILES

When a program starts, three files are automatically opened: the standard input, the standard output, and the standard error output. We are familiar with the standard input and standard output; the standard error output is where error messages should be written to distinguish them from normal output. The file pointers corresponding to these files are `stdin`, `stdout` and `stderr`, and are defined in *stdio.h*. These file pointers are constants, and no assignment can be made to them.

Using `stdin` and `stdout`, we can define `getchar` and `putchar` as macros that expand into calls to `getc` and `putc`:[3]

```
#define getchar()    getc(stdin)        /* next char from std input */
#define putchar(c)   putc(c, stdout)    /* next char from std output */
```

Although `printf` and `scanf` cannot be defined as macros because they can be passed a variable number of arguments, `fprintf` with `stdout` is equivalent to `printf`:

```
printf("Hi dad!\n");                  /* both write to */
fprintf(stdout, "Hi dad!\n");         /*    stdout */
```

Similarly, `fscanf` with `stdin` is equivalent to `scanf`:

```
scanf("%d", &value)                   /* both read from */
fscanf(stdin, "%d", &value)           /*    stdin */
```

Error messages are usually written to `stderr` so that they will show up on the terminal, even if the standard output has been redirected. We illustrate the use of `stderr` in the function `our_fopen`, shown in Figure 11.4. `our_fopen`'s parameters are a file name and a mode, which are passed to `fopen` to open the file. If the open fails, an error message is printed on the standard error; otherwise, `our_fopen` returns the file pointer returned by `fopen`. Since `our_fopen` handles the errors, the functions that use it are simpler because they no longer have this responsibility.

EXERCISES

11-9 Write a function (or macro), `our_fclose`, that takes a file pointer and closes the file only if the file pointer it is passed is not `NULL`. □

11-10 Modify `file_copy` to use `our_fopen` to open files and `our_fclose` to close them. Does this simplify the function significantly? □

[3]This is how it is done in most standard I/O library implementations.

```
/*
 * Open a file, writing error message if it fails.
 */
#include <stdio.h>

FILE *our_fopen(file_name, mode)
char *file_name,                            /* file to open */
     *mode;                                 /* "r", "w" or "a" */
{
  FILE *fp = fopen(file_name, mode);        /* open the file */

  if (!fp)                                  /* did open fail */
    fprintf(stderr, "Can't open file \"%s\" for %s\n", file_name,
                   (*mode == 'r')
                    ? "reading"
                    : ((*mode == 'w') ? "writing" : "appending"));
  return fp;
}
```

FIGURE 11.4 A function to open a file, printing any necessary error message onto the standard error.

> **11-11** Many errors are caused by passing an incorrect mode. Make `our_fopen` verify that it has been given a reasonable mode. □

> **11-12** Write versions of the functions in *getnum.c* that read from files instead of the standard input. □

11.3

FILES, COMMAND LINE ARGUMENTS, AND OPTIONS

To illustrate the full power of command line arguments, we write a small program (called *wc*) that counts the number of lines, words, and characters in the files specified by its arguments. In addition to file names, we allow the user to specify the desired counts in optional arguments appearing before the names of the files to be processed. It has become traditional for these optional arguments to begin with a dash ("–"), so *wc*'s options will be "–c" to count characters, "–w" to count words and "–l" to count lines. For ease of use, we allow these options to be specified as either a single argument or separate arguments. Here are some example uses of *wc*:

wc –l datebook termpaper	lines only
wc –c –w datebook termpaper	characters and words only
wc –cw datebook termpaper	characters and words only
wc datebook termpaper	characters, words and lines

wc is a simplified version of the UNIX utility with the same name.

It seems natural to break *wc* into two pieces, the first handling argument processing and file opening and closing, and the second counting the characters, words, and lines in the file. The first part, the main program, is shown in Figure 11.5.

wc's design is typical of most programs that have options. First, the optional arguments are processed and their values recorded. The first argument that does not begin with a dash signals the end of the options. When an argument does begin with a dash, each character of the argument is examined and a flag is set with its value. Any unrecognized options causes an error message describing the program's normal usage to be written to `stderr`. Figure 11.6 shows the relationships between the various pointers used to process the arguments.

Once the options have been processed, each subsequent argument is assumed to be a file name and is opened using `our_fopen` (Figure 11.4). Following a successful file open, the file pointer and option flags are passed to `file_count`, which does the counting. We are careful to close each file after it is printed to avoid running out of files when there are many arguments.

An interesting case occurs when there are no arguments. Instead of printing an error message, the program assumes that the user wants to use the standard input, and `file_count` is called with `stdin` as its file pointer.

Going through a file and counting the words is simple and is shown in Figure 11.7. The only tricky part consists of defining a word. We have defined a word as a sequence of alphanumeric or punctuation characters. To test this definition, we use the library functions `isalnum` and `ispunct`, part of the set of character-testing functions discussed in Chapter 6 and listed in Appendix 6.

Command line options to control a program's functioning are a powerful and useful idea. Unfortunately, many programs use them to provide different and often unrelated features. These extra features are used infrequently, if at all, but they make the program significantly harder to read and debug. To avoid falling into this trap, first write a simple version of the program that performs its main task correctly. Options should be added only after the program has been used for a while, and adding certain features will clearly make the program more useful.

EXERCISES

11-13 Have *wc* print a grand total line if it is given more than one argument. Add an option to suppress the new default action. □

```
/*
 *   Count words, lines and characters in file
 */
#include <stdio.h>
#include "boolean.h"

main(argc, argv)
int argc;                               /* argument count */
char **argv;                            /* list of arguments */
{
  FILE *fp, *our_fopen();               /* next file to process */
  BOOLEAN bad_opt, chars, lines, words; /* option flags */
  char **last_ptr = &argv[argc - 1];    /* pointer to last argument */
  int i;                                /* index to option */
  void file_count();                    /* does the counting */

  /* Process optional arguments */

  bad_opt = chars = lines = words = FALSE;
  while (++argv <= last_ptr && (*argv)[0] == '-')
    for(i = 1; (*argv)[i] != '\0'; i++)
      switch ((*argv)[i])               /* in row of options */
        {
          case 'c':  chars = TRUE;   break;
          case 'w':  words = TRUE;   break;
          case 'l':  lines = TRUE;   break;
          default:   fprintf(stderr,"wc: bad option %c\n", (*argv)[i]);
                     bad_opt = TRUE;
        }
  if (!chars && !words && !lines)       /* no options means all of them */
    chars = words = lines = TRUE;

  /* Process other arguments */

  if (bad_opt)
    fprintf(stderr,"Usage: wc [-c][-w][-l] [files...]\n");
  else if (argv > last_ptr)             /* use stdin if no args */
    file_count(stdin, "Standard Input", chars, words, lines);
  else                                  /* otherwise arg specifies file */
    while (argv <= last_ptr)
    {
      if (fp = our_fopen(*argv,"r"), fp != NULL)
      {
        file_count(fp, *argv, chars, words, lines);
        fclose(fp);
      }
      argv++;
    }
}
```

FIGURE 11.5 Program to count characters, words, and lines in the files that are given to it as arguments.

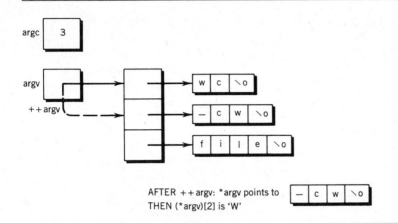

FIGURE 11.6 Processing the optional arguments. | `argv` points to the argument, `(*argv)[i]` is the next character in the argument.

11-14 Many of the programs written in earlier chapters should be extended to process external files. Among them are *num* (Chapter 1), *isort* (Chapter 1), *Uniq* (Chapter 3), *Histo* (Chapter 4), and *Xref* (Chapter 10). Modify these programs to use external files. □

11-15 Add three new options to the *Uniq* program of Chapter 3. The first, −c, causes a count of the number of occurrences of any line of output to be printed before the line. The second, −u, causes only those lines that appear uniquely to be output. The last, −d, causes only those lines that are duplicated to appear in the output. What should *Uniq* do when combinations of these options are specified? □

11-16 Write a program, *sort*, that sorts the files specified as arguments, using any of the sorting methods we have discussed. Note that *sort* simply prints the sorted files onto `stdout` without changing the files. Add a new option to *sort*, −r, that reverses the sense of the sort. □

11.4

LINE ORIENTED I/O

For many programs (such as *Uniq*), it is more natural to process the input a line at a time instead of a character at a time. The standard I/O library provides four functions that do line-at-a-time I/O. The most general of

```
/*
 * Count words, characters and lines.
 */
#include <stdio.h>
#include <ctype.h>
#include "boolean.h"

#define PRINT(flg,cntl,thing) ((flg) ? printf(cntl, thing) : 0)

void file_count(fp, fname, chars, words, lines)
FILE *fp;                                       /* file pointer */
char *fname;                                    /* file name */
BOOLEAN chars, words, lines;                    /* flags */
{
  long c_cnt = 0, w_cnt = 0, l_cnt = 0;         /* counters */
  int c;                                        /* next character */
  BOOLEAN inword = FALSE;                        /* are we in a word */

  while ((c = getc(fp)) != EOF)
  {
    c_cnt++;                                     /* one more character */
    if (c == '\n')
      l_cnt++;                                   /* one more word */
    if (!isalnum(c) && !ispunct(c))
      inword = FALSE;                            /* end of word */
    else if (!inword)
    {
      inword = TRUE;                             /* start of word */
      w_cnt++;
    }
  }
  PRINT(chars, "%10ld", c_cnt);                  /* print counters */
  PRINT(words, "%10ld", w_cnt);
  PRINT(lines, "%10ld", l_cnt);
  PRINT(fname, " %s", fname);                    /* and file name */
  putchar('\n');
}
```

FIGURE 11.7   Function to count characters, words and lines in a file.

these functions are `fputs` and `fgets`.   `fputs` takes a string and a file
pointer and writes the string to the file. For example,

```
fputs("For a good time, call 555-1212\n", fp);
```

writes a single line to the file specified by `fp`.   `fputs` provides a convenient and more efficient way to print a string than `printf`. One drawback, however, is that the file pointer is its last argument instead of its first
argument, as with `fprintf`.

`fgets` reads a line of input from a file and is somewhat similar to get_line (Chapter 3). fgets takes three parameters: a character array, its size, and a file pointer. It reads characters until a newline is read or the array is full. The array is terminated with a null, and to accommodate the null, the number of characters read will be, at most, one less than the number of characters in the array. The line's trailing newline is included in the array.

```
char buffer[MAXLINE];
    . . .
fgets(buffer, MAXLINE, fp)
```

reads up to MAXLINE − 1 characters, placing them into buffer.

fgets and get_line differ in their handling of longer than expected input lines. If the line (including the trailing newline) is too long, more calls to fgets can be used to read the rest of the line; get_line ignores the rest of the line.   fgets returns NULL when end of file is reached, otherwise returning its first argument, a pointer to a character.   get_line returns the number of characters read.

As an example, Figure 11.8 shows a version of file_copy written using fgets and fputs instead of getc and putc. The line-copying version produces the same result as the character-copying version, albeit a little slower, since fgets and fputs are usually written using getc and putc.

A problem with fgets is that there is no way to determine if the entire input line was read without examining the returned string, making fgets significantly less useful than it would be if it returned the line length, as get_line does.

The functions gets and puts are closely related to fgets and fputs, and are just different enough to cause confusion. gets takes a character array, reading a line from stdin and placing it into the array, terminating the array with a null character. gets returns a pointer to the array's first character, or NULL when the end of file is reached. Unlike fgets, gets does not place the terminating newline into the array. puts is simpler and more useful, taking a string and writing it and a trailing newline onto the standard output.

The most common uses of puts and gets are to prompt the user for input and to read the response, as shown below.

```
char response[MAX_LINE];
    . . .
puts("What's your name?");
if (gets(response) != NULL)
  printf("Hi %s!  Are you free Friday night?\n", response);
```

The usefulness of gets is limited because there is no way to limit the number of characters it reads, which causes the program to "bomb" if more characters are read than the array can accomodate. We prefer get_line.

```
/*
 * Copy "source" into "dest" a line at a time.
 */
#include <stdio.h>

#define MAX_LINE  256                    /* longest input line */

int file_copy(dest, source)
char *dest,                              /* source file name */
     *source;                            /* destination file name */
{
  FILE *sfp,                             /* source file pointer */
       *dfp,                             /* destination file pointer */
       *our_fopen();                     /* our file opener */
  char line[MAX_LINE];

  if ((sfp = our_fopen(source,"r")) != NULL)
  {
    if ((dfp = our_fopen(dest,"w")) != NULL)
    {
      while (fgets(line, sizeof(line), sfp))   /* copy source into */
        fputs(line, dfp);                       /* destination */
      fclose(dfp);
    }
    fclose(sfp);
  }
  return sfp && dfp;
}
```

FIGURE 11.8 Copy files line by line. Surprisingly, this is slower than character by character copying.

EXERCISE

11-17 Write `fgets`, `fputs`, `puts`, and `gets`, using `getc` and `putc`. How can these functions be changed to make them more useful? Make these changes. □

11.5

RANDOM FILE ACCESS

So far, all file processing has been sequential. There are times, however, when we are interested only in a particular part of a file and want to access that part without having to read all the preceding data. In effect, we want to treat a file like an array, indexing any byte in the file as we would an array element. There are three standard I/O functions to support this random file access: `rewind`, `ftell`, and `fseek`.

`rewind` takes a file pointer and resets the current position to the beginning of the file. A `rewind` is done implicitly whenever a file is opened with `fopen` for reading or writing, but is of course not done when a file is opened for appending. Any input function immediately following a `rewind` will start reading the file's first character. `rewind` allows a program to read through a file more than once without having to open and close the file.

`ftell` takes a file pointer and returns a `long` containing the current offset in the file, the position of the next byte to be read or written. An `ftell` at the beginning of the file returns the position of the file's first byte. Using `ftell`, a program can save its current position in the file in order to return to it later without having to read all the intervening data.

`fseek` moves the current file position to a given location within the file. It takes three arguments—a file pointer, a `long` offset, and an `int` specifier—and resets the current byte position within the file. The new position is computed by adding the offset to the part of the file specified by the specifier, which can have one of three values: zero means the beginning of the file, one means the current position, and two means the end of the file. Here are some example `fseek`s:[4]

```
long n;
...
fseek(fp, 0L, 0);          /* go to the start: same as rewind(fp) */
fseek(fp, 0L, 1);          /* stay where we are (not too useful!) */
fseek(fp, 0L, 2);          /* go to the end of the file */
fseek(fp, n, 0);           /* go to the nth byte in the file */
fseek(fp, n, 1);           /* skip ahead n bytes */
fseek(fp, -n, 1);          /* go backwards n bytes */
fseek(fp, -n, 2);          /* go to n bytes before the file's end */
```

It is a common mistake to forget that `fseek`'s second parameter is a `long`; passing any other type will produce unpredictable results.

`fseek` returns zero if the file pointer can be moved to the desired position and minus one if there is an error such as attempting to seek past the file's boundaries. We have ignored `fseek`'s return value in these examples; however, by checking it, we can verify that the file position was changed.

Using these functions, we can write the function `read_bytes` (Figure 11.9), which allows us to read a group of bytes starting from any byte in the file. `read_bytes` takes a file pointer, a position, a number of bytes to read, and a place to put those bytes. It moves to the desired position and

---

[4]On some systems the offset to `fseek` must be a value returned by `ftell` and is not simply the desired byte number. For these examples, however, we are assuming that this is not the case.

then uses `getc` to read the requested number of bytes into the specified place. `read_bytes` returns the number of bytes read, which may be fewer than the number requested if we start reading too far into the file. If there is an error, minus one is returned. We are careful to test `fseek`'s return value, because the file pointer's position will not change if we specify an invalid location to which to move.

11.5.1 INDEXED FILES

When we do not process files in a sequential fashion, we can use `fseek` to speed processing. As an example, we will write a program (called *view*) that allows a user to examine the contents of a file in any order. To view a line, the user specifies the line number. For instance, specifying 50 causes the 50th line in the file to be printed.

If we assume that many different line numbers will be specified during a run of the program, doing a sequential search for each line will be time-consuming. And in general, since the file's line lengths can vary, we cannot use a formula to determine where each line starts. However, by reading through the file once, we can create a table (called an *index* table) that contains the starting position of each line in the file. Once this table is created, when we are given a line number we access the desired line in the file by moving to the file position contained in its corresponding table entry, as shown below.

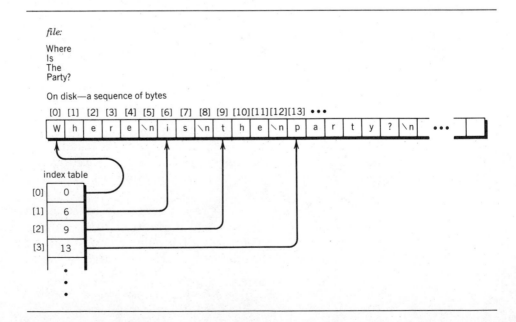

```
/*
 * Read a group of bytes, given position in file.
 */
long read_bytes(fp, pos, num, place)
FILE *fp;                                    /* file to read from */
long pos, num;                               /* position and number */
char place;                                  /* place to put them */
{
  long nread = -1L;                          /* bytes actually read */
  int c;

  if (fseek(fp, pos, 0) == 0)
    for (nread = 0; nread < num && (c = getc(fp)) != EOF; nread++)
      place[nread] = c;
  return nread;
}
```

FIGURE 11.9   Reading a group of bytes from a specified location in a file. This allows us to treat a file as if it were an array.

Figure 11.10*a* contains make_index, a function that builds an index table.   make_index builds the table by opening the file to be indexed and, reading through it sequentially, recording the current file position with ftell each time a newline is read.   Once we have the index, it is easy to write the function print_line, shown in Figure 11.10*b*, which prints the desired line.   print_line uses the line number to index the table, and then uses fseek to set the file's current position to the position indexed in the table.

Given make_index and print_line, it is easy to write *view*, shown in Figure 11.11.   main opens the file (the name is the program's argument) and calls make_index to build the index table.   Then main reads in line numbers from the user, displaying the line using print_line, or printing an error message if the line cannot be found.   As usual, we use getnum and skip_garbage for reading input values, and our_fopen to open files.

If we know that a file we want to examine frequently rarely changes, we can store the index table in a file.   Then the program that lets us examine the file can use the positions in the index file to access the requested lines.   In this way, the overhead of building the table occurs only when the file changes, instead of each time the lookup program is run.   We will use this idea in the data base case study at the end of the chapter.

EXERCISES

11-18 Extend *view* to handle more than one file. *view* should go on to the next file if it is given a negative line number.   □

```
/*
 *  Create index, and print indexed lines.
 */
#include <stdio.h>

int make_index(fp, index_tab, max_ind)        /* build the index table */
FILE *fp;                                      /* file to index */
long index_tab[];                              /* table of indices */
int max_ind;                                   /* maximum number of indices */
{
  long *next_ptr = index_tab,                  /* ptr to next index */
       *last_ptr = index_tab + max_ind - 1;    /* ptr to end of index table */
  int c, lastch;                               /* next and last character */

  for (lastch = '\n'; c = getc(fp), c != EOF; lastch = c)
    if (lastch == '\n')                        /* save position of line */
      if (next_ptr <= last_ptr)                /* as long as room */
        *next_ptr++ = ftell(fp) - 1;
      else                                     /* no room in table, give up */
        break;
  return next_ptr - index_tab;                 /* number of indices in table */
}
```

(a) `make_index`: *build an index table*

```
void print_line(fp, index_tab, lineno)         /* print a line */
FILE *fp;                                      /* file we're looking at */
long index_tab[];                              /* index table */
int lineno;                                    /* line number to print */
{
  int c;                                       /* next character */

  if (fseek(fp, index_tab[lineno], 0) != 0)    /* get to line */
    fprintf(stderr, "Can't read line %d at %ld\n", lineno, index_tab[lineno]);
  else
  {
    while(c = getc(fp), c != EOF && c != '\n') /* print the line */
      putchar(c);
    putchar('\n');
  }
}
```

(b) `print_line`: *print a line given its line number*

FIGURE 11.10 Building and using an index table.

11-19 We can make *view* more efficient by building the index table as we read. That is, the first time we are asked for a line, if the line does not already have an index, we build the part of the index table corresponding to the part of the file preceding that line. Make this change. □

```
/*
 * View: a program to allow random display of lines.
 */
#define MAX_INDEX 2000

main(argc, argv)
int argc;
char *argv[];
{
  long index_tab[MAX_INDEX], next;   /* index table, next number */
  int lines,                         /* lines in table */
      inpres;                        /* result of reading number */
  FILE *fp, *our_fopen();            /* file */
  void print_line(), skip_garbage();

  if (argc != 2)
    fprintf(stderr,"Usage: %s file - name\n", argv[0]);
  else if ((fp = our_fopen(argv[1], "r")) != NULL)
  {
    if ((lines = make_index(fp, index_tab, MAX_INDEX)) != 0)
      while (printf("Line? "), (inpres = getnum(&next)) != EOF)
        if (!inpres)
        {
          fprintf(stderr,"Skipping garbage...\n");
          skip_garbage();
        }
        else if (next < lines)
          print_line(fp, index_tab, (int) next);
        else
          fprintf(stderr,"Line %ld not found\n", next);
    (void) fclose(fp);
  }
}
```

FIGURE 11.11 A program to display selected lines within a file.

11-20 Use the index table approach to print a file in reverse order. Is this more efficient than the alternative method suggested in Chapter 8? Can you come up with an even more efficient method? □

11-21 What does *view* do if the file has more lines than anticipated? The program's behavior can be improved by using doubly-linked lists to hold the indexes. Make this improvement. □

11-22 Write a function, file_len, that computes the number of characters in a file without reading any characters. Is this function portable? Why or why not? □

11-23 Write a function, `tail`, that prints out the last *n* bytes of a file without reading through the file. Extend `tail` to print out the last *n* lines.   □

11.6

BINARY I/O

The functions from the standard I/O library that we have used so far are designed to read and write characters or character arrays. C also provides two functions that can be used to read and write arbitary types: `fread` reads an array from a file and `fwrite` writes an array to a file. Both are passed four parameters: a pointer to the array's first element (`char *`), the size (in bytes) of an element, the number of elements in the array, and a file pointer. Both return the number of elements successfully read or written; zero indicates the end of file or an error. Notice that the file pointer is the last argument. (Isn't consistency wonderful?)

We can use `fwrite` to write an array, `x`, containing 10 integers to a file as follows:

```
int x[10], n;
   . . .
n = fwrite((char *) x, sizeof(int), 10, fp);
```

Because `fwrite` expects its first parameter to be a pointer to a character and `x` points to an integer, we must cast `x` into a pointer to a character. After the call to `fwrite`, n will contain the number of elements that were written. Note that all our example `fwrite` does is to write 10 × `sizeof(int)` bytes to the file, the first byte coming from `&x[0]`.

We can read the file back into `x` in a similar way:

```
int x[10], n;
   . . .
n = fread((char *) x, sizeof(int), 10, fp);
```

After the call to `fread`, n contains the number of elements that were read. Like the previous call to `fwrite`, this call to `fread` simply reads 10 × `sizeof(int)` bytes from the file, placing them into `x`.

`fread` and `fwrite` provide a convenient and efficient way to save internal tables between program runs. We can use `fwrite` to save an internal table when the program finishes and `fread` to read it the next time the program starts. This method is much more efficient than using `fprintf` and `fscanf` but has the disadvantage that the saved table is not text and cannot be easily examined.

While the use of `fread` and `fwrite` is portable, the files read and written by them are not. To see why, let us look at a file containing 10 ints written using `fwrite`. If ints are 4 bytes, this file takes 40 bytes. Now suppose the file is transported to a machine with 2-byte ints, and we try to read it using `fread`, telling `fread` to read 10 ints. `fread` will read only the first 20 bytes of the file. The moral: files that are transferred between machines should not be written with `fwrite`.

11.6.1 RECORD I/O

The arrays read and written by `fread` and `fwrite` can contain elements of any type, including structures. As an example, suppose we are writing a game and wish to maintain a table of the game's top 10 scores and their scorers, perhaps so that this list can be updated and printed when the game finishes. The program can store this table internally as an array of structures:

```
struct score_rec
{
  int  score;                        /* score */
  char scorer[40];                   /* scorer's name */
};
     . . .
score_rec scoretab[MAX_SCORES];      /* score table */
```

The table is read from the file when the program starts, updated after the game is played, and written to the file before the program finishes.

The module used to manage the scores file is shown in Figure 11.12. `read_scores` reads the score, scorer pairs from the scores file into the table, returning the number of table entries. `write_scores` writes the table to the scores file. A single `fwrite` creates the table, and a single `fread` reads it. The major difference between these functions and those in our previous example is that each table element is now a `struct score_rec` instead of an `int`.

EXERCISES

11-24 Extend `read_scores` and `write_scores` to manage a score file in which the table of scores is preceded by a single integer containing the number of entries in the table. Why might this be a good idea? □

11-25 Write a program that can create an indexed file, using `fwrite` to write the table of indices. (*Hint*: use `make_index` as a starting point.) Then

```
/*
 *  Score file management.
 */
#include <stdio.h>

int read_scores(scores, table, n)          /* get scores from file */
char scores[];                              /* scores file name */
struct score_rec table[];                   /* scores table */
int n;                                      /* scores to read */
{
  FILE *fp = our_fopen(scores, "r");        /* reading scores file */
  int nread;                                /* scores read */

  if (fp)
  {
    nread = fread((char *) table, sizeof(struct score_rec), n, fp);
    fclose(fp);
  }
  return nread;
}

int write_scores(scores, table, n)          /* put scores to SCORES file */
char scores[];                              /* scores file name*/
struct score_rec table[];                   /* score table */
int n;                                      /* scores to write */
{
  FILE *fp = fopen_good (scores, "w");       /* writing scores file */
  int nwrite;                               /* scores written */

  if (fp)
  {
    nwrite = fwrite((char *) table, sizeof(struct score_rec), n, fp);
    fclose(fp);
  }
  return nwrite;
}
```

FIGURE 11.12 Module to manage a score file for a game. The score file is kept as a binary file.

rewrite the lookup program of Figure 11.11 to use `fread` to input the index table. How can the program know the number of table entries to read? □

11-26 Implement `fread` and `fwrite` using `getc` and `putc`. □

11.7

CASE STUDY — AN INDEXED DATA BASE

We bring together many of the concepts covered in this text with the implementation of a small indexed data base containing names, addresses, and phone numbers—a computerized little black book. We will write two programs to manage the data base: *make-index* and *lookup*. *make-index* creates an index file that is used by *lookup* to quickly find the address and phone number associated with a particular name.

The data base is made up of a text file, *addresses*, and an index file, *index*, as illustrated in Figure 11.13. *addresses* is divided into records, with the first line of each record containing a name and the following lines containing the corresponding address and phone number. A record ends with a line containing only a period ("."). To make it easy to create and maintain this file using a text editor, there are no restrictions on the number of lines per record or the order of the records in the file.

index is a binary file, with records that contain a name and the starting position of the corresponding record in *addresses*. *make-index* must be run whenever *addresses* is edited to create an up-to-date index file; *index* is not a text file and should not be edited.

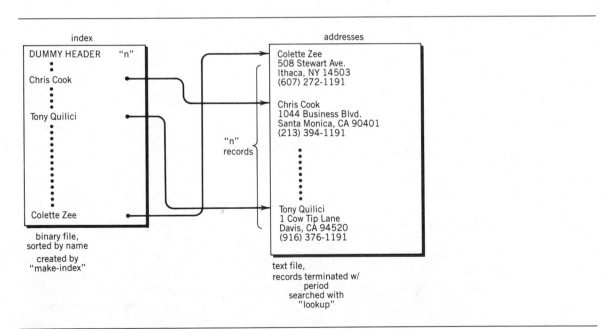

FIGURE 11.13 The organization of the data base, and its maintenance programs.

make-index creates the index file by reading through *addresses* and building a table of names and record positions. When all records have been processed, *make-index* writes the table into the file *index*, sorted by name. When *lookup* needs to find the address and phone number corresponding to a given name, it can use binary search to look up the name in *index*, and can use the position found there to access the record in *addresses*. This makes searching for an address reasonably efficient.

We also want to create the index file efficiently, so we need an intelligent data structure for the index table. Since the index file is sorted, we must either keep the table sorted or sort it before we save it. While either choice is reasonable, we have chosen to keep it sorted. To do so, we keep the table as a binary tree (see Chapter 10), with each node pointing to a structure containing a name and a position. As *make-index* reads each record in *addresses*, its name and starting position are placed in one of these structures and inserted into the correct place in the tree.

When *addresses* has been completely processed, we traverse the tree, using `fwrite` to write the index structures into *index*. Before we write any records, however, we write a dummy record containing the number of names that are indexed, so that this information will be available when we search *index*. A sample index tree shown in Figure 11.14.

Since both programs need the definition of an index structure, it is placed in the header file *index.h*, shown in Figure 11.15. *index.h* also contains constants for the data base file names, the input line length, and the end-of-record delimiter.

make-index (Figure 11.16) is straightforward despite its long length, using `make_tree` to build the tree and `save_tree` to save it. `make_tree` reads records from *addresses*, using `insert_tree` to save the key and its position. `insert_tree` is a recursive version of the tree insertion function in Chapter 10.

To simplify the program's control structure we use a new version of `our_fopen`, shown in Figure 11.17, to open files. The new version is similar to the old version, except that if it cannot open the file it terminates the program instead of returning a null pointer. To do this, `our_fopen` uses another library function, `exit`. `exit` stops a program, closing any open files. It takes a single integer parameter that is returned to the operating system as the program's exit status. Traditionally, only successful programs return zero.

Once we have run *index* to build the sorted index table, we can run *lookup*, shown in Figure 11.18, to search for entries. The main program prompts for user names, using `bsearch` to do a binary search of *index* for the position of the name's record in *addresses*. `bsearch` searches the file for the name, using `fseek` to access the next index record to examine. Once we have the position of the name's record in *addresses*, we use `fseek` to move to that position, printing out the name, address, and phone number found there.

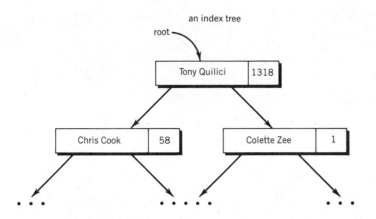

FIGURE 11.14 A sample index tree.

EXERCISES

11-27 Modify *make-index* and *lookup* to allow the data base files to be specified as optional arguments. □

11-28 As we mentioned in Chapter 5, binary search can be slower than sequential search for small tables. Determine where this trade-off occurs with *lookup* and modify it to use sequential search for smaller tables. □

```
/*
 * Definitions to use indexes.
 */
#define MAX_LINE    256                     /* maximum line length */
#define MAX_KEY     40                      /* maximum key size */
#define ADDR_FILE   "addresses"             /* the data base */
#define INDEX_FILE  "index"                 /* the index file */
#define END_REC     ".\n"                   /* end of a record */

struct index_rec                            /* index record */
{
  char key[MAX_KEY];                        /*    name */
  long pos;                                 /*    position */
};

typedef struct index_rec INDEX;
```

FIGURE 11.15 *index.h* – the data base header file.

```
/*
 *  Creating the index table.
 */
#include <stdio.h>
#include "index.h"                              /* definition of INDEX */
#include "boolean.h"                            /* Chapter 7 */

struct tree_node                                /* node in tree */
{
  struct tree_node *l_ptr, *r_ptr;             /* left and right pointers */
  INDEX *data_ptr;                              /* data pointer */
};

typedef struct tree_node TREE_NODE;

main()
{
  FILE *afp, *ifp, *our_fopen();               /* the files */
  TREE_NODE *root, *make_tree();               /* index tree */
  static INDEX header = {"DUMMY HEADER", 0};   /* dummy header node */
  void save_tree();

  afp = our_fopen(ADDR_FILE, "r");
  if ((root = make_tree(afp, &header.pos)) !- NULL)
  {
    ifp = our_fopen(INDEX_FILE, "w");
    (void) fwrite((char *) &header, sizeof(header), 1, ifp);
    save_tree(root, ifp);
    (void) fclose(ifp);
    printf("%ld records\n", header.pos);
  }
  (void) fclose(afp);
  exit(0);
}

/* Make the index tree. */

TREE_NODE *make_tree(fp, cnt_ptr)
FILE *fp;                                       /* file */
long *cnt_ptr;                                  /* count of records */
{
  TREE_NODE *root = NULL,                       /* tree */
            *temp_ptr, *insert_tree();          /* add node to tree */
  char line[MAX_LINE], *malloc();               /* next line */
  long start_pos = 0;                           /* record count, position */
  INDEX *next_ptr;                              /* next key, pos pair */
  BOOLEAN new_record = TRUE, have_mem = TRUE;   /* starting with new record */
```

FIGURE 11.16 *make-index.c* – creates an indexed data base.

```
    *cnt_ptr = 0;
    while (start_pos = ftell(fp), have_mem && fgets(line,sizeof(line), fp))
    {
      if (new_record)
      {
        if ((next_ptr = (INDEX *) malloc(sizeof(INDEX))) != NULL)
        {
          strncpy(next_ptr->key, line, MAX_KEY);
          next_ptr->pos = start_pos;
          if ((temp_ptr = insert_tree(root, next_ptr, cnt_ptr)) != NULL)
            root = temp_ptr;
        }
        have_mem = next_ptr && temp_ptr;
      }
      new_record = strcmp(line, END_REC) == 0;
    }
    if (!have_mem)
      fprintf(stderr,"Out of memory.  Key: %s\n", line);
    return root;
}

/* Save the index tree into a file. */

void save_tree(root, fp)
TREE_NODE *root;                   /* the tree */
FILE *fp;                          /* file pointer */
{
  if (root)
  {
    save_tree(root->l_ptr, fp);    /* save left subtree */
    (void) fwrite(root->data_ptr,sizeof(INDEX), 1, fp);
    save_tree(root->r_ptr, fp);    /* save right subtree */
  }
}
/* Add record to tree. */

TREE_NODE *insert_tree(root, rec_ptr, cnt_ptr)
TREE_NODE *root;                           /* pointer to tree */
INDEX     *rec_ptr;                        /* record to install */
long      *cnt_ptr;                        /* nodes in tree */
{
  char *malloc();

  if (root)                                /* empty tree? */
  {
    int cmp = strncmp(rec_ptr->key, root->data_ptr->key, MAX_KEY);

    if (cmp < 0)                           /* left side? */
      root->l_ptr = insert_tree(root->l_ptr, rec_ptr, cnt_ptr);
    else if (cmp > 0)                      /* right side? */
      root->r_ptr = insert_tree(root->r_ptr, rec_ptr, cnt_ptr);
    else                                   /* duplicate */
      fprintf(stderr,"Duplicate key: %s\n", rec_ptr->key);
  }
```

FIGURE 11.16 (continued)

```
      else if (root = (TREE_NODE *) malloc(sizeof(TREE_NODE)), root)
      {
        root->data_ptr = rec_ptr;
        root->l_ptr = root->r_ptr = NULL;
        (*cnt_ptr)++;
      }
      return root;
  }
```

FIGURE 11.16 (continued)

11-29 The entire name must be specified in order to find its address. Modify *lookup* to allow partial matches and to print all records matching the given name. □

11-30 Modify *lookup* to get the names to look up from command line arguments. □

11-31 *make-index* does not allow duplicate names. Is this a good idea? Why or why not? Modify it to allow duplicate names.   □

11-32 Write a program, *print-labels*, that prints the entire data base in a format suitable for mailing labels.   □

```
/*
 *  Open a file, writing an error message if it fails.
 */
#include <stdio.h>

FILE *our_fopen(file_name, mode)
char *file_name,                          /* file to open */
     *mode;                               /* "r", "w" or "a" */
{
  FILE *fp = fopen(file_name, mode);      /* open the file */

  if (!fp)                                /* did open fail? */
  {
    fprintf(stderr, "Can't open file \"%s\" for %s\n", file_name,
                (*mode == 'r')
                   ? "reading"
                   : ((*mode == 'w') ? "writing" : "appending"));
    exit(1);                              /* quit early */
  }
  return fp;
}
```

FIGURE 11.17 our_fopen—using exit to end a program if an error occurs.

```
/*
 * Lookup addresses/phone numbers given name.
 */
#include <stdio.h>
#include "index.h"

main()
{
  FILE   *afp, *ifp, *our_fopen();    /* address and index files */
  char   line[MAX_LINE];              /* holds user input, record output */
  INDEX  header;                      /* header containing cnt */
  long   pos, bsearch();              /* position of record, search function */
  int    c;

  afp = our_fopen(ADDR_FILE, "r");
  ifp = our_fopen(INDEX_FILE, "r");
  if (fread((char *) &header, sizeof(INDEX), 1, ifp) == 0)
    fprintf(stderr, "Can't read header of \"%s\"\n", INDEX_FILE);
  else
    while (printf("Name? "), fgets(line, sizeof(line), stdin))
      if ((pos = bsearch(ifp, 1L, header.pos, line)) == -1)
        printf("Couldn't find: %s\n", line);
      else if (fseek(afp, pos, 0) != 0)
        fprintf(stderr,"Can't read record at position %ld\n", pos);
      else
        while (fgets(line, sizeof(line), afp) && strcmp(line,END_REC) != 0)
          fputs(line,stdout);
  (void) fclose(ifp);
  (void) fclose(afp);
  exit(0);
}

/* Search index file for name. */

long bsearch(ifp, first, last, target)
FILE *ifp;                            /* file to index */
long first, last;                     /* range to search */
char *target;                         /* what we're looking for */
{
  long  pos, mid = (first + last) / 2; /* next and mid positions */
  INDEX next;                          /* to hold record */
  int   cmp;                           /* holds comparison result */

  if (mid < first || fseek(ifp, mid * sizeof(INDEX), 0) != 0 ||
          fread((char*) &next, sizeof(INDEX), 1, ifp) == 0)
    pos = -1;                          /* couldn't find, or error */
  else
    pos = ((cmp = strncmp(target, next.key, MAX_KEY)) == 0)
            ? next.pos
            : ((cmp < 0) ? bsearch(ifp, first, mid - 1, target)
                         : bsearch(ifp, mid + 1, last, target));
  return pos;
}
```

FIGURE 11.18 *lookup* – searching an indexed data base.

11-33 Add an option to *make-index* to create an additional indexed file based on the phone number. Assume that the phone number is the last line in the record. When might this be useful?   □

SELECTING THE RIGHT LIBRARY FUNCTION

The standard I/O library has several useful functions. Unfortunately, there are so many that at times it can be hard to decide which functions to use. Here are some simple guidelines:

- Whenever possible, use character input and output. The functions getc, putc, getchar, and putchar are more efficient than the other library functions and are easier to use.

- Use the line-oriented functions fgets, fputs, puts, and gets in applications that naturally process their input a line at a time. They are not as efficient as the character I/O functions but are more efficient than the formatted I/O functions. Watch out, however, for longer than expected lines.

- Save the formatted functions for those times when they are really needed: reading and writing formatted input and output. Because of the overhead of parsing the control string, these are much slower and larger than any of the other I/O functions.

- Use binary I/O functions for writing record I/O and for saving tables between program runs. Beware, however, of using them where a textual representation will suffice, since they are not text files and cannot be edited using a text editor.

PORTABILITY AND EFFICIENCY

By now you have been exposed to all of C's features and should feel comfortable with the language. We now discuss portability and efficiency — two issues that are important when writing real programs and are, unfortunately, often thought to work against each other. When we write programs to be easily transported to different computers, we often eschew constructs that are fast and save storage on the development machine. Conversely, techniques that speed up programs or save storage space are often peculiar to a particular machine. However, the two concerns can be complementary; we often achieve faster, more compact programs through careful algorithm and data structure design, not through code diddling and machine-dependent tricks.

In this chapter we show how to write programs that are both portable and efficient. We first present a series of problems and solutions to writing portable programs, and then conclude with two case studies — Radix sort and "The Game of Life" — in which we reduce their running times substantially without hurting their portability.

12.1
PORTABILITY

What do we mean by portability? Ideally, a portable program would not need any changes to run with different input or output devices, to run under a different operating system,[1] to run on a different computer, or any combination of these factors. In other words, a portable program can run unmodified in different environments. Unfortunately, the ideal is almost always impossible to attain. To understand why, consider the common environmental differences listed below.

Word size	32 bits versus 16 bits.
Memory size	Virtual addressing (16M bytes) versus fixed memory space (64K bytes).
Hardware capabilities	Floating point accelerator versus floating point in software.
External storage	200M-byte disk versus two 360K byte floppies.
Operating system calls	Highly flexible operating system versus small set of operating system calls.
Displays	Full color versus black and white. Mouse input versus cursor movement keys.
Compiler/linker differences	Long names versus short names.
Character set	ASCII versus EBCDIC.

There are so many differences that it is clear that careful program design and coding are required to achieve any degree of portability between systems that differ as widely as these.

Since writing portable programs requires extra effort, you might wonder why we care about portability. If you always develop and run your code on the same machine, you probably do not care. However, it is rare for a program to spend its entire lifetime on a single machine. Much software, such as most applications programs that run on Apple Macintoshs, IBM-PCs, and in fact virtually all micros, are developed – written, tested, and debugged – on larger and faster development machines. Many compilers (since writing a complete, *correct* compiler for a given programming language is a major task) are written in an elaborate verification mode on one machine, and then ported to other target machines. And, because highly interactive or graphics-based programs take a great deal of effort to write, such programs should be able to run on many output devices – from low-resolution character CRTs to high resolution, full-color devices.

---

[1] Such as on a DEC VAX running either UNIX or VMS.

12.1.1 SOME SOLUTIONS TO THE PROBLEMS OF PORTABILITY ACROSS MACHINES

Once we have even a simple set of descriptions of alternative computers and displays, suggestions for portability quickly come to mind. Most of them have already been pointed out. Our suggestion is to use the following guidelines as a checklist for all code where portability is of concern.

> ***Do not assume that*** `ints` ***are 32 bits. Use*** `longs` ***instead of*** `ints` ***whenever the range of an integral variable may be a problem.***

This assures that the representation for most integral values will be the same, at least 32 bits.[2] If code is being developed on 36- or 60-bit machines (such as PDP-10s or CDC machines), it is best to assume that an integral type may not be larger than 32 bits on another machine. On both 16- and 32-bit machines, there is no integral type that is larger than 32 bits.

If an integer is being used to represent a quantity that is always constrained in some small range (such as a boolean value or the number of values in a small array), an `int` will port safely to all machines. Again, the C standard requires `ints` to be at least 16 bits. Avoid using `shorts` to represent small values unless space is at a premium. Do not use `chars` to hold small integers, since their size (and whether they are signed) varies among machines.

The problem of overflow does not disappear just because we use `longs` instead of `ints`. When integer overflow is possible, the programmer is responsible for guarding code and devising suitable schemes for protecting against overflow, including using `floats` or `doubles` instead.

We can use the preprocessor to help solve some of the problems involved with different word sizes, as illustrated in Figure 12.1. We define variable type names that reflect their use using `#define` or `typedef`, tailoring their definition to the machine used. Thus, a `SMALL_COUNTER` (used to count from 0 to 255) can be a `char` on one machine and an `unsigned short` on another.

> ***Do not assume that all pointers are the same size. Cast from one pointer type to another.***

We have been consistent in always casting the type of the pointer returned from `malloc`:

---

[2] The draft C standard requires that `longs` be at least 32 bits. This minimum length was never specified in the original description of the language, although virtually all compilers are in conformance with it.

```
temp = (NODEPTR) malloc(sizeof(struct node));
```

We do this for two reasons. The first reason is that `malloc` is defined to return a type pointer to `char`, and pointers to different types may be different sizes. If this is the case, the automatic type conversion between the pointer to `char` and the pointer to `struct node` (in the above example) may use different bits in the word from the explicit cast. The assumption is that the compiler does the right thing on casting between pointer types. The second reason is a more theoretical one: strong typing. When all variables are typed and all conversions between types are specified in the program, program correctness is enhanced and program verification is made easier.

Do not assume dynamic allocation will never fail.

All programs we have written in this book that use dynamic storage allocation (via calls to `malloc`) test the return from the storage allocation functions. At the least, a program should terminate gracefully when out of storage. Because there is such a wide variety of heap storage space (our sample machines varied from 64K to 16M bytes per program), the need for error handling or recovery is clear.

Do not assume that pointers are integers.

As an example, it is occasionally necessary to print the address of a variable. However, address types are not well defined in the language;

```
#ifdef vax
  typedef  unsigned char    SMALL_COUNTER      /* 0..255 */
#endif
#ifdef tops20
  typedef  unsigned short   SMALL_COUNTER      /* 7-bit chars, must use short */
#endif
   . . .
```

(a) Data definitions in an include file "TYPES.h"

```
#include "TYPES.h"

main ()
{
  SMALL_COUNTER    n = 0;
     . . .
```

(b) Using the defined type SMALL_COUNTER in a program

FIGURE 12.1 Use of defined types to isolate the underlying actual type.

they may be ints or longs, and they may be one on one machine, another on another, or they may be both on the same machine. Instead of worrying about the issue, simply print addresses as if they were longs, casting so that the types match:

```
printf("Address of x: %ld\n", (long) &x);
```

Do not assume file opens and file writes (see Chapter 11) cannot fail.

When a disk is full, it is possible for a write to fail. As with dynamic storage allocation, we must test the return from the various standard I/O library routines. It might be suspected that on a machine with a large disk, this would be unlikely to happen, but because disk space is like Murphy's law (files expand to fill up all available space), large systems are as likely to run out of space as small ones.

Attempting to write to disk when the file system is full is always a serious problem. A familiar situation is that of a text editor. At the end of a long session of editing, we give a write command to copy out the in-core version of the file, only to find that the file system is full. If we immediately exit with the message, "Too bad, file system full. Can't write your file. All your work is lost," users are understandably upset. Often it is best to wait for a while and, then try again. Full file systems are often temporary, and the editor file write will succeed at some later time. On floppy disk systems, all that may be needed is a message requesting the user to insert a new disk.

Floating point speed varies enormously. For efficiency, use integer arithmetic whenever possible.

There are rarely representation problems with floating point numbers, but portable code implies that response characteristics are similar across environments. Such is not the case when floating point operations are used, however. When arithmetic can be done with integers, performance is often improved. But that brings up the problem of ints versus longs. You win some, you lose some.

All machines use more space for a double than for a float (typically, 32 bits for floats, 64 for doubles). There are no inherent portability problems with floating point numbers, since the sizes are more clearly specified and since there are no "unsigned" floating point types.

EXERCISES

12-1 If you have access to more than one machine, take a sizeable program that you have written and used on one machine and port it to another. How much work did you have to do to port it? Where were your portability problems? Does the program have identical run-time behavior on both machines?   □

12-2   Suppose you have to write a program that requires a 100,000 element array of integers and that, in addition, it must be able to run on a machine with 16M bytes of virtual memory and on a machine where arrays are limited to 64,000 bytes. Assume that the only operations on the table are to access an element and to store a value in an array element. Write functions for these operations that use an in-memory array if there is enough room, or store the array in an external file if there is not. Should the callers of these functions be aware of how the array is actually accessed?   □

12.1.2 SOME SOLUTIONS TO THE PROBLEMS OF PORTABILITY ACROSS DISPLAYS

Just as we can present guidelines that solve most machine problems, once we indicate the kinds of differences we are likely to find in displays, it is simple to generate guidelines for dealing with those differences. The most important point is that displays should be viewed as virtual devices. That is, we should not write code that is specific to one particular device. Rather, we should write programs or routines that are generic to the functions that need to be performed. The interpretation of those routines, converting them into the requirements of a specific device, is performed by a *device driver*.

Even with basic CRTs, virtually every terminal maker has its own ideas about the codes needed to perform these functions. Obviously we do not want to include specific direct cursor movement codes in a `printf` statement such as

```
printf("%cY%d[%d;", ESC, row, col);        /* move to "row" and "col" */
```

which is the code for one particular terminal. Instead, we want to call a function, `move_cursor(row, col)`, and then have that function determine the correct action for the terminal.

A function like `move_cursor` can be written portably using two different techniques. If the program can determine the terminal type it will run on at compile time, we can use the preprocessor to define `move_cursor` appropriately. If not, we can write it as shown in Figure 12.2*a*. The terminal type is an enumeration type and is used to select the appropriate action in a `switch` statement. To add another terminal, we add an entry to the enumeration type and another `case` to the `switch` statement in `move_cursor`. No other code needs to be changed. Another method is to put all terminal information into a file and then read that file when the program starts. Whichever technique is used, we want to keep the details of terminal control hidden from all other parts of the program.

How does the program find out the terminal type? If this information is available through the operating system (as it is in UNIX), an operating system call can be made. If not, it is necessary to ask the user for the terminal. A program that uses direct cursor positioning can begin with a function, `get_term_type`, that returns an enumeration type, the user's terminal, that becomes global to the entire program. Functions such as `move_cursor` are written to use this type. Figure 12.2*b* shows how `get_term_type` can be written to accommodate an operating system function, if available, or a direct request for the terminal type, and how `move_cursor` uses the terminal enumeration type.

As with output displays, input device drivers can be written so that their workings are portable and hidden from main programs. In graphics programs, certain devices have a generic capability. Equipment used for pointing, such as mice, tablets, and joysticks, are called *locators*. These devices return two values, an *x* and a *y* screen coordinate. Programs that need locator input should use a generic call like

```
read_locator(&x, &y);
```

rather than placing the locator-accessing code (which can be quite messy) in-line. If a new device is installed or if the code is ported to a machine with a locator different from the one for which it was written, the `read_locator` function can be rewritten.

EXERCISE

12-3 Provide versions of the functions `get_term_type` and `move_cursor` that work in the environment your programs are running under. What other terminal accessing functions (such as clear screen, or clear to end of line) should be provided? □

12.1.3 SPECIFIC C PROBLEMS RELATED TO PORTABILITY

When code is written to be ported to machines and compilers that are different from the ones on which the program was written, we need to be aware of the way C is connected to the rest of the world. Many limitations (such as short identifier names) are not caused by lack of support within the compiler, but instead are restrictions imposed by linking loaders and by historical association between C and certain computers and operating systems. In this section we look at the restrictions that are most troublesome.

```
/*
 *  Move the cursor to the indicated row and column.
 */
void move_cursor(row, col)
int     row, col;
{
    extern enum TERMTYPE   terminal;        /* access the global "terminal" */

    switch (terminal)
    {
    case vt100:    printf(...);
                   break;

    case wyse:     printf(...);
                   break;

    case gt101:    printf(...);
                   break;
        . . .
    }
}
```

(a) Moving the cursor in a terminal-independent manner

```
/*  Get the terminal type from the operating system, if possible;
 *  otherwise, ask the user for the type. The global enumerated type  "terminal"
 *  must be set appropriately.
 */
void get_term_type(terminal)
enum TERMTYPE   *terminal;
{
  char *term;
#ifdef unix
  {
    term = getenv("TERM");
        . . .
  }
#else

    Ask for terminal type

#endif
        . . .
}
```

(b) Getting the terminal type appropriately

FIGURE 12.2 Two functions `get_term_type` and `move_cursor`, written to be portable across operating systems.

Identifier Names and Length

Almost all C compilers allow variables to be mixed case, and most allow long identifier names (31 or more characters). However, if a program includes separately compiled modules or modules written in another programming language, the pieces must be combined using a linking loader. Loaders themselves are programs that may not have been written with the specific needs of C programs in mind. Historically, languages such as FORTRAN have required identifiers to be single case, with six or fewer characters. Consequently, it is necessary to limit external variable and function names to six or fewer characters, mono case, to ensure portability. It is often possible to use longer names, though, as long as they differ within the first six characters.

The use of short names may conflict with the goal of writing readable programs. When two names are identical in the first six characters, we should rename them slightly so that they vary. For example, two variables used for screen manipulation:

```
int     screenlocx, screenlocy;
```

could be renamed to be different in their first character instead of their last:

```
int     xscreenloc, yscreenloc;
```

Another way to provide readable identifier names is to use #defines to cause longer variable names to be converted by the preprocessor to shorter names. Using an existing program with a large number of variables such as

```
int     screenlocx, screenlocy, screenlocz, . . .;
```

a header file can be created to redefine them to shorter names, and the file can be included at the start of the program to be ported. A similar technique can be used with mixed-case identifiers.

```
/* Header file "names.h" */

#define  screenlocx     sclx
#define  screenlocy     scly
#define  screenlocz     sclz
          . . .
#define  GetInputData   gtdata
          . . .
```

We can apply this technique when initially writing programs. We can still use long function or variable names internally, using the preprocessor to make shorter names externally visible. The only problem with this practice is that error messages from the loader or from a run-time debugger will be related to the externally visible names, so that a redefinition like

```
#define  longstackpush  _X17
```

will cause all references to `longstackpush` to be reported as `_X17` by the loader.

Operating System Dependencies

Because of the historic association between the language and the PDP-11s and VAXs, and the UNIX operating system, code is often written that makes subtle use of low-level machine details or that makes operating system calls as if they were part of the C language.[3] Using UNIX operating system calls is easy to do because they are simply library calls. However, UNIX system calls are *not* part of the C language or its standard libraries and are not portable.

To aid portability, we should place all system calls in generically named routines instead of threading specific calls throughout the code. By *generic*, we mean that routines should be named to indicate the function they perform. The generically named function can be written to take into account all machines and operating systems the code will be ported to by protecting the routines with appropriate `#ifdefs`. A simple example is shown in Figure 12.3, a program that prints the size of a file named *junk*.

Note that in Figure 12.3 including all the operating system-specific code, guarded by `#defines`, makes the code within the function difficult to read. However, the main program itself is more readable, since the purpose of the unusually named system calls are now clear.

Machine Dependencies

Machine dependencies crop up in at least three places: sign conversions, right shifts, and byte ordering. We pointed out in Chapter 2 that conversions between unsigned and signed types, particularly when there is a change in the length of the data type, are not specified in the language. Some machines sign extend, and others zero extend. When converting from a longer to a shorter type, truncation occurs. Are the most or least significant bits retained? The result is machine or compiler dependent.

On right shifts, zeroes are *always* shifted in if the variable is an unsigned type. If it is a signed type, zeroes are always shifted in if the

---

[3] We recommend the book *The UNIX Programming Environment*, by Brian Kernighan and Rob Pike (Prentice-Hall, 1984), or *The UNIX System*, by Steve Bourne (Addison-Wesley, 1984) for a discussion of the UNIX operating system calls available through C.

```
/*  Print the size of file "junk".  */
#include <stdio.h>
#define  UNKNOWNSIZE     -1L

main ()
{
  long    file_size(), fs;

  if ((fs = file_size("junk")) == UNKNOWNSIZE)
    puts("Can't get size of junk\n");
  else
    printf("Size of junk: %ld\n", fs);
}

/*
 * Determine the size of the given file.  Makes use of specific
 * operating system calls.  Returns UNKNOWNSIZE if the file doesn't
 * exist or if its size cannot be determined.
 */
long file_size(file)
char    *file;                          /* name of file to size */
{
#ifdef unix

#include <sys/types.h>                  /* UNIX specific include file */
#include "stat.h"                       /* UNIX specific include file */
{
  struct stat    statbuf;

  return (stat(file, &statbuf) == -1) ? UNKNOWNSIZE : (long) (statbuf.st_size);
}
#endif

#ifdef tops30                           /* a mythical operating system */

#define FILESIZEJSYS     197

  return  (long) jsys(FILESIZEJSYS, file);

#endif

  return UNKNOWNSIZE;                    /* unknown o.s. - unknown file size */
}
```

FIGURE 12.3 A program that prints the size of a file. The main program makes a generic call to `file_size`, which in turn calls specific operating system routines.

value is positive. If the value is negative, the shifted-in bits are machine dependent. Left shifts always shift in zeroes, so the problem does not occur.

Unfortunately, the order of bytes in a word is different on different machines. A correct compiler will always extract the bytes in a consistent order, but programmer assumptions about where bytes are stored in a word leads to portablity problems. For example, in one 32-bit byte-addressable machine, strings are arranged so that characters are packed in a word with the first character in the right-most byte of the first word, the second character in the next byte to the left, and so on. The fifth through the eighth characters are in the next higher word, and so on, until all characters are stored, as in Figure 12.4a. However, in another 36-bit, word-addressed machine, the characters are stored left to right in a word, with the first character in the lowest address. This machine uses seven bits per character, storing five characters in a word (with one bit unused), as in Figure 12.4b.

Using the Standard Libraries

Although some programmers may use minus one for EOF and zero for NULL, this is not advisable, since their specific values may be different across machines or compilers. Instead, use the symbolic constants and the other standard input and output routines in *stdio.h*.

The standard string library defines the functions strcmp, strlen, strcpy, and others. These functions are presumably written to be efficient, and their use is portable across virtually all C compilers. Even though it is fun and tempting to write our own versions, it is good practice to use these standard routines.

Programming is easier and portability enhanced, by using the *ctype.h* include file. This file declares various standard character comparison functions. It is clearer and portable across character sets to use:

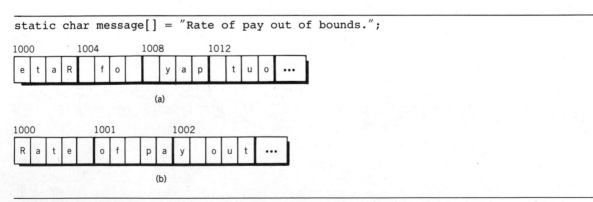

```
static char message[] = "Rate of pay out of bounds.";
```

FIGURE 12.4 (a) Byte ordering and word ordering of strings in a typical 32-bit machine. (b) Byte ordering and word ordering of strings in a typical 36-bit machine.

```
#include <ctype.h>
    . . .
while (islower(c))
    . . .
```

rather than the specific character comparisons in

```
    . . .
while (c >= 'a' && c <= 'z')
    . . .
```

The comparison in the second `while` loop implies that the lowercase letters are contiguous, with no intervening non-lowercase characters, but such is not the case with all character sets (although it is true with ASCII). In theory, `islower` is portable across all character sets, since a table lookup is used, as in the version we wrote in Chapter 6.

EXERCISES

12-4 Some popular C compilers do not provide all of the features we have discussed in this book. Does this mean programs desiring to be portable should avoid these features? Why or why not? □

12-5 `file_size` currently gives up if there is no library function that returns the length of a file. Can the length of a file be computed without using a library function? Modify `file_size` to do so. □

12-6 Write a program to search for identifier names that are similar in the first n characters. n should be provided as an optional command line argument that defaults to eight. □

12-7 Find out what the machine-dependent operations actually do on your machine. Do any of your programs take advantage of them? If any do, how difficult are they to rewrite to avoid these operations? □

12.1.4 PORTABILITY — CONCLUSION

You should now understand the difficulties involved in writing portable programs. However, many of these problems can be overcome by careful design and good coding style. Isolate the nonportable, machine-, operating system-, and device-dependent code in as small an area as possible. Use the standard libraries for input and output, for string handling, and for character manipulations, since the use of these functions is portable. Test returns from functions that give error indications, such as file routines and dynamic storage routines, so that a failure on a different machine does not cause your program to bomb. Be aware from the start of machine dependencies in operations and word sizes and try to avoid them wherever possible. If you follow these suggestions and keep portability in mind when writing your programs, they will will be much easier to port to other machines or operating systems.

EXERCISE

12-8 How portable are the programs in this book? Try compiling and running them on different machines. □

12.2
PROGRAM EFFICIENCY — RADIX SORTING

We want our programs to be fast and compact. Saving memory and reducing computing time is usually beneficial. Surprisingly, the best way to write efficient programs is to avoid thinking about efficiency as long as possible, and instead, to concentrate on selecting the best algorithms and data structures to solve the problem at hand. If we select an appropriate algorithm and write our code cleanly, we will have gone far in meeting the need for compactness and speed. A sorting program that uses $n \log_2 n$ sorts such as quicksort or tree sort will always be faster (as n gets large) than one that uses an n^2 sort like insertion sort, regardless of the coding tricks or machine-dependent features used in coding the insertion sort program.

Nonetheless, no matter how efficient the algorithm or clever the data structure, there are times when even more efficiency is desired, and we must further reduce the running time or the amount of memory required by a program. In this section, we present some techniques for increasing the efficiency of our programs, illustrated by a series of improvements in another sorting program. We pay special attention to certain routines and methods in C that are convenient but that reduce performance.

12.2.1 A CASE STUDY — RADIX SORT

Are you tired of sorting? There are hundreds of sorting techniques, and new results occur regularly in classifying methods and extracting their relevant time and space properties. Usually, we think of sorting methods as being either n^2 or $n \log_2 n$ in time complexity. However, there are methods that are order of n instead, and as n becomes large, the time differences can be substantial.

One special technique is radix sort. It is an order of n method, but it does require special properties of the input. If the input is numerical, all values must be integers with D or fewer digits. We then make D passes over the data, sorting one digit at a time. On the first pass, we sort on the units digit; on the second pass on the 10s; on the third pass, on the 100s; and so on, until we reach pass D, when we sort on the 10^{D-1}s. The sorting is done by taking each value in turn and placing it into a queue, based on the value of its digit. For example, on the first pass, the number 7863 is placed at the end of the '3' queue and the number 820 is placed at the end of the '0' queue. To start the second pass, the numbers are removed from the queues back to the original array, and the processs repeats with the next digit.

A queue is an abstract data type, usually represented as a list, with certain restrictions: additions to the list may be made only at the rear, removals only from the front. A typical example is a movie theatre line; you pay your money and join the end of the line. Patrons are allowed in only from the front. In an abstract data type, it is the programmer's responsibility to make sure that the restrictions are not violated; in a movie queue, it is the general sense of social responsibility that maintains the queue discipline.

Figure 12.5 shows a small set of input values and the arrangement of the 10 queues after sorting on the first digit.

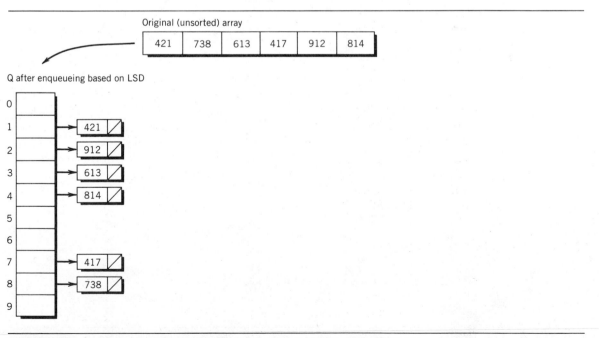

FIGURE 12.5 (a) Input values. (b) Arrangement of the 10 buckets or queues, after sorting on the first digit.

After the numbers have been enqueued based on the first digit, they are dequeued back to the original array, and the process is repeated, this time enqueueing based on the second digit, and so on, until the process has been completed for all D digits. In Figure 12.6 we show the rest of the process after enqueueing on the second, third, and last digits, using the same input values as in Figure 12.5.

Data and Program Structure for Radix Sorting

The description of the process makes it appear simple, and it is. We read the original values into an array using `get_data`, and then enqueue and dequeue back and forth, based on the current digit, until we are done. For debugging purposes, we also print the sorted values, guarding the printing statements with an `#ifdef`. When we do timing runs with large input files, we can easily recompile the code with output turned off. After all, who wants to see 5000 integers flash across the terminal?

Because we do not know in advance how many numbers will end up in any of the queues, we use dynamically allocated linked lists. Since there are two access points for a queue (add at the *rear*, remove from the *front*), we must be able to access these two places in the list separately and quickly. There are several ways we can do this. One is to maintain a

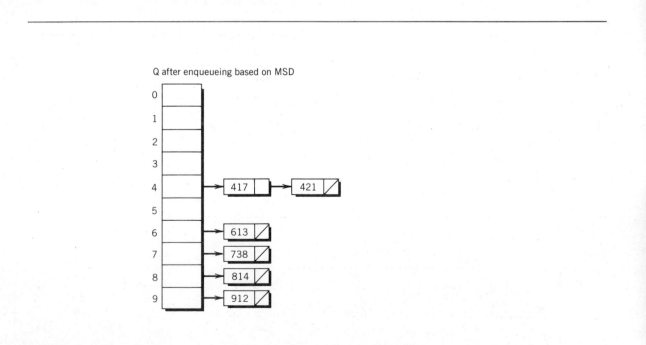

FIGURE 12.6 Stages in enqueueing and dequeueing the values from Figure 12.5. After all D passes, the original array is sorted from low to high.

linked list with a pointer to the front and a separate pointer to the rear, packaging the two together in a structure, as we did with the cross-referencer in Chapter 10:

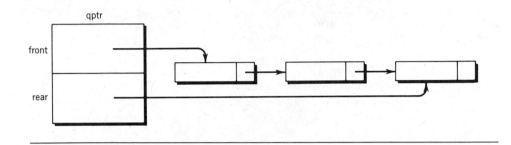

We can save the additional pointer to the rear by using a circular linked list instead. In a circular linked list, the queue pointer points to the rear of the list. We have to make one hop to get to the front. Figure 12.7 shows what a circular linked list looks like for an empty queue, a queue with a single element, and a queue with several elements.

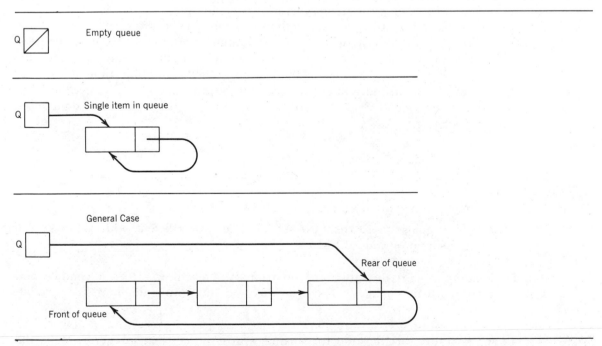

FIGURE 12.7   Examples of circular linked lists used for queues.

TABLE 12.1 Number of values, time needed to sort, and time divided by number for radix sort.

Number of Vals (N)	Time in Seconds (T)	1000 T/N
100	0.37	3.7
200	0.77	3.9
400	1.22	3.1
800	2.52	3.2
1000	3.10	3.1
2000	6.37	3.2
5000	15.50	3.1

Figure 12.8*a* shows the radix sort main program. It includes a file of data definitions, *RXSORT.h*, shown in Figure 12.8*b*.

This program uses two new functions: `enqueue` takes a value and a queue and places the value at the end of the queue; and `dequeue` removes values from an array of queues and returns them to the array `vals`. The two functions are straightforward and work as expected. Enqueueing is a matter of correctly setting links, particularly when enqueueing into an empty queue. Dequeueing is a matter of traversing a circular linked list and knowing when to stop. The functions are shown in Figure 12.9. Note that they assume the definitions in the include file *RXSORT.h*.

Putting all the pieces together, we ran the program on a DEC VAX 11/780 with files of various sizes containing randomly distributed integers, each of five digits. Table 12.1 shows the computing time, and also the time divided by N times 1000. Clearly, the computing time is close to being linear in the number of values to be sorted. (Actually, it is linear in N, the number of values to be sorted, times D, the number of digits used for sorting.)

EXERCISES

12-9 Before going on to the next section, see how efficient you can make the radix sort program. □

12-10 Compile and run radix sort on your own machine. Does it compile and run with no changes? Have we followed our own guidelines for portability? □

12-11 Can radix sort be used for sorting words rather than integers? Make the changes to our version of radix sort to sort words. □

```
/*
 *  Test program for radix sorting.
 */
#include "RXSORT.h"                        /* constants for rxsort */

main ()
{
  long  DF = 1,                     /* div factor for selecting digit */
        vals[MAX];                  /* the input values */
  int   i, j, n,                    /* number of vals. read */
        get_data(),                 /* read input values */
        mem_space = 1,              /* dynamic space available? */
        thequeue;                  /* the selected digit */
  QPTR  Q[BASE];                    /* array of queues */
  void  dequeue();                  /* ret. vals to array */

  n = get_data(vals, MAX);          /* read input data */

  for (i = 1; i <= NDIGITS && mem_space; i++)     /* enqueue one digit at a time */
  {
    for (j = 0; j < BASE; j++)          /* set queues to empty */
      Q[j] = NULL;

    for (j = 0; j < n; j++)             /* enqueue each number in "vals" */
    {
      thequeue = (vals[j]/DF) % BASE;  /* put into this queue */
      if (!(mem_space = enqueue(vals[j], &Q[thequeue])))
      {
        puts("Out of internal memory space.\n");
        break;                     /* out of internal mem_space */
      }
    }


/* This one digit has been enqueued.  Read back into "vals". */

    dequeue (Q, vals, BASE);
    DF *= BASE;
  }

#ifdef printing
  if (mem_space)
  {
    puts("\nSorted output:");
    for (i = 0; i < n; i++)
      printf("%ld\n", vals[i]);
  }
  else
    puts("\nInsufficient internal storage. Values not sorted.\n");
#endif
}
```

(a) The radix sort main program

FIGURE 12.8 (*a*) The main program for radix sort. (*b*) The include file *RXSORT.h*.

```
#include <stdio.h>

#define  BASE       10          /* base of number system */
#define  MAX         5000        /* max no. of input values */
#define  MAXVAL     99999       /* max value */
#define  NDIGITS     5          /* max no. of digits per val */

typedef  struct QUEUENODE    *QPTR;      /* ptr to a queue node */

struct QUEUENODE                          /* node in a queue */
{
        long     value;
        QPTR     next;
};
```

(b) The include file "RXSORT.h"

FIGURE 12.8 (continued)

```
/*
 * Enqueue "val" into the queue, "Q".
 * Returns zero if out of storage, nonzero otherwise.
 */

int enqueue(val, Q)
long    val;                           /* value to enqueue */
QPTR    *Q;                            /* the queue */
{
  QPTR  temp;
  char  * malloc();

  /* Get new queue node. */

  if ((temp = (QPTR) malloc (sizeof(struct QUEUENODE))) != NULL)
  {
    temp->value = val;
    if (*Q == NULL)                    /* insert into empty queue? */
      temp->next = temp;
    else                               /* general case */
    {
      temp->next = (*Q)->next;
      (*Q)->next = temp;
    }
    *Q = temp;                         /* the queue points to the new node */
  }
  return temp != NULL;                 /* returns zero if malloc fails */
}
```

(a) enqueue, *a function that places a value at the end of a queue*

FIGURE 12.9 *(a)* enqueue, a function that places a value at the end of a queue. *(b)* dequeue, a function that returns all values to an array.

```
/*
 *  Dequeue "n" queues into the given array "vals".
 */
void dequeue (Q, vals, n)
QPTR    Q[ ];                           /* array of queue pointers */
long    vals[ ];                        /* array to dequeue into */
int     n;                              /* number of queues in the array */
{
   int   i = 0, j;                      /* loop counters */
   QPTR  temp,                          /* ptr to given queue */
         temp1;                         /* ptr to queue - for free() */

   for (j = 0; j < n; j++)
      if ((temp = Q[j]) != NULL)
      {
         do
         {
            temp1 = temp;
            vals[i++] = temp->next->value;
            temp = temp->next;
            (void)free ((char *) temp1);
         } while (temp != Q[j]);
      }
}
```

(b) dequeue, *a function that returns all values to an array*

FIGURE 12.9 (continued)

12-12 Radix sort sorts on the least significant digit first. Describe the results if the program sorts on the most significant digit first. □

12-13 The times given in Table 12.1 demonstrate that radix sort is an order N sorting routine. Compare the sorting times with runs of insertion sort and quick sort. How large must N be for radix sort to be the sorting method of choice (given that that input meets its special limitations)? □

The Computing Time of Radix Sort I

We would like to make radix sort as fast as possible. To do so, we profiled the program to find out how its time is spent. Table 12.2 shows the output of an execution profiler for radix sort run on a file of 5000 randomly distributed integers, using five digits for the sorting. This is the output of one run; the times vary from run to run, depending on system loading and other factors. However, the average over a few dozen runs was quite close to the time for this run, about 15.5 seconds; only routines accounting for more than about one percent of the total time are shown. Note that several system-supplied routines account for a substantial percentage of the total running time of this program, including the profiling code. The function mcount keeps a record of each function called and the time spent in it. Note that this function alone accounted for more than 11 percent of the total running time for the program. Obviously, if the monitoring routines are not compiled into the program, the overall time is reduced.

What can we conclude from Table 12.2? First, that the program is spending more than 26 percent of its time in dynamic storage management, the functions malloc and free. Furthermore, it is spending almost 25 percent of its time reading data – the functions innum, doscan, ungetc, scanf, and read, all called from get_data. Although these are system-supplied routines, and we use them because they provide a useful service, we can still attack them as sources of inefficiency.

12.2.2 RADIX SORT II — A FASTER METHOD

Since dynamic storage allocation appears to account for the largest percentage of time, we work on that first. The problem with malloc and free is that they are general-purpose storage manipulation routines. They allocate and return blocks of arbitrary size, and this flexibility causes them to engage in quite a bit of activity each time they are called. In particular, because blocks can be requested and freed in arbitrary order, free merges adjacent blocks, so that contiguous blocks are as large as possible,

TABLE 12.2 Execution profile for radix sort, sorting 5000 randomly distributed integers.

Function	% Time	Cum. Seconds	Notes
malloc	20.2	3.12	
innum	16.2	5.63	System routine
main	15.4	8.01	
mcount	11.8	9.83	Profiling code
enqueue	10.6	11.46	
dequeue	9.1	12.86	
free	6.3	13.83	
doscan	4.5	14.52	System routine
get_data	1.6	14.77	
ungetc	1.3	14.97	System routine
monstartup	1.2	15.15	Profiling code
scanf	1.0	15.30	
read	0.9	15.44	System routine

making it less likely that `malloc` will fail when a request for a large piece of storage is made. In addition, `malloc` requests its space through an operating system call (in UNIX this is `sbrk`), which is usually fairly expensive. In Table 12.2 `malloc` alone accounted for over 20 percent of the program's time.

To improve efficiency we avoid using `free` and instead manage our own free storage pool. We `malloc` all the space we need after we read the values, keeping these queue nodes in our own linked list, pointed to by a pointer named `FSP` (for free storage pointer).

Once we've created our own free storage pool, we need only modify `enqueue` and `dequeue` so that nodes come from the list and are returned to the list pointed to by `FSP`. No calls to `malloc` or `free` are needed. Instead, we have writen our own routines, called `ALLOCQPTR` and `FREEQPTR`, respectively. The changes needed in `enqueue` and `dequeue` are minor. The new versions are shown in Figure 12.10. Notice how simple the changes are from the original versions of these functions.

Figure 12.11 diagrams how nodes are allocated and freed with our own free storage pool.

In Figure 12.12, we show the routines that build and manage the free storage pool. `init_storage` calls on `malloc` to request all the space we need, assigning the global `FSP` to point to the start of the storage pool. `ALLOCQPTR` and `FREEQPTR` provide nodes, and return nodes, to the storage pool, respectively.

When we run the new version of radix sort, the average time decreases from about 15.5 to about 13.9 seconds, a saving of about 10 percent.

Table 12.2 shows that the second source of inefficiency is reading data. To correct this problem, we need some insight into `scanf`. As we have pointed out, this function is fine for building programs but poor for actually using them, mainly because it provides little error detection or handling. In addition, because of its generality, it is rather slow and takes a great deal of space. To overcome these problems, we substitute `getnum` from Chapter 6 in `get_data` to handle our input.

In several runs with identical files of 5000 randomly distributed integers, the new version of radix sort (incorporating both our own free storage manager and the replacement for `scanf`) required about 11.5 seconds, for a saving of 26 percent over the original version. Often when we recode for efficiency we lose something in the process – such as clarity of code, modularity, functional separation, and the like. In this case, we actually gain a great deal: better error control. The function `getnum` does precisely what we want it to do on invalid data (because we wrote it ourselves) and returns a flag indicating whether the data are valid. By combining our own storage manipulation and our own input routines we have reduced the computing time from 15.5 to 13.9 to 11.5 seconds. In addition, the compiled program has been reduced in size from 15K to 11K

```
/*
 *  Enqueue "val" into the queue "Q", using its own internal storage allocator
 *  for speed.
 */
void enqueue(val, Q)
long    val;                            /* value to enqueue */
QPTR    *Q;                             /* the queue */
{
  QPTR  temp, ALLOCQPTR();

  temp = ALLOCQPTR();                   /* get new queue node */
  temp->value = val;
  if (*Q == NULL)                       /* insert into empty queue */
    temp->next = temp;
  else                                  /* general case */
  {
    temp->next = (*Q)->next;
    (*Q)->next = temp;
  }
  *Q = temp;                            /* the queue points to the new node */
}
```

(a) Routines for enqueueing, using our own free storage allocator

```
/*
 *  Dequeue "n" queues into the given array "vals"
 */
void dequeue (Q, vals, n)
QPTR    Q[];                            /* array of queue pointers */
long    vals[];                         /* array to dequeue into */
int     n;                              /* number of queues in the array */
{
  int   i = 0, j;                       /* loop counters */
  QPTR  temp,                           /* ptr to given queue */
        templ;                          /* ptr to queue - for FREEQPTR() */
  void  FREEQPTR();

  for (j = 0; j < n; j++)
    if ((temp = Q[j]) != NULL)
      do
      {
        templ = temp;
        vals[i++] = temp->next->value;
        temp = temp->next;
        FREEQPTR(templ);
      } while (temp != Q[j]);
}
```

(b) Routines for dequeueing, using our own free storage deallocator

FIGURE 12.10 New versions of enqueue and dequeue using our own storage allocation functions.

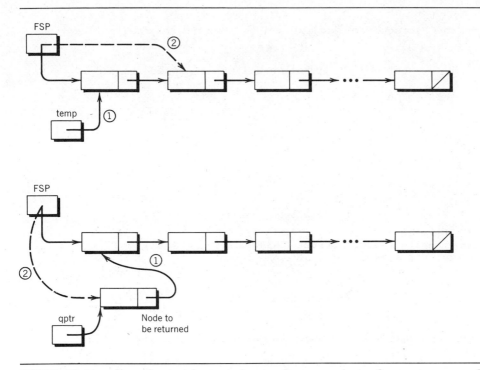

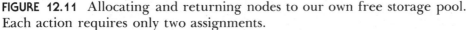

FIGURE 12.11 Allocating and returning nodes to our own free storage pool.
Each action requires only two assignments.

bytes, a space saving of bettter than 26 percent. At this point, we have
made substantial progress in speeding up radix sort. Table 12.3 is the
profiled output from one run, again with 5000 random integers. Routines
that accounted for less than one percent of the total time are not included.

EXERCISES

12-14 Code the storage management functions as macros. Does this make the
program noticably more efficient? □

12-15 Modify radix sort to use pointers instead of array subscripts in those places
where it is traversing arrays. Does this result in a significant performance
improvement? □

12-16 Before reading further, can you think of any other ways to speed up radix
sort? Make these changes. □

```
/*
 *  Manage our own Free Storage Pool.
 */

QPTR     FSP;                         /* global to all other procedures */

/*  Initialize local FSP to "n" nodes */

int init_storage(n)
int   n;
{
  int    i;
  QPTR   temp;
  char  * malloc();

  FSP = NULL;
  for (i = 0; i < n; i++)
    if ((temp = (QPTR) malloc(sizeof(struct QUEUENODE))) != NULL)
      temp->next = FSP, FSP = temp;
    else
      break;
  return temp != NULL;                /* returns zero if malloc failed */
}
```

(a) Routine to initialize our own free storage pool.

```
/* Return a node from the FSP. */

QPTR ALLOCQPTR()
{
  QPTR   temp = FSP;

  FSP = FSP->next;
  return temp;
}


/* Return a pointer to the FSP. */

void   FREEQPTR(qptr)
QPTR     qptr;
{
  qptr->next = FSP, FSP = qptr;
}
```

(b) Routines for allocating and deallocating space, using our own free storage management.

FIGURE 12.12 Routines for managing our own free storage pool. `init_storage` must be called once from the main program.

TABLE 12.3 Execution profile for radix sort, after providing our own input converter, `getnum`.

Function	% Time	Cum. Seconds	Notes
main	23.3	2.65	
mcount	16.8	4.57	Profiling code
getnum	11.6	5.89	
dequeue	11.6	7.20	
enqueue	9.9	8.34	
ALLOCQPTR	7.0	9.14	
FREEQPTR	5.8	9.80	
malloc	5.8	10.47	
monstartup	2.6	10.77	Profiling code
get_data	2.0	11.00	
read	1.3	11.15	System routine
sbrk	1.2	11.29	System routine
init_storage	1.0	11.40	

12-17 Can the memory management techniques discussed in this section be used to speed up other programs in the book? Which ones? Make these improvements. □

12.2.3 RADIX SORT III — AN EVEN FASTER METHOD

The next possible change is either coding some of the expensive routines in-line or rewriting them as macros. There are several functions that are called thousands of times, and there is `dequeue`, although called only 5 times, which accounts for more than 11 percent of the total execution time. But we are not going to change this yet. Instead, we will reconsider our internal management of the various queues.

In order to produce a clean, elegant design, we reuse the array of queues on each pass over the data, copying (via a call to `dequeue`) from the queue array back to the input array. Then we again queue values from the array into the queues. Why do we need to copy back to the original array each time? The answer is, we do not. Instead, we can use two arrays of queues, queueing up values back and forth between them. The first time we have to read from the input array, and the last time we have to dequeue back into the array. At all other times, we just enqueue and dequeue back and forth between the queue arrays, as in Figure 12.13.

Since we save the process of dequeueing back to the original array each time, we expect some performance improvement, but this occurs at the expense of additional space. In fact, it appears that we need twice as much queue space.

We will redesign the input array to make use of the new technique and to save storage. Instead of reading into an array of longs, we read values into an array of structures. The first element in the structure is the input value, a long, and the second is like a pointer to the next element in the current queue. Instead of pointers, however, we use array indexes. Figure 12.14 illustrates how the array will look after the first few values have been read.

Since each element in the array is a structure, and there are MAX of them, we can define the vals array as follows. Note that the definitions use the same names as those in the original version of the program. The only change is in the definition of QPTR in *RXSORT.h*. Keeping data type names consistent makes rewriting the program simpler.

```
      . . .
typedef int     QPTR;                    /* <- QPTR is now an int */

struct QUEUENODE
{
        long    value;                   /* value of this element */
        QPTR    next;                    /* index of next element in queue */
}
```

In the main program we must change the definition of vals to the global:

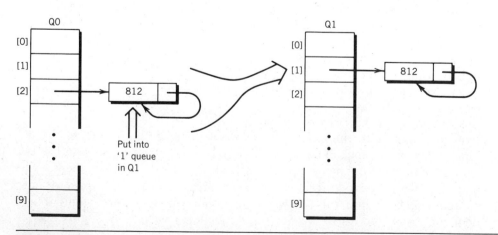

FIGURE 12.13 Enqueueing and dequeueing between two arrays of queues.

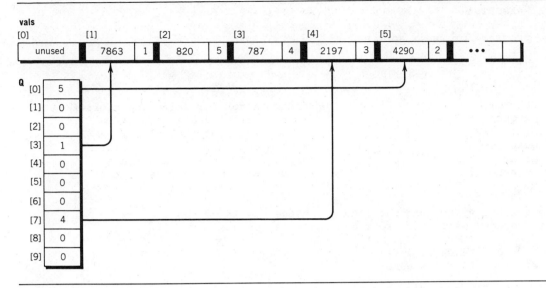

FIGURE 12.14 An array of queues, each containing a pointer to (the index of) the rear of its queue, in the structure array `vals`.

```
struct QUEUENODE  vals[MAX+1];   /*    vals now an array of QUEUENODEs */
```

With this new representation, the main program structure uses two queues stored as a two-dimensional array. The first dimension selects the queue number (zero or one), and the second selects the bucket for enqueueing the current digit. The queues are declared as:

```
QPTR  Q[2][BASE];
```

Figure 12.15 is the new main program.

As we can see, the program's structure remains simple and obvious. The important change is in the input array, `vals`. We make this a global array of structures. The first component of the structure is the numerical value, a `long`; the second component is the index of the next entry in the appropriate queue. Using this new representation, the functions `enqueue` and `requeue` have to be rewritten and are shown in Figure 12.16, along with the routine that reads the values initially and places them into the correct queue (function `queue_data`). Again, they assume the new definitions in *RXSORT.h*.

The payoff from all these changes is a computing time below 6 seconds, for sorting the same 5000 integers, as we see in Table 12.4 (routines that accounted for less than one percent of the total time have again

```
#include "RXSORT.h"                    /* constants for rxsort */

/*  Test program for radix sorting. */

main ()
{
  int    i = 0, j,                     /* number of vals. read */
         DF = 10,                      /* div factor for selecting digit */
         nxtqueue = 0;                 /* the current queue array */
  QPTR   Q[2][BASE];                   /* two arrays of queues */
  void   queue_data(),                 /* read and enqueue input vals */
         print_vals(),                 /* print elements in a queue */
         requeue();                    /* move vals between queues */

  /*
   *  Read input values and put into first queue.  If we run out
   *  of storage, we'll just sort the first "n" values.
   */
   for (i = 0; i < BASE; i++)
     Q[0][i] = Q[1][i] = NULL;


  queue_data(Q, MAXVAL);               /* read input data into Q */


  for (i = 2; i <= NDIGITS; i++)       /* enqueue one digit at a time */
  {
    nxtqueue = !nxtqueue;              /* alternate queue arrays */
    DF *= BASE;

    requeue(Q, nxtqueue, DF);          /* Requeue to "nxtqueue" */
  }

#ifdef printing
  for (puts("Sorted Values:\n", j = 0; j < BASE; j++)
    print_vals(Q[nxtqueue][j]);
#endif
}
```

FIGURE 12.15 Main program for radix sort, using two queues.

been removed from the table). The time averaged about 5.5 seconds, compared with the first-version time of about 15.5 seconds, a total savings of about 65 percent.

From this point on, there are several changes that can be made to reduce the time further. Table 12.4 shows that the program is spending more than 50 percent of its time in requeue. Analyze that function care-

```
/*
 *  Read input values and enqueue each in turn into the first queue,
 *  using the function "getnum" from Chapter 6.
 */
void queue_data(Q, maxval)
QPTR    Q[][BASE];
long    maxval;                             /* max. allowable input value */
{
  long  next;                               /* next input value */
  int   valid;                              /* returned from "getnum" */

  while ((valid = getnum(&next)) != EOF)
    if (valid && next >= 0 && next <= maxval)
        if (!enqueue(next, &Q[0][next % BASE]))
          break;
}
```

(a) The function `queue_data` that performs the initial input, using `getnum` from Chapter 6

```
/*
 *  Enqueue a single long, "val", into the queue, "Q".
 *  Returns zero if out of storage, nonzero otherwise.
 */
int enqueue(val, Q)
long    val;                                /* value to enqueue */
QPTR    *Q;                                 /* the queue */
{
  QPTR  temp;
  static int    nxt_cell = 1;

  /* Get new queue node */
  if ((temp = nxt_cell++) < MAX )
  {
    vals[temp].value = val;                 /* vals is a global array */
    if (*Q == NULL)                         /* insert into empty queue */
     vals[temp].next = temp;
    else                                    /* general case */
    {
      vals[temp].next = vals[*Q].next;
      vals[*Q].next = temp;
    }
    *Q = temp;                              /* the queue points to the new node */
  }
  return (temp<MAX);                        /* returns zero if too many input vals */
}
```

(b) Final version of `enqueue` using an array rather than dynamically allocated space

FIGURE 12.16 Final versions of `enqueue`, `queue_data`, and `requeue`.

```
/*
 * Move values from one queue to the next, based on "digit".
 */
void requeue (Q, q, digit)
QPTR    Q[][BASE];                          /* two-dimensional array of queue pointers */
int     q,                                  /* queue TO this queue */
        digit;                              /* queue using this digit */
{
  int    i, iq;                             /* queue array indexes */
  QPTR   front, nxt;

  for (i = 0; i < BASE; i++)
    if (Q[!q][i] != NULL)                   /* pick all entries in this queue */
    {
      front = vals[Q[!q][i]].next;          /* vals is a global array */
      vals[Q[!q][i]].next = NULL;           /* NULL the "next" field */
      Q[!q][i] = NULL;                      /* NULL the current queue ptr */

      while (front != NULL)                 /* traverse until NULL */
      {
        nxt = vals[front].next;

        /* "value" goes into the "iq" queue */
        iq = ((vals[front].value) % digit) / (digit/BASE);

        if (Q[q][iq] == NULL)               /* insert into empty queue */
          vals[front].next = front;
        else                                /* general case */
        {
          vals[front].next = vals[Q[q][iq]].next;
          vals[Q[q][iq]].next = front;
        }

        (Q[q][iq]) = front;
        front = nxt;
      }
    }
}
```

(c) Function `requeue` *that moves values between queues*

FIGURE 12.16 (continued)

---

fully and consider what can be done to increase speed by using pointers rather than direct array access and other techniques. We think we have done the best we can with radix sort without resorting to tricks. We have used special knowledge of C and the run-time libraries and we have made use of a rich collection of data structures available in C.

TABLE 12.4 Execution profile for radix sort, using arrays for the queues, rather than dynamically-allocated space.

Function	% Time	Cum. Seconds	Notes
requeue	52.2	2.85	
getnum	29.3	4.45	
queuedata	6.7	4.82	
enqueue	6.4	5.17	
mcount	3.0	5.34	Profiling code
read	2.1	5.45	System routine

EXERCISES

12-18 Take the latest version of radix sort and try to reduce its computing time. Use the suggestions about efficiency presented in earlier chapters, particularly Chapter 8, which demonstrated certain performance improvements by using pointers to access arrays.   □

12-19 Implement a hybrid sorting routine that sorts D-digit numbers using both radix and quick sort. On the first pass, sort the numbers based on the most significant digit. Then sort each of the buckets independently. Finally, combine the sorted lists using a list merge techique.[4] Compare the time to sort 5000 randomly distributed five-digit integers with both conventional radix sort, and with quick sort.   □

12-20 When using radix sort for strings, there may be large differences in the length of the strings. Implement a variation of radix sort for strings that makes an initial pass over the data to find the longest string (of length *max*), and sorts only those strings first (again on the least significant character). On the next pass, sort these strings along with all strings with *max* − 1 characters. Continue in this manner until all strings have been sorted. Work with some hand examples first to fully understand the algorithm. Why is this method more efficient than always sorting each string?   □

---

[4] See for example, Alfred V. Aho, John E. Hopcroft, and Jeffrey D. Ullman, *The Design and Analysis of Computer Algorithms* (Addison-Wesley Publishing Company, Reading, Mass., 1974).

12.3

PROGRAM EFFICIENCY — THE GAME OF LIFE

Radix sorting illustrated the gains we can expect when we use performance monitoring to examine and analyze where a program is spending its time. By working first on the most time-consuming routines, we were able to improve the program's running time substantially. The programs in the previous section also demonstrate the advantage of examining a program's performance from a data structures point of view. We saw that excessive data movement was wasteful, and by combining together our original input array with two queues needed for the sorting, we gained a large improvement in the running time of the program. In this section we use performance monitoring to gain the *perception* of a faster program. Specifically, we will see that the way the output display is refreshed substantially affects our perception of how fast a program runs. We also rewrite the program using pointers rather than array indexing and gain even greater speed.

To illustrate these efficiency techniques, we conclude this chapter by implementing the Game of Life, a simulation of population growth dynamics developed by the British mathematician John Horton Conway. In Life, a board represents the world, each cell in the board symbolizing a single location. Each cell is either empty or occupied by a single inhabitant. The game models the changes in the world's population over time, using three simple rules:

1. *Survival.* An inhabited cell remains inhabited if two or three of its neighboring cells are inhabited. (A cell has eight neighbors: four adjacent orthogonally and four adjacent diagonally.)
2. *Birth.* An uninhabited cell becomes inhabited if exactly three of its neighbors are inhabited.
3. *Death.* An inhabited cell becomes uninhabited if fewer than two or more than three of its neighbors are occupied. (The former represents death from loneliness, the latter from overcrowding.)

All births and deaths occur simultaneously, together causing the creation of a new generation.

Figure 12.17 shows some sample initial configurations and their first few generations. Unfortunately, it appears that most worlds eventually become uninhabited. It is comforting, however, to find that some worlds develop into a stable, inhabited population, while others reach a dynamically stable population that oscillates between states. The game is usually run until a stable population is detected.

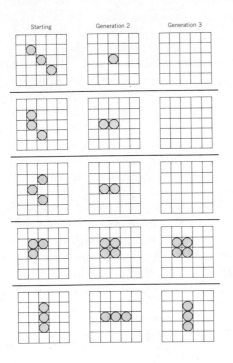

Starting   Generation 2   Generation 3

FIGURE 12.17 Various worlds for the game of Life and their population changes

12.3.1 THE LIFE PROGRAM

The Life program reads an initial configuration describing the size of the world and the positions of its initial inhabitants, and then computes and displays the resulting generations. The world is a two-dimensional array of BOOLEANs; TRUE indicates an inhabited cell.

Life divides itself nicely into three basic tasks: reading an initial configuration, displaying a generation, and computing the next generation. Each task corresponds to a single function. inp_world reads the initial configuration and does simple error checking. inp_world is passed a world, pointers to variables to fill in with the world's size, the number of its occupants and the number of generations to display, and returns a BOOLEAN that indicates whether any errors have occurred.

out_world displays a generation in a nice format indicating occupied cells. out_world is passed a world, its size, the number of the current generation and the total number of generations to be displayed. It displays the world, indicating its border with an X, inhabited cells with a #, and uninhabited cells with a blank. In addition, a line is printed identifying this generation, and the total number of generations to be output.

nxt_world computes the next generation by examining each cell of the current generation and noting whether the cell should be inhabited in the next. When a cell is examined, its inhabited neighbors are counted, and then the game's rules are applied to determine if it is to be inhabited in the next generation. Because all changes in a world must be made at the same time, nxt_world is passed another world where the next generation can be recorded, and a pointer to a counter where the number of inhabitants in this world can be stored. The main program can then swap worlds, making the next generation the current one, as well as determining easily if a generation has been annihilated. nxt_world returns a BOOLEAN indicating whether the new generation is the same as the old one.

The Life program is shown in Figure 12.18. The type WORLD is defined as a two-dimensional array of BOOLEANs to simplify the passage of entire worlds as parameters. To simplify later counting of a cell's neighbors, a WORLD includes an extra uninhabited border of cells surrounding the world, that is examined but not displayed. The displayable world is 20 rows by 78 columns; this is the space left on the average CRT after writing a border around the world and a line identifying the current generation. These values are determined by constants MAXROW and MAXCOL.

Life uses inp_world to get an initial world and then iterates through the requested number of generations, using out_world to display a generation and nxt_world to compute the next generation. The loop stops when a stable state has been reached or the requested number of generations has been displayed.

12.3.2 A MORE EFFICIENT VERSION OF LIFE

The Life program in Figure 12.18 works, but when simulating large worlds it is slow in displaying successive generations, annoying those watching the program's output. To determine where the program's time was spent, we profiled it as it ran through the first 10 generations of a large world; the results are shown in Table 12.5. Clearly, to make the program more efficient, we should concentrate on improving nxt_world and out_world, since the program spends almost 97 percent of its time in these two functions.

Both functions are almost entirely devoted to traversing a two-dimensional array representing a world, using two-dimensional subscripting to access the array's elements. Because the array elements are accessed sequentially within rows, and the rows are accessed sequentially within the

```
/*
 *  Conway's Game of Life.
 */
#include <stdio.h>
#include "boolean.h"                        /* boolean type from Chapter 7 */
#include "defs.h"                           /* macros/constants from Chapter 7 */

#define  BORDER    'X'                       /* output border around world */
#define  MARKER    '#'                       /* marker for occupied cell */
#define  MAXCOL    78                        /* legal cells: 1..MAXCOL */
#define  MAXROW    20                        /* ...and 1..MAXROW */
#define  NUMCOLS   (MAXCOL + 2)              /* extra cell surrounding world */
#define  NUMROWS   (MAXROW + 2)              /* ...to make tests simpler */

typedef  BOOLEAN   WORLD[NUMROWS][NUMCOLS];  /* two-dimensional array of cells */
typedef  BOOLEAN   (*ROW_PTR)[NUMCOLS];      /* pointer to row in the world */

main()
{
  static WORLD  current = {0},               /* current and future worlds */
                future = {0};
  ROW_PTR       curr_ptr = current,          /* pointer to current ... */
                fut_ptr = future;            /*    and future worlds */
  int           rows, cols,                  /* actually considered part */
                count,                       /* inhabitants in world */
                gen, last_gen;               /* current and final generations */
  BOOLEAN       inp_world(), nxt_world();    /* read in world, compute next */
  void          out_world();                 /* display world */

  if (inp_world(curr_ptr, &rows, &cols, &count, &last_gen))
  {
    for (gen = 0; gen < last_gen; gen++)
    {
      ROW_PTR temp_ptr;

      out_world(curr_ptr, rows, cols, gen, last_gen);
      if (!count || !nxt_world(curr_ptr, fut_ptr, rows, cols, &count))
        break;
      SWAP(temp_ptr, curr_ptr, fut_ptr);     /* switch current and future */
    }
    printf("%s after %d generation(s)\n",
           !count ? "All inhabitants are dead" :
                 ((gen == last_gen) ? "Finished" : "Stable"), gen);
  }
}
```

(a) The main program for the Game of Life

FIGURE 12.18 The Game of Life and the routines it calls.

```
/*
 *  Read in world size and inhabitants.
 */
BOOLEAN inp_world (world, rows_ptr, cols_ptr, count_ptr, numgen_ptr)
WORLD    world;
int      *rows_ptr,
         *cols_ptr,
         *count_ptr,
         *numgen_ptr;
{
  int    inpres,                        /* scanf return value */
         col,                           /* next inhabitant's position */
         row;

  if ((inpres = scanf ("%d%d%d", numgen_ptr, rows_ptr, cols_ptr)) != 3)
    printf ("Nonnumeric board size or number of generations.\n");
  else {                                /* verify world size */
    if (!INRANGE (*rows_ptr, 1, MAXROW) || !INRANGE (*cols_ptr, 1, MAXCOL)) {
      printf ("World size %d by %d is invalid--using maximum of %d by %d\n",
              *rows_ptr, *cols_ptr, MAXROW, MAXCOL);
      *rows_ptr = MAXROW, *cols_ptr = MAXCOL;
    }

  /* Get inhabitants' positions, marking their cell. */

  while ((inpres = scanf ("%d %d", &row, &col)) == 2)
    if (!INRANGE (row, 1, *rows_ptr) || !INRANGE (col, 1, *cols_ptr))
        printf ("Position %d,%d is invalid--ignored\n", row, col);
    else
        if (!world[row][col])
        {
            world[row][col] = TRUE;
            (*count_ptr)++;
        }
  if (inpres != EOF)
    printf ("Nonnumeric inhabitant position found.\n");
  return inpres == EOF;
}
```

(b) inp_world, *the routine to read the initial Life configuration*

```
/*
 *  Print a generation in a nice format.
 */
void out_world(world, rows, cols, gen, last_gen)
WORLD    world;
int      rows, cols,
         gen, last_gen;
{
  int    col,                           /* together index next element */
         row;
```

FIGURE 12.18 (continued)

```
  printf("Generation: %d (out of %d)\n\n", gen, last_gen);
  for (col = 0; col <= cols + 1; col++)
    putchar(BORDER);
  putchar('\n');
  for (row = 1; row <= rows; row++)
  {
    putchar(BORDER);
    for (col = 1; col <= cols; col++)
      putchar(world[row][col] ? MARKER : ' ');
    putchar(BORDER);
    putchar('\n');
  }
  for (col = 0; col <= cols + 1; col++)
    putchar(BORDER);
  putchar('\n');
}
```

(c) out_world, *the routine that writes a Life configuration to the screen*

```
/*
 * Compute next generation, returning nonzero if nonstable.
 */
BOOLEAN nxt_world(current, future, rows, cols, count_ptr)
WORLD     current,
          future;
int       rows,
          cols,
          *count_ptr;
{
  int     changed = 0,              /* number of inhabitants died, or created */
          col, row;                 /* next column and row processed */

  for (*count_ptr = 0, row = 1; row <= rows; row++)
    for (col = 1; col <= cols; col++)            /* count neighbors */
    {
      int neighbors = current[row - 1][col - 1] + current[row - 1][col] +
                      current[row - 1][col + 1] + current[row + 1][col] +
                      current[row + 1][col - 1] + current[row][col - 1] +
                      current[row + 1][col + 1] + current[row][col + 1];

      /* Note if lived or died and note any changes. */

      if ((future[row][col] =
             (neighbors == 3 || (neighbors == 2 && current[row][col]))) != 0)
        (*count_ptr)++;
      changed += future[row][col] != current[row][col];
    }
  return changed;                              /* zero if stable */
}
```

(d) nxt_world, *the routine that computes the next generation, following the rules of Life*

FIGURE 12.18 (continued)

TABLE 12.5 Profile of the Life program's execution after running for 10 generations.

Function	% Time	Cum. Seconds
nxt_world	80.6	3.73
out_world	16.2	4.48
inp_world	0.0	4.48
main	0.0	4.48
System calls	3.2	4.63

world, we should be able to improve the function's performance by using pointers to traverse the array.

Figure 12.19 is the pointer version of nxt_world. The pointer row_ptr is used to traverse the rows of the current world. Once a row is selected, col_ptr is used to traverse the elements of the row. Since cells in the previous and following rows must be examined to count neighboring cells, two additional pointers, prev_ptr and next_ptr, are used to traverse the elements in those rows. The dummy cells surrounding the world are skipped by adding one to the pointers traversing the rows when they are initialized.

We can make similar changes to out_world, and in addition, we can make Life faster and more impressive by rewriting out_world to display the world in a fixed part of the screen, reprinting only those cells that change in subsequent generations. To do this, we use the include file *cursor.h* (Chapter 7). We specify the terminal type before including the file, and macros to clear the screen and move the cursor will be defined for us. out_world then uses these macros extensively in writing the world. This new and final version of out_world is shown in Figure 12.20.

We reran this new, improved version for 10 generations again, yielding the timing profiles shown in Table 12.6. The total time has decreased from about 4.6 to 1.5 seconds, a saving of more than 75 percent. It is always useful to try to understand why these kinds of savings occur and to determine their effect on users. Here, we gained about 75 percent of the time saving by replacing array subscripting by pointer indexing and 25 percent by direct cursor movement.

For someone watching Life run (and it is fun to do) the benefit comes from moving the cursor exactly where we want it. The result is that the screen updates virtually instantaneously, rather than by the original line-by-line method. Previously, the screen was painted a line at a time, and then there was an uncomfortably long pause while the program calculated the next generation.

```
/*
 * Compute next generation, returning nonzero if nonstable.
 */
BOOLEAN nxt_world(row_ptr, fut_row_ptr, rows, cols, count_ptr)
ROW_PTR row_ptr,
        fut_row_ptr;
int     rows,
        cols,
        *count_ptr;
{
  ROW_PTR end_row_ptr = row_ptr + rows;      /* pointer to last row */
  int     changed = 0;                        /* number of changes made to world */

  *count_ptr = 0;
  while (++row_ptr <= end_row_ptr)
  {
    BOOLEAN *prev_ptr   = *(row_ptr - 1) + 1,  /* ptr to first column in */
            *curr_ptr,                         /*   previous, current and */
            *next_ptr   = *(row_ptr + 1) + 1,  /*   next rows */
            *last_ptr   = *(row_ptr) + cols,   /* ptr to end of current row */
            *future_ptr = *++fut_row_ptr + 1;  /* ptr to column in future */

    for (curr_ptr = *row_ptr + 1; curr_ptr <= last_ptr; prev_ptr++, next_ptr++)
    {                      /* count number of neighbors */
      int  neighbors = prev_ptr[-1] + prev_ptr[0] + prev_ptr[1] +
                       next_ptr[-1] + next_ptr[0] + next_ptr[1] +
                       curr_ptr[-1] + curr_ptr[1];

      /* Note if lived or died, and note any changes. */

      if ((*future_ptr = (neighbors == 3 || (neighbors == 2 && *curr_ptr))) != 0)
        (*count_ptr)++;
      changed += *future_ptr++ != *curr_ptr++;
    }
  }
  return changed;                              /* nonzero if not stable */
}
```

FIGURE 12.19 Pointer version of nxt_world.

12.3.3 EFFICIENCY — CONCLUSIONS

For almost any piece of code, the following guidelines, based on the examples in this chapter, should yield savings in time and space:

- Use your own input scanner rather than scanf.
- malloc extracts a substantial performance overhead for its generality. If all nodes are the same size, try to malloc all the space

```
/*
 * Print a generation in a nice format.
 */
#include "cursor.h"                              /* direct cursor movement (Chapter 7) */
#define HEADER_LINE   0                          /* header message */
#define TOP_CELLS     2                          /* first line with cells */
#define FIRST_CELL    2                          /* first column with cells */

void out_world(row_ptr, past_row_ptr, rows, cols, gen, last_gen)
ROW_PTR           row_ptr, past_row_ptr;
int               rows, cols, gen, last_gen;
{
  static int   printed = FALSE;                  /* first printing? */
        int    col, row;                         /* current column/row */

  if (!printed)                                  /* clear screen and write border */
  {
    CLEAR_SCREEN();
    MOVE_CURSOR(TOP_CELLS - 1, FIRST_CELL - 1);            /* top border */
    for (col = 0; col <= cols + 1; col++)
      putchar(BORDER);
    MOVE_CURSOR(TOP_CELLS + rows, FIRST_CELL - 1);         /* bottom border */
    for (col = 0; col <= cols + 1; col++)
      putchar(BORDER);
    for (row = TOP_CELLS; row < TOP_CELLS + rows; row++)
    {
      MOVE_CURSOR(row, FIRST_CELL - 1), putchar(BORDER);
      MOVE_CURSOR(row, FIRST_CELL + cols), putchar(BORDER);
    }
    printed = TRUE;
  }
  MOVE_CURSOR(HEADER_LINE, FIRST_CELL - 1);               /* header line */
  printf("Generation: %d (out of %d)", gen, last_gen);
  for (row = TOP_CELLS ; row < TOP_CELLS + rows; row++)
  {
    BOOLEAN *curr_ptr = *++row_ptr,              /* pointer to current column */
            *past_ptr = *++past_row_ptr;         /* pointer to past word column */

    for (col = FIRST_CELL; col < FIRST_CELL + cols; col++)
      if (*++curr_ptr != *++past_ptr)            /* move and write only if change */
      {
        MOVE_CURSOR(row, col);                   /*    character didn't change */
        putchar(*curr_ptr ? MARKER : ' ');
      }
  }
  MOVE_CURSOR(TOP_CELLS + rows + 1, FIRST_CELL - 1);
}
```

FIGURE 12.20 Function `out_world` using absolute addressing of pointer version.

TABLE 12.6 Execution times of the version of Life using pointers and direct cursor movement.

Function	% Time	Cum. Seconds
nxt_world	58.9	0.8
out_world	25.0	1.2
inp_world	1.1	1.2
main	0.0	1.2
System calls	15.0	1.5

you need initially, and then manage your own free storage pool. In any event, be certain to return unused space with `free` so that `malloc` will need to make fewer operating system calls and is less likely to fail.

- Reuse data structures rather than allocate new space for several different uses.
- Avoid substantial data movement. Whenever possible, use the structures that data comes in, rather than copying into special-purpose structures.
- Replace array accessing with pointer indexing.
- Look for ways to speed up output. Direct cursor movement is faster than line-by-line writing. This works with Life because most of the screen is empty. In this case, we use special properties of the structures and representations.

EXERCISES

12-21 The system calls alluded to in Table 12.6 primarily involve `scanf`. Rewrite Life to eliminate `scanf` by using `getnum` from Chapter 6, as we did with radix sort. Does this make a difference in running time? How does it affect the size of the program? □

12-22 Modify Life so that the space for the world is dynamically allocated. Run this version and compare its running time with our version. Is it faster or slower? Now apply the lessons of this chapter to modify this new version for efficiency. □

12-23 According to Table 12.6, Life is still spending almost 60 percent of its time in one routine, `nxt_world`. This routine may be made more efficient by using methods that require certain board configurations to be precomputed. Then a table lookup can be used to map current board configurations into the next generation. Rewrite `nxt_world` to use this scheme. Is it faster or slower? □

12-24 `out_world` currently moves the cursor even if it is already at the location where it should be. Modify it so that it doesn't. □

12-25 Pick one of the case studies from the earlier chapters and apply the techniques discussed in this chapter to make it as efficient as possible. The cross-referencer (Chapter 10) and the address book (Chapter 11) are two good candidates. □

WHY WE USE C — PORTABILITY AND EFFICIENCY

It may seem strange to try to summarize a chapter that is, after all, summary itself. But this is the end of the end, and so it is appropriate to consider the entire book and review what we have learned. Here are some comments about the C programming language, its strengths, its weaknesses, and how they relate to concerns about portability and efficiency.

- *C is compact and rather simple in its capabilities.* However, it comes wrapped in a rich collection of standard additions: the preprocessor and the various run-time libraries. Even though the language itself seems to be composed of rather small pieces, so much has been created for us, particularly I/O and string functions, that the language is as powerful as most high-level languages.

- *The language appears to be both strongly and weakly typed.* The compiler complains when variables are not typed or are used in a way that is different from their type. In contrast, there are capabilities for type conversions – casts, automatic conversions, and the like – and some types may be used interchangeably with others, so that we can often use the language as if it were an untyped assembly language.

- *Portability of programs can never be taken for granted.* There are subtle machine and operating system dependencies, as well as word size representations, that creep into even the most thoughtfully constructed program. Using program development tools (such as *lint* in the UNIX operating system) is a great aid. As with abstract data types, where we try to hide the underlying structures and algorithms, hiding the machine- and system-dependent material in separate modules aids portability.

- *C is inherently efficient.* Compilers have been written for optimization, and the language's run-time support is relatively unencumbering; there are no run-time array bounds checks, for example. Programs in C can often be made to run faster by converting array indexing to pointer referencing. Often programs written in C are as fast as assembly language programs for performing the same task.

- *And C is fun to program in!* A great deal of code is now written in C. Why is everyone using it? Because it is lean and mean. Because it rewards the tinkerer while still making the more conventional programming styles efficient. And because it is accessible to a wide range of programming needs and programmer experiences.

APPENDIXES

OCTAL AND HEXADECIMAL NUMBERING SYSTEMS

There is a class of representations known as the *base systems*. Some commonly used bases are binary (base 2), octal (base 8), decimal (base 10), and hexadecimal (base 16). Each of these systems is centered on an integer, other than zero or one, called the *base* or *radix*.

Each base uses a finite number of symbols. In binary the allowable symbols are 0 and 1. In octal the symbols used are 0, 1, 2, 3, 4, 5, 6, and 7. In hexadecimal we need a way to represent the values 10, 11, 12, 13, 14, and 15. The letters A, B, C, D, E, and F, respectively, have been chosen to symbolize them.

In a base system, a value is represented by a string of symbols. Each place occupied by a symbol corresponds to a power of the base. The rightmost place corresponds to the base raised to the zero power (which is one for any choice of base). Each move to the left multiplies the current place value by the base. In octal, the rightmost place corresponds to 1s; the next place to the left corresponds to 8s; the place one more to the left corresponds to 64s, and so on. In hexadecimal, the rightmost place also corresponds to 1s, the next place to the left corresponds to 16s; the third place to the 16×16s, or 256s, and on up.

The following table illustrates the correspondence between position and value in binary, octal, and hexadecimal. It is convenient to start numbering the positions at zero from the right so that the position value will be equal to the power of the base.

	n	Position 4	3	2	1	0
Binary	2^n	16	8	4	2	1
Octal	8^n	4,096	512	64	8	1
Hexadecimal	16^n	65,536	4,096	256	16	1

To compute the base 10 value of a number $a_n a_{n-1} \cdots a_1 a_0$ in base B, compute $\sum_{i=0}^{n} a_i \times B^i$. To convert the number 742_8 to base 10 evaluate $(7 \times 8^2) + (4 \times 8^1) + (2 \times 8^0)$ to obtain the value 482_{10}. To convert the number $A2C_{16}$ to base 10 you evaluate $(10 \times 16^2) + (2 \times 16^1) + (12 \times 16^0)$ to get 2604_{10}.

There is a simple and direct relationship between binary, octal, and hexadecimal numbers. To convert from binary to octal, group the number from the right in three-bit units and convert each to an octal number. To convert to hexadecimal, group in four-bit units, converting each group in turn. For hexadecimal, values from 0 to 9 convert to the same digit; 10 converts to A, 11 to B, 12 to C, 13 to D, 14 to E, and 15 to F.

```
Binary:  0 0 1 1 1 0 1 1 1 0 1 0
Octal:   |____|____|____|____|
            1    6    7    2

Binary:  0 0 1 1 1 0 1 1 1 0 1 0
Hex:     |_____|_____|_____|
             3      B      A
```

To convert a number, X, from base 10 to base B, recursively divide X by B. The remainder becomes the leftmost digit of the converted number and the quotient becomes the next X. When the new quotient becomes zero, the process is complete.

APPENDIX 2

THE ASCII CHARACTER SET

0	1	2	3	4	5	6	7	8	9	10	11	12	13	14	15
^@	^A	^B	^C	^D	^E	^F	^G	^H	^I	^J	^K	^L	^M	^N	^O

16	17	18	19	20	21	22	23	24	25	26	27	28	29	30	31
^P	^Q	^R	^S	^T	^U	^V	^W	^X	^Y	^Z	esc				

32	33	34	35	36	37	38	39	40	41	42	43	44	45	46	47
sp	!	"	#	$	%	&	'	(	)	*	+	,	-	.	/

48	49	50	51	52	53	54	55	56	57	58	59	60	61	62	63
0	1	2	3	4	5	6	7	8	9	:	;	<	=	>	?

64	65	66	67	68	69	70	71	72	73	74	75	76	77	78	79
@	A	B	C	D	E	F	G	H	I	J	K	L	M	N	O

80	81	82	83	84	85	86	87	88	89	90	91	92	93	94	95
P	Q	R	S	T	U	V	W	X	Y	Z	[		]	^	_

96	97	98	99	100	101	102	103	104	105	106	107	108	109	110	111
'	a	b	c	d	e	f	g	h	i	j	k	l	m	n	o

112	113	114	115	116	117	118	119	120	121	122	123	124	125	126	127
p	q	r	s	t	u	v	w	x	y	z	{			}		del

APPENDIX 3

THE EBCDIC CHARACTER SET

0	1	2	3	4	5	6	7	8	9	10	11	12	13	14	15
NUL	SOH	STX	ETX	PF	HT	LC	DEL			SMM	VT	FF	CR	SO	SI

16	17	18	19	20	21	22	23	24	25	26	27	28	29	30	31
DLE	DC1	DC2	TM	RES	NL	BS	IL	CAN	EM	CC	CU1	IFS	IGS	IRS	IUS

32	33	34	35	36	37	38	39	40	41	42	43	44	45	46	47
DS	SOS	FS		BYP	LF	ETB	ESC			SM	CU2		ENQ	ACK	BEL

48	49	50	51	52	53	54	55	56	57	58	59	60	61	62	63
		SYN		PN	RS	UC	EOT				CU3	DC4	NAK		SUB

64	65	66	67	68	69	70	71	72	73	74	75	76	77	78	79
SP										cents	.	<	(	+	|

80	81	82	83	84	85	86	87	88	89	90	91	92	93	94	95
&										!	$	*	)	;	corner

96	97	98	99	100	101	102	103	104	105	106	107	108	109	110	111
/											,	%	-	>	?

112	113	114	115	116	117	118	119	120	121	122	123	124	125	126	127
										:	#	@	'	=	"

128	129	130	131	132	133	134	135	136	137	138	139	140	141	142	143
	a	b	c	d	e	f	g	h	i						

144	145	146	147	148	149	150	151	152	153	154	155	156	157	158	159
	j	k	l	m	n	o	p	q	r						

160	161	162	163	164	165	166	167	168	169	170	171	172	173	174	175
		s	t	u	v	w	x	y	z						

176	177	178	179	180	181	182	183	184	185	186	187	188	189	190	191

APPENDIX 3

THE EBCDIC CHARACTER SET

192	193	194	195	196	197	198	199	200	201	202	203	204	205	206	207
	A	B	C	D	E	F	G	H	I						

208	209	210	211	212	213	214	215	216	217	218	219	220	221	222	223
	J	K	L	M	N	O	P	Q	R						

224	225	226	227	228	229	230	231	232	233	234	235	236	237	238	239
		S	T	U	V	W	X	Y	Z						

240	241	242	243	244	245	246	247	248	249	250	251	252	253	254	255
0	1	2	3	4	5	6	7	8	9						

APPENDIX 4

THE MATH LIBRARY

Here is a table of C mathematical functions. To use these functions, include *math.h*. Some of the functions expect a `double` as an argument, but because of C's automatic type conversions (section 5.3.1), a `float` can be passed instead. But note that many of them return a `double`, so be careful of the type of the variable being assigned to.

```
int abs(x)
int x;
```

Absolute value of `x`. Cannot be used to take the absolute value of a `long`.

```
double acos(x)
double x;
```

Arc cosine of `x` in radians. Returns zero if `x` not in range minus one to one.

```
double asin(x)
double x;
```

Arc sine of `x` in radians. Returns zero if `x` not in range minus one to one.

```
double atan(x)
double x;
```

Arc tangent of `x` in radians. Sometimes called `arctan`.

```
double atan2(y, x)
double y, x;
```

Arc tangent of `x/y` in radians. Result machine dependent if `x` and `y` are both zero.

```
double ceil(x)
double x;
```

`x` rounded up to the nearest integer.

```
double cos(x)
double x;
```

Cosine of `x` (x in radians).

```
double cosh(x)
double x;
```

Hyperbolic cosine of **x**. Returns largest possible double on overflow.

```
double exp(x)
double x;
```

e to the **x** power. Returns largest possible double on overflow.

```
double fabs(x)
double x;
```

Absolute value of **x**.

```
double floor(x)
double x;
```

x rounded down to the nearest integer.

```
double fmod(x,y)
double x, y;
```

Remainder when **x** is divided by **y**.

```
double frexp(x, nptr)
double x;
int    *nptr;
```

Finds *f* and *n* such that *f* is between 0.5 and 1.0, and $fr^n = x$, where *r* is the radix used by the internal representation; returns *f*, and puts *n* in the place pointed to by `nptr`.

```
long int labs(x)
long x;
```

Absolute value of **x**.

```
double ldexp(x)
double x;
```

xr^y, where *r* is the radix used by the internal representation.

```
double log(x)
double x;
```

Natural log of **x**. Returns largest negative double if **x** is less than zero.

```
double log10(x)
double x;
```

Base 10 log of x. Returns largest negative double if x is less than zero.

```
double modf(x, nptr)
double x;
int    *nptr;
```

Splits x into a fraction and an integer; the fraction is returned, and the integer is put in the place pointed to by nptr.

```
double pow(x, y)
double x, y;
```

x to the y power. Returns largest possible double on overflow; returns largest negative double if x is negative and y is not an integer, or if x is zero and y is not positive.

```
int rand()
```

Random number between zero and the largest positive double (inclusive). May be initialized with srand(x).

```
double sin(x)
double x;
```

Sine of x (x in radians).

```
double sinh(x)
double x;
```

Hyperbolic sine of x. Returns largest positive double on overflow; unpredictable results on underflow.

```
double sqrt(x)
double x;
```

Square root of x. Returns zero if x is negative.

```
srand(seed)
unsigned seed;
```

No value returned; initializes rand. Same seed produces same numbers.

```
double tan(x)
double x;
```

Tangent of **x** (**x** in radians).

```
double tanh(x)
double x;
```

Hyperbolic tangent of **x**.

APPENDIX 5

THE CTYPE LIBRARY

Here is a table of C character functions.[1] To use these functions, include *ctype.h*. Assume that `c` has been declared as a `char`.

```
isalnum(c)
```

Nonzero if `c` is alphabetic or numeric; zero otherwise.

```
isalpha(c)
```

Nonzero if `c` is alphabetic; zero otherwise.

```
isascii(c)
```

Nonzero if `c` is an ASCII character; zero otherwise. `isascii` also works on any `int`; if `c` has no ASCII value, zero is returned.

```
iscntrl(c)
```

Nonzero if `c` is a control char; zero otherwise.

```
iscsym(c)
```

Nonzero if `c` can be a valid character within an identifier; zero otherwise.

```
iscsymf(c)
```

Nonzero if `c` can be the first letter of an identifier; zero otherwise.

```
isdigit(c)
```

Nonzero if `c` is a digit; zero otherwise.

```
isgraph(c)
```

Nonzero if `c` is any printing character other than space; zero otherwise.

```
islower(c)
```

Nonzero if `c` is a lowercase letter of the alphabet; zero otherwise.

[1]Not all of these functions are available in all C environments. Consult your local reference manual for details.

```
isodigit(c)
```

Nonzero if c is an octal digit; zero otherwise.

```
isprint(c)
```

Nonzero if c is printable; zero otherwise.

```
ispunct(c)
```

Nonzero if c is a punctuation character; zero otherwise.

```
isspace(c)
```

Nonzero if c is any white space character; zero otherwise.

```
isupper(c)
```

Nonzero if c is an uppercase letter of the alphabet; zero otherwise.

```
isxdigit(c)
```

Nonzero if c is a hex digit; zero otherwise.

```
toascii(c)
```

ASCII value of c; if c is not in the range of ASCII characters, truncates to lowest seven bits.

```
toint(c)
```

Decimal value of a hex digit; minus one if c is not a hex digit.

```
tolower(c)
```

c in lowercase

```
toupper(c)
```

c in uppercase

```
char _tolower(c)
```

c in lowercase; defined only for uppercase c.

```
char _toupper(c)
```

c in uppercase; defined only for uppercase c.

APPENDIX 6

THE STANDARD I/O LIBRARY

Here is a table of C I/O functions. All of the streams are assumed to be open for input and output unless otherwise stated. Include *stdio.h* before using these functions.

```
    EOF
```

Returned by functions when end of file is reached.

```
    int fclose(stream)
    FILE *stream;
```

Closes a stream that was open for input and output.

```
    int feof(stream)
    FILE *stream;
```

If end of file is detected on an input stream, a nonzero value is returned; otherwise zero is returned.

```
    int fgetc(stream)
    FILE *stream;
```

Returns integer value of next character of input stream.

```
    char *fgets(s, n, stream)
    char *s;
    int n;
    FILE *stream;
```

Reads n characters from stream into s; stops reading on newline or end of file.

```
    FILE *fopen(path, type)
    char *path, *type;
```

Opens a file for input and output. type is one of:

"r"   Open the file for reading from the beginning.
      If the field doesn't exist, NULL is returned.
"w"   Open the file for writing. If the file exists, it is truncated
      to zero length. If it doesn't exist, it is created.
"a"   Open the file for updating. If the file exists, writes
      will occur at the end. If it doesn't exist, it is created.

```
int fprintf(stream, format, argl, arg2,...)
File *stream;
char *format;
```

Writes arguments to a specified stream using a given format (see `printf`).

```
int fputc(c, stream)
char c;
FILE *stream;
```

Writes the character `c` to the stream and returns the value of `c` as an int.

```
int fputs(s, stream)
char *s;
FILE *stream;
```

Writes the string `s` to the stream.

```
int fread(ptr, ptr_size, n, stream)
char *ptr;
unsigned ptr_size;
int n;
FILE *stream;
```

Reads a block of binary data into a buffer from a stream and returns the number of items read.

```
int fscanf(stream, format, ptrl, ptr2, ...)
FILE *stream;
char *format;
```

Reads formatted input from a specified stream (see `scanf`).

```
int fseek(stream, offset, type)
FILE *stream;
long offset;
int type;
```

Allows positioning within a stream for input or output.

```
long ftell(stream)
FILE *stream;
```

Returns current position within an open stream.

```
int fwrite(ptr, ptr_size, n, stream)
char *ptr;
unsigned ptr_size;
int n;
FILE *stream;
```

Writes a block of binary data from a buffer to a stream; returns number of items written.

```
int getc(stream)
FILE *stream;
```

Macro version of `fgetc`; true function equivalent to `fgetc` in operation.

```
int getchar()
```

Returns integer value of next character from standard input.

```
char *gets(s)
char *s;
```

Reads a string from the standard input until newline or end of file.

```
int printf(format, argl, arg2,...)
char *format;
```

Formats output and writes to stdout. Formatting specifications consist of six components. The first is a percent sign indicating output formatting.

The second component is a flag used to indicate the presence of a plus sign for positive numbers, zero or space padding, and right or left justification. These flags are:

0 Pad with zeroes rather than blanks. E.g. `printf("[%08d]\n",val)` produces

`[00000015]`

while `printf("[%8d]\n",val)` produces

`[      15]`

—   Left justify within the field.
`printf("[%-8d]\n",val)` produces

`[15      ]`

This can be especially important for strings. Using the `"%s"` format, strings will align on the right. Using `"%-s"` they will align on the left:

Left Aligned	Right Aligned
miller, larry	miller, larry
quilici, alex	quilici, alex
cohen, danny	cohen, danny
brooks, jan	brooks, jan
kay, david	kay, david
swenson, marcy	swenson, marcy

+	Print with a sign, + for positive numbers, − for negative numbers.
space	Use a space for positive numbers, − for negative numbers.
#	Use an alternative representation, described below.

The third component is a minimum field width, given as a (decimal) integer constant. A variable may not be used as a field width, as it may in some other languages. We have used this form throughout the book, and in the above examples, to place output in fixed size fields. The field specifies a minimum. If the value is larger, it will take up more space, (again, some languages are guaranteed never to exceed the field width—asterisks are used if a value will not fit into the specified field). If the value is a string that is larger than the field width, only the specified number of characters is printed.

The fourth component is used for floating point output. It is a period followed by the numer of spaces used for the fractional part of the number (it must be a nonnegative decimal integer constant). Reals are rounded to the indicated precision. E.g.:

```
float fval = 2.0/3.0;
printf("[%7.2f]\n",fval);
```

produces

```
[   0.67]
```

The fifth component, the letter l, is used to indicate a long argument. This is valid only with the formats d (for decimal integer), o, (for octal integer) u, (for an unsigned decimal integer) x, (for hexadecimal integer) X, (for hexadecimal integer).

Finally the sixth component is the argument type, one of:

c	character
d	decimal integer
e	floating point 'e' notation
E	floating point 'e' notation
f	floating point fractional notation
g	'e' or decimal notation determined at run time
G	'e' or decimal notation determined at run time
o	octal integer
s	string
u	unsigned integer
x	hexadecimal integer
X	hexadecimal integer
%	percent sign

In all cases, the value to be printed should match in type the corresponding format specifier. If it does not, certain automatic conversions may be applied (for example, a `float` is always promoted to a `double`), or the results may be unpredictable.

The # flag is used as an optional output form specifier for the %e, %E, %f, %g, %G, %o, %x, and %X format specifiers. For %e, %f and %g, # means do not strip off nonsignificant trailing zeroes. For %o, # means prepend the digit 0. For %x or %X, # means prepend 0x or 0X, respectively.

```
int putc(c, stream)
char c;
FILE *stream;
```

Puts character c into specified stream; returns character as a value of type int.

```
int putchar(c)
char c;
```

Same as putc but writes character to standard output.

```
int puts(s)
char *s;
```

Writes string s to standard output.

```
int scanf(format, ptrl, ptr2,...)
char *format;
```

Reads characters from standard input according to a specified format; choices for format include:

%d	signed decimal
%hd	signed short decimal
%ld	signed long decimal
%u	unsigned decimal
%hu	unsigned short decimal
%lu	unsigned long decimal
%ou	unsigned octal
%ho	unsigned short octal
%lo	unsigned long octal
%x	unsigned hex
%hx	unsigned short hex
%lx	unsigned long hex
%c	character(s)
%s	right-adjusted string
%-s	left-adjusted string
%f, %e, %g	signed decimal float
%lf, %le, %lg	signed decimal double
%%	percent sign

```
int sscanf(s, format, ptrl, ptr2,...)
char *s, *format;
```

Reads characters from string s according to specified format (see scanf).

```
extern FILE *stderr;
```

Stream to which error messages may be written.

```
extern FILE *stdin;
```

Stream from which normal input is read, usually the terminal.

```
extern FILE *stdout
```

Stream to which normal output is written, usually the terminal.

```
int ungetc(c, stream)
char c;
FILE *stream;
```

Next character c is put back on the specified stream; getc from same stream will return this character.

```
system(command)
```

An operating system command is run and its exit status is returned. Though originally defined for the UNIX operating system, now found on most others.

APPENDIX 7

THE STRING LIBRARY

Here is a table of C string functions.[2] All strings should end with the null character ('\0'); if a string without a null character is passed to one of these functions, the results are unpredictable at best. Include *string.h*[3] before using the following functions.

```
char *strcat(s1, s2)
char *s1, *s2;
```

s2 appended to s1. Returns a pointer to s1. Unpredictable results if s1 and s2 share any memory.

```
char *strchr(s, c)
char *s, c;
```

A pointer to the first occurrence of c in s; a NULL pointer if c does not occur in s. Sometimes called index.

```
int strcmp(s1, s2)
char *s1, *s2;
```

An int, less than zero if s1 is less than s2, zero if s1 equals s2, and greater than zero if s1 is greater than s2.

```
char *strcpy(s1, s2)
char *s1, *s2;
```

The contents of s2 are copied into s1. Returns a pointer to s1. Unpredictable results if s1 and s2 share any memory.

```
int strcspn(s, set)
char *s, *set;
```

Number of characters in s before encountering a character in set. Returns length of s if no characters in set are also in s; sometimes called instr.

---

[2]As with the other libraries, some of these functions may not be available on your machine.
[3]Some systems call this file *strings.h*, and others do not have it at all.

```
int strlen(s)
char *s;
```

Number of characters in s before the temrinating null. Sometimes called `lenstr`.

```
char *strncat(s1, s2, n)
char *s1, *s2;
int n;
```

First n characters of s2 are appended to s1; returns pointer to s1. Unpredictable results if s1 and s2 share any memory.

```
int strncmp(s1, s2, n)
char *s1, *s2;
int n;
```

Compares first n characters of s1 and s2. Returns an integer less than zero, zero, or greater than zero depending on comparison of the first n characters as with `strcmp`.

```
char *strncpy(s1, s2, n)
char *s1, *s2;
int n;
```

Copies n characters to s1 from s2; if s2 is less than n, s1 is padded with null characters to length n; returns a pointer to s1. If s2 greater than or equal to n, s1 is not null terminated.

```
char *strpbrk(s, set)
char *s, *set;
```

A pointer to the first character in s that is also in set; NULL if s and set have no intersection.

```
int strpos(s, c)
char *s, c;
```

The position of the first occurrence of c in s; minus one if c not in s. Some versions have a variant called `scnstr`.

```
char *strrchr(s, c)
char *s, c;
```

A pointer to the last occurrence of c in s; NULL if c not in s.

```
char *strrpbrk(s, set)
char *s, *set;
```

A pointer to the last occurrence in s of a character in set; NULL if s and set have no intersection.

```
int strrpos(s, c)
char *s, c;
```

The position of the last occurrence of c in s; minus one if c not in s.

```
int strspn(s, set)
char *s, *set;
```

Number of characters in s before encountering a character not in set. Returns length of s if all characters in set are also in s; sometimes called notstr.

APPENDIX 8

STORAGE ALLOCATION FUNCTIONS

Here are the functions provided for allocating and freeing storage. The storage allocation functions all return a pointer to a contiguous block of storage of at least the requested size. The functions return type `char *`, and should be cast to the appropriate type. The storage is guaranteed to be properly aligned to the requirements of the underlying hardware. These functions return NULL (defined in *stdio.h*) if there is not enough free space available.

The storage freeing routines require a pointer to a contiguous block of storage previously allocated by one of the storage allocation functions. They return the pointed-to block to the free storage pool. The type of the argument is `char *`, and should be cast as appropriate. These functions should never fail.

```
char *calloc(n, size)
unsigned n, size;
```

Allocates n blocks of storage, each of `size` bytes. All bits in the allocated space are set to zero.

```
cfree(ptr)
char  *ptr;
```

Returns space previously allocated by `calloc` to the free storage pool.

```
char *clalloc(n, size)
unsigned long n, size;
```

Similar to `calloc`, except the arguments are `long`s allowing for larger blocks of storage to be allocated.

```
free(ptr)
char  *ptr;
```

Returns space previously allocated by `malloc` to the free storage pool.

```
char *malloc(size)
unsigned  size;
```

Allocates a contiguous block of storage of at least `size` bytes, and returns a pointer to the first byte in the block, or `NULL` if there is not enough space.

```
char *mlalloc(size)
unsigned long  size;
```

Similar to `malloc`, except that the argument is of type `long`, so that more space may be requested.

```
char  *realloc(ptr, size)
char      *ptr;
unsigned size;
```

Takes a pointer to a block of storage and "grows" it to the requested size. A pointer to the new block is returned. Returns NULL if the amount of space requested is not available. NOTE – in some installations if `realloc` fails, the original space may be lost.

INDEX

419

FUNCTIONS AND PROGRAMS (By Function Name)

FUNCTIONS AND PROGRAMS
(By Function Description)

M